# VETERAN POETICS

In this first full-length study of the war veteran in literature, Kate McLoughlin draws new critical attention to a figure central to national life. Offering fresh readings of canonical and non-canonical works, she shows how authors from William Wordsworth to J. K. Rowling have deployed veterans to explore questions that are simultaneously personal, political and philosophical. What does a community owe to those who serve it? What can be recovered from the past? Do people stay the same over time? Are there right times of life at which to do certain things? Is there value in experience? How can wisdom be shared? *Veteran Poetics* features veterans who travel in time, cause havoc with their reappearances, solve murders, refuse to stop talking about the wars they have been in and refuse to say a word about them. Through this last trait, they also prompt consideration of possible critical responses to silence.

KATE MCLOUGHLIN is a Professor of English Literature at the University of Oxford.

# VETERAN POETICS

*British Literature in the Age of Mass Warfare, 1790–2015*

KATE MCLOUGHLIN

*University of Oxford*

CAMBRIDGE
UNIVERSITY PRESS

# CAMBRIDGE
## UNIVERSITY PRESS

University Printing House, Cambridge CB2 8BS, United Kingdom

One Liberty Plaza, 20th Floor, New York, NY 10006, USA

477 Williamstown Road, Port Melbourne, VIC 3207, Australia

314–321, 3rd Floor, Plot 3, Splendor Forum, Jasola District Centre, New Delhi – 110025, India

79 Anson Road, #06-04/06, Singapore 079906

Cambridge University Press is part of the University of Cambridge.

It furthers the University's mission by disseminating knowledge in the pursuit of education, learning, and research at the highest international levels of excellence.

www.cambridge.org
Information on this title: www.cambridge.org/9781107195936
DOI: 10.1017/9781108350754

First published 2018

Printed in the United States of America by Sheridan Books, Inc.

*A catalogue record for this publication is available from the British Library.*

ISBN 978-1-107-19593-6 Hardback

*In memory of Angela Bolton and Jennifer Fisher*

# Contents

# Acknowledgements

It is my great pleasure to thank the friends and colleagues who helped in the writing of this book in various ways, none of whom bear any responsibility for the final text: Rebecca Beasley, Karen Benavente, Celeste-Marie Bernier, Carolyn Burdett, Sandie Byrne, Monika Class, Nick Caddick, Steve Connor, Santanu Das, Rex Ferguson, Nick Freeman, Holly Furneaux, Carl Gardner, Konstantina Georganta, Claire Gorrara, Richard Hamblyn, Jen Hui Bon Hoa, Ian Isherwood, Keith Krause, Vassiliki Kolocotroni, Nigel Leask, Hermione Lee, Esther Leslie, Marina Mackay, Ankhi Mukherjee, Charles Mundye, Chris Oakey, Muireann O'Cinneide, Sam Perry, Luke Pitcher, Gill Plain, Neil Ramsey, Graham Riach, Ravenel Richardson, Lynn Robson, Phil Shaw, Kevin Spruce, the late Jon Stallworthy, Fiona Stafford, Victoria Stewart, Matthew Taunton, Andrew Van Der Vlies, Hope Wolf and Nigel Wood.

In particular, I would like to thank three friends who nobly read chapters in draft and provided me with wonderfully helpful feedback at a relatively late stage: David Dwan, Finn Fordham and Alexandra Harris.

Lieutenant Colonel Christopher Keeble, DSO MSc FCMI, supernumerary fellow of Harris Manchester College, cast his expert eye over things to ensure that I have got military matters right. I take full responsibility for any errors that remain and am grateful to Chris and to all the other former and currently serving military personnel who advised me and who did not want to be personally identified.

In the course of writing this book, I tried out ideas in a number of venues. I was always met with invaluable feedback and, knowing from my own experience that organizing such talks is no small thing, I am very grateful to the following for giving me the opportunity to listen, learn and improve: Emily Senior and the Eighteenth-Century Reading Group at Birkbeck, University of London; Emma Parker and the Graduate Seminar in Twentieth-Century English Literature at the University of Leicester;

Maggie Andrews and the Remembrance seminar at the National Memorial Arboretum; Jennifer Cooke and the Research Seminar Series at the Department of English and Drama, University of Loughborough; John Gorman and the Wirral Festival of Firsts; Eoin Flannery and the English and Modern Languages Research Seminar Series at Oxford Brookes University; Amy Cameron and the National Army Museum; Isabel Davies and the Staff Research Seminar at Birkbeck; Rachel Hewitt, the Oxford Centre for Life Writing and Wolfson College, Oxford; Christina Britzolakis and the Northern Modernism Seminar at the University of Warwick; Ingrid Hanson and the English Research Seminar at the University of Hull; Deborah Lea Madsen and the Département de Langue et Littérature Anglaise at the University of Geneva; Santanu Das and the participants in the British Academy Landmark Conference *The First World War: Literature, Culture, Modernity*; Patrick Hayes and the Modern Literature Graduate Seminar at the Faculty of English, University of Oxford; Justine Shaw, Sara Crangle, Hope Wolf, the Centre for Modernist Studies and the English Colloquium at the University of Sussex.

The staff of the Bodleian Library, Oxford; the British Library; the Imperial War Museum; the National Archives; the Templer Study Centre at the National Army Museum; the University of Geneva Libraries; and the Cheshire Archive and Local Studies Service at the Cheshire Record Office, Chester, were all enormously helpful: thank you. My particular gratitude goes to Sue Killoran, librarian of Harris Manchester College, Oxford, who gets the books I ask for seemingly before I have pressed 'send' on the emails. I am also most grateful to Noranne Griffiths of the Central Legal Services, Ministry of Defence, for taking the time to respond to my query.

Ray Ryan, commissioning editor at Cambridge University Press, has been an extraordinary source of support and encouragement. The editorial team at Cambridge University Press is second to none: my thanks to everyone involved. I am also hugely grateful to the manuscript readers, whom I now know to be Vincent Sherry and Lyndsey Stonebridge, for their incisive feedback. I owe special thanks to Ian Finlay, who has been a meticulous proofreader.

I would like to acknowledge the support of the British Academy in awarding me a mid-career fellowship in 2013 and to my colleagues at Birkbeck for taking over my responsibilities in that year of leave. The work I was able to do in that time laid the foundation for all the rest, and the book wouldn't have happened without it. A version of some of the ideas contained in Chapter 5 appears in *The First World War: Literature, Culture,*

*Modernity, Proceedings of the British Academy* 213 (published for the British Academy by Oxford University Press in 2018), which I co-edited with Santanu Das, and I am grateful again to the British Academy for permission to use the material.

Finally, thanks to Nick Trefethen, who has rooted for *Veep*, as we came to call *Veteran Poetics*, or *VP*, from the day I climbed into the hammock with the *Odyssey* in Le Petit Pey.

# Introduction

## Veteran Poetics

Veterans inaugurate the Western canon: the Greek and Trojan warriors of Homer's *Iliad* and the homecoming protagonist of his *Odyssey* are a vocational summons to imaginative literature, whose eternal subject matter is human experience. The veteran has been a charged figure since antiquity. As a social persona, the ex-soldier is a focal point for debate about what a community owes to those who serve it and how that community relates to others; the answers to such questions can shape a nation as much as a village. As a private person – parent, offspring, partner, friend – the former fighter raises and confronts questions that are as personal as they are philosophical: what can be recovered from the past? To what extent do people stay the same over time? What is the value of experience? How can what has happened be communicated to others?

Veterans bring the real world into literature: they are figures at the heart of historical events, active agents in the processes of change. To meet a veteran (I speak as a civilian) is to be confronted with the fact and face of armed conflict – a living synecdoche; de-anonymized and re-individualized former members of the military, each one brings war home in very human terms. Veterans are inescapable reminders of a nation's conduct on the world stage but they also require us to think beyond 'the exceptional, marked event' and into 'the landscape of the mind'.[1] Ex by definition, they embody *having-been-ness*; they do the opposite of soldiering on. Returnees from afar, they live out the age-old connection between seeing and comprehending the world. They pose questions about how gender roles are understood; about parenthood, filiality and spousage. They bring us to reflect on merit, need and desert, on gratitude, debt and reward, on

[1]  Margaret R. Higonnet and Patrice L.-R. Higonnet, 'The Double Helix', *Behind the Lines: Gender and the Two World Wars*, ed. Margaret R. Higonnet, Jane Jenson, Sonya Michel and Margaret Collins Weitz (New Haven, CT: Yale University Press, 1987), 31–48: 46.

I

heroism, brokenness and exploitation. They ask us to confront the nature and necessity of our remembering and memorialization.

Central to national life, arousing conflicting reactions from adulation to fear, the veteran has extraordinary potential as a literary figure. But it is as though he – and it is almost invariably a he – has been hiding in plain sight in works of literature, treated as a sentimental or comic character or diagnosed as traumatized or overlooked entirely by critics. This book attempts something different: to illuminate how the figure has been deployed in literature of the age of mass warfare to represent ideas relating to being, knowing and communicating. The literary veteran, I suggest, challenges biographical decorum (the idea that certain things should happen at certain times of life), questions the notion of an enduring self, puts the relationship between the community and the Other under scrutiny, probes the nature of problem-solving, disrupts the discourses of politeness and reason, and expresses the limitations of experientially based knowledge and its transmission.

In view of the last of these, *Veteran Poetics* is, among other things, a book about a later, post-Enlightenment version of modernity.[2] In Théodor Adorno and Max Horkheimer's thesis, Enlightenment leads to totalitarianism, a process 'consummated by means of dictators and wars'.[3] That seemingly ineluctable process, I argue, meets an opposing tendency in the temporally unbound, deracinated, unfathoming and unfathomable *xenos* that is the veteran encountered in literary texts of the age of mass warfare. I take the inception of that age – which is ongoing – to coincide with the outbreak of the French Revolutionary Wars, and later in this Introduction I say more about why the kind of warfare that was waged from that juncture can be considered different to what went before. Here, though, it can briefly be stated that the French Revolutionary Wars, and the Napoleonic Wars that succeeded them, were unprecedentedly intense, massive in scale (in terms both of involvement of personnel and geographical extent) and subject, as never formerly, to high degrees of uncertainty.[4] The sheer

---

[2] The terms 'Enlightenment' and 'modernity' have a wide range of usage. Robert Pippin, for example, uses them 'interchangeably' (*Modernism as a Philosophical Problem: On the Dissatisfactions of European High Culture* (Oxford: Blackwell, 1991/1999), 4). I am distinguishing here between the modernity that the Enlightenment indisputably inaugurated and a later phase, which I discuss fully in Chapter 5.

[3] Théodor Adorno and Max Horkheimer, *Dialectic of Enlightenment* (*Dialektik der Aufklärung*) [1944], trans. John Cumming (London: Verso, 1979), XII.

[4] On this last point, see Anders Engberg-Pedersen, *Empire of Chance: The Napoleonic Wars and the Disorder of Things* (Cambridge, MA: Harvard University Press, 2015), which I return to later in this Introduction and in Chapters 3 and 5.

numbers of veterans they gave rise to, moreover, had not hitherto been known. Enlightenment led to the production *en masse* of a figure apt to counter Enlightenment, that is.

This is not the only Enlightenment it is possible to hypothesize, nor the only enlightenment that literary veterans illuminate.[5] As the texts discussed in this book demonstrate, they reveal the deep love of comradeship, draw attention to the reach of compassion and embody the sadness of things being over. They also lead us, I suggest – particularly in the guise of the ex-combatant who, despite expectations, fails to tell war stories – towards a respectful *not* knowing, which attends to the not said. 'Veteran poetics', then, comprise not only what fictional veterans do in and for literary texts, but also a way of reading that registers and values silences. This way of reading has been developed by the theoretical 'new ethicists',[6] among them Gayatri Chakravorty Spivak, whose famous and much-revised essay 'Can the Subaltern Speak?' cautions against either speaking for the silenced or empowering them to speak in a hostile system, and Judith Butler, who has proposed a conception of ethics 'that honors what cannot be fully known or captured about the Other'.[7] In her essay 'Values of Difficulty', Butler notes the refusal of Catherine Sloper in *Washington Square* either to promise her father not to marry Morris Townsend or, when her father is dead, actually to marry him.[8] Her final communication to the bemused Morris, Butler writes, 'does not take the form of words but rather an extended silence, as if whatever meaning this refusal has for her will not and cannot appear in speech'.[9] Like Morris, the reader is left 'exasperated, cursing, staring'.[10] But, despite the frustration, Butler recommends that we refrain from judging Catherine. Instead, we might 'affirm what is enigmatic [...], what cannot be easily or ever said, what marks the limits of the sayable'.[11] The non-storytelling veterans I discuss in Chapter 5 similarly

---

[5] As Dan Edelstein writes, 'the Enlightenment was a heterogeneous phenomenon, to the extent that some historians insist on speaking of it only in the plural' (*The Enlightenment: A Genealogy* (Chicago: The University of Chicago Press, 2010/2014), 3).

[6] See Dorothy J. Hale, 'Aesthetics and the New Ethics: Theorizing the Novel in the Twenty-First Century', *PMLA* 124.3 (May 2009), 896–905: 899.

[7] Judith Butler, 'Values of Difficulty', *Just Being Difficult: Academic Writing in the Public Arena*, ed. Jonathan Culler and Kevin Lamb (Stanford, CA: Stanford University Press, 2003), 199–215: 208.

[8] With her embroidery and refusal of numerous suitors, Catherine is a Penelope-figure, but, unlike Homer's Penelope, Catherine ultimately protects 'what we might be tempted to call her autonomy' (ibid., 208).

[9] Ibid., 208.

[10] Ibid., 208.

[11] Ibid., 208.

mark the limits of what can be said: noting and affirming those limits are the hallmark of veteran poetics.

## Poetics and Veterancy

In positing a veteran poetics, I recognize the distinguished, if largely unacknowledged, role that veterancy – real-life and fictional – has played in the history of literary aesthetics. As English Literature developed as an academic discipline in Britain in the twentieth century, it was profoundly shaped by people who had seen military service. In the First World War these included J. R. R. Tolkien (Second Lieutenant in the Lancashire Fusiliers, combatant in the Battle of the Somme),[12] F. R. Leavis (medical orderly with the Friends' Ambulance Unit),[13] C. S. Lewis (Second Lieutenant in the Somerset Light Infantry, wounded at the Battle of Arras),[14] Edmund Blunden (Second Lieutenant in the Royal Sussex regiment, awarded the Military Cross),[15] G. Wilson Knight (motorcycle dispatch rider in the Royal Engineers in Mesopotamia, India and Persia)[16] and Nevill Coghill (Second Lieutenant in the trench mortar division of the Royal Artillery in Salonika and Bulgaria).[17] In the Second World War there was Ian Watt (junior infantry officer, wounded during the surrender of Singapore, prisoner of war in the Far East from 1942 to 1945),[18] Richard Ellmann (member of the US Navy),[19] Raymond Williams (Second Lieutenant, later Captain, in the 21st Anti-Tank Regiment in the Normandy campaign)[20] and Richard Hoggart (anti-aircraft gunner in the Royal Artillery in North

---

[12] T. A. Shippey, 'Tolkien, John Ronald Reuel (1892–1973)', *Oxford Dictionary of National Biography* (Oxford University Press, 2004), online edition.

[13] Ian MacKillop, 'Leavis, Frank Raymond (1895–1978)', *Oxford Dictionary of National Biography* (Oxford University Press, 2004), online edition.

[14] J. A. W. Bennett, 'Lewis, Clive Staples (1898–1963)', rev. Emma Plaskitt, *Oxford Dictionary of National Biography* (Oxford University Press, 2004), online edition.

[15] Bernard Bergonzi, 'Blunden, Edmund Charles (1896–1974)', *Oxford Dictionary of National Biography* (Oxford University Press, 2004), online edition.

[16] Francis Berry, 'Knight, (George) Richard Wilson (1897–1985)', *Oxford Dictionary of National Biography* (Oxford University Press, 2004), online edition.

[17] John Carey, 'Coghill, Nevill Henry Kendal Aylmer (1899–1980)', *Oxford Dictionary of National Biography* (Oxford University Press, 2004), online edition.

[18] Marina Mackay, 'The Wartime Rise of *The Rise of the Novel*', *Representations* 119.1 (2012), 119–43: 120, 119.

[19] John Kelly, 'Ellmann, Richard David (1918–1987)', *Oxford Dictionary of National Biography* (Oxford University Press, 2004), online edition.

[20] Dai Smith, 'Williams, Raymond Henry (1921–1988)', *Oxford Dictionary of National Biography* (Oxford University Press, 2004), online edition.

Africa and Italy).[21] There is much valuable work to be done on revealing the connections between these figures' veterancy and their literary thinking – Marina Mackay's article on Ian Watt sets a sterling example[22] – and there is insufficient space to do more than point to some resonances here. But one can mention, for example, Lewis's experience of trench camaraderie – 'a kind of love between fellow-sufferers' – and his claims for the role of 'the mutual love of warriors' in helping to render the conventions of courtly love acceptable;[23] Tolkien's 'taste for fairy-stories', which was 'wakened by philology' but 'quickened to full life by war';[24] what Leavis witnessed as an ambulance orderly and his commitment to discerning organic, vital morality in literature ('[w]e forget, when Leavis invokes "life"', wrote his former student Howard Jacobson, 'that its quite literal opposite is death; that when he began reshaping what was meant by English literature he was pulling matter out of the fire');[25] and the apparent connection between Williams's sense of losing his 'full human perspective' in war and his life-long project to uncover 'structures of feeling'.[26] Mackay has gone much further in Watt's case, persuasively arguing that experience of 'war's characteristic involuntary collectivities' accounts for his emphasis, in *The Rise of the Novel* (1957), on the eighteenth-century novel's advancement of individualism.[27] Watt 'knew more than most', writes Mackay, of the 'struggle for survival in the bleak perspectives' that Defoe portrayed; '[l]ittle could have qualified him better to speak of them than his experience as a prisoner of war'.[28] Though the reactions to combat service in the work of these literary critics are varied, what shines through them all is a predilection for lucidity (which can come via myth or realism), an aversion to rhetorical pettifoggery and a commitment to the values inherent in comradeship. While it's true that war can make literary criticism seem irrelevant – as Ezra

---

[21] John Ezard, 'Richard Hoggart Obituary', *Guardian* (10 April 2014), www.theguardian.com/books/2014/apr/10/richard-hoggart.

[22] See also Kate McLoughlin, 'New Impressions XVI: *The Great War and Modern Memory*', *Essays in Criticism* 64.4 (October 2014), 436–48, on the American veteran critic Paul Fussell.

[23] C. S. Lewis, *Surprised by Joy: The Shape of my Life* (London: Fontana, 1955/1959), 152; C. S. Lewis, *The Allegory of Love: A Study in Medieval Tradition* (Oxford: The Clarendon Press, 1936), 9.

[24] J. R. R. Tolkien, 'On Fairy-Stories', *The Monsters and the Critics and Other Essays*, ed. Christopher Tolkien (London: George Allen and Unwin, 1983), 109–61: 135.

[25] Howard Jacobson, 'Howard Jacobson on Being Taught by F. R. Leavis', *Telegraph* (23 April 2011), www.telegraph.co.uk/culture/books/8466388/Howard-Jacobson-on-being-taught-by-FRLeavis.html.

[26] Raymond Williams, *Politics and Letters: Interviews with New Left Review* (London: New Left Books, 1979), 57; Williams coined the phrase 'structures of feeling' in *Preface to Film* (1954) and developed it throughout his work.

[27] Mackay, 'The Wartime Rise of *The Rise of the Novel*', 124.

[28] Ibid., 119.

Pound suggests in his excoriation of *belletrism* in 'Hugh Selwyn Mauberley' (1920) or, more practically, as Vera Brittain made clear in her decision to switch from English Literature to History when she returned to Oxford after nursing in the First World War[29] – the work of these scholars, critics and theorists ensures that veterancy runs through literary studies, driving methodologies, forming canons, shaping syllabuses.

Complementing the influence of real-life veterans on English Literature as a discipline is the role that certain key fictional veterans have played in critical theorizings. In his classic work of criticism, *The Wound and the Bow* (1941), for instance, Edmund Wilson, himself a First World War veteran,[30] argued that the ancient Greek story of Philoctetes, possessor of an invincible bow and irreparably injured in the Trojan War, is the story of creative endeavour: 'genius and disease, like strength and mutilation, may be inextricably bound up together'.[31] The bow is nothing without the wound, that is – and vice versa. But it is another fictional veteran from antiquity who has most inspired philosophico-critical thought – Homer's Odysseus. Scholars have turned to the *Odyssey* for support for a variety of ideas and approaches: Piero Boitani to illustrate the proximity of poetry and history in *The Shadow of Ulysses* (1991) and Jonathan Shay to illuminate post-traumatic stress disorder in *Odysseus in America* (2002), for instance – two examples that demonstrate the range of application. Four *Odyssey* readers in particular merit special attention, given the significance of their ideas to this book. Erich Auerbach, Théodor Adorno, Max Horkheimer and Emmanuel Levinas – all Jewish, all deracinated by the Nazis (the first three forced to flee Germany, the last held in a Prisoner of War camp near Hannover)[32] – were in exile themselves when they contemplated Odysseus'

[29] Brittain accounted for the change by saying that she now believed it was her job 'to find out all about it' and prevent it happening again (*Testament of Youth: An Autobiographical Study of the Years 1900–1925* [1933] (London: Virago, 2008), 431).

[30] Wilson served as a nurse and, later, as a translator with the US Army in France during the First World War (Jeffrey Meyers, *Edmund Wilson: A Biography* (Boston: Houghton Mifflin, 1995), 33–9). 'In general, I loathed the Army,' he wrote (quoted on 32).

[31] Edmund Wilson, *The Wound and the Bow: Seven Studies in Literature* [1941] (London: Methuen, 1961), 259.

[32] Erich Auerbach, born in Berlin in 1892, fought with the German Army in the First World War and took refuge from the Nazis in Istanbul, where, at the Turkish National University, he wrote *Mimesis* (1946/1953) (René Wellek, 'Erich Auerbach (1892–1958)', *Comparative Literature* 10.1 (1958), 93–5: 93). Max Horkheimer, born in Stuttgart in 1895, moved to New York in 1934 and returned to Germany in 1948/9 (J. C. Berendzen, 'Max Horkheimer', *The Stanford Encyclopedia of Philosophy*, ed. Edward N. Zalta (Winter 2016), https://plato.stanford.edu/archives/win2016/entries/horkheimer/). Théodor Adorno, born in Frankfurt in 1903, left Germany for America in 1938, returning in 1949 (Tom Huhn, 'Introduction: Thoughts Beside Themselves', *The Cambridge Companion to Adorno*, ed. Tom Huhn (Cambridge: Cambridge University Press, 2002), 1–18: 1, 2). Emmanuel Levinas, born in Kaunas, Lithuania, in 1906, studied at the University of Strasbourg and was drafted into

*nostos*,[33] his return home to Ithaca. It would have been understandable if it had reinforced in them a desire for a similar safe return to the familiar, but it did the opposite, stimulating instead ideas about the nature of being based upon acceptance of incompletion, risk-taking and love of the Other.

In *Dialectic of Enlightenment*, working out their theory as to why the Enlightenment led to the death camps, Adorno and Horkheimer saw the whole process unfolding in the *Odyssey*. In packed, meticulous sentences, each one compacting a philosophy, they explain that the *nostos* was a return to kingly domination of territory: back in Ithaca, Odysseus could sleep with a 'quiet mind', knowing that servants were ready to chase away thieves and wild animals.[34] Enlightenment was just that – sleeping easy: the mastery of nature in the form of scientific knowledge that, finding doubt its anathema or 'paralyzed by fear of the truth', had only one reaction to what was foreign to it: relentless eradication.[35] Levinas takes the idea further. Contrasting Homeric odyssey with Abrahamic errand, the journey home to the familiar with the journey out to the unknown,[36] he hypothesizes at the outset of *Totality and Infinity* (1961) a 'metaphysical desire' for 'a land not of our birth, for a land foreign to every nature, which has not been our fatherland and to which we shall never betake ourselves'.[37] For Levinas, the untroubled sleep of Odysseus in Ithaca would be delusional at best, at worst its own form of bondage, for '[f]reedom consists in knowing that freedom is in peril'.[38] Better the 'truly human' state of Abraham, whose tent remains open to all-comers, than the palace in lock-down.[39]

Like Levinas, Auerbach also drew inspiration from the contrasting stories of Odysseus and Abraham. In the middle of the episode in which

the French army in 1939, serving as an interpreter of Russian and German. He was taken prisoner in 1940 and spent most of his captivity in a camp in Fallinpostel (Simon Critchley, 'Emmanuel Levinas: A Disparate Inventory', *The Cambridge Companion to Levinas*, ed. Simon Critchley and Robert Bernasconi (Cambridge: Cambridge University Press, 2002), xv–xxx: xv, xix).

[33] *Nostos* (homecoming) is derived from νέομαι (return home) (Marigo Alexopoulou, *The Theme of Returning Home in Ancient Greek Literature: The Nostos of the Epic Heroes* (Lewiston, ON: The Edwin Mellen Press, 2009), 1).

[34] Adorno and Horkheimer, *Dialectic of Enlightenment*, 14.

[35] Ibid., xiii.

[36] Emmanuel Levinas, *Totality and Infinity: An Essay on Exteriority* (*Totalité et Infini: essai sur l'extériorité*) [1961], trans. Alphonso Lingis (Pittsburgh, PA: Duquesne University Press, 2007), 103. See also Adriaan Peperzak, *To the Other: An Introduction to the Philosophy of Emmanuel Levinas* (West Lafayette, IN: Purdue University Press, 1993), 44, 67, 68.

[37] Levinas, *Totality and Infinity*, 33–4; see also 103, and Peperzak, *To the Other*, 44, 67, 68.

[38] Levinas, *Totality and Infinity*, 35.

[39] Emmanuel Levinas, *Nine Talmudic Readings* (*Quatre lectures talmudiques*, 1968; *Du sacré au saint: cinq lectures talmudiques*, 1977), trans. Annette Aronowicz (Bloomington, IN: Indiana University Press, 1968/1990), 99.

Eurycleia, washing her disguised master's feet, recognizes him from the scar on his thigh, Homer interpolates the story of the boyhood boar-hunt in which Odysseus acquired the original wound. Auerbach opens his classic work *Mimesis* (1946) with a section called 'Odysseus's Scar', in which he presents the interpolation as evidence of the 'fully externalized form' of Hellenic literature.[40] Unlike Hebraic literature that, as instanced by the story of Abraham and Isaac, can 'indicate thoughts which remain unexpressed', the Homeric style, for Auerbach, 'knows only a foreground, only a uniformly illuminated, uniformly objective present'.[41] Auerbach is analysing literary aesthetics rather than, as Adorno, Horkheimer and Levinas, ideas of ethical being. But the fully externalized literary mode has this in common with the ontological refuge in the familiar: it is a form of safety. For all four thinkers, albeit loosely, the arc described by the *Odyssey* is shorthand for mastering reality by nothing less than attempting to know everything about it.

The *Odyssey* also informs *Veteran Poetics*. I begin each chapter except the last with a vignette from the epic, drawing on it to illuminate points about the *curriculum vitae*, interaction between the community and the Other, problem-solving and the inhospitality of talking too much. But the subject of my last chapter lacks antique precedent. In my reading, the unfathomable veteran of mass warfare finds no ancient avatar in the easy-sleeping Odysseus. Rather, as already suggested, he is an impediment in the onward flow of the Enlightenment's 'dissolvent rationality'.[42] In this case, it is the absence of Homeric parallel that makes the point most forcefully. In using vignettes from the *Odyssey* in the first four chapters, my methodology is both less ambitious and messier than what T. S. Eliot had in mind when, referring to the manipulation of the parallel between contemporaneity and antiquity in Joyce's *Ulysses* (1922), he declared 'the mythical method' to be a means of 'controlling' and of 'ordering' an 'immense panorama of futility and anarchy'.[43] What I am attempting to do is closer to Rita Felski's characterization of actor-network theory as 'trudg[ing] like an ANT', alert to 'intricate ecologies and diverse micro-organisms', thinking 'temporal

---

[40] Erich Auerbach, *Mimesis: The Representation of Reality in Western Literature* (Princeton, NJ: Princeton University Press, 1953), 5.

[41] Ibid., 11, 7. In a section also titled 'Odysseus's Scar', Terence Cave provides an alternative reading to Auerbach's, arguing that '[r]ecognition reaches back most often to painful or problematic narrative events hidden in the past': '[t]he crisis of the adolescent [Odysseus] is re-enacted in the crisis of the middle-aged man' (*Recognitions: A Study in Poetics* (Oxford: The Clarendon Press, 1988), 22, 23).

[42] Adorno and Horkheimer, *Dialectic of Enlightenment*, 6.

[43] T. S. Eliot '*Ulysses*, Order and Myth' [1923], *Selected Prose of T. S. Eliot*, ed. Frank Kermode (London: Faber and Faber, 1984), 175–8: 178.

interdependency without telos, movement without supersession', noticing the past in the present and vice versa.[44] So, rather than the paradigmatic, 'controlling' deployment of Homer that Eliot discerned in Joyce, I offer echoes and inter-connections. Hence, it is important to note that when I quote from the *Odyssey* it is from the 1946 translation for Penguin by E. V. Rieu. Emile Victor Rieu served in the Maratha Light Infantry during the First World War and translated the *Odyssey* during the Second while serving as a Major in the Home Guard, completing the first draft 'as France fell' and revising it to the accompaniment of 'the sound of V1 and V2 explosions and the crash of shattering glass'.[45] In this volume, Odysseus is a veteran's veteran; the *Odyssey* a veteran's text. The joint work of Homer and Rieu traverses *Veteran Poetics* like Odysseus the voyager: persistent, interfering, infuriating, inspiring.

More: it is – except as regards the final chapter – *knowing*. What it means for a text to know has been best articulated by Seamus Heaney who, citing the final chorus of *Doctor Faustus*, the opening lines of *Paradise Lost* and the whole of Wallace Stevens's 'The River of Rivers in Connecticut', identified an 'affective power' that 'has not to do simply with [an] author's craft' but that 'comes from a kind of veteran knowledge which has gathered to a phonetic and rhythmic head, and forced an utterance'.[46] Throughout *Veteran Poetics* the affective power of the *Odyssey* wells up, except, as indicated, in the last chapter, on whose subject – the unfathomable – the well runs dry. And if the *Odyssey* is a veteran text, another kind of textual veterancy belongs to the reader. Reading is not the same as fighting in a war or being in the army, but its processes of accumulating knowledge, growing familiar, making personal investment, following direction, encountering difficulties, repeating certain actions, testing hypotheses, waiting in uncertainty, becoming skilled in recognition, persisting over time, making gains, suffering losses and emerging changed endow it with qualities that veterancy shares.[47] The likeness between the reader and the war veteran is metaphorical and, to preserve the special quality of having been at war, I treat it with the lightest of touches in this book,

[44] Rita Felski, 'Context Stinks!', *New Literary History* 42.4 (Autumn 2011), 573–91: 577.

[45] P. J. Connell, 'Rieu, Emile Victor (1887–1972)', *Oxford Dictionary of National Biography* (Oxford University Press 2004), online edition; www.us.penguingroup.com/static/pages/classics/history. html. The *Odyssey* was the first Penguin Classic.

[46] Seamus Heaney, 'Dylan the Durable? On Dylan Thomas', *Salmagundi* 100 (Fall 1993), 66–85: 76.

[47] Textual veterancy is acknowledged in Margot Norris, *Virgin and Veteran Readings of Ulysses* (Basingstoke: Palgrave Macmillan, 2010/2011).

drawing on it principally to illuminate the sense of *having come through* on which interpretation of a text can depend.

Both real-life and fictional veterancy generate poetics, whether in the form of providing a metaphorical vehicle for philosophical ideas or shaping literary thinking or suggesting a model for textual behaviour or readerly experience. But what – or who – exactly is a 'veteran'? In the following section I give a definitional history of the term.

### The Meaning of 'Veteran'

The word 'veteran' comes from the Latin *vetus*, meaning 'old', which is itself related to the inferred Proto-Indo-European *wetos-, meaning 'year'.[48] In theory, therefore, it is possible to become a veteran simply by growing older[49] – I'm veterating as I'm writing this; you're veterating as you're reading it – and, as will be seen in Chapters 3 and 5, this aspect of veterancy is key to the literary deployment of the figure to express epistemological ideas based on experience accrued over time. The related and more familiar usage – 'One who has long experience in military service; an old soldier' – is first recorded by the *Oxford English Dictionary* as occurring in 1509, in a reference in Stephen Hawes's *The Pastime of Pleasure* to 'the noble veterane syr Consuetude'.[50] 'Consuetude' is an old word for 'habit' or 'custom', both dependent upon the accumulation of time: hence the noble knight's name matches his military status. The *OED*'s next recorded instance combines these senses of combat service and temporal extension: in *The Remaining Medical Works of that Famous and Renowned Physician Dr. Thomas Willis* (1681), 'Veterans' are defined as 'Old Soldiers, or any thing that hath served long in a place'.[51] A report in the *Post Boy and Historical Account* for 6–8 August 1695 refers to the 'Veteran Forces' of the King of Sweden, a usage that seems to denote experienced soldiers, as opposed to aged or former servicemen.[52]

By the end of the eighteenth century – the beginning of the period with which this book is concerned – the word 'veteran' is appearing with

---

[48] 'Veteran, n. and adj.', *Oxford English Dictionary* (Oxford University Press), online edition.

[49] The *OED*'s second definition is 'One who has seen long service in any office or position; an experienced or aged person' ('Veteran, n. and adj.', 2, *Oxford English Dictionary* (Oxford University Press), online edition).

[50] 'Veteran, n. and adj.', 1a., *Oxford English Dictionary* (Oxford University Press), online edition.

[51] Thomas Willis, *The Remaining Medical Works of that Famous and Renowned Physician Dr. Thomas Willis* (London: T. Dring, 1681), unpaginated.

[52] Anonymous, 'Lisbon, July Th 5th 1695', *Post Boy and Historical Account* (Gale-Cengage 17th–18th Century Burney Newspaper Collection).

some frequency in the press, regularly associated with experience, longevity, calmness and, consequently, wisdom.[53] (In the 1790s, the Royal Navy's fleet included a man-of-war called the *Veteran*, the vessel's name no doubt reflecting its formidable qualities.)[54] On 14 February 1793, the French correspondent of the *St James's Chronicle* interviewed a 'worthy veteran' of the Irish Brigade on the subject of his fellow countrymen. The man prefaces his remarks with 'Well, I'll tell you with the frankness of an old soldier that has fifty scars on his body', claiming the unimpeachable credentials of age and battle experience along with the corporeal evidence to prove them.[55] A report on the Battle of Avesnes in the *Sun* on 30 October 1793 quotes 'several veteran Officers, who made the Campaigns of the Seven Years Wars against the Turks' to the effect that 'the fire was so dreadful' that they had never 'seen the like'.[56] In this instance, veterancy represents a corpus of experiential knowledge capable of substantiating what is unprecedented. In a more quotidian example, a letter published in the *Sun* on 29 November 1793 about donating 'winter cloathing' notes that 'the experienced Veteran' (a possible tautology) is the best authority on the 'means of alleviating the miseries of a Winter Campaign'.[57] An obituary published in the *Evening Mail* for 22–24 June 1796 of one Lieutenant-Colonel Robert Malcolm, killed in action in St. Lucia, declares that he 'combined the most heroic bravery with the coolness and the knowledge of a veteran of consummate abilities':[58] in this case, veterancy is associated not only with insight amassed over a number of years but also with a corresponding *sang-froid* of judgement and action.

Its connection with experience accrued over time is further evident in wider applications of the term 'veteran': the Irish actor Charles Macklin is described as 'a venerable veteran' who 'ought to write a treatise on long

[53] Cf. James Thomson's praise of Viscount Cobham's 'veteran skill' in l. 1081 of 'Autumn' (added to *The Seasons* in 1744) (James Thomson, *The Seasons and The Castle of Indolence*, ed. James Sambook (Oxford: Oxford University Press, 1984), 118).

[54] The *Veteran*'s movements are recorded in the press, for example in Anonymous, Untitled, *Lloyd's Evening Post* (12–14 February 1794) (Gale-Cengage 17th–18th Century Burney Newspaper Collection).

[55] Anonymous, 'The Diary', *Diary or Woodfall's Register* (14 February 1793) (Gale-Cengage 17th–18th Century Burney Newspaper Collection).

[56] Anonymous, 'Brussels, Oct. 28', *Sun* (30 October 1793) (Gale-Cengage 17th–18th Century Burney Newspaper Collection).

[57] F. E., 'To the Conductor of the Sun', *Sun* (29 November 1793) (Gale-Cengage 17th–18th Century Burney Newspaper Collection).

[58] Anonymous, 'Lieutenant-Colonel Malcolm', *Evening Mail* (22–24 June 1796) (Gale-Cengage 17th–18th Century Burney Newspaper Collection).

life';[59] the President of the Royal Academy, Benjamin West, is termed a 'veteran of the pencil';[60] and the Rector of Lincoln College, Oxford, calls Dr Vicesimus Knox 'a veteran in pedantry'.[61] Providing a slight but significant variation on these patterns of usage, an advertisement in the *Diary or Woodfall's Register* of 14 February 1793 for Tobias Smollett's *The Expedition of Humphrey Clinker* mentions an engraving of the scene featuring 'the veteran Admiral Balderick and other ancient friends, who had been roughly treated by life'.[62] The alignment between 'veteran' and 'ancient' highlights not only the oldness connoted by veterancy, but also its anteriority, its condition of being something no longer[63] – a strand of meaning that has resonances in the literary use of the veteran figure to express certain ontological concepts, not least in Samuel Taylor Coleridge's 'The Rime of the Ancient Mariner' (discussed in Chapter 4).

At the beginning of the nineteenth century, then, 'veteran' is established in a multiplicity of associations – age, long life and long service, experience, insight and the quality of being former – as well as denoting an exserviceman. Analysis of the word 'veteran' in the corpus of British English from 1760 to 2008 using Google's Ngram viewer reveals that usage has remained buoyant throughout the period.[64] But alongside the usages of the word so far encountered, there also exist other, 'official' definitions, created to determine who qualifies for veteran compensation and benefits. To give two international comparators: in the United States, veterans are defined as 'personnel who have served for a minimum period of service and have

[59] Anonymous, Untitled, *Diary or Woodfall's Register* (26 June 1793) (Gale-Cengage 17th–18th Century Burney Newspaper Collection).

[60] Anonymous, 'Exhibition of Pictures', *Times* (30 April 1793) (Gale-Cengage 17th–18th Century Burney Newspaper Collection).

[61] Anonymous, 'Dr. Knox.', *Morning Chronicle* (10 September 1793) (Gale-Cengage 17th–18th Century Burney Newspaper Collection). The associations are not always positive: in *Caleb Williams* (1794), for example, the loathsome landlady of the robbers' abode is described as a 'hoary veteran' (William Godwin, *Caleb Williams*, ed. Pamela Clemit (Oxford: Oxford University Press, 2009), 221).

[62] Anonymous, 'Advertisement', *Diary or Woodfall's Register* (14 February 1793) (Gale-Cengage 17th–18th Century Burney Newspaper Collection).

[63] 'Ancient' derives from the Latin *ante* (before) ('Ancient, adj. and n.', 1, *Oxford English Dictionary* (Oxford University Press), online edition). Geoffrey Hudson notes that, of 9,194 veterans granted pensions by the Royal Hospital for Seamen at Greenwich between 1714 and 1790, 28 per cent were under the age of 50, 13 per cent were under the age of 40 and some were as young as 12 ('Arguing Disability: Ex-Servicemen's Own Stories in Early Modern England, 1590–1790', *Medicine, Madness and Social History: Essays in Honour of Roy Porter*, ed. Roberta Bivins and John V. Pickstone (Basingstoke: Palgrave Macmillan, 2007), 105–17: 112).

[64] The British English corpus was searched for instances of the word 'veteran' (case insensitive) between 1760 and 2008 (the cut-off point of the corpus). There were peaks in usage in 1804, 1818, 1828, 1833 and 1851.

been discharged with at least the status of "honorable" despite the fact that they may not have served on operations', while in Australia, veterans are 'personnel who have served in an active deployment overseas'.[65] The UK Ministry of Defence uses what has been described as the 'most inclusive of definitions available': '[t]hose who have served for at least a day in HM Armed Forces, whether as a Regular or as a Reservist'.[66] This definition requires neither longevity of service (as in the United States) nor combat experience, overseas or otherwise (as in Australia); moreover, the Armed Forces Covenant adopted in 2011 extends the population of those who qualify for veterans' benefits to include 'relevant family members'.[67] Christopher Dandeker et al. suggest that this expansive definition can be attributed to the British home front experience in the Second World War: the 'sharing of suffering' by military and civilians in that conflict has ensured that the idea of the veteran with 'its implied meaning of exclusivity' has not been favourably regarded by British eyes.[68] Certainly, the Armed Forces Covenant[69] supports the idea of such vicarious veterancy, which

[65] Christopher Dandeker, Simon Wessely, Amy Iversen and John Ross, 'What's in a Name? Defining and Caring for "Veterans": The United Kingdom in International Perspective', *Armed Forces and Society* 32.2 (January 2006), 161–77: 166.

[66] Anonymous, *The Armed Forces Covenant* (London: Ministry of Defence, 2011), 5.

[67] Ibid., 5.

[68] Dandeker et al., 'What's in a Name?', 163.

[69] Despite pressure from the Royal British Legion and the Labour Party, the Armed Forces Covenant was not enshrined in statute (see Nick Hopkins, 'MPs Block Military Covenant', *Guardian* (17 February 2011), www.theguardian.com/uk/2011/feb/17/mps-block-miltary-covenant). It does not, therefore, have legal force per se, but section 2 of the Armed Forces Act 2011 inserted a new Part 16A into the Armed Forces Act 2006, which provides that the Secretary of State for Defence must report annually to Parliament on the Covenant's implementation. Part 16A does not contain a definition of 'veteran' but its interpretative provisions (section 343B) defines 'service people' as:

(a) members of the regular forces and the reserve forces;

(b) members of British overseas territory forces who are subject to service law;

(c) former members of any of Her Majesty's forces who are ordinarily resident in the United Kingdom; and

(d) relevant family members.

Dandeker et al., writing in 2006, state that 'The United Kingdom has recently formalized its approach to veterans, using the most inclusive of the definitions available: all personnel who have served more than one day (together with their dependants)' ('What's in a Name?', 166). No source is given for this statement. Howard Burdett et al. similarly claim that 'Everyone who has performed military service for at least one day and drawn a day's pay is termed a veteran' ('"Are You A Veteran?" Understanding of the Term "Veteran" Among UK Ex-Service Personnel: A Research Note', *Armed Forces and Society* 39.4 (2013), 751–9: 752, citing R. H. Talbot Rice, *The Next Generation of Veterans: Their Critical Needs and Their Emerging Rights* (London: Royal College of Defence Studies, 2009). Colonel Talbot Rice writes, 'In 2001 the UK Ministry of Defence formally defined the word "veteran" as a person who has served more than one day in any of the 3 services, together with his/her dependents' (unpaginated). Again, no source is given for this claim. It seems that Colonel Rice's statement has been relied on by subsequent writers (e.g. Jim McDermott, 'Old Soldiers Never Die: They Adapt Their Military Skills

encompasses not only secondary trauma (the trauma of being close to a traumatized person) but also carrying memories or witnessing for another (a phenomenon akin to Marianne Hirsh's postmemory).[70] The long-term future of the United Kingdom's generous definition is in some doubt, however: the Veterans' Transition Review carried out by Lord Ashcroft in 2014 recommended a re-examination of the term 'veteran' to produce 'an acceptable qualification with greater credibility and exclusivity'.[71]

Not everybody works by dictionary and governmental definitions, of course. A 2002 survey of public perceptions of veterans in the UK yielded some intriguing results: 57 per cent of those surveyed believed that a 'veteran' was only someone who had been in the First or Second World Wars. Interviews of personnel who had recently left the military conducted for a 2007 thesis by ex-soldier Jim McDermott corroborated this view: 'veterans were second world war chaps, first world war chaps, there's very few of them left', suggested one respondent.[72] These recent army-leavers emphasized the importance of combat service to veterancy: '[i]n my mind a "veteran" is an ex-serviceman who has seen "extensive action" like in the WW2 days or Korea or even the Falklands conflict (proper shooting matches)'; 'I don't consider myself a veteran as I associate that with the real soldiers at the sharp end, but ex serviceman covers it nicely'.[73] This view was shared by the 29 per cent of those responding to the 2002 survey who thought that veterans were people who had 'served overseas' on 'campaigns'.[74] Dandeker et al. accordingly suggest that, in the UK, the 'norm' has been 'to use *ex-service* to describe those who have been employed in the armed forces, with the term veteran reserved for those who have served in military operations'.[75] That British usage has tended to associate the term 'veteran' with participation in a particular campaign is evident in the names of ex-servicemen's organizations such as the 1940 Dunkirk Veterans' Association

---

and Become Successful Civilians. What Factors Contribute to the Successful Transition of Army Veterans to Civilian Life and Work?', unpublished PhD thesis (University of Leicester, 2007), 49) but I have been unable to find any statutory definition of this kind or of this time, and nor could the Central Legal Services of the Ministry of Defence point me to one.

[70] 'Postmemory is a powerful and very particular form of memory precisely because its connection to its object or source is mediated not through recollection but through an imaginative investment and creation' (Marianne Hirsch, *Family Frames: Photography, Narrative, and Postmemory* (Cambridge, MA: Harvard University Press, 1997), 22).

[71] Michael Ashcroft, 'The Veterans' Transition review', www.veteranstransition.co.uk/vtrreport .pdf, 24.

[72] McDermott, 'Old Soldiers Never Die', 132.

[73] Ibid., 132.

[74] Dandeker et al., 'What's in a Name?', 166.

[75] Ibid., 165, original emphasis.

and the Normandy Veterans' Association. Expanding use of the term in the UK may reflect a growing Americanization and politicization of the constituency, reflecting the considerable lobbying power of organizations such as Veterans of Foreign Wars in the United States.

Paul Fussell, American Second World War veteran and author of the book that has had one of the greatest impacts on cultural understanding of the First World War – *The Great War and Modern Memory* (1975) – was in no doubt on the matter. Criticizing J. Glenn Gray's *The Warriors* (1959) as showing 'every sign of error occasioned by remoteness of experience',[76] he notes: 'Division headquarters is miles – *miles* – behind the line where soldiers experience terror and madness and relieve those pressures by crazy brutality and sadism. Indeed, unless they actually encountered the enemy during the war, most "soldiers" have very little idea what "combat" was like.'[77] Fussell quotes William Manchester's remark that '[a]ll who wore uniforms are called veterans, but more than 90 per cent of them are as uninformed about the killing zones as those on the home front' and commends Manchester's fellow marine E. B. Sledge for 'thoughtfully and responsibly invok[ing] the terms *drastically* and *totally* to underline the differences in experience between front and rear, and not even the far rear, but the close rear'.[78] Fussell's remarks, made in the course of arguing who may legitimately pronounce on the ethics of dropping the atom bomb on Hiroshima, demonstrate a visceral certainty that veterancy is coincident with front-line combat experience.[79]

The authors of the literary works explored in this book were not concerned with dictionary or statutory definitions; nor did they all share Fussell's conviction that veteran status requires a hostile encounter with an enemy. Nonetheless, all but one of the literary veterans we shall encounter satisfy the British, American and even Australian definitions of the term. The exception is Coleridge's Ancient Mariner, and the justification for his inclusion is made in Chapter 4. It is true, too, that as they exploited the multiple associations surrounding the figure, the authors discussed here perceived veterans in a

---

[76] Paul Fussell, *Thank God for the Atom Bomb and Other Essays* (New York: Summit Books, 1988), 29.

[77] Ibid., 29–30.

[78] Ibid., 29–30.

[79] This is an example of what James Campbell identified as 'combat gnosticism', the belief that armed combat 'represents a qualitatively separate order of experience' that is 'difficult if not impossible to communicate to any who have not undergone an identical experience' (James Campbell, 'Combat Gnosticism: The Ideology of First World War Criticism', *New Literary History* 30 (1999), 203–15: 203).

non-specialist way. They were not necessarily aware, that is, of the regulatory framework governing the treatment of ex-service personnel and their views of veterans were often the result of general impressions, rather than informed knowledge. But the reader of this book deserves to have that knowledge, if only to understand the generality of the impressions. Rather than lengthen this Introduction with the information, though, I have provided a potted history of the veteran in English/British life and culture in the Appendix for consultation at the reader's convenience.

## Modern Warfare

In parameter-setting mode, I also need to elaborate upon the time frame that *Veteran Poetics* focuses on. Literary veterans from before the age of mass warfare – from Chaucer's Knight to Othello to Uncle Toby in *Tristram Shandy* – could be enlisted to demonstrate many of the ideas and themes I am concerned with. But cut-off points have to be made and, as already noted, there is agreement among military, political and cultural historians that the French Revolutionary and Napoleonic Wars inaugurated a new kind, and therefore a new experience, of armed conflict. Briefly put, the veteran of these and subsequent wars can be associated with an uncertainty that had not hitherto been known, or not known so intensely. In literary texts, therefore, such a veteran is an ideal vehicle via which to probe and confound received notions, whether they are about personal identity or social identity or problem-solving or communication. More specifically, as mentioned earlier, my argument in the final chapter is that modern mass warfare has produced, *en masse*, the figure apt to convey a post-Enlightenment *Weltanschauung* – another reason to confine my attention to literary works from the 1790s onwards.[80] Having made these claims, it behoves me to say more about the novelty of the warfare dating from that juncture.

Complete breaks with the past are impossible to prove but there is consensus that the French Revolutionary and Napoleonic Wars constituted a new way of waging war. 'An astonishing transformation' is the phrase David A. Bell uses to describe what happened to warfare in the 1790s; Peter Paret calls it nothing less than a 'revolution'.[81] What was different? Carnage

---

[80] Michel Foucault, for other reasons, also associated this period with a 'mutation' in 'the entire Western episteme' (*The Order of Things: An Archaeology of the Human Sciences* (*Les mots et les choses: Une archéologie des sciences humaines*) [1966], translator unknown (New York: Vintage, 1973), 205).

[81] David A. Bell, *The First Total War: Napoleon's Europe and the Birth of Modern Warfare* (London: Bloomsbury, 2007), 5; Peter Paret, *Understanding War: Essays on Clausewitz and the*

was certainly nothing new. The Thirty Years War, fought between various European powers, including England, between 1618 and 1648, was particularly bloody: one of its leading historians, Geoffrey Parker, calls it 'by far the most traumatic period in the history of Germany' up to 1939.[82] Wars of the early and mid-eighteenth century might have been 'a sort of theatre of the aristocracy', but to participate in them was still 'an indescribably bloody horror'.[83] But even these episodes of destruction and bloodshed were 'qualitatively and quantitatively different'[84] from what began in that century's last decade.

The difference was not to do with weaponry. As Michael Howard notes, Napoleon's armaments 'were almost identical with those of Frederick the Great'.[85] There were some tactical innovations – re-structuring of armies into autonomous divisions, use of free-moving, free-firing skirmishers, more flexible use of artillery, deployment of the column rather than the line as a unit of attack[86] – and though these did make combat an experience that was sensorially maximal, they were the outward manifestations, rather than the cause, of war's 'radically new scope'.[87] The newness derived from ideology: a revolutionary re-conceptualization of the relationship between the individual and the state. As Howard puts it, once the state was no longer seen as the ' "property" of dynastic princes' but the 'embodiment of some absolute Good' – 'Liberty', 'Nationality', 'Revolution' – it became an entity for which 'no price was too high, no sacrifice too great to pay'.[88] The logic of egalitarianism is that everyone will fight for it. And if this was

*History of Military Power* (Princeton, NJ: Princeton University Press, 1992), 75. Though insisting that the 'military profile' of the French Revolutionary and Napoleonic Wars points to 'quite the opposite of dramatic change', Michael Broers nonetheless accepts that what *was* new was the 'role and character of the state in raising troops' and the response of rural societies to that state ('Changes in War: The French Revolutionary and Napoleonic Wars', *The Changing Character of War*, ed. Hew Strachan and Sibylle Scheipers (Oxford: Oxford University Press, 2011), 64–78: 64).

[82] Geoffrey Parker, *The Thirty Years War* (London: Routledge), 192.

[83] Bell, *The First Total War*, 5, 44.

[84] Clive Emsley, *British Society and the French Wars 1793–1815* (London: Macmillan, 1979), 1.

[85] Michael Howard, *War in European History* (Oxford: Oxford University Press 1976/2000), 76. That is, mortars, furnace bombs, grapeshot, canister shots, muskets, pistols, swords, bayonets and pikes (see Terence Wise, *Artillery Equipments of the Napoleonic Wars* (Oxford: Osprey, 1979)).

[86] Howard, *War in European History*, 76. See also Broers, 'Changes in War' and David Gates, 'The Transformation of the Army 1783–1815', *The Oxford History of the British Army*, gen. ed. David G. Chandler, associate. ed. Ian Beckett (Oxford: Oxford University Press, 2007), 132–60. Guerrilla fighting made for particularly savage encounters (see Broers, 'Changes in War', 65, and Bell, *The First Total War*, 3).

[87] Bell, *The First Total War*, 8.

[88] Howard, *War in European History*, 75.

the fervour energizing the forces of revolutionary France, their opponents in battle had to meet it in kind. Bell calls the result 'the first total war'.[89]

Ideology, then, was the dynamo that made the French Revolutionary and Napoleonic Wars qualitatively different to what had gone before, and the new quality was intensity, reflected in quantity – a scale 'unprecedented since the barbarian invasions', 'not matched again until World War II'.[90] Previous warfare, particularly in the eighteenth century, had, to a great extent, been a form of show: securing the capitulation of an enemy by demonstrating what could be inflicted upon it, rather than pursuing that enemy's obliteration and losing manpower in the process.[91] By contrast, the goal of the French revolutionary government and, later, Napoleon, was, purely and simply, 'the crushing, in decisive engagement, of an adversary's means and will to resist'.[92] It was war as annihilation, war, in Clausewitz's view, that most nearly approached 'its true character, its absolute perfection'.[93] Everyone – in theory, at least – was involved in it. The *levée en masse* issued to the French population on 23 August 1793 proclaimed:

> Young men will go off to fight; married men will forge weapons and transport food supplies; women will make tents and clothing and will provide the service in hospitals; children will shred old linen; old men will be taken to the public squares to offer encouragement to the warriors and to preach the hatred of kings and the unity of the Republic.[94]

These, then, were the combined forces that Britain had been facing since 1 February of that year – the date on which France declared war on her and the Netherlands. Britain's own military resources fell into three categories: the

---

[89] Bell, *The First Total War*, 7.

[90] Howard, *War in European History*, 75; Bell, *The First Total War*, 3. Cf. 'It was the French Revolution, the revolutionary wars and the rise and fall of Napoleon, which for the first time made history a *mass experience*' (Georg Lukács, *The Historical Novel* (*Der Historische Roman*) [1937], trans. Hannah Mitchell and Stanley Mitchell (Lincoln, NE: University of Nebraska Press, 1983), 23, original emphasis). As Stephen Pinker makes clear, the *horribleness* of violence is nothing new (*The Better Angels of Our Nature: Why Violence Has Declined* (New York: Penguin, 2001), ch. 1).

[91] To get a sense of the scale of previous wars involving England/Britain, see John Childs, *The British Army of William III, 1689–1702* (Manchester: Manchester University Press, 2007) on the Glorious Revolution and the War of the Spanish Succession (102–3) and H. C. B. Rogers, *The British Army of the Eighteenth Century* (London: George Allen and Unwin, 1977) on the War of the Spanish Succession (19) and the Seven Years War (25).

[92] Gates, 'The Transformation of the Army 1783–1815', 139.

[93] Carl von Clausewitz, *On War* (*Vom Kriege*) [1832], trans. Michael Howard and Peter Paret (Princeton, NJ: Princeton University Press, 1976), 593.

[94] Quoted in Ute Frevert, 'War', *A Companion to Nineteenth-Century Europe: 1789–1914*, ed. Stefan Berger (Oxford: Blackwell Reference Online, 2006), unpaginated. For more on the *levée en masse*, see Paret, *Understanding War*, 53–74.

established Army and Navy, the Militia and the Volunteers. Of these, given our focus on active armed combat, only the Army and Navy concern us. In 1789, the Army was some 40,000 men strong; by 1813, the figure had risen to 250,000.[95] Before 1789, there were 16,000 in the Navy; by 1812, there were 140,000.[96] By 1815, as noted previously, some 350,000 men had served in the regular forces.[97] As in France, women were also part of the war effort, buying and sending uniforms to troops and raising public subscriptions to support the armed forces.[98] In consequence, war became, as Linda Colley, quoting Clausewitz, puts it, 'the business of the people'.[99]

It was a bloody business. As war with France went on, Britain was incurring 16,000 to 24,000 casualties every year.[100] Death became routine. The country lost a greater proportion of her population than she would in the First World War and a 'lemminglike quality' has been noted in the soldiers of these times that foreshadowed the 'mass acceptance of death so characteristic of the great industrial wars of the twentieth century'.[101] The scale of attrition was matched by the temporal span and geographical range: together, the French Revolutionary and Napoleonic Wars occupied Britain, with some intervals, from 1793 to 1815; reached from Europe to the Middle East to the Caribbean; and involved fighting in the Mediterranean Sea and Atlantic and Pacific Oceans.

If revolutionary ideology produced a warfare unprecedented in intensity, battle conditions in turn gave rise to new ways of thinking. Anders Engberg-Pedersen has recently noted that these wars necessitated a move from the ' "optical-acoustic presence" of the commander on the battlefield' as the centre of direction towards 'long-distance management of multiple divisions and distinct battles'.[102] Military leaders and rank-and-file soldiers both faced a 'tremendously complex epistemic field of probabilities, possibilities, conjectures, averages, modalities' – a new 'empire of chance' that left reason 'incapacitated' and instead 'activated the sensorium to the utmost degree'.[103] Yuval Noah

[95] Linda Colley, *Britons: Forging the Nation 1707–1837* (New Haven, CT: Yale University Press, 2009), 293.

[96] Ibid., 293.

[97] Ibid., 318.

[98] Mark Philp, 'Revolution', *An Oxford Companion to the Romantic Age: British Culture 1776–1832*, ed. Iain McCalman (Oxford: Oxford University Press, 1999), 17–26: 24.

[99] Colley, *Britons*, 291, quoting Clausewitz, *On War*, 592.

[100] Gates, 'The Transformation of the Army 1783–1815', 138.

[101] Robert O'Connell, *Of Arms and Men: A History of War, Weapons and Aggression* (Oxford: Oxford University Press, 1989), 185.

[102] Engberg-Pedersen, *Empire of Chance*, 43.

[103] Ibid., 4. The phrase 'empire of chance' is from Georg Heinrich von Berenhorst, *Betrachtungen über die Kriegskunst, über ihre Fortschritte, ihre Widersprüche und ihre Zuverlässigkeit* [1797–9], 3/3 vols

Harari dates the epistemological revolution half a century earlier, to 1740, but he, too, endorses the idea that 'extreme bodily conditions' on the battlefield, reinforced by Sensationist and Romantic philosophy (in particular the notion of the individual as *tabula rasa*), resulted in a new sense of combat as a 'quasi-mystical experience of revelation' based on the body.[104] The 'flesh-witnessing' of which only the combat veteran is capable, Harari argues, superseded both 'the rationalist authority of logical thinking' and 'the scientific authority of objective eye-witnessing'.[105] I return to the arguments of Engberg-Pedersen and Harari in Chapters 3 and 5 and, in the latter, my claim is that even flesh-witnessing proves inadequate in the face of modern warfare.

Let me be clear: fighting in the French Revolutionary and Napoleonic Wars was not the same as fighting in the World Wars of the twentieth century. But the experiences had this in common: they exposed those fighting in them to an unprecedented uncertainty, intense and fundamentally unsettling, on an enormous scale. And what was felt in these wars was also felt in the reign of Queen Victoria. As John Ruskin asked of an audience of young veterans in 1865:

> If, finally, having brought masses of men, counted by hundreds of thousands, face to face, you tear those masses to pieces with jagged shot, and leave the fragments of living creatures countlessly beyond all help of surgery, to starve and parch, through days of torture, down into clots of clay – what book of accounts shall record the cost of your work?[106]

The warfare in which his listeners had participated was 'modern war, – scientific war, – chemical and mechanic war'.[107] Ruskin's adjectives are apt not only to characterize the wars of his century but those of the next century, and beyond.

For many, the veteran of modern mass warfare – and all he stands for – would appear to be quintessentially Modern*ist*. I therefore need to say a word about the applicability of this term as a descriptor. Certainly,

---

(Osnabrück: Biblio, 1978), 437, quoted in Engberg-Pedersen, *Empire of Chance*, 51. In an argument that complements Engberg-Pedersen's, Mary Favret suggests that the unprecedented numbers of combat deaths in the French Revolutionary and Napoleonic Wars 'set feeling into motion', evoking 'unsettled passion' ('A Feeling for Numbers: Representing the Scale of the War Dead', *War and Literature*, ed. Laura Ashe and Ian Patterson (Cambridge: D. S. Brewer, 2014), 185–204: 193, 197).

[104] Yuval Noah Harari, *The Ultimate Experience: Battlefield Revelations and the Making of Modern War Culture, 1450–2000* (Basingstoke: Palgrave Macmillan, 2008), 7, 1.

[105] Ibid., 7.

[106] John Ruskin, *The Crown of Wild Olive: Three Lectures on Work, Traffic, and War* (New York: John Wiley, 1866), 76–7.

[107] Ibid., 77.

the term fits the conceptual unsettlings described in this book. Philip Weinstein links the emergence of the 'unknowing' subject to ideas at the heart of Modernist movements: Freud's unconsciousness, which worked as a 'destabilizer of ego and deformer of space and time' and the reconceptualization by F. H. Bradley, Henri Bergson, Franz Brentano and Edmund Husserl of 'the embodied subject's way of inhabiting and registering the exterior world'.[108] These ways of being and knowing are immediately discernible in the time-warping unfathomable *xenos*. In his revelatory *Modernism and the Reinvention of Decadence* (2015), Vincent Sherry traces the decline of '[t]hat grand romantic adagio of harmonized and reconciled times, which holds the moments of childhood and adulthood in a single continuum of imaginatively coherent feeling' into a Decadent, then Modernist, sense of 'a stopping of the time of progress' or 'anti-futurity'.[109] In this volume, I am describing the phenomenon that Sherry perceives from an angle that is more epistemological, though not without attendant affect. Sherry's Decadent/Modernist 'anti-futurity' is coincident with the collapse of experiential epistemology – or, put more simply, the disappearance of the ability to hand on wisdom – figured by the non-storytelling veteran of mass warfare. The accompanying 'counterconventional' activities and 'counter-natural values' that he identifies, such as the protagonist of J. K. Huysman's *Against Nature* (*À Rebours*) (1884) sleeping by day or the 'Nineties figure of genius dying young', are of the same species as the temporal disruptions that I discuss in Chapter 1.[110]

Modernism resists an exhaustive definition – though we know its traits when we see them – and its chronological span is equally difficult to pin down. Though conventionally and roughly associated with the forty years from 1890 to 1930, it can justifiably be stretched back to the mid-nineteenth-century works of Baudelaire. My arguments in this book present the opportunity to extend it even further back, to the 1790s. If I do not avail myself of this opportunity, it is because what matters are not the labels but the philosophical leanings and their forms of expression. Rather than get bogged down in the applicability of a certain term, I prefer to trace a complex intellectual history free of taxonomic constraints.

---

[108] Philip Weinstein, *Unknowing: The Work of Modernist Fiction* (Ithaca, NY: Cornell University Press, 2005), 83, 162.
[109] Vincent Sherry, *Modernism and the Reinvention of Decadence* (Cambridge: Cambridge University Press, 2015), 42, 27, 29.
[110] Ibid., 37, 49, 192.

**Further Particulars**

There are a few further parameters of *Veteran Poetics* to set out. The literary veterans who appear in these pages include not only former members of armies, but also of navies and air forces – references to 'ex-soldiers' include, where appropriate, ex-sailors and ex-pilots. All but one is male (the exception is a character in Robert Henriques's *The Journey Home* (1944), discussed in Chapter 2). This is due to the fact that front-line military service in the period covered by the volume has been almost exclusively a male preserve. But the effect on, engagement with and understanding of veterancy by women are not ignored: indeed, they are crucial to the expression of literary and philosophical ideas in the texts under consideration. The texts in which these literary veterans appear are all by British writers, and I have kept examples of non-British real-life veterans to a minimum. This is not for lack of material: the veteran is a figure of interest across literatures, and I would have loved to have included examples from them – the homecoming scenes in Erich Maria Remarque's *All Quiet on the Western Front* (*Im Westen nichts Neues*) (1929) and Wolfgang Borchert's *The Man Outside* (*Draußen vor der Tür*) (1946); what Pierre Bezuhov learns from the old soldier Platon Karataev in Tolstoy's *War and Peace* (1869); the linguistic surfeiting of Joyce's *Ulysses* (which would have been the perfect text to demonstrate my arguments in Chapter 4); the traumatic legacies in Hemingway's 'Soldiers Home' (1924), Tim O'Brien's *In the Lake of the Woods* (1995) and Kevin Powers's *The Yellow Birds* (2012); the unclassifiable scene in Philip Roth's *The Human Stain* (2000) in which a Vietnam veteran undergoes exposure therapy in a Chinese restaurant. American literature of the Vietnam War is particularly rich in veteran representations and I regret its absence. But extending the book to other literatures in addition to British would have meant detailing how veterans are perceived in those other cultures: an enormous task, to which a single volume would have been inadequate. I also regret the absence of depictions of veterans in other media, in particular painting (one thinks of the caricatures by James Gillray and Isaac Cruikshank, John Cawse's *A Soldier Relating His Exploits in a Tavern* (1821), David Wilkie's *The Chelsea Pensioners Reading the Waterloo Dispatch* (1822), Henry Nelson O'Neil's *The Soldier's Return* (1861), Charles Martin Hodge's *Home Sweet Home* (1890)) and film (*The Best Years of Our Lives* (1946), *It's Always Fair Weather* (1955), *Tunes of Glory* (1960), *The Manchurian Candidate* (1962), *The Deer Hunter* (1978), *Born on the Fourth of July* (1989), the *Rambo* series (1982–2008), *American*

*Sniper* (2014)).[111] There is a huge amount to say about representations of the veteran in these media but, in addition to the considerations of space, they require scholarly expertise I do not lay claim to. I hope, though, that the ideas in *Veteran Poetics* may translate across media boundaries.

## Being, Knowing, Storytelling

The arc of this book is from the ontological to the epistemological, though who we are, what we know and how we convey it to others are always inter-related. The first two chapters illustrate how literary veterans enact and question certain notions about personal and social identity: that we live our lives in sequential order, that we remain the same person over time, that mutual respect is the best basis for our relations with others. Chapter 1, 'Life Times', analyses Robert Merry's 'The Wounded Soldier' (1795), Jane Austen's *Persuasion* (1818) and Alfred Lord Tennyson's 'Ulysses' (1833) to illustrate the concept of biographical decorum, or doing the 'right' thing at the 'right' time of life. Prematurely aged, the veteran disrupts such decorum. If children can become older than their parents, if it is possible to grow younger rather than older, if soonness and lateness get mixed up, then the assumption that life can be proceeded through in linear fashion is shaken.

The subject of Chapter 2, 'Strangers', is the veteran as *xenos*, a term that can signify a range of Others, from enemy, foreigner and stranger to guest-friend.[112] Returned from the wars, the veteran poses the question 'is the person who has come back the same as the one who went away?' It is a question both for the individual and the community to answer. The person who is at once much changed and deeply familiar is ontologically troubling, and this is not the only way in which the veteran disrupts the community – he represents a range of threats from non-conformity to violence. This chapter examines the ways in which communities respond to such threats, from assimilation to expulsion. The fundamental issue is that of hospitality. The familiar stranger tests Kant's notion of universal conditional hospitality and its successor, Jürgen Habermas's theory of supranational human rights, to their limits. Mutual respect is key to these ideas

---

[111] On representations of veterans in British art in the late eighteenth and early nineteenth centuries, see Philip Shaw, *Suffering and Sentiment in Romantic Military Art* (Farnham: Ashgate, 2013) and, from 1815–1914, J. W. M. Hichberger, *Images of the Army: The Military in British Art, 1815–1914* (Manchester: Manchester University Press, 1988), ch. 9. On representations of veterans in film, see Emmett Early, *The War Veteran in Film* (Jefferson, NC: McFarland, 2003).

[112] Wendy Olmsted, 'On the Margins of Otherness: Metamorphosis and Identity in Homer, Ovid, Sidney, and Milton', *New Literary History* 27.2 (1996), 167–84: 168.

and it is undermined variously by veterans in the literary works discussed. These are a cluster of Second World War novels: Betty Miller's *On the Side of the Angels* (1945), Helen Ashton's *The Captain Comes Home* (1947), Nigel Balchin's *Mine Own Executioner* (1945) and *A Sort of Traitors* (1949), J. B. Priestley's *Three Men in New Suits* (1945) and Robert Henriques's *The Journey Home* (1944). Miller's novel features a character impersonating a veteran, a deception that is itself inhospitable since it exploits trust. The presence of this impostor in a small village induces unease in members of the community. But, in a sense, *all* returning veterans are impostors, in that they are expected in each case to be the same person as the one who went away. By extension, imposture can be regarded as an ineluctable element of identity. Drawing attention to the prospect of universal deception, *On the Side of the Angels* puts pressure on the very foundation of conditional hospitality. Ashton's novel centres on the trial of a returned veteran who has committed a (justifiable) act of violence. This veteran is ultimately expelled from the village community, albeit to a respectable life of scholarship. Conditional hospitality has failed to accommodate the human relict of modern mass warfare. In the novels by Balchin, Priestley and Henriques, inhospitality on the part of the returned veteran ranges from non-conformity to incitement to revolution. The revolutionary potential is contained, but this is more due to the veterans' own sense of decorum rather than to any hospitable welcome extended to them. Reason-based conditional hospitality, these texts show, strains to deal with the threatening Other.

The remaining three chapters are about knowledge and its articulation. Chapter 3, 'Problem-Solving', concerns the intersection of epistemology, heuristics and pedagogy. In the thriving genre of veteran detective fiction, it emerges that forensic methods – the offspring of the scientific revolution – are insufficient in themselves to catch criminals. Hunches, gut feelings, strong impressions, all rooted in knowledge of the ways of the world, must be drawn on, too. These forms of knowledge, deriving from Lockean empiricism, were conceptualized in the twentieth century by, among others, Walter Benjamin. Benjamin's *Erfahrung*, which this chapter explores in some detail, is both experience accrued over time and the insight derived from that experience: what life teaches you, in other words. The veteran – the person who has literally 'been through the wars' – is apt both to figure *Erfahrung* and, just as importantly, this chapter argues, to question its soundness and the possibility of handing it on. The texts discussed are Arthur Conan Doyle's *The Sign of Four* (1890), Dorothy L. Sayers's *The Unpleasantness at the Bellona Club* (1921) and the three so-far extant Cormoran Strike novels by J. K. Rowling writing as Robert Galbraith – *The Cuckoo's Calling* (2013), *The Silkworm* (2014) and *Career of Evil* (2015). If Sherlock Holmes is a virtuoso of forensic reasoning, his veteran assistant, confidant and chronicler, Dr Watson, solves life's problems by virtue of being a man of the world. The epistemological mismatch finds expression in generic dissonance: Holmes's scientific rigour fits Watson's 'fantasies' like a square peg in a round hole. Since Watson's Holmes is brilliant but inimitable, concern begins to surround the transmissibility of expertise: despite Holmes's constant injunctions, neither Watson nor the reader will be able to apply his methods successfully. In *The Unpleasantness at the Bellona Club*, Sayers pinpoints the exact moment in the murder investigation in which forensic reasoning gives way to experientially based heuristics. From fingerprints and blood stains, Lord Peter Wimsey turns to the catch in a voice and taste in books. But, in a further twist, he expresses himself dissatisfied at the end by the absence of conclusive evidence, suggesting a certain unease about the alternative methodology. His discomfort is shared by the detective partnership in Rowling's Cormoran Strike novels. Like Dr Watson, Strike is an Afghanistan veteran, in his case a former member of the military police. A classic example of having learned things the hard way, he draws on his toughening experiences to understand human behaviour. But, like Wimsey, Strike has to face up to the fact that hunches and gut feelings must be corroborated with proof capable of scientific verification. Reinforcing the point that experience only goes so far are the problems he has in transmitting his know-how to his assistant, Robin Ellacott. Experience can be a useful foundation for knowledge, Watson, Wimsey and Strike intimate, but what is known will be known imperfectly and will be difficult to hand on.

Chapters 4 and 5 look further at the problem of transmissibility in an epistemological context. Given that the returned veteran is almost inevitably prevailed upon to describe what he has seen and been through, he is a particularly appropriate figure through which to explore the process of conveying what has happened in a different place and time. Chapter 4, 'Telling Tales', is about communication that, because excessive, is ultimately empty. This is exemplified by veterans who tell unsolicited tales or who will not stop talking about the war(s) they have been in. Their prolixity is, in the terms discussed in Chapter 2, *inhospitable*. Breaching the boundaries of polite discourse, a discourse associated since the seventeenth century with reason and empiricism, it also expresses anxieties about the capacities of such epistemologies to accommodate the fact and effects of mass warfare. The first text discussed is the anonymously authored poem

'The Soldier's Return' (1804). In this work, fearing that his family will be fatally overwhelmed on seeing him again, a young soldier returning home from the Napoleonic Wars decides on impulse to disguise himself as an aged veteran and, in that guise, gradually to reveal the fact of his own continued existence. This is a 'feign'd story' – a lie – and hence already in some sense excessive. As a deception, it is also impolite, since dissembling inevitably involves lack of respect for the person(s) being misled. Though ultimately harmless, the tale indicates anxieties about the capacities of polite, reason-based discourse. An unsolicited story is followed by an unwanted story: Coleridge's 'The Rime of the Ancient Mariner' (1797–1834) is the example *par excellence* of an utterance that, tsunami-like, smashes the constraints of politeness and reason. Its auditor may (finally) escape from the encounter 'a sadder and a wiser man', but the sadness and wisdom are likely to consist of pity and the determination not to succumb to such extended button-holing in the future, rather than sympathy or true edification. Insight has signally failed to be passed on. The last text discussed, Henry Green's *Back* (1946), abstracts excessive veteran utterance into the repetition of a single word. In a novel teeming with doublings and multiplications, 'rose' is reiterated so many times that it becomes empty of signification. As in the other works discussed, both communicative and epistemological anxieties can be inferred from the linguistic surplusage surrounding the former combatant.

From garrulous veterans to silent veterans: the subject of Chapter 5, 'The End of the Story', is veterans who are, in Ted Hughes's words, 'buffeted wordless', by what they have been through.[113] If Chapter 3, tracing the fortunes of an experientially based epistemology against scientific methodology, found a certain unease surrounding the former, Chapter 5 charts its collapse. The utter failure of experiential epistemology goes beyond casting doubt on Lockean empiricism to form an obstacle in the larger Enlightenment endeavour that, in Adorno and Horkheimer's thesis already discussed, is of knowing and mastering the world. The non-storytelling veteran, that is, figures the inability to fathom experience, whether one's own or that of other people. This figure appears in William Wordsworth's 'The Discharged Soldier' (the fragment of 1798 and its incarnation in the 1805 *Prelude*), Rebecca West's *The Return of the Soldier* (1918) and Virginia

---

[113] 'My father sat in his chair recovering / From the four-year mastication by gunfire and mud, / Body buffeted wordless' ('Out' (1967)); cf. 'My post-war father was so silent / He seemed to be listening' ('Dust as We Are' (1989)) (Ted Hughes, *Collected Poems*, ed. Paul Keegan (London: Faber and Faber, 2003), 165, 753).

Woolf's *Mrs Dalloway* (1925). The first of these is a completely impenetrable character, encountering whom leaves the Wordsworthian persona wholly unedified. The image of a dropped staff reveals that this veteran of the French Revolutionary Wars will not be handing on experientially based wisdom. Imported into Wordsworth's epic autobiographical poem, *The Prelude*, the episode lies inertly, an epistemological non-starter in the great learning project. In West's novel, an amnesiac First World War veteran is physically older but mentally de-aged, unable to say anything at all about his combat experiences. Woolf, too, writes of a de-veterated veteran, Septimus Warren Smith's dead sergeant, Evans, who appears in Septimus's dream with 'no mud on him'. Septimus himself speaks only in terms incomprehensible to others. It is not that experience is shown to be unprofitable in West's and Woolf's novels; it has been stripped away. No insight is passed on: the story ends in silence.

With Zadie Smith's *White Teeth* (2000) as the centrepiece, the Conclusion reflects on how such silences might be read. At first glance, the possibilities are unpromising. Silence potentially thwarts the capacity to understand other people, the enlargement of which is the *raison d'être* of imaginative literature. At least, it is according to the long-standing view that empathy is increased by the act of imagining oneself in another's shoes. But it is possible to respect another person without usurping their footwear. As already noted, new ethicists including Gayatry Chakravorty Spivak, Dipesh Chakrabarty, Judith Butler and Dorothy Hale have variously developed a notion of critical non-judgement that emphasizes caring for the Other without trying to rationalize that Other. In the Conclusion, I draw on their ideas to suggest a critical deep listening that registers and affirms silence while preserving its unfathomable qualities. Such listening will have its due solemnity. But, inspired by the veteran silences it hearkens to, it will also know wonderment and glee.

# CHAPTER I

# *Life Times*

### *Odyssey* 1: Time Travel

In Book 2 of the *Odyssey*, the situation in his absent father's palace having reached a point beyond which it can no longer be tolerated, Telemachus calls his fellow Ithacans together to discuss what to do. The old lord Halitherses addresses the assembly. 'Odysseus is not going to be parted from his friends much longer,' he assures his compatriots:

> I speak from ripe experience. [...] Has not everything fallen out as I warned that self-reliant man when he embarked for Ilium with the Argive army? I said it would be nineteen years before he got home, after much suffering, with all his comrades lost, and that no one would know him when he did. See how my prophecies are coming true!
>
> (2.163, 170–6)

Veterancy is a temporal condition. Joining the military immediately posits a potential future (or, more accurately, a future perfect): at some point, if he survives, the recruit *will have been* a soldier. For those left at home, a backwards look towards the person last seen departing for war oscillates with a forwards look towards his return. Poems and songs across the entire period covered by this book – from 'On A Late Victory At Sea' (1794)[1] to Vera Lynn's classic Second World War number 'We'll Meet Again' (1939),[2] to the Military Wives' 2011 Christmas hit 'Wherever You Are'[3] – demonstrate this by combining

---

[1] 'With fond impatience did the virgin moan / Her hero's absence [...] / The helpless orphan, ignorant of woes, / Oft lisping, doth require his sire's return' ('T. O.', 'For the *European Magazine*: On a Late Victory at Sea', *European Magazine, and London Review* 26 (December 1794), 438–9: 438; quoted in Betty T. Bennett, ed., *British War Poetry in the Age of Romanticism: 1793–1815* (New York: Garland, 1976), 131).

[2] See Kate McLoughlin, 'Vera Lynn and the "We'll Meet Again" Hypothesis', *From Self to Shelf: The Artist Under Construction*, ed. Sally Bayley and William May (Newcastle: Cambridge Scholars Publishing), 109–25.

[3] Lyrics and music by Paul Mealor, who created the lyrics from letters written by couples separated by military service.

memories of the absent loved one with a desire for reunion. Veteran status itself implies both experience accrued over time and the quality of formerness. Halitherses, a veteran soothsayer himself, covers a number of temporalities in his speech: referring to the past, forecasting the future and noting the fulfilment of prophecies in the present. He is not alone: Odysseus' entire trajectory is hedged around with expectations, premonitions, predictions, votive promises, optative petitions, analepses and prolepses, not to mention Penelopean temporizing. These reckonings with time take their place within broader temporal issues. The veteran who has returned deeply changed by combat ('no one would know him') raises questions about the recoverability of the past. The ongoing nature of veterancy focuses attention on how to conceptualize the present. The uncertainty regarding a soldier's return tests the status of knowledge about the future. But these statements themselves indicate a particular, 'tensed', view of time that the veteran, in whom past, present and future clash and merge, potentially disrupts anyway.[4]

Veterans are time travellers: visitors from the past en route to the future, anticipating retrospect, recalling expectation. As such, they are apt to figure an age in which ideas of temporality – scientific, philosophical and historiographical, as well as literary – underwent radical transformation. To give a specific example of such radical re-thinking: on 5 October 1793, just six weeks after the *levée en masse*, the French Legislative Assembly passed into law a new calendar that declared 1792 to be the 'Year I', renamed the months with reference to climate and agricultural activities and rearranged the week into *décades*.[5] The revolutionaries' 'new sense of time' was a fuzzy mixture of the linear and the cyclical (what they had done was cast both as 'rupture' *and* 'regeneration', a new beginning and a *re*newal) but the *calendrier républicain* at least proved the point that temporality could be toyed with.[6] The idea of starting history again from scratch (also a Christian notion) is one of a constellation of cognate if sometimes clashing concepts that posit alternatives to what Newton in *Principia Mathematica* (1687–1726) called 'absolute time':[7] these range from Kant's denial in the

---

[4] A 'tensed' view of time contrasts with an 'untensed' view that, in Mark Currie's words, 'generally holds that there is no ontological distinction between the past, present and future' (*About Time: Narrative, Fiction and the Philosophy of Time* (Edinburgh: Edinburgh University Press, 2007), 15).

[5] Matthew Shaw, *Time and the French Revolution: The Republican Calendar 1789–Year XIV* (Woodbridge: Royal Historical Society/Boydell Press, 2001), 1–2.

[6] Sanja Perofic, *The Calendar in Revolutionary France: Perceptions of Time in Literature, Culture, Politics* (Cambridge: Cambridge University Press, 2012), 4, 7.

[7] 'Absolute, true, and mathematical time, of itself and from its own nature, flows uniformly, without regard to anything external' (Isaac Newton, *Philosophiae Naturalis Principia Mathematica* [1687], trans. Andrew Motte, rev. Florian Cajori, vol. 1/2 (Berkeley, CA: University of California Press, 1966), 6).

*Critique of Pure Reason* (1781) that time has any claim to 'absolute reality [...] independent of any reference to the form of our sensible intuition'[8] to Nietzsche's notion of eternal recurrence to Bergson's *durée vécue* to Einstein's relativity to post-colonial understandings of 'a plurality of times existing together'.[9]

Crisscrossing past, present and future, the veteran lends himself to literary attempts to confound unidirectional time. But in this chapter, I want to concentrate upon a very specific kind of temporality and its disruption, the nature of which is hinted at by Halitherses. An 'I told you so' on an epic scale, his speech conveys a sense of lateness. His prediction was that Odysseus would be away too long; now he *has* been away too long. If someone is overdue, it follows that there was a 'right' time for him to come home. The ancient Greeks called the concept of the 'right' time *kairos* (καιρος), and *kairos* can be understood as the best or most opportune moment ('to strike while the iron's hot' sums it up perfectly).[10] Since ancient times, *kairos* has been a matter of seasonableness (*tempestivitas*),[11] rooted in the predictable recurrence of natural phenomena that can be used to inform human activity. Hesiod's *Works and Days* (eighth century BCE), for example, recommends the carrying out of various agricultural tasks according to the occurrence of astronomical patterns, weather changes, leaf-fall and animal behaviour, while Galen and the medical writers of the Hippocratic Corpus warn physicians to prepare for certain maladies at certain times of year. Most famously the third-century BCE biblical wisdom book Ecclesiastes proclaims: 'To every thing there is a season, and a time to every purpose under the heaven: A time to be born, and a time to die; a time to plant, and a time to pluck up that which is planted.'[12] In these lovely, pendular lines, the connection between season and agricultural intervention ('a time to plant') is accompanied by the idea of a natural life-course ('a time to be born and a time to die'). Later versicles – 'a time to love and a time to hate'[13] – omit the seasonal attachment but propose that there are appropriate points for (non-agricultural) activities and events in

---

[8] Immanuel Kant, *Critique of Pure Reason* (*Kritik der reinen Vernunft*) [1781], trans. Norman Kemp Smith (London: Palgrave, 2003), 78.

[9] Dipesh Chakrabarty, *Provincializing Europe: Postcolonial Thought and Historical Difference* (Princeton, NJ: Princeton University Press, 2000), 109.

[10] Emily R. Wilson defines it as 'the right moment or qualitative time' (*Mocked with Death: Tragic Overliving from Sophocles to Milton* (Baltimore, MD: The Johns Hopkins University Press, 2004), 8).

[11] See J. A. Burrow, *The Ages of Man: A Study of Medieval Writing and Thought* (Oxford: Oxford University Press, 1988), 1.

[12] Ecclesiastes 3.1–2 (King James Version).

[13] Ibid., 3.8.

the life course. Ecclesiastes makes the notion that there are 'right' times in life to do certain things seem as natural as sowing seeds in spring.[14]

Edward Said uses the term '*timeliness*' for *kairos*, intending it to convey 'that what is appropriate to early life is not appropriate for later stages, and vice versa'.[15] In this chapter, to specify the notion that certain things ought to happen at certain times of life I am coining the phrase 'biographical decorum'.[16] (Biographical decorum could itself be said to be a sub-species of 'historiographical decorum', the intuition that a particular development is 'right' as a particular point in history – a sense exhibited, for example, by those who felt in the 1830s that the time was 'ripe' for constitutional reform.)[17] Though derived from natural rhythms and often necessarily contingent upon biological developments, this sense of decorum is also affected by the 'inner expectations' of individuals, their families and their peer groups and is subject to 'generational transmission'.[18] Biographical decorum forms our sense of how long a person should live, of whether someone has died 'too young' or has 'outlived his

---

[14] On classical and medieval conceptions of the *curriculum vitae*, see further Burrow, *The Ages of Man*, and Mary Dove, *The Perfect Age of Man's Life* (Cambridge: Cambridge University Press, 1986).

[15] Edward Said, *On Late Style* (London: Bloomsbury, 2006), 5, original emphasis.

[16] The term 'biographical decorum' is sometimes used to refer to the etiquette governing those writing biographies (see, for example, Max Saunders, *Self Impression: Life-Writing, Autobiografiction, and the Forms of Modern Literature* (Oxford: Oxford University Press, 2010), 434), but I deploy it here in preference to the more etymologically accurate but less euphonious 'bio-decorum'. Helen Small demonstrates an instance of biographical decorum in the sense in which I am using it when she refers to 'the idea that someone who has died young, say at 18, has died prematurely' (*The Long Life* (Oxford: Oxford University Press, 2007), 95).

[17] Lord John Russell, for example, in a Reform Bill debate, noted that after 50 years of constitutional discussion, the matter was now 'ripe for deliberation' and could be entered upon 'without any imputation that we have undertaken it rashly' (*House of Commons Hansard*, 24 June 1831, series 3, vol. 4, col. 322). The notion of historiographical decorum also arises elsewhere. In *Sartor Resartus*, first serialized in 1833–4, Thomas Carlyle's Professor Teufelsdröch speaks of the 'World-Phoenix' whose ashes are 'blown about' even as new 'organic filaments [...] mysteriously spin themselves', a figure suggesting that political regimes have 'natural' ends and beginnings' (*Sartor Resartus*, ed. Kerry McSweeney and Peter Sabor (Oxford: Oxford University Press, 1987), 185). In his 1830 'Spirit of the Age' articles in the *Examiner*, John Stuart Mill expresses the idea that mankind has 'outgrown old institutions and old doctrines' with an image uniting historiographical, biographical and sartorial decorum: 'A man may not be either better or happier at six-and-twenty, than he was at six years of age: but the same jacket which fitted him then, will not fit him now' (*Newspaper Writings*, ed. Ann P. Robson and John M. Robson (Toronto: University of Toronto Press, 1986), 230). (Both quoted in Chris R. Vanden Bossche, *Carlyle and the Search for Authority* (Columbus, OH: Ohio State University Press, 1991), 41, 43.) Historiographical decorum is a complex idea, clearly involving cultural and political manipulation, but it is still worth noting that a sense that 'the time is right' was pervasive in the years contemporaneous with the last work discussed in this chapter, Tennyson's 'Ulysses'.

[18] Tamara K. Haraven, 'Synchronizing Individual Time, Family Time, and Historical Time', *Chronotypes: The Construction of Time*, ed. John Bender and David E. Wellbery (Stanford, CA: Stanford University Press, 1991), 167–82: 171.

or her usefulness' – indeed, of whether someone should die before or after someone else. It influences our view of when childhood starts and finishes, and adolescence, adulthood and old age. It shapes our perceptions of when someone should leave home, get married, have children, retire from work. The idea was well established by the outset of the time frame of this book and, in particular, came to the fore in cases of so-called 'May–December' marriages.[19] In August 1797, for example, a London newspaper reported on a 70-year-old veteran of Doncaster who had married 'a blooming damsel of seventeen'.[20] Some women 'saluted the bridegroom with sods and mud' so that the 'fond pair' were forced to take shelter in an adjoining house and afterwards cross the river in a boat 'to avoid their congratulations'.[21] Though the story is told with loving relish, the underlying sense that biographical decorum has been breached is clear: this septuagenarian has no business marrying a 17-year-old.

The proper places of old and young was a live issue concerning veterans (in the sense of long-serving soldiers) in the period of the French Revolutionary and Napoleonic Wars, and frequently reported in the press. On 21 January 1795, Colonel Thomas Maitland deplored in the House of Commons the practice of allowing wealthy men to raise regiments with the result that 'boys from school were set over the heads of veteran officers'.[22] An opinion piece in the *Oracle and Public Advertiser* on 18 August 1796 reiterated the point: 'Nothing could be more beneficial to the service, than to prevent lads and children from being elevated over the heads of veteran Officers.'[23] On 5 January 1797, the *Telegraph* reported the following anecdote: 'The late Earl of Sandwich, when First Lord of the Admiralty, meeting an old Lieutenant in the Navy, expressed some surprize at seeing him grow so bald. "Ah," said the veteran tar, "so many young Lieutenants have walked over my head, that it is a wonder I am not quite scalped." '[24] The point of decorum on which these examples are founded is that age equates to seniority, the message being conveyed in

[19] The *senex amans* (old lover) is a figure of classical origins, as is the *puer senex* (the youth wise beyond his years) (see Burrow, *The Ages of Man*, 3).
[20] Anonymous, 'Postscript', *London Packet* (4–7 August 1797), 4 (Gale-Cengage 17th–18th Century Burney Newspaper Collection).
[21] Ibid., 4.
[22] Anonymous, 'British Parliament: House of Commons', *Morning Chronicle* (22 January 1795), 2 (Gale-Cengage 17th–18th Century Burney Newspaper Collection).
[23] Anonymous, 'London, August 18', *Oracle and Public Advertiser* (18 August 1796), 1 (Gale-Cengage 17th–18th Century Burney Newspaper Collection).
[24] Anonymous, Untitled, *Telegraph* (5 January 1797), 3 (Gale-Cengage 17th–18th Century Burney Newspaper Collection).

all three cases with a metaphor of relative altitude ('over the head') that the 'veteran tar' jokingly literalizes. Violating that perceived precedence is, the press of the period shows, consistently disturbing to the point of being newsworthy.[25]

The indignation in these instances depends upon a number of assumptions regarding age, experience, aptitude and seniority, as well as certain ingrained notions of hierarchy. The veteran is a natural focal point for all these concepts, making him a particularly apt literary vehicle for expressing temporal fluidity or what Philip Weinstein calls 'unbound time'.[26] More specifically, he works as a reminder of future retrospect in the manner explained by Mark Currie:

> If in reading a narrative we decode the preterite as a kind of present, the process is one of presentification, whereas in living we use a kind of envisaged preterite to deprive the today of its character as present. Put simply, it is possible that the reading of narrative fiction, in instructing us in the presentification of the past, also robs us of the present in the sense that it encourages us to imagine looking back on it.[27]

To conceptualize the veteran as preterite is to remember that he is an ongoing *has-been*, a temporal condition roomy enough also to accommodate the future perfect: he *will always have been*.

'It is a hopeless curiosity that wants to know what other kinds of intellects and perspectives there might be [...] whether some beings might be able to experience time backward, or alternately forward and backward,' wrote Nietzsche in *The Gay Science* (1882).[28] The literary veteran not only experiences time forward and backward but confounds the very idea of due

---

[25] Shakespeare draws on the same sense of offended order in *King Lear*:

> Edmund: I have heard him oft
> maintain it to be fit, that, sons at perfect age,
> and fathers declining, the father should be as
> ward to the son, and the son manage his revenue.

> Gloucester: O villain, villain! His very opinion in
> the letter. Abhorred villain! Unnatural, detested,
> brutish villain!

> (1.2.71–7).

[26] Philip Weinstein, *Unknowing: The Work of Modernist Fiction* (Ithaca, NY: Cornell University Press, 2005), 76.

[27] Currie, *About Time*, 30.

[28] Friedrich Nietzsche, *The Gay Science* (*Die fröhliche Wissenschaft*) [1882], trans. Walter Kaufmann (New York: Vintage Books, 1974), 336.

course. Such temporal transgressions are evident in the texts I now turn
to: Robert Merry's 'The Wounded Soldier' (1795), Jane Austen's *Persuasion*
(1818) and Alfred Lord Tennyson's 'Ulysses' (1833).

## Nature Reversed: Robert Merry's 'The Wounded Soldier' (1795)

Robert Merry's poem 'The Wounded Soldier' contains what must count
among the most extreme reactions in imaginative literature to the
(re)appearance of a war veteran: two people collapse – one fatally – and
another bursts into tears. The poem was first published in the *Courier*, a
radical London daily newspaper,[29] in 1795; reappeared the same year in
*Cabinet of Curiosities*, a pro-revolutionary, anti-Pitt compendium of satires,
sketches and songs; and came out again in *The Spirit of Public Journals*, an
annual digest, in 1799. It opens on a tranquil evening lit by glow-worms
and the crescent moon, the relative obscurity immediately informing the
reader that conditions are far removed from the well-illuminated venues of
Enlightenment certainties.[30] Henry, a wounded soldier, is moving 'feebly'
along a country path (l. 10):[31]

> On Crutches borne, his mangled Limbs he drew,
> Unsightly remnants of the Battles rage
>
> (ll. 13–14)

Like Odysseus, Henry can barely recognize his native environs:

> 'How chang'd' he cried 'is the fair scene to me,
> Since last across this narrow Path I went.'
>
> (ll. 25–6)

He remembers with nostalgia working in the fields in the seasons of spring
and harvest, a time when his 'Vigour' and 'manly Mien' drew admiration
from his beloved Lucy (l. 40). But he recalls with regret the moment when
a 'gaudy Sergeant caught [his] wond'ring Eye' and 'of War and Honor
spake' (ll. 50, 51), leading to his enlistment and hurried transit to:

---

[29] The *Courier* was described on 9 July 1798 by its rival, the *Anti-Jacobin*, as a 'seditious morning
post' (M. Ray Adams, 'Robert Merry, Political Romanticist', *Studies in Romanticism* 2.1 (Fall 1962),
23–37: 34).

[30] See Michael Charlesworth, 'The Ruined Abbey: Picturesque and Gothic Vales', *The Politics of the
Picturesque: Literature Since 1770*, ed. Stephen Copley and Peter Garside (Cambridge: Cambridge
University Press, 1994), 62–80: 72–4.

[31] Robert Merry, 'The Wounded Soldier', *The Spirit of the Public Journals* II (1799), 126–9. Line
numbers are given in the text. 'The Wounded Soldier' is also available in Bennett, ed., *British War
Poetry in the Age of Romanticism*, 242–5.

> a Scene of Strife;
> To painful Marches, and the din of Arms,
> The wreck of Reason and the waste of Life.
>
> (ll. 66–8)

Battle was attritional – 'Thousands of Wounds and Sickness left to Die' (l. 79) – but now the ex-soldier beholds the 'well known Prospect' of his home, those picturesque staples 'The Farm, the Cot, the Hamlet and the Mill' (ll. 19, 20). His arrival at the 'Threshold of his Father's shed' is unexpected, since his relatives 'knew not of his Fate, yet mourn'd him lost, / Amidst the Number of the unnam'd Dead' (ll. 94–6). When those within hear his 'well remember'd voice', they 'rejoice': 'Our Henry lives' (ll. 97, 99). Yet joy is short-lived:

> [...] when he entered in such horid guize,
> His Mother shriek'd, and dropp'd upon the Floor;
> His Father look'd to Heaven with streaming Eyes,
> And Lucy sunk, alas! to rise no more.
>
> (ll. 101–4)

The concluding stanza expresses the desire that the monitory tale will 'Give due contrition' to 'the self-call'd great' (l. 106).

'The Wounded Soldier' is a meeting-place of eighteenth-century sentiment and revolutionary radicalism. Nicknamed 'Liberty' Merry,[32] its author was an enthusiastic supporter of the French Revolution.[33] In his early twenties, he purchased an army commission, but never saw active service, instead living 'the dissipated life of a Guards officer' until 1780.[34] After some years of travel, he arrived in Florence, became a member of the literary coterie led by Hester Lynch Piozzi and wrote poetry under the name of 'Della Crusca', thereby showing his support for Italian independence, which the Accademia Della Crusca promoted. The Della Cruscan

---

[32] Adams, 'Robert Merry, Political Romanticist', 27.

[33] The biographical information about Merry given here is derived from Adams, 'Robert Merry, Political Romanticist'; Jerome J. McGann, *The Poetics of Sensibility: A Revolution in Literary Style* (Oxford: Oxford University Press, 1996), 74–93; Jon Mee, 'Merry, Robert', *An Oxford Companion to the Romantic Age: British Culture, 1776–1832*, ed. Iain McCalman (Oxford: Oxford University Press, 1999), 601–2; Corinna Russell, 'Merry, Robert (1755–1798)', *Oxford Dictionary of National Biography* (Oxford University Press), online edition; Jon Mee, '*The Magician No Conjuror*: Robert Merry and the Political Alchemy of the 1790s', *Unrespectable Radicals?: Popular Politics in the Age of Reform*, ed. Michael T. Davis and Paul A. Pickering (Aldershot: Ashgate, 2008), 41–55; and Rachel Rogers, 'Vectors of Revolution: The British Radical Community in Early Republican Paris 1792–1794', unpublished PhD thesis (University of Toulouse, 2012), esp. 245–63.

[34] Mee, '*The Magician No Conjuror*', 43.

school was associated with high sentimentalism: Jon Mee notes that Merry
became famous as 'the man of feeling Della Crusca' in the pages of *The
World* while, less politely, M. Ray Adams reports that he 'c[a]me to stand
in the history of English literature for sentimental bombast'.[35] On the fall
of the Bastille, Merry rushed to Paris; two years later, on 14 July 1791, his
ode on this event was 'Recited and Sung'[36] to 1,500 English sympathizers
at the Crown and Anchor in London (meeting place of the radical Society
for Constitutional Information), and Merry dined with Thomas Paine
the same night at the Shakespeare Tavern.[37] In a long roster of works in
various genres, including 'Inscription written at La Grande Chartreuse'
(1790), *The Laurel of Liberty* (1790), *The Picture of Paris* (1790), the 'Fall of
the Bastille' ode and *The Magician No Conjurer* (1792), Merry praised and
promoted the ideals of the Revolution and denigrated the Prime Minister,
William Pitt the Younger.

Merry's radicalism permeates 'The Wounded Soldier', whose protagonist treads 'where peasant Footsteps marked the way', recalls sharing a
'frugal meal', returns to a 'humble Cot' (ll. 9, 35, 64) and is keenly alert to
the illegitimacy of the cause to which he has been recruited:[38]

> [S]uch to my dull sense it was explain'd,
> The Cause of Monarchs, Justice and the Laws
> [...]
> My King and Country seem'd to ask my aid,
> [...]
> Ah! sure Remorse their savage Hearts must rend
> Whose selfish, des'prate phrenzy could decree,
> That in one mass of Murder MAN should blend,
> Who sent the Slave to fight against the Free.
>
> (ll. 59–60, 62, 81–4)

Lured into fighting for George III against the forces of Revolutionary
France,[39] Henry now feels the injustice of subjects, or 'Slaves', combating
'Free' citizens. In a reading that highlights the ideological tenor of the

---

[35] Ibid., 43; Adams, 'Robert Merry, Political Romanticist', 23.
[36] Anonymous, Classified Advertising, *Times* (14 July 1791), 1 (The *Times* Digital Archive).
[37] Adams, 'Robert Merry, Political Romanticist', 29.
[38] For a reading that emphasizes the class politics in the poem, see James Gillinder Masland, 'Narratives of Romantic Masculinity within the Long Eighteenth Century', unpublished PhD thesis (University of California Los Angeles, 2008), 173–80.
[39] Simon Bainbridge, *British Poetry and the Revolutionary and Napoleonic Wars* (Oxford: Oxford University Press, 2003), 42.

poem, Simon Bainbridge remarks that, when wars are fought 'not to pro-
tect the home but to stifle "fair Freedom's call", the ultimate cost of conflict
is the home itself'[40] – in this case as manifested in the soldier's family unit.
The final stanza of the poem is in no doubt as to where blame lies:

> O may this Tale, which agony must close,
> Give deep Contrition to the self-call'd great;
> And shew the Poor, how hard's the lot of those,
> Who shed their Blood, for Ministers of State.
>
> (ll. 105–8)

Two audiences are implicated here: Henry's story should chasten the self-
nominated 'great' but also 'shew' something to the poor. The last two lines
would be a call to arms except that their specific purpose is to warn the
labouring classes *not* to fight – not to fight in the state's cause, at any rate.

In the context of a highly political poem, challenges to biographical
decorum might seem a subsidiary matter. In fact, they enrich the politics. The governing idea of 'The Wounded Soldier' is that of 'nature [...]
revers'd'. This reversal occurs, it should be noted, alongside the 'wreck of
reason', posited in the poem as an effect of battle on the individual but
also possible to understand as a general collapse of rationally based norms.
Conditions are right for time to warp. Young and old swap places, as do the
living and the dead. Having been absent from the village – for how long is
unspecified – Henry is someone who seems to have emerged directly out of
the past. His appearance, as he approaches his home, is such that 'Pity, in
his youthful form, might view / A helpless Prematurity of Age' (ll. 15–16).
Overripe, he has aged before his time ('helpless' suggests both the involuntary nature of the process and the pitifulness of his condition). That he
finds his home greatly changed since his departure reinforces this sense of
the alienness of the past: his being out of time is conveyed by his feeling
out of place. As he nears the cottage, those inside hear him before they
see him. Since he has long been thought dead, the sound of his voice has
the effect of resurrecting him.[41] But if his 'well remembered voice' (l. 97)

---

[40] During the War of the First Coalition (1792–7), the first phase of the French Revolutionary Wars,
Britain supported revolts against Republican France.

[41] There is a significant strand of literary veterans straddling the boundary between life and death.
Balzac's Colonel Chabert rises from his interment in a ditch of corpses after the Battle of Eylau
asking 'Am I dead or alive?' ('Suis-je mort ou suis-je vivant?') (Honoré de Balzac, *Le Colonel Chabert*
[1832] (Paris: Librio, 2013), 40 (my translation)). On the dead/alive superpositional state produced
by war, see Kate McLoughlin, *Authoring War: The Literary Representation of War from the* Iliad *to Iraq*
(Cambridge: Cambridge University Press, 2011), 122–31.

is unchanged, his haggard form is unnaturally aged. Excessively old, he presents in 'horid guize' that is literally unsupportable: unable to co-exist with it, his parents and lover immediately remove it from their consciousness by averting their eyes or collapsing. Indeed, Henry's accelerated ageing actually causes his lover's own premature death. But Lucy is not the only young person to die at the wrong time of life: as Henry muses elsewhere in the poem, the global effect of war is that 'The Son now weeps not on the Father's Bier' but 'grey Hair'd Age [...] Drops o'er his Children's Grave an Icy tear' (ll. 90–2). For a child to predecease a parent violates a deeply felt sense of what is biographically decorous.[42] With his 'helpless Prematurity', Henry is now in some sense older than his mother and father: a further disturbance of the natural biography of things.

Biographical indecorousness works as a broad-brush metaphor for times of revolution when regimes are brought down and society upended. But the infringements of 'due course' contained in 'The Wounded Soldier' have a more particular application. The poem belongs to an *oeuvre* deeply critical of a prime minister who was widely perceived to be too young. William Pitt was known as 'the younger' to distinguish him from his father who had the same name, but the epithet also highlights his precocity – a prodigious child, he became prime minister at the very young age of 24. Writing in 1865, the French poet and politician Alphonse de Lamartine 'recompose[d]' the 22-year-old Pitt from the reminiscences of Pitt's niece, Lady Hester Stanhope: 'not yet touched by the feverish and mephitic breath of assemblies', his cheeks 'had the bloom, the transparency, and so to speak, the virginity of adolescence'.[43] Nonetheless, he exuded the 'precocious gravity of the novice in state affairs'.[44] For those less admiring, Pitt's youth was an obvious point of satire: a 'parliamentary eclogue' published in a volume entitled *An Asylum for Fugitive Pieces* in 1789 set Pitt against his rival Edmund Burke under the title 'The Angry Boy and the Calm Veteran'.[45] Merry himself was a joyful and inventive Pitt-satirist. The

---

[42] Infant mortality is not the issue here, but it is still worth noting that infant mortality rates in England in the late eighteenth century were 'low' – *c.*175 per 1,000 births in 1801 (R. Woods, 'Infant Mortality in Britain: A Survey of Current Knowledge on Historical Trends and Variations', *Infant and Child Mortality in the Past*, ed. Alain Bideau, Bertrand Desjardins and Héctor Pérez Brignoli (Oxford: Oxford University Press, 1997), 74–88: 75–7) – and so unlikely to have normalized the experience of outliving a child.

[43] Alphonse de Lamartine, *Biographies and Portraits of Some Celebrated People. Volume 1: Lord Chatham. William Pitt. Shakespeare* (London: Tinsley Brothers, 1866), 56.

[44] Ibid., 57.

[45] Anonymous, 'An Angry Boy and A Calm Veteran', *An Asylum for Fugitive Pieces, in Prose and Verse, Not in Any Other Collections: With Several Pieces Never Before Published* (London: J. Debrett, 1798), 79–80 (Eighteenth Century Collections Online).

first instalment of a Della Cruscan publication, *Cabinet of Curiosities*,[46] published in London in 1795 – which, as noted, includes 'The Wounded Soldier' – demonstrates this in pieces such as 'Mustapha's Adoration of the Sublime Sultan Pittander the Omnipotent' and 'Theatrical Extraordinary. Pittachio's Theatre Royal' (it is not impossible that the word 'pittance' in 'The Wounded Soldier' (l. 47) belongs with these Pitt-puns).[47] The satires in the *Cabinet* repeatedly set critiques of the Prime Minister's foreign policy, including his treatment of the armed forces, in the context of nature-surpassing wonders. 'Mustapha's Adoration' lavishes the ironical praise that 'Thou sendest out armies conquering and to conquer, and when they are discomfited thou becomest exceeding wroth, and orderest forth others to be again destroyed; for thy power and thy glory are without end',[48] while 'Wonderful Exhibition […] Signor Guglielmo Pittachio, the Sublime Wonder of the World' promises that its star will explain such enigmas as 'By running backward, we get forward' and display his 'master trick' of being 'six different places at one and the same time'.[49] Pittachio/ Pitt is, as M. Ray Adams remarks, 'a mountebank belonging to the tradition of the *commedia dell'arte*',[50] and the spirit and illogic of that tradition are evident in Merry's satire. So, too, is the influence of an established tradition of characterizing 'the British system of government as a deception of one kind or another'.[51] Jon Mee traces the 'specific identification' between the Pitt administration and 'the arts of conjuration' from the 'satirical assaults' organized by the Sheridan circle from the mid-1780s to Thomas Paine's *The Rights of Man* (1791).[52] (While the Government kept up 'the clamour of French intrigue, arbitrary power, popery, and wooden shoes', the nation was 'easily allured and alarmed into taxes', wrote Paine. 'These

---

[46] Given that Merry, following the lead of Sheridan's *Political Miscellanies* (1787) that created 'Signor Pinetti the Conjuror', published a series of playbills in the radical London dailies mocking the Prime Minister as 'Signor Pittachio' in 1794 (Mee, 'The Magician No Conjuror', 47), it can be assumed that he was also the author of these pieces.

[47] On 18 January 1792, the *Diary or Woodfall's Register* published a open letter to Pitt from 'Mercator' (Sir John Gladstone), 'Otherwise, a Seaman, moored head and stern, with a breast-fast run out, and secured to the Rock of Despair', entreating him to pay veteran officers 'their poor scanty pittance' ('To the Right Honourable William Pitt', *Diary or Woodfall's Register* (18 January 1792), 2 (Gale-Cengage 17th–18th Century Burney Newspaper Collection)).

[48] Robert Merry, 'Mustapha's Adoration of the Sublime Sultan Pittander the Omnipotent', *Cabinet of Curiosities* (London: publisher unknown, 1795), 26–30: 26–7.

[49] Robert Merry, 'Wonderful Exhibition', *Cabinet of Curiosities* (London: publisher unknown, 1795), 82–7: 83, 85.

[50] Adams, 'Robert Merry, Political Romanticist', 34 n44.

[51] Jon Mee, 'The Magician No Conjuror', 47.

[52] Ibid., 47.

days are now past: deception, it is to be hoped, has reaped its last harvest.')[53] For present purposes, the most noteworthy marvel is that Pittachio/Pitt can defy unidirectional time. In addition to the feats of going forward by running backward and being in six different places at once, Merry has Pittachio/Pitt turning old into young. In 'Theatrical Extraordinary', the Signor produces 'old men in youthful characters':[54] 'Mansmead[55] has one foot in the grave and the other scarcely out of it, and yet he scrapes and grasps with all the vigour of youth: so gross an improbability might very well be omitted.'[56] The gross improbability of an old man in the guise of a young man belongs to the same fluid temporality as 'The Wounded Soldier' in which parents outlive their children, senescence is accelerated and individuals die too soon. Less personally satirical of Pitt than the other *Cabinet of Curiosities* sketches – though still focused upon one of the key criticisms of the Prime Minister's administration: the inadequate payment of members of the armed forces – the poem contributes to the nimbus of irrationality and incredibleness fostered around the government's programme by its opponents.

'O that I could sleep two centuries like the youths of Ephesus and then awake to a new order of things!' Merry wrote to his friend the poet Samuel Rogers on 12 December 1794.[57] The new order of things he had in mind was political – his ideals were those of 'pacifism, liberty and direct democracy'[58] – but 'The Wounded Soldier' also points to a revised temporal order in which the path of time's arrow is no longer straight. (In the story of the Seven Sleepers of Ephesus, one version of which is told in the Qur'an, young men sleep in a sealed cave for a couple of hundred years yet age only a day.) But the figure of the veteran gives Merry scope to attempt a different form of persuasion than the Pittachio/Pittander satires. If those marvels belong to the circus, prematurely aged veterans come home in the real world. The French Revolutionary and Napoleonic Wars were resulting in parents outliving their children in significant numbers. The ravaged young veteran character, therefore, allows Merry to bring his criticisms of Pitt up close and personal as he vividly demonstrates the effect of the

[53] Thomas Paine, *Rights of Man, Common Sense and Other Political Writings*, ed. Mark Philp (Oxford: Oxford University Press, 1998), 287.

[54] Robert Merry, 'Theatrical Extraordinary. Pittachio's Theatre Royal', *Cabinet of Curiosities* (London: publisher unknown, 1795), 87–90: 88.

[55] Sir James Mansfield?

[56] Merry, 'Theatrical Extraordinary', 88–9.

[57] Quoted in Mee, '*The Magician No Conjuror*', 41. The letter is in the University College, London, Special Collections: Sharpe Papers 15 f.214.

[58] Rogers, 'Vectors of Revolution', 247.

government's neglect of its former soldiers. In the next text for discussion, by contrast, Jane Austen's novel *Persuasion*, a veteran returns from naval service in the pink. The text contains another time lapse, again accompanied by challenges to biographical decorum. But if Merry's target was precocity, Austen questions the apparent connection between wisdom and age.

### Complexions: Jane Austen, *Persuasion* (1818)

In chapter 10 of *Persuasion*, two people hide themselves within a hedgerow. The concealed pair wish to remove themselves from public view; at least one of them has flirtatious intentions. But although they are 'quite out of sight and sound' at first (109),[59] they re-enter audible range and become subject to eavesdropping. The hidden two are Captain Wentworth and Louisa Musgrove, and the eavesdropper is Anne Elliot, who, sitting down to rest on a 'sunny bank' (109), by chance overhears their conversation. Captain Wentworth picks a hazelnut to illustrate to Louisa what he is trying to explain to her about human nature:

> 'Here is a nut,' said he, catching one down from an upper bough, 'to exemplify: a beautiful glossy nut, which, blessed with original strength, has outlived all the storms of autumn. Not a puncture, not a weak spot anywhere. This nut,' he continued, with playful solemnity, 'while so many of his brethren have fallen and been trodden under foot, is still in possession of all the happiness that a hazel nut can be supposed capable of.' Then returning to his former earnest tone – 'My first wish for all whom I am interested in, is that they should be firm. If Louisa Musgrove would be beautiful and happy in her November of life, she will cherish all her present powers of mind.'
>
> (110)

Unlike her sister Henrietta, Louisa – in Wentworth's view – possesses admirable qualities of 'decision and firmness' (110). He purports to find the same qualities in the glossy nut, which has remained whole throughout 'all the storms of autumn'. If Louisa can maintain those admirable attributes of 'fortitude and strength of mind' (110) through to and beyond the autumn of her life, she will be 'beautiful and happy' and – so is the implication – at his side. At first glance, the parable seems directly applicable to Anne Elliot, an application reinforced by the dramatic irony of her overhearing it. Anne, after all, has very evidently not demonstrated decision and

[59] Jane Austen, *Persuasion* [1818], ed. D. W. Harding (Harmondsworth: Penguin, 1965/1985). Page numbers are given in the text.

firmness but did the wrong thing eight and a half years previously when she was all too easily persuaded to break off Wentworth's suit. Eight and a half years on, she is – again very evidently – neither beautiful nor happy.

But there is something misleading about Wentworth's analogy. In *Persuasion* Jane Austen is not interested in the hazelnut that has remained upon the tree so much as in the one that has fallen and been trodden underfoot. That nut might not reach the end of the storm 'beautiful and glossy', but its 'original strength' may nonetheless allow it to survive. It is those 'punctured' and with 'weak spots', but still enduring – veterans, that is – that the novel will reward. But, this being Jane Austen, the reward is tinged with caution: advancing in wisdom is not necessarily the same as advancing in years.

*Persuasion*, of all Austen's works, is the most concerned with military representation, a fact that binds it inexorably to the long critical debate concerning its author's engagement with national and international concerns. 'How horrible it is to have so many people killed! And what a blessing that one cares for none of them!':[60] Austen's comment on the enormous losses sustained at the Battle of Albuera (1811) has been taken as indicative of her general indifference to the mass warfare and geopolitics of her era. 'The year may be 1815, but Waterloo is as far off as Cathay,' commented one reviewer of a theatrical production of *Emma* staged in the last year of the Second World War,[61] exemplifying the critical tendency to berate Austen for insularity and ignorance. It was V. S. Pritchett who proposed, in the 1969 Clark Lectures, the idea of 'Jane Austen, War Novelist', 'formed very much by the Napoleonic wars, knowing directly of prize money, the shortage of men, the economic crisis and change in the value of capital'.[62] The French Revolutionary and Napoleonic Wars can be – have been – traced in Austen's novels in the presence of military personnel and passing references to actual events:[63] among them, General Tilney and Captain Frederick Tilney in *Northanger Abbey*; Colonel Brandon, veteran of the East Indies, in *Sense and Sensibility*;[64] the militia encamped in *Pride and*

---

[60] Jane Austen, *Jane Austen's Letters*, ed. Deirdre Le Faye (Oxford: Oxford University Press, 1995), 191.

[61] Ivor Brown, 'Theatre and Life', *London Observer* (11 February 1945), 2; quoted in Mary Favret, *War at a Distance: Romanticism and the Making of Modern Wartime* (Princeton, NJ: Princeton University Press, 2010), 45.

[62] V. S. Pritchett, *George Meredith and English Comedy* (London: Chatto and Windus, 1970), 28.

[63] See, for example, Warren Roberts, *Jane Austen and the French Revolution* (London: Macmillan, 1979), 95–106; Gillian Russell, 'The Army, the Navy, and the Napoleonic Wars', *A Companion to Jane Austen*, ed. Claudia L. Johnson and Clara Tuite (Chichester: Wiley-Blackwell, 2009), 261–71.

[64] Warren Roberts describes Brandon as 'an eighteenth-century soldier who found life in India harsh, not for military reasons but because of the hot climate and mosquitoes' (*Jane Austen and the French Revolution*, 96).

*Prejudice* and the entanglements of members of the 'cluster of redcoats' with members of the Bennett family;[65] and the Antigua episode and Midshipman William Price's service in *Mansfield Park*.[66] When Austen came to write her last completed novel, *Persuasion*, therefore, she was herself an experienced creator of war-related characters and motifs. But even at the opposite end of the critical spectrum from that which finds her parochial, scholars emphasize the subtlety and muteness of her engagement with the large events of history. Brian Southam quotes a comment from the 1870 memoir by Austen's nephew, James Edward Austen-Leigh – 'with ships and sailors she felt herself at home' – before reaching in apparent disappointment the conclusion that, in her works, 'we have to be content with sailors' tales and sailors safe on shore'.[67] Mary Favret, by contrast, finds the domestication of the warlike a critical opportunity: in *Persuasion*, she argues, 'the everyday [is] informed by the language, the features, and the affective resonance of wartime' and hence exhibits the 'survivor's perspective'.[68] My thinking is similar to Favret's. Veteran poetics inform *Persuasion*, not as a scheme of naval references, but in terms of the novel's treatment of the passing of time and the accrual of wisdom, particularly as figured in the weather and the seasons, and their effects on people's faces.[69]

At the centre of *Persuasion* is an eight-and-a-half-year gap. Narratologically, this missing period forms a chronological reference point ( '"That was in the year six"; "That happened before I went to sea in the year six" ' (88)) and sets up an oscillation between analepsis and prolepsis as discussion ranges back across it and forwards into the future. Thematically, it prompts characters to regret past decisions, compare their present selves

---

[65] Jane Austen, *Pride and Prejudice* [1813], ed. James Kinsley (Oxford: Oxford University Press, 2004), 74.

[66] William 'had been in the Mediterranean – in the West Indies – in the Mediterranean again – had often taken on shore by the favour of his Captain, and in the course of seven years had known every variety of danger, which sea and war together could offer' (*Mansfield Park* [1814], ed. Tony Tanner (Harmondsworth: Penguin, 1985), 245).

[67] J. E. Austen-Leigh, *A Memoir of Jane Austen and Other Family Recollections*, ed. Kathryn Sutherland (Oxford: Oxford University Press, 2002), 18; quoted in Brian Southam, *Jane Austen and the Navy*, 2nd ed. (London: National Maritime Museum, 2005), 3.

[68] Favret, *War at a Distance*, 147, 149.

[69] *Persuasion*'s figurative scheme of complexion and maturity is anticipated by a piece Austen wrote in her teens, *Jack and Alice: A Novel*, dedicated to her brother, Francis William Austen, then a Midshipman on the *Perseverance*. One evening, 'somewhat heated by wine', Alice goes to Lady Williams to confide her love for Charles Adams (*Catharine and Other Writings*, ed. Margaret Anne Doody (Oxford: Oxford University Press, 1993), 15). Lady Williams refers to a woman who has 'too much colour' (16) and Alice questions how 'any one can have too much colour?' (16). During a circular argument that does not improve as it matures, Alice's own 'reddening' (16) face proves that there is no connection between wisdom and the signs of wear and tear.

with their younger ones, ruminate on lost opportunities and speculate as to what they would do if re-presented with similar circumstances. The temporal deficit therefore produces a subjunctive ambiance: should those involved have acted as they did? Would they make the same mistakes again? How can we ever know when the time is 'right'?

The facts are these. In 1806, Captain Frederick Wentworth, aged 23, newly promoted to Commander for his part in the British action off St Domingo, had asked for the hand of the then 19-year-old Anne Elliot, daughter of Sir Walter Elliot, Baronet, of Kellynch Hall, Somersetshire. Sir Walter, a 'conceited, silly father' (36), had refused to consent to the engagement, considering it a 'degrading alliance' (55). Lady Russell, a friend of the late Lady Elliot and a quasi-maternal figure to Anne, also advised against the match, 'persuading' her not to throw away 'all her claims of birth, beauty and mind' on a young man 'who had nothing but himself to recommend him, and no hopes of attaining affluence' (55). The novel's backstory, therefore, sets up a conflict between elders and youngsters on the grounds of the former knowing better than the latter. Wisdom has, at least ostensibly, been aligned with age, folly with youth.

Sir Walter's judgement, however, is shown to be flawed from the outset. The 'beginning and the end' of his character is 'vanity', the reader is told as the novel opens; indeed, '[f]ew women could think more of their personal appearance than he did' (36). The key to Sir Walter's appearance is that he 'had been remarkably handsome in his youth; and, at fifty-four, was still a very fine man' (36). He has not, that is, aged visibly over time to any significant degree. This fact is a source of immense pride to Sir Walter, who enjoys regarding himself ('Such a number of looking-glasses!' comments Admiral Croft (143)) and who immediately notices the effects of ageing in others. His objection to the navy is not only that it raises 'persons of obscure birth into undue distinction' but also that it 'cuts up a man's youth and vigour most horribly; a sailor grows old sooner than any other man' (49). This explains his indignation at having to give place to an Admiral Baldwin, 'the most deplorable looking personage you can imagine, his face the colour of mahogany, rough and rugged to the last degree, all lines and wrinkles, nine grey hairs of a side, and nothing but a dab of powder at top' (49). Sir Walter predicts that, since Admiral Croft was 'in the Trafalgar action' and has been stationed in the East Indies since, his face will be 'as orange as the cuffs and capes of my livery' (Mr Shepherd confirms that Admiral Croft is 'a very hale, hearty, well-looking man, a little weather-beaten, to be sure, but not much' (51)) and is gratified when the Admiral is reported to have gout ('Gout and decrepitude? [...] Poor old gentleman' (177)). The thrust of Sir Walter's prejudices is that experience and maturity, figured by worn or aged complexions and associated with naval veterancy,[70] are less valuable than an ancient pedigree, and can never trump or match it.

In fact, the characters in the novel who have weather-beaten or aged faces display more attractive qualities than their more youthful-looking associates. Admiral Croft is modest, socially and manually adroit, kind, humorous and tactful. His wife has a 'reddened and weather-beaten complexion, the consequence of her having been almost as much at sea as her husband', which makes her 'seem to have lived some years longer in the world than her real eight and thirty' (74). A veteran of the East Indies, Lisbon, Gibraltar, Cork and four Atlantic crossings, Mrs Croft literally and metaphorically keeps a steady hand on the reins to guide the couple's carriage, a metaphor that resonates powerfully with the novel's theme of (appropriately) persuading or steering others.[71] Mrs Smith is another quasi-veteran, and tells tales to prove it. Having suffered through poverty and illness and become transformed in the space of twelve years from 'the fine-looking, well-grown Miss Hamilton' into a 'poor, infirm, helpless widow' (165), she is remarkably un-self-pitying, keen to help those even less fortunate than herself and in possession of 'good sense and agreeable manners' (166). Undermining the ostensible opposition between wise age and foolish youth implied by Sir Walter and Lady Russell knowing better than Anne and Wentworth in 1806 is a more subtle endorsement of altruism and mature wisdom derived from (often harsh) experience.

It is now 1814.[72] After an absence of eight and a half years, Anne learns, Captain Wentworth has returned to Kellynch. The novel derives an early narratological momentum from their imminent reunion: 'he was expected, and speedily' (78). After the two meet again, their long separation continues

---

[70] Overseas military service here complicates the long-standing association between tanned skin and outdoor labour. Cf. Sir Harry Beaumont's (aka Joseph Spence) comment in *Crito: Or, A Dialogue on Beauty* (1752) that '[t]he honest Rustic can think himself happy in his Woman of a good strong Make, and Sunburnt frowsy Complexion' (*Crito: Or, A Dialogue on Beauty*, ed. Edmund Goldsmid (Edinburgh: privately printed, 1885), 59).

[71] There are distinct similarities between Mrs Croft and Mrs Bagnet (aka 'the old girl') in Dickens's *Bleak House*. Both have assumed the veterancy of their husbands – and the tanned complexion that goes with it.

[72] The year 1814 is historically significant: the Peace of Paris was signed on 30 May (temporarily) ending war between Britain and Napoleonic France and resulting in the return of naval personnel to civilian life 'in large numbers' (Southam, *Jane Austen and the Navy*, 273, 271). Unlike ordinary seamen, returning naval officers did not leave the navy but remained on half-pay. In 1814, the Admiralty introduced a new pay-scale based on seniority in the Captains' List (rather than on the rating of the officer's last vessel). Without prize money, Southam suggests, half-pay 'would provide only a bare minimum to live on' (292; see also 271).

to form the basis for questions regarding time and personal growth. Central to such questions is the effect the intervening eight and a half years has had on both of them. Wentworth has enjoyed a distinguished naval career. After commanding a sloop, the *Asp*, to the West Indies and taking 'privateers enough to be very entertaining' (90), he has been promoted to captain and posted to a frigate, the *Laconia*, at the age of 25 (promotion beyond this would have been made on grounds of seniority rather than merit), taking her to Gibraltar, the Azores and the Mediterranean. He has made a 'handsome fortune' of twenty-five thousand pounds (58).[73] If his service in the West Indies gives Wentworth something in common with Wordsworth's Discharged Soldier, his wealth wholly distinguishes him from that destitute figure – and so too does his ability to tell tales. Indeed, his verbosity is explicitly commented upon: '[h]is profession qualified him, his disposition led him, to talk' (88). His sea stories produce 'surprise' 'amazement', 'shudderings', 'pity and horror' (89, 90, 91) in his audience, and an obvious pleasure in reminiscence in Wentworth himself.

But there is something odd about Captain Wentworth. Though he is a much-travelled naval officer with the tales to prove it, his exterior appearance is not consonant with his experience, nor with the amount of time that has passed. In the novel's scheme for indicating such experience, he should have a weather-beaten aspect. In fact, he has 'not altered, or not for the worse' (85). If anything, he has acquired a 'more glowing, manly, open look' (86), 'foreign climes' and 'active service' not having 'robb[ed] him of one personal grace' (188). Notably, Sir Walter now pronounces him 'a very well-looking man' (197). His revised opinion on Wentworth's suitability for Anne is couched as follows: '[W]hen he saw more of Captain Wentworth, saw him repeatedly by daylight and eyed him well, he was very much struck by his personal claims, and felt that his superiority of appearance might be not unfairly balanced against her superiority of rank' (250). That Wentworth is not weather-beaten or otherwise physically attenuated by his naval service suggests something unusual about the passage of time.

In fact, it is Anne who exhibits signs of veterancy. She is described with a recurrent image of fading bloom. The missing years have 'destroyed her youth and bloom' (86), leaving her 'with every beauty excepting bloom' (166) or even in 'ruins' (96).[74] Learning that Wentworth considers her '[a]ltered

---

[73] Ibid., 272; see also 276.

[74] A 'rosy' facial colour in women was prized in the period in which Austen was writing. The Scottish physiologist, novelist and journalist Alexander Walker opined in 1836: 'the forehead, the temples,

beyond his knowledge' is a 'mortification' (85). Austen explicitly associates 'declining happiness' with autumn in Anne's mind (107) ('images of youth and hope, and spring' are also combined (107)), reinforcing the (apparent) applicability of Wentworth's hazelnut analogy to her. She has also acquired a veteran consciousness (aptly described by Mary Favret as an 'affective state of simultaneous belatedness and anticipation'):[75] at 27, she thinks 'very differently from what she had been made to think at nineteen' (57). Her present mode of thought is reflective, regretful and wary. Above all, she is preoccupied with the missing years: 'What might not eight years do? Events of every description, changes, alienations, removals, – all, all must be comprised in it [...] It included nearly a third part of her own life' (85). The implication is clear: she would not – will not – make the same mistake again.

But retrospection does not render clear-cut the decision that should have been made eight and a half years ago. As Robert Hopkins points out in a critical approach that matches the novel's own speculative epistemology, if Anne had married Wentworth in 1806, he might have been lost at sea without making a fortune, leaving her a destitute widow.[76] (The ontological status of such a parallel fictional universe is unclear, but the hypothesis usefully illustrates the problems of hindsight.) Suggestions that what is at stake is constancy are also misleading. In chapter 23, Anne and Captain Harville enter a discussion – with Wentworth listening – about whether men or women are the more faithful. Harville remarks that he has never 'opened a book in [his] life which had not something to say about woman's inconstancy. Songs and proverbs, all talk of women's fickleness' (237). Anne counters:

> We certainly do not forget you, so soon as you forget us. It is, perhaps, our fate rather than our merit. We cannot help ourselves. We live at home, quiet, confined,

the eyelids, the nose, the upper part of the superior lip, and the lower part of the inferior lip, ought in woman to be of a beautiful and rather opaque white. The approach to the cheeks and the middle of the chin ought to have a slight teint of rose-color, and the middle of the cheeks ought to be altogether rosy, but of a delicate hue. – Cheeks of an animated white are preferable to those of a red color, although less beautiful than those of rosy hue' (*Beauty; Illustrated Chiefly by an Analysis and Classification of Beauty in Woman* (New York: Henry G. Langley, 1845), 247–8). On complexions of the period, see further Lynn Festa, 'Cosmetic Differences: The Changing Faces of England and France', *Studies in Eighteenth-Century Culture* 34 (2005), 25–34; Tassie Gwilliam, 'Cosmetic Poetics: Coloring Faces in the Eighteenth Century', *Body and Text in the Eighteenth Century*, ed. Veronica Kelly and Dorothea von Mücke (Stanford, CA: Stanford University Press, 1994), 144–62; and Michael Prince, 'The Eighteenth-Century Beauty Contest', *MLQ* 55.3 (September 1994), 251–79.

[75] Favret, *War at a Distance*, 163.

[76] Robert Hopkins, 'Moral Luck and Judgment in Jane Austen's *Persuasion*', *Nineteenth-Century Literature* 42.2 (September 1987), 143–58: 144–5.

and our feelings prey upon us. You are forced on exertion. You have always a profession, pursuits, business of some sort or other, to take you back into the world
immediately, and continual occupation and change soon weaken impressions.

                                                                              (236)

This speech is more notable for what it says about the psychological
conditions in which Anne has spent the last eight and a half years than
about women's essential steadfastness. She has, indeed, been faithful to
Wentworth – or, at least, to her idea of Wentworth – rejecting other
suitors, and, the reader is told, '[h]er attachment and regrets had, for a
long time, clouded every enjoyment of youth; and an early loss of bloom
and spirits had been their lasting effect' (57). Over the same span of time,
Anne appears to have lived longer than Wentworth.

But as her renewed acquaintance with Wentworth develops, something
remarkable begins to happen to Anne's looks. She is assured that 'she has
not lost one charm of her earlier youth' (245) and, indeed, is said to have
'improved looks' (158). Wentworth sees in her 'something like Anne Elliot
again' (125) and when they are fully reunited he goes so far as to contra-
dict his earlier statement ('he said, "You were so altered he should not
have known you again"' (85)), insisting that 'to my eye you could never
alter' (245). Anne herself entertains hopes for 'a second spring of youth and
beauty' (139) and proclaims herself 'not yet so much changed' (229). The
'second spring' thesis posits a striking temporal reversion: Anne seems to
be actually growing younger instead of older. Indeed, this state of affairs is
prefigured at the outset of the novel in the authorial comment that '[s]he
had been forced into prudence in her youth, she learned romance as she
grew older' (58). If the 19-year-old Anne was prematurely old, the 27-year-
old Anne is belatedly young. But there is no hard evidence that she now
'knows better': age is not, in this novel, the same as wisdom, and wisdom is
not the same as prudence. The decision she must make at 27 – whether or
not to marry Wentworth – is not the same decision that she faced at 19, for
the excellent reason that Wentworth is now prosperous and of senior rank.
Her accepting him second time round, therefore, is not in itself proof that
she has attained mature judgement, just that times have changed.

*Persuasion* rewards Anne and Captain Wentworth not, presumably, for
wisdom acquired over time (they were no more foolish in 1806) nor for
being less susceptible to persuasion (they are still being persuaded, not
least by each other) nor for steadfastness (which in some lights looks like
obstinacy or a plain refusal to accept reality), but for resilience, flexibility
and for showing good faith second time round – what Austen in another

context in the novel calls 'elasticity of mind' (167). What is endorsed is not the hazelnut that emerges from the storms 'beautiful and glossy' (even though Anne does miraculously recover some of her youthful bloom) but the one that, having fallen, nonetheless survives. In veterancy, Austen finds a suggestive ambivalence, as is evident not only in what happens to the main protagonists' faces, but in the work's repeated, unsettled questioning of past and future behaviour, its speculative nature and its obsession with lost time. In the text discussed next, Tennyson's 'Ulysses', the question of what individuals ought to do at certain times in their lives becomes even more acute as a superannuated veteran provides a means of marking the injustice of a young man's early death.

## Late: Alfred, Lord Tennyson, 'Ulysses' (1833)

Early in October 1833, 24-year-old Alfred Tennyson received the news that his beloved friend, Arthur Hallam, 22, was 'no more'.[77] The death (which the expression 'no more' couched as a form of *being late*)[78] came as 'a sudden and brutal stroke' that 'annihilated' him.[79] But, despite professing to be 'crushed' and 'paralysed',[80] in the next few weeks Tennyson produced one of his most celebrated works: a poem about the archetypal war veteran Odysseus/Ulysses.[81] His choice of protagonist in the circumstances is striking, at first glance even inapposite. What could an old man who has lived too long have to do with a young man who has died too soon? 'Ulysses' reflects the power of veterancy as an idea and as a source of figurative expression, in particular of the pain of caducity. 'You are [perceived as] a past-it has-been,' commented one twenty-first-century army veteran in

---

[77] Letter from Henry Elton, Hallam's uncle, to Alfred Tennyson, quoted in Hallam Tennyson, *Alfred, Lord Tennyson: A Memoir* 1/2 vols (London: Macmillan, 1897), 105. Christopher Ricks notes that Tennyson 'was sent the news' on 1 October but may not have received it until 6 October (Alfred, Lord Tennyson, *The Poems of Tennyson*, ed. Christopher Ricks, 3 vols (Harlow: Longman, 1969), 2.304–5). References to Tennyson's poems are to this edition. Line numbers are given in the text.

[78] 'Late, adj. 1', 5b: 'That was recently [...] but is not now', *Oxford English Dictionary* (Oxford University Press), online edition.

[79] Charles Tennyson, *Alfred Tennyson* (London: Macmillan, 1949), 145.

[80] Alfred, Lord Tennyson, *The Letters of Alfred Lord Tennyson*, ed. Cecil Y. Yang, 3 vols (Oxford; The Clarendon Press, 1982–1990), 1.112.

[81] 'Ulysses' was completed by 20 October 1833 (Tennyson, *The Poems of Tennyson*, ed. Ricks, 1.613.). In the weeks and months following Hallam's death, Tennyson also produced 'On a Mourner'; 'Tithon' (later 'Tithonus'), which he described as a 'pendent' to 'Ulysses' (letter of 26 December 1859, *The Letters of Alfred Lord Tennyson*, ed. Yang, 2.605); 'Morte d'Arthur'; a long section of 'Tiresias' (the 75-line exhortation to Menoeceus (see David F. Goslee, 'Three Stages of Tennyson's "Tiresias"', *The Journal of English and Germanic Philology* 75.1/2 (January–April 1976), 154–67: 154); and 'Break, Break, Break'.

an interview,[82] reflecting the fact that the ex-soldier is inescapably defined by what he was formerly but is no longer. Veterancy allows the 'has-been', Ulysses, to reach out to the 'never-waser', Hallam. Both are outside their primes, the former through over-living, the latter through under-living; the one exhausting his usefulness, the other not fulfilling his promise. The lateness of veterancy, in the senses both of its connection with late life and its quality of being former, provided Tennyson with a state of temporal disjuncture – time 'out of joint'[83] – via which it was possible to articulate the unacceptability of Hallam's untimely death.

Critics have been preoccupied with Ulysses as a man of (in)action. A. A. Markley's description of the character as 'a perfect embodiment of a tireless, masculine hero, craving action and shunning domestic tranquillity'[84] typifies a strand of critical readings of the poem in which the doing or not doing of deeds is gender-inflected. A variation on this approach has been to treat the poem as a study in old age or late life. Explicitly connecting waning virility with old age, Robert Langbaum sees the poem as the dramatization of 'an old man's appetite exceeding potency'.[85] For John Batchelor, Tennyson 'aged twenty-four played the role of an old man preparing for death and summoning the will to confront it courageously'.[86] In his view, 'Ulysses' ends with courageous defiance and stoical acceptance'.[87] Defiance and acceptance are a tricky combination to bring off, though both responses are symptomatic of late life. Tony Robbins also picks up on the character's 'heterogeneous awareness' but, *contra* Batchelor, concludes that 'it is in the face of death that Ulysses' will to live is strongest'.[88] For Robbins, the 'simple heroic refusal to die' outweighs the protagonist's other priorities in late life.[89] Francis O'Gorman politicizes Ulysses' motives, suggesting that, in the context of the 1832 Reform Bill, his unwillingness to right the 'injustices' of Ithaca resembles the failure of the leaders of the Reform lobby at the beginning of the 1830s to remedy

---

[82] Quoted in Jim McDermott, 'Old Soldiers Never Die: They Adapt Their Military Skills and Become Successful Civilians: What Factors Contribute to the Successful Transition of Army Veterans to Civilian Life and Work?', unpublished PhD thesis (University of Leicester, 2007), 165.

[83] *Hamlet* 1.5.188.

[84] A. A. Markley, *Stateliest Measures: Tennyson and the Literature of Greece and Rome* (Toronto: University of Toronto Press, 2004), 125.

[85] Robert Langbaum, *The Poetry of Experience: The Dramatic Monologue in Modern Literary Tradition* (London: Chatto and Windus, 1957), 90.

[86] John Batchelor, *Tennyson: To Strive, To Seek, To Find* (London: Chatto and Windus, 2012), 79.

[87] Ibid., 79.

[88] Tony Robbins, 'Tennyson's "Ulysses": The Significance of the Homeric and Dantesque Backgrounds', *Victorian Poetry* 11.3 (Autumn, 1973), 177–93: 177, 178.

[89] Ibid., 177, 178.

'the "unequal laws" of their own island'.[90] In O'Gorman's conception, Ulysses becomes a 'Wellington', another 'veteran hero' who 'distanced [himself] from the pressing issues of domestic politics.[91] Another group of critics finds Ulysses *too* politically engaged; in the words of Alan Sinfield, he is 'a colonizer who requires ever more remote margins to sustain his enterprise'.[92] In descriptions that pick up the entropic tendencies endemic in the imperialist endeavour, critics have commented that the character 'sounds for all the world like a bored colonial official somewhere in the back of beyond' or 'a colonial administrator turning over the reins to a successor just before stepping on the boat to go home'.[93] The hero of Homer and Dante starts to come across as a gin-soaked Foreign Office hand recklessly calling for one last hurrah.

My intention here is to build on the work of those critics who have read the poem as an exploration of old age, and to inquire concertedly into the significance of 'lateness' in terms of biographical decorum. Arthur Hallam himself nodded towards this notion when he wrote in his essay 'On Sympathy' (1830), 'how often does our actual self desire different objects from those which allured us in a previous condition!'[94] Hallam's reference to 'desire' provides a convenient entry point for our inquiry, since Ulysses is described as 'yearning in desire' (l. 30).[95] What is this 'desire'? What does Ulysses want out of life, and, more specifically, what does he want at this particular point in his life? As scholars have noted – Robbins mentions not only 'heterogeneous awareness' but also 'divided intentions'[96] – the

---

[90] Francis O'Gorman, 'Tennyson's "The Lotos-Eaters" and the Politics of the 1830s', *Victorian Review* 30.1 (2004), 1–20: 11, 12. Cf. Matthew Bevis's reading of the poem in the context of the 1833 Abolition Bill (*The Art of Eloquence: Byron, Dickens, Tennyson, Joyce* (Oxford: Oxford University Press, 2007), 165–71).

[91] O'Gorman, 'Tennyson's "The Lotos-Eaters"', 12.

[92] Alan Sinfield, *Alfred Tennyson* (Oxford: Basil Blackwell, 1986), 53. For post-colonialist readings of 'Ulysses' see also Patrick Brantlinger, *Rule of Darkness: British Literature and Imperialism, 1830–1914* (Ithaca, NY: Cornell University Press, 1988), 36, and Bevis, *The Art of Eloquence*, 166–71. In fact, references to territorial conquest by force are scarce in the poem. Only after rehearsing his travels through civilian societies does this famous veteran mention having 'drunk delight of battle with my peers' (l. 16), though his reference to 'rust[ing] unburnished' (l. 23) suggests that he associates himself with weaponry.

[93] Victor Kiernan, 'Tennyson, King Arthur and Imperialism', *Culture, Ideology and Politics: Essays for Eric Hobsbawm*, ed. Raphael Samuel and Gareth Stedman Jones (London: Routledge and Kegan Paul, 1983), 126–48: 131–2; Matthew Rowlinson, 'The Ideological Moment of Tennyson's "Ulysses"', *Victorian Poetry* 30.3/4 (Autumn–Winter 1992) (Centennial of Alfred, Lord Tennyson: 1809–1892), 265–76.

[94] Arthur Hallam, *Remains in Verse and Prose* (London: John Murray, 1863), 104.

[95] Dante's 'ardore' (26.97). The edition of Dante used is *The Divine Comedy of Dante Alighieri. Volume 1. Inferno*, trans. and ed. by Robert M. Durling (Oxford: Oxford University Press, 1996). Canto and line numbers are given in the footnotes.

[96] Robbins, 'Tennyson's "Ulysses"', 178.

answer is not wholly clear. As an incarnation of Homer's Odysseus, Ulysses is the subject of a prophecy: in the destiny projected by Tiresias (identified by Tennyson as a source for the poem), he travels on from Ithaca and dies a 'gentle' death in 'sleek old age'.[97] Prophecy gives narratological compulsion to Ulysses' wish to set off again, a compulsion audible in the lines 'I cannot rest from travel; I will drink / Life to the lees' (ll. 6–7). Tennyson's son, Hallam Tennyson, noted of the character, 'the craving for fresh travel seizes him',[98] and this resonates with evidence in the poem that the driving force is a simple thirst for novelty or motion. Ulysses welcomes 'new things' (l. 28), looks towards a 'newer world'[99] – a world that will be sought rather than constructed. Hallam had also written of the attraction of newness in 'On Sympathy': '[t]o become something new, to add a mode of being to those we have experienced, is a temptation alike to the lisping infant in the cradle and the old man on the verge of the grave.'[100] Conflating the agendas of early and late life, Hallam proposes that the lure of novelty might transcend biographical decorum. This craving for the new is expressed at various points in the poem as a need to be in motion. The second line of the poem introduces the idea of 'stillness', which Ulysses will contrast unfavourably with movement. 'I cannot rest from travel' (l. 6), 'For always roaming' (l. 12), 'For ever and for ever when I move' (l. 21), 'my purpose holds / To sail beyond the sunset [...] / Until I die' (ll. 59–60): these lines express a longing for movement for movement's sake, which articulates the longing for newness for newness's sake. Aurally, the iambic pendulum, particularly in lines containing repetition – 'For ever and for ever' (l. 21), 'life. Life piled on life' (l. 24), 'we are, we are' (l. 67) – creates the impression of perpetual motion, or at least of its possibility. There emerges from the poem a dynamic version of the desire of those other Homeric veterans, the Lotos-Eaters, to disengage with the 'now'.

---

[97] Tennyson, *The Poems of Tennyson*, ed. Ricks, 1.613. The prophecy is contained in *Odyssey* 11.100–37.
[98] Quoted in Tennyson, *The Poems of Tennyson*, ed. Ricks, 1.613.
[99] Seamus Perry draws attention to the restricted ambition of 'newer' as opposed to 'new' (*Alfred Tennyson* (London: Northcote House, 2005), 77): the restriction resonates with the sense of waning powers on Ulysses' part.
[100] Hallam, *Remains in Verse and Prose*, 102. In 'The Nature of Gothic' (1853), John Ruskin stated the 'greatness' of the 'Gothic spirit' to be 'love of *Change*': 'that restlessness of the dreaming mind, that wanders hither and thither among the niches, and flickers feverishly around the pinnacles, and frets and fades in labyrinthine knots and shadows along wall and roof, and yet is not satisfied, nor shall be satisfied' (*Selected Writings*, ed. Dinah Birch (Oxford: Oxford University Press, 2004), 57). Ruskin could be describing Ulysses' state of mind.

But it would be unfair to sum up Ulysses' motivation in the faux syllogism of 'I must do something. This is something. I must do this.' The kernel of the character's urgings is contained in the first five lines of the poem:

> It little profits that an idle king,
> By this still hearth, among these barren crags,
> Matched with an agèd wife, I mete and dole
> Unequal laws unto a savage race,
> That hoard, and sleep, and feed, and know not me.
>
> (ll. 1–5)

'Profit', with its faint hint of Mark 8.36,[101] suggests the desire for gain of some kind. The idleness Ulysses disparages – no Lotos-Eater he, after all – connotes not only lack of activity (an 'idol' king?) but also lack of purpose and lack of output (the latter reinforced by the nearby 'barren').[102] The members of the 'savage race' who merely sleep and feed are both inactive and unproductive. 'Hoard' is, at first glance, an unlikely addition to the list, but contrasts with the idea of profit. Those who hoard make no profit – not even by way of interest – and Ulysses later calls hoarding 'vile' (l. 29). In sum, the lines endorse industriousness and productivity, an endorsement that is reinforced throughout the poem.

Critical concentration on the cerebral – as opposed to martial – nature of Ulysses' aspirations has somewhat obscured this emphasis on usefulness. It need not: information-gathering enhances productivity. Ulysses' reputation as theorist derives from lines such as 'Much have I seen and known; cities of men / And manners, climates, councils, governments' (ll. 14–15) – a kind of political science version of the Homeric boast. The lines resonate with Tennyson's Dantean source, canto 26 of the *Inferno*. In Hell, in H. F. Cary's 1805 translation,[103] Dante's Ulisse speaks of the 'zeal' he had:

> T' explore the world, and search the ways of life,
> Man's evil and his virtue.[104]

---

[101] 'For what shall it profit a man, if he gain the whole world, and lose his own soul?'

[102] 'Idle, adj. and noun', 3a. 'Of things: Serving no useful purpose, useless'; 4a. 'Of persons: Not engaged in work, doing nothing, unemployed', *Oxford English Dictionary* (Oxford University Press), online edition.

[103] Ricks posits that Cary's was the translation that Tennyson probably used (Tennyson, *The Poems of Tennyson*, ed. Ricks, 1.614). But Tennyson 'owned at least eleven copies of Dante' and his 'favourite' was in Italian (Robert Pattison, *Tennyson and Tradition* (Cambridge, MA: Harvard University Press, 1979), 167).

[104] Canto 26, ll. 97–9. Quoted in Tennyson, *The Poems of Tennyson*, ed. Ricks, 1.614. Dante's original reads: 'l'ardore / c'i' ebbi a divenir del mondo esperto, / e de li vizi umani e del valore'.

He bids his mariners:

> Call to mind from whence ye sprang:
> Ye were not form'd to live the life of brutes,
> But virtue to pursue and knowledge high.[105]

As Tony Robbins points out, Ulisse's ambition is to acquire *canoscenza* (verifiable knowledge),[106] to become an expert in the ways of human-kind. In Tennyson's poem, Dantean *canoscenza* stands behind Ulysses' claim to have 'known' much and his desire 'To follow knowledge like a sinking star, / Beyond the utmost bound of human thought' (ll. 30–2). His reference to the 'untravelled world' (l. 20) also reinforces *canoscenza*-driven aspirations: this is Dante's 'mondo sanza gente', more accurately translated by Cary as 'unpeopled'. Tennyson's substitution of 'untravelled' for 'unpeopled' suggests again that Ulysses' desire is for insight into human society,[107] rather than for territorial conquest. Cumulatively, and curiously, given his history, Ulysses' clear preference is for acquisition of knowledge over martial accomplishment.[108] The preference is clearest in the absence of a particular word. In the line 'Souls that have toiled and wrought and thought with me' (l. 46), nothing would have been more natural to use the verb 'fought' instead of 'thought', but Tennyson declines the opportunity, preferring to emphasize work, production and mental activity.[109]

Ulysses' elevation of the arts of civilization over military advances is relevant to the fact of his being in late life, as is discussed later. But at this juncture, it is important to note that the character is not determined simply to expand his theoretical understanding of political science, statecraft and mores. His

---

[105] Canto 26, ll. 118–20. Quoted in Tennyson, *The Poems of Tennyson*, ed. Ricks, 1.614. Dante's original reads: 'Considerate la vostra semenza: / fatti non foste a viver come bruti, / ma per seguir virtute e canoscenza.'

[106] Robbins, 'Tennyson's "Ulysses"', 189.

[107] 'Untravelled' does raise the question of 'untravelled by whom?' I concur with Robbins, who writes, Odysseus has a 'delight in experience for its own sake, and particularly in getting knowledge of human societies unknown to him' (ibid., 189), providing as evidence Odysseus' interest in the Cyclopes' customs, which 'prompts him unnecessarily to explore the island, and subsequently to await Polyphemus' return to his cave' (*Odyssey* 9.127ff) (184n).

[108] Lines 31–2 could indicate sexual knowledge. As David Goslee discusses, these lines first appeared in an eight-line opening to 'Tiresias', begun before Hallam's death, which expresses Tiresias' guilt about the 'intellectual and sexual forces within his own nature' ('Three Stages of Tennyson's "Tiresias"', 156).

[109] The emphasis is a re-routing of attention from the bloodier aspects of armed combat to a more reassuring narrative, which seems to form a distinct strand in Victorian literature of war, a strand that contributes to what Daniel Hack has termed a 'resistance to the demands of Victorian masculine self-discipline' ('Wild Charges: the Afro-Haitian "Charge of the Light Brigade"', *Victorian Studies* 54.2 (Winter 2012), 199–225: 218).

greatest ambition is to be an active agent. In his exclamation 'How dull it is to pause, to make an end, / To rust unburnished, not to shine in use!' (ll. 22–3), the words 'end' and 'use' interact suggestively.[110] The kind of 'end' he aspires to is not a conclusion but a purpose,[111] and having a purpose is on the way to being useful. What Ulysses begins to feel his way towards is the idea of useful work.[112] 'Old age hath yet his honour and his toil', he muses, 'Some work of noble note [...] / Not unbecoming men that strove with Gods' (ll. 50, 52–3). The work he envisages must be both appropriate and noteworthy, the latter quality suggesting that it will live on beyond its executors in a manner reminiscent of the character's own indefinitely stretching forth plans.[113] Albeit with some inconsistency, then, Ulysses reveals his intentions of doing useful, honourable, appropriate and productive work – and of being noticed doing so. He hopes, like Tithon, not just for more life or simply to continue being,[114] but to be publicly valued in purposeful existence ('to shine in use'). In his conception, late life is not a matter of decline, graceful or otherwise, but a (final) flourish.

That Ulysses is in late life – or understands that he is perceived as being in late life – is insisted upon in the poem. He is 'Matched with an agèd wife' (l. 3). He refers to himself as a 'gray spirit' (l. 30). He remarks that of his life 'little remains' (l. 7). Having told his mariners in no uncertain terms, 'you and I are old' (l. 49),[115] he rubs the painful fact in: 'We are not now that strength which in old days / Moved heaven and earth' (ll.

---

[110] Cf. '[A] trope that is central both to Tennyson's poetics – in "Ulysses" and its pendent poem "Tithonus" as well as elsewhere – and to his politics [is] the metonymic interchange of beginnings and endings, of early and late' (Matthew Rowlinson, 'The Ideological Moment of Tennyson's "Ulysses"', 270).

[111] '[E]nd' means 'death' when it occurs again in l. 51. Cf. '[T]he stayings-still of repetition are always likely to incite the question that stirs in so much Tennyson, "is this the end? Is this the end?" (*In Memoriam*, 12.16)' (Perry, *Alfred Tennyson*, 19).

[112] Karen Chase notes that the 'capacity for work' lent 'increasing value' to the 'chronological definition' of old age in the Victorian period (*The Victorians and Old Age* (Oxford: Oxford University Press, 2009), 2). The ability to work, that is, belied calendrical age.

[113] Cf. 'The Lotos-Eaters', who fear their 'great deeds' will be 'half-forgotten' (l. 123). Ulysses' desire for ongoing renown resonates ironically with Kipling's poem 'The Last of the Light Brigade' (1890), in which the now-destitute veterans of the charge at Balaclava determine to ask Tennyson to write new verses exposing their current plight: ' "You wrote we were heroes once, sir. Please, write we are starving now" ' (*Rudyard Kipling's Verse: Inclusive Edition. 1885–1918* (New York: Doubleday, 1922), 230).

[114] An existence also imagined in 'Love and Duty' ('year by year alone / Sit brooding in the ruins of a life, / Nightmare of youth, the spectre of himself') and 'Supposed Confessions of a Second-Rate Sensitive Mind' ('living, but that he shall live on').

[115] This derives from Dante's 'Io e' compagni eravam vecchi e tardi' (26.106). Cary translates this as 'Tardy with age were I and my companions' (quoted in Tennyson, *The Poems of Tennyson*, ed. Ricks, 1.614). Tennyson does not translate 'tardi', which, as well as meaning 'slow', carries the connotations of 'late'.

66–7). But these are only the explicit references to being elderly. In less obvious ways, Tennyson further conveys Ulysses' advanced years. The first three lines of the poem contain a grammatical anomaly, beginning in the third person ('It little profits that an idle king') and continuing in the first person ('I mete and dole'). This anomaly could have been removed with the insertion of a comma after 'that' ('It little profits that, an idle king, / [...] I mete and dole'), though, admittedly, such punctuation would make the opening sound like a bout of grumbling, rather than the ringing proclamation Tennyson rendered it. Without a comma, a productive confusion is created between the first and third persons, which suggests that Ulysses does not fully identify with his present state. Throughout the poem, moreover, he tends to speak about old age in the plural. This bespeaks both a reluctance to embrace ageing personally but also a sense of aloneness, a fear of being the last of his kind.[116] His remark that 'all experience is an arch wherethrough / Gleams that untravelled world, whose margin fades / For ever and for ever when I move' (ll. 19–21) defers the end of life to an indefinite future, a variation on the habit, identified by Kathleen Woodward, of 'push[ing] ahead' old age so that it always denotes an age older than the person defining it.

Woodward further notes the 'psychological phenomenon' whereby: 'when we age, we increasingly separate what we take to be our real selves from our bodies. [...] Our bodies are old, we are not. Old age is then understood as a state in which the body is in opposition to the self.'[117] The examples given already illustrate Ulysses' unwillingness to identify with his current corporeal incarnation: elsewhere in the poem, he speaks of himself and his comrades as 'Made weak by time and fate, but strong in will' (l. 69). The body is weak – old – but the 'real' internal self is not. In Woodward's words, the body has become a 'foreign body',[118] and she accordingly posits a 'mirror stage' of old age in which the mirror image is

---

[116] Fiona Stafford, in her study of this phenomenon, comments that 'writers of the eighteenth and nineteenth centuries were faced with an increasingly secular society and a future uncontrolled by providential destiny' and so 'the image of the last of the race as an isolated sufferer, burdened with memories, and cut off from others, became a common figure' (*The Last of the Race: The Growth of a Myth from Milton to Darwin* (Oxford: The Clarendon Press, 1994), 11). Stafford names Tennyson's 'The Passing of Arthur' as another example of the genre (302).

[117] Kathleen Woodward, *Aging and Its Discontents: Freud and Other Fictions* (Bloomington, IN: Indiana University Press, 1991), 62. Cf. Hallam, writing 'On Sympathy': 'To know a thing as past, and to know it as similar to something present, is a source of mingled emotions. There is pleasure, in so far as it is a revelation of self; but there is pain, in so far that it is a divided self, a being at once our own, and not our own, a portion cut away from what we feel, nevertheless, to be single and indivisible' (*Remains in Verse and Prose*, 105).

[118] Woodward, *Aging and Its Discontents*, 62.

rejected as 'uncannily prefiguring the disintegration and nursling depend-ence of advanced age'.[119] This explains Ulysses' preoccupation with public 'note', with 'shining in use': his image in the eyes of others must also be one of not-old (hence his dissatisfaction with the fact that his subjects 'know not me' (l. 5)). The late life body/self split may also explain his emphasis on the arts of government and his strange disinclination to dwell on his martial prowess: as non-physical but still productive activities, these arts divert attention from the body to the mind, accentuating his remaining strengths. This is a sophisticated portrayal of agency in old age that, rather than crudely equate it with physical capacity, configures it as social and interactional.[120]

Writing on 'late style' (itself established by the Victorians as a 'self-reflexive phenomenon'),[121] Gordon McMullan illuminates the signifi-cance of these symptoms for the associated concept of late life. McMullan notes in individual responses to lateness or lastness or the imminence of death a 'serene' and an 'irascible' version ('irascible' derives from Adorno's description of late subjectivity as an 'irascible gesture' towards capit-alism).[122] The dichotomy lacks nuance, not least because an individual is not exclusively restricted to one version or the other, but the irascible version, with which Ulysses' state of mind has the greatest affinities,[123] is illuminating in the present context because it permits the idea of late style as a 'late flowering', the product of 'late renewed energy'.[124] This in turn enables the construction of late style in terms of what McMullan calls 'a kind of coda, a supplementary phase of the creative life manifesting itself at the same time as a renewal, a rediscovery, a renaissance [...] pre-dictive of styles yet to be established by the artist's successors [...] as work, in other words, that stands outside its own time'.[125] Far from a decline,

[119] Ibid., 67. See further Amelia DeFalco, *Uncanny Subjects: Aging in Contemporary Narrative* (Columbus, OH: The Ohio State University Press, 2010).

[120] Katharina Boehm, Anna Farkas and Anne-Julia Zwierlein emphasize that agency in old age is 'always embedded in social relations and larger communities' ('Introduction', *Interdisciplinary Perspectives on Victorian Old Age*, ed. Katharina Boehm, Anna Farkas and Anne-Julia Zwierlein (London: Routledge, 2014), 1–17: 4).

[121] Gordon McMullan, *Shakespeare and the Idea of Late Writing: Authorship in the Proximity of Death* (Cambridge: Cambridge University Press, 2007), 172.

[122] Ibid., 150; Théodor Adorno, *Beethoven: The Philosophy of Music. Fragments and Texts (Philosophie der Musik: Fragmente und Texte)* [1938–], trans. Edmund Jephcott, ed. Rolf Tiedemann (Cambridge: Polity, 1998), 125.

[123] The 'irascible' version is the 'do not go gentle into that good night' model of ageing, which Woodward regards as a 'dreadful cliché' but that resonates in this context because its addressee, Dylan Thomas's father, was himself an army veteran (Woodward, *Aging and Its Discontents*, 44).

[124] McMullan, *Shakespeare and the Idea of Late Writing*, 25.

[125] Ibid., 25.

late style is considered a 'renewal', a kind of added extra or bonus or 'supplement'. And, as McMullan points out, the supplementary has not only 'the straightforward sense of "additional"' but also 'the slightly more elusive deconstructive sense in which, by claiming finally to complete something previously considered complete, the supplement demonstrates the impossibility of completion'.[126]

McMullan's terminology – the 'coda', the 'supplement' that 'stands outside its own time' – is consistent with a progressive model of personal development (which Helen Small traces to Aristotle's framework in the *Nicomachean Ethics* for understanding our lives as 'accruing their meaning over the passage of time').[127] Performing what old-age theorists term a 'late life review' – an 'evaluative backward glance' – Ulysses, *prima facie*, endorses this model.[128] The model underpins what might be called the 'careers advisor' version of biographical decorum: the belief that certain achievements are fitting, even requisite, at certain points in a lifetime.[129] When these norms are departed from, there arise feelings of prematurity and belatedness. Both prematurity and belatedness are pertinent to 'Ulysses': switching the natural temporal order in accordance with the spirit of this chapter, I shall take the latter first.

In its *OED* definitions, 'belated' can mean '[o]vertaken by the lateness of the night; hence, overtaken by darkness' ('The long day wanes: the slow moon climbs' (l. 55)) and '[d]etained beyond the usual time, coming or staying too late, behind date'.[130] When Ulysses protests that ' 'Tis not too late', he is expressing a desire to be within the 'usual time', not to be outside it or to have run out of it, and he also wants to be what he was lately (recently). Existing 'beyond the usual time' – or living too long – is a version of biographical indecorum explored by Emily Wilson, who notes the 'uneasiness' elicited in others by someone who 'should' have died.[131] Ulysses, who understands biographical decorum ('Old age hath yet his honour and his toil' (l. 50)) even as he purports to transcend it, elicits, with

---

[126] Ibid., 2.

[127] Small, *The Long Life*, 89, and see also ch. 3.

[128] De Falco, *Uncanny Subjects*, 18, 23.

[129] Cf. 'Tennyson evidently felt the attraction of the idea that there are specific virtues proper to the different periods of a man's life' (Helen Small, 'Tennyson and Late Style', *Tennyson Bulletin* 8.4 (2005), 226–50: 229). In *Maud* (1855), Tennyson introduces a variation on the idea of biographical decorum: 'ah, wherefore cannot I be / Like the things of the season gay?' asks the tormented speaker, suggesting that certain feelings are 'right' at certain times of year – the pathetic fallacy rendered as seasonality (4.1.2–3).

[130] 'Belated, adj.' 1, 2, *Oxford English Dictionary* (Oxford University Press), online edition.

[131] Wilson, *Mocked with Death*, 1.

his self-contradictions and gnawing fear that he has outlived his usefulness, a similar sense of unease.[132] Should this character be proposing to set off on another voyage, or should he, an attenuated version of his former glorious self, be dead?

These questions arise in relation to a poem inspired by someone who many people thought should have lived far longer than he did.[133] 'This is a loss which will most assuredly be felt by this age, for if ever man was born for great things he was,' commented Hallam's friend, the historian John Kemble.[134] Tennyson himself, in *In Memoriam*, hypothesized a distinguished future for Hallam, based on what he knew of his friend's potential:

> For can I doubt, who knew thee keen
> In intellect, with force and skill
> To strive, to fashion, to fulfil –
> I doubt not what thou wouldst have been:
>
> A life in civic action warm,
> A soul on highest mission sent,
> A potent voice of Parliament,
> A pillar steadfast in the storm.
>
> (113.5–12)

---

[132] In *Odyssey* 5.306–12 Odysseus claims to envy those who died at Troy because they received due burial rites and their fame is assured: he already has a sense of having lived too long.

[133] In a queer reading of *In Memoriam*, Jeff Nunokawa links Hallam's premature death with Tennyson's depiction of his own homosexual feelings as a temporary adolescent stage ('dwarf'd [...] growth' (61.7)): 'The funeral that Tennyson hosts for his own puerile homoerotic desire [...] has its afterlife in the glamorous rumor of pre-ordained doom that bathes the image of live-fast-die-young gay boys such as Dorian Grey [sic], Montgomery Clift, James Dean, Joe Orton, and, most recently, a French-Canadian airline steward who came to be known as Patient Zero' ('*In Memoriam* and the Extinction of the Homosexual', *ELH* 58.2 (Summer 1991), 427–38: 436). If it violates biographical decorum – and, as Judith Halberstam has shown, 'queer temporality' disrupts 'the normal narratives of time' (Judith Halberstam, *In a Queer Time and Place: Transgender Bodies, Subcultural Lives* (New York: New York University Press, 2005), 152–3) – Hallam's early death satisfies the literary decorum of (queer) elegy, a genre in which the expression of love is predicated on death. For further discussion of elegy and same-sex love, see George E. Haggerty, 'Desire and Mourning: The Ideology of the Elegy', *Ideology and Form in Eighteenth Century Literature*, ed. David H. Richter (Lubbock: Texas Tech University Press, 1999), 184–206; George E. Haggerty, 'Love and Loss: An Elegy', *GLQ: A Journal of Lesbian and Gay Studies* 10.3 (2004), 385–405; and Matthew Curr, *The Consolation of Otherness: The Male Love Elegy in Milton, Gray and Tennyson* (London: McFarland, 2002). On the way that queerness 'challenges a modern ideology of progressive time in general', see Vincent Sherry, *Modernism and the Reinvention of Decadence* (Cambridge: Cambridge University Press, 2015), 25–6.

[134] The letter is in Hallam Tennyson, *Alfred, Lord Tennyson*, 106.

'To strive' links Hallam to Ulysses (l. 70), another soul bent on 'civic action': here, Tennyson projects a late(r) life for Hallam of a kind that would fulfil his promise – a needed supplement to what was cruelly left unfinished. It is the late life to which Ulysses aspires.

But if the incomplete nature of Hallam's life was cause for grief, Ulysses, in another mirror image, values the idea of incompletion. In this poem, indefiniteness becomes both an art and a form of existence. As Matthew Rowlinson points out, the character 'does not seem to know where he is'.[135] He might be 'inside, outside, by his hearth, on the beach, in private, in public'.[136] Nor is the extent of his readiness to act clear. The poem's opening and the subjunctive mood in the passage beginning 'Life piled on life / Were all too little' sound like an attempt at (self-)persuasion, but there are other indications that Ulysses has already decided to depart. 'To whom I leave the sceptre and the isle' (l. 34) might even constitute a speech act by which power is transferred. But the line 'There lies the port; the vessel puffs her sail' (l. 44) introduces further doubt. The ship is ready but the deixis both distances Ulysses from it spatially and suggests a futurity to the embarkation. Demonstrating what Seamus Perry praises as Tennyson's 'genius for *pending*' and T. S. Eliot and Christopher Ricks criticized, respectively, as his 'lack of narrative gift' and his 'stagnancy',[137] Ulysses is *stranded*; in the words of Tennyson's contemporary Goldwin Smith 'for ever a listless and melancholy figure on the shore'.[138] The spatial uncertainty and open-ended narrative create and preserve a 'space apart'. I take the phrase from Jahan Ramazani's *Poetry of Mourning*, where it is used to denote the site of mourning in modern elegy – a site that, as Ramazani points out, has affinities with Adorno's 'social antithesis' or 'negative responses to dominant social forms'.[139] Rather than a mourning space, for Ulysses the space carved out by his hortatives and subjunctives is a site of aspiration, equally at odds with social expectations.

Above all, lines such as 'Old age hath *yet* his honour and his toil' (l. 50, emphasis added), 'something ere the end' (l. 51), 'Though much is taken,

---

[135] Rowlinson, 'The Ideological Moment of Tennyson's "Ulysses"', 267.

[136] Ibid., 267.

[137] Perry, *Alfred Tennyson*, 20; T. S. Eliot, '*In Memoriam*' [1936], *Selected Prose of T. S. Eliot*, ed. Frank Kermode (London: Faber and Faber, 1984), 239–47: 241; Christopher Ricks, *Tennyson* (Basingstoke: Macmillan, 1989), 118. See also Christopher Decker, 'Tennyson's Limitations', *Tennyson Among the Poets: Bicentenary Essays*, ed. Robert Douglas-Fairhurst and Seamus Perry (Oxford: Oxford University Press, 2009), 57–75: 59.

[138] Goldwin Smith, 'The War Passages in "Maud"', *Saturday Review* 1.1 (3 November 1855), 14–15: 15.

[139] Jahan Ramazani, *Poetry of Mourning: The Modern Elegy from Hardy to Heaney* (Chicago: The University of Chicago Press, 1994), 14; Théodor Adorno, *Negative Dialectics (Negative Dialektik)* [1966], trans. Robert Hullot-Kentor, ed. Gretel Adorno and Rolf Tiedemann (London: Continuum, 2004), 9.

much abides' (l. 65) yield the poignant sense of wanting something not to be over. It is on this basis that Ulysses rejects veteran status because to be a veteran is to be former, to be a has-been, to be 'no more'. This sense is evident, too, in *In Memoriam* in the passages in which Tennyson expresses his wish that his friend's life, and their youth and friendship, were not over:

> Ah dear, but come thou back to me:
> Whatever change the years have wrought,
> I find not yet one lonely thought
> That cries against my wish for thee.
>
> (90.21–5)

The second line of this stanza measures, if only implicitly, the speaker's 'change' against Hallam's lack of it: he has remained young, that is, while his contemporaries have aged. Visiting Hallam's grave in 1859, Benjamin Jowett was struck by the same thought: 'It is a strange feeling about those who are taken young that while we are getting old and dusty they are as they were.'[140] The young-person-who-should-be-old is uncanny, provoking fears that he might not be recognized if he should return.[141] Ulysses, looking forward to the possibility of seeing again a former comrade who, having died, will not have aged as he and his mariners have ('It may be we shall touch the Happy Isles, / And see the great Achilles, whom we knew' (ll. 63–4)), appears not to notice the potential for misrecognition and rejection – though Tennyson gives the faintest of hints that awareness of it may be present in his subconscious in the poignant juxtaposition of 'the great Achilles, whom we knew' and 'Though much is taken, much abides' (ll. 64–5)). Having thought about Achilles, that is, Ulysses' mind moves (albeit in glass-half-full mode) to his own deterioration. The juxtaposition illuminates equally poignantly the temporal deficit that had opened and would widen between the poet and his friend.[142]

---

[140] Quoted in Ricks, *Tennyson*, 119.

[141] On Hallam and change, see *In Memoriam* 30.22–4; 82.1–4; 121.17–20. Return after a long time induces anxiety elsewhere in Tennyson's works, for example in 'The Lotos-Eaters' (ll. 114–25) and 'Enoch Arden'.

[142] Martin Heidegger's *Being and Time* (*Sein und Zeit* [1927]) provides an illuminating framework for the temporal themes in 'Ulysses', although I am reserving it to this footnote as it runs the risk of producing an over-schematized reading. Heidegger argues that authentic being (Dasein) constantly anticipates its own death, a state of affairs that both casts it back towards its past (or 'having been' (*Being and Time*, trans. John Macquarrie and Edward Robinson (San Francisco, CA: HarperSanFrancisco, 1962), 373, H326) and energizes its present. ('Past', 'present' and 'future' are not to be understood as sequential tenses, according to Heidegger, but as 'ecstasies' or orientations outside time (401, H350).) Incomplete until it reaches its 'wholeness' in death (281, H237), Dasein is characterized by a constitution in which there is *constantly something still to be*

Dying at the wrong time, Hallam became late too soon, his death 'out of time' because premature. Ulysses, by contrast, has lived too long, becoming 'out of time' by being belated. His aspirations for late life – a swansong – are imbued with pathos, but at the same time are not without effectiveness. In projecting beyond his current state, he ensures it remains unfinished. 'Ulysses' is also unfinished in narrative terms (do they go or not?), its open-endedness contrasting with the decisive blow of Hallam's death. But the poem is not simply a narratological means of refusing to allow something to be over. In Ulysses' unwanted veterancy, Tennyson responded to the unfairness of his best friend's non-veterancy: the unbearable eternal fact of his missing life.

## Conclusion

Veterancy plays havoc with lifetimes: the ageing process is speeded up; children outstrip their parents; individuals can look back upon having anticipated becoming has-beens. The period of mass, globalized, industrialized warfare began with a radical redrafting of the calendar and the demands of military service produced in real life the lapses in biographical decorum that are exploited in literary texts to question very ancient ideas of seasonality and the *curriculum vitae*. If Austen's Anne Elliot weathers her personal storms, the protagonists of Merry's 'The Wounded Soldier' and Tennyson's 'Ulysses' are caused considerable pain by the differences between their past and present selves. A wobbling sense of personal identity points us towards the next chapter, which continues to explore veterancy as an expression of thinking about the self, but that shifts attention to social identity and the relationship between the veteran and the community.

---

settled' (278, H236), a 'not-yet' (286, H242) that is 'always [...] *still* outstanding' (279, H236). Ulysses' awareness of death ('Death closes all' (l. 51)), his overwhelming sense of 'having been' and his unquenchable urge to achieve more things before he dies ('something ere the end [...] / may yet be done' (ll. 51–2)) match these qualities of Dasein. But the fact that Ulysses' 'Being-towards-Death' is stimulated by the death of Hallam challenges Heidegger's assertion that '*No one can take the Other's dying away from him*' (284, H240). (H-numbers refer to the pagination in the seventh edition of *Sein und Zeit* (Tübingen: Neomarius Verlag, 1953. Original emphases.)

# CHAPTER 2

# *Strangers*

## *Odyssey 2: Xenos*

In Phaeacia, Odysseus' appearance in King Antinous' hall provokes a stunned reaction: 'at the sight of this man in their midst a silence fell on all the banqueters up and down the hall. They stared at Odysseus in amazement [...] from the whole company there came not a sound' (7.144–5).

One can imagine the turned heads, the dropped jaws, the forgotten food. Not a single person thinks of welcoming the arrival. Indeed, though Odysseus eventually asserts, and can assume, his true name, he remains a 'stranger' (7.24) in Phaeacia, and, as Athene advises him, 'the people here have little affection for strangers' (7.32). (The name 'Odysseus' itself is etymologically linked to anger and hatred,[1] and these will emerge as common responses to veteran homecomers.) In Phaeacia and pending his re-admittance to Ithacan society, Odysseus is a *xenos* (ζένος),[2] a term that can signify a range of 'others', from enemy, foreigner and stranger to guest-friend.[3] Very often, the *xenos* is an irritant in the community in which he finds himself: different, ill-fitting, impossible to ignore, odious, enraging. Here in Phaeacia, his hosts press Odysseus for information, working on what they see as his emotional weaknesses, until they are satisfied with his answers. Later, in Ithaca, his physical appearance magically altered, he will be regarded as an alien. His identity will be categorically denied ('You are not my father [...] you are not Odysseus' (16.194)) and he will be doubted, asked for proof and subjected to tests and trials. For his own part, he will

[1] W. B. Stanford, 'The Homeric Etymology of the Name Odysseus', *Classical Philology* 47.4 (October 1952), 209–13: 209.

[2] Marigo Alexopoulou, *The Theme of Returning Home in Ancient Greek Literature* (Lewiston, ON: The Edwin Mellen Press, 2009), 31.

[3] Wendy Olmsted, 'On the Margins of Otherness: Metamorphosis and Identity in Homer, Ovid, Sidney, and Milton', *New Literary History* 27.2 (1996), 167–84: 168.

be threatening, punitive, abusive and violent. Hospitality will be tested to its limits.

Like Odysseus, a veteran may *never* entirely lose the association of the *xenos*. As such, he attracts attention, requires reading, provokes concern, elicits judgement. As Thomas Paine put it at the outset of the period dealt with by this book, the soldier in the civilian world is 'shunned by the citizen on apprehension of their being enemies to liberty'.[4] In many instances, the veteran's presence is *too* disquieting, and what ensues is the palliation, phasing or outright rejection of his return, often involving another departure. In this chapter, my focus turns from the issues of personal identity discussed in the previous chapter to identity as experienced and perceived socially, and, more particularly, to what the reception and treatment of the veteran-as-*xenos* reveals about the community (whether local or national) he returns to or otherwise finds himself in. From this angle, what the veteran figures – or, more precisely, reflects – is a society's own image of itself, its norms, values, aspirations and fears. For, as Julia Kristeva put it, the foreigner who 'lives within us' is 'the hidden face of our identity'.[5] In the course of analysing socially constructed identity, I draw attention to the pressure that the veteran puts on notions of reason-based mutual hospitality, as adumbrated by Kant in his essay 'To Perpetual Peace' ('Zum Ewigen Frieden. Ein Philosophischer Entwurf') (1795) and developed in Jürgen Habermas's more recent discourse ethics and political theory. Behaving inhospitably, the veteran provokes inhospitable reactions, questioning the capacity of Kantian and Habermasian mutual respectfulness to accommodate the outcome of mass warfare. Though the veteran-as-*xenos* is a theme of long standing, in this chapter – due to the resonances among them – I concentrate on a cluster of texts relating to the Second World War: novels by Betty Miller, Helen Ashton, Nigel Balchin, J. B. Priestley and Robert Henriques.[6]

## Dissonance and Hospitality

Long before his arrival home, the soldier is subject to suspicion and expectation. 'Who knows,' asks Nestor, more hopefully than speculatively, 'whether some day Odysseus may not come back [...] and pay these Suitors

---

[4] Thomas Paine, *Rights of Man, Common Sense and Other Political Writings*, ed. Mark Philp (Oxford: Oxford University Press, 1998), 321.

[5] Julia Kristeva, *Strangers to Ourselves* (*Étrangers à nous-mêmes*) [1988], trans. Leon S. Roudiez (New York: Columbia University Press, 1994), 1.

[6] I am grateful to Victoria Stewart and Gill Plain for drawing these texts to my attention.

out for all their violence?' (3.216–7). In Ithaca, as noted in Chapter 1, old Halitherses has long foretold that no one will know the king when he finally arrives (2.176). For his part, Odysseus prays that he will find his wife and dear ones 'safe and sound in my home when I reach it' (13.42–3). From one side, violence, revenge and unfamiliarity are anticipated; from the other, intact domesticity. Before Odysseus has even set foot on Ithaca, assumptions and preconceptions are dissonant.

The return of a combat veteran in the age of mass warfare has even greater potential to maximize such dissonance.[7] Consider a soldier's experience. Cut off from his family and from family life, he has been absorbed in what Jim McDermott, after Etienne Wenger, terms a 'community of practice':[8] a 'highly organized social world' that is 'intense', 'compact' and 'replete with meaning'.[9] He has undergone formal and informal training and become accustomed to a daily routine 'repeated over and over again'.[10] Uniquely in human experience, he has been liable 'to use lethal force, to risk [his] own life but also those of others by ordering them to do the same'.[11] He has, in more vivid words, had a 'rendezvous with death'.[12] A 'special sort of impurity' clings to him, 'still tainted with the slaughter of war'.[13] He has grown used to being 'expendable'.[14] He may be injured or disabled. Upon his return, he may encounter obstacles in obtaining civilian employment. His family and friends may not understand or want to hear what has happened to him; he may be seen – and see himself – as 'toxic',

---

[7] On the returned veteran as threat, see Willard Waller, *The Veteran Comes Back* (New York: Dryden Press, 1944); Helen Margaret McClure, 'Alienated Patriots: A Sociological Portrait of Military Retirees', unpublished PhD thesis (University of California Berkeley, 1992); Jonathan Shay, *Odysseus in America: Combat Trauma and the Trials of Homecoming* (New York: Scribner, 2002); Christopher Dandeker, Simon Wessely, Amy Iversen and John Ross, *Improving the Delivery of Cross Departmental Support and Services for Veterans. Joint Report* (London: Department of War Studies and Institute of Psychiatry, 2003); Jim McDermott, 'Old Soldiers Never Die: They Adapt Their Military Skills and Become Successful Civilians. What Factors Contribute to the Successful Transition of Army Veterans to Civilian Life and Work?', unpublished PhD thesis (University of Leicester, 2007); David Finkel, *Thank You for Your Service* (New York: Sarah Crichton Books, 2013); Jaremey McMullin, 'Integration or Separation? The Stigmatization of Ex-Combatants after War', *Review of International Studies* 39.2 (April 2013), 385–414.

[8] McDermott, 'Old Soldiers Never Die', 23; Etienne Wenger, *Communities of Practice: Learning, Meaning and Identity* (Cambridge: Cambridge University Press, 1999), 45.

[9] Waller, *The Veteran Comes Back*, 26.

[10] McDermott, 'Old Soldiers Never Die', 31.

[11] Dandeker et al., 'Improving the Delivery of Cross Departmental Support and Services for Veterans', 17 n3.

[12] Waller, *The Veteran Comes Back*, 15.

[13] René Girard, *Violence and the Sacred* (*Violence et le sacré*) [1972], trans. Patrick Gregory (Baltimore, MD: Johns Hopkins University Press, 1977), 41.

[14] Waller, *The Veteran Comes Back*, 15.

capable of harming others with his knowledge of war, even of carrying 'the taint of a killer, of blood pollution'.[15] For some, he may represent unpalatable truths about a specific war or about war more generally.[16] He may be held responsible for unpopular government decisions or collective action. For his part, the veteran may be coping with a radical loss of trust and confronting the loss of respect, obedience, status, security and comradeship.[17] 'While the truth of war is that it's always about loving the guy next to you', writes David Finkel, 'the truth of the after-war is that you're on your own'.[18] Civilian existence may seem 'smaller, dingier, more sordid' than the ex-combatant remembers it,[19] and less stimulating than life in the military. The veteran may find it difficult to deal with other people 'who have wills of their own and a right to them'.[20] The 'habits of war', such as those described by Robert Graves – 'commandeering anything of uncertain ownership that I found lying about', 'stopping cars for a lift', 'unbuttoning by the roadside without shame, whoever might be about'[21] – may be hard to shed but are problematic in civilian society. In 1944, the American sociologist Willard Waller summed up the veteran's situation in the following powerful terms:

> The veteran who comes home is a social problem, and certainly the major social problem of the next few years. Not always but all too often he is a problem because of his misfortunes and his needs, because he is maimed, crippled, demented, destitute, cold and enhungered; these things he is, these wants he has, from no fault and no desire of his own but solely because of what we have done to him; only because we have used him as an instrument of national policy; because we have used him up, sacrificed him, wasted him. No man could have a better moral claim to the consideration of his fellows. And no man could have a better right to bitterness. [...] But the veteran, so justly entitled to move us to pity and to shame, can also put us in fear. Destitute he

[15] Shay, *Odysseus in America*, 83, 152.
[16] Terry Eagleton makes this point in relation to Elizabeth Gaskell's *Sylvia's Lovers* (' "Sylvia's Lovers" and Legality', *Essays in Criticism* 26.1 (January 1976), 17–27: 26), and Simon Parkes writes of 'the truth that is represented in the revenant veteran, not-Orlando' in Charlotte Smith's *The Old Manor House* (1793) 'manifesting as the disturbing force of war returning home' (' "More Dead Than Alive": The Return of Not-Orlando in Charlotte Smith's *The Old Manor House*', *European Romantic Review* 22.6 (2011), 765–84: 765).
[17] Shay, *Odysseus in America*, xv; McDermott, 'Old Soldiers Never Die', 39.
[18] Finkel, *Thank You for Your Service*, 148.
[19] Waller, *The Veteran Comes Back*, 93.
[20] Ibid., 31.
[21] Robert Graves, *Good-Bye to All That* [1929] (New York: Anchor, 1957), 28; quoted in Shay, *Odysseus in America*, 32.

may be, friendless, without political guile, unskilled in the arts of peace; but weak he is not. [...] Unless and until he can be renaturalized into his native land, the veteran is a threat to society.[22]

In similar vein, if more pithily, the American psychiatrist Jonathan Shay, who treats veterans with post-traumatic stress disorder at the Department of Veterans' Affairs outpatients' clinic in Boston, describes returned ex-servicemen as 'social and political nitroglycerine'.[23]

But this model of the veteran as outcast, as scapegoat,[24] simultan-eously to be pitied and feared, has, of late, been revisited. Though both Waller and Shay speak from extensive personal experience of interviewing and observing returned servicemen, and though the soldier *may* have experienced some or all of the feelings and situations described above, a more nuanced construction of the figure is possible. In a recent study of ex-combatants in Liberia, Jaremey McMullin has shown how 'threat' and 'resentment' narratives about veterans – imposed externally by both the media and by aid agencies – obscure other causes of social disruption, dis-miss individual behaviours, confuse visibility with threat and ignore the fact that ex-combatants may be sources of conflict resolution.[25] McDermott, an army veteran himself, concurs with this, agreeing that most civilians gain their ideas of ex-servicemen from the media and suggesting that, if the military does 'institutionalize' its members, it does so by fostering 'self-reliance', 'self-esteem', 'confidence' and 'integrity'.[26] Two of McDermott's veteran interviewees confirm this, commenting that to have served in the army 'adds an air of mystique to the individual' and confers a 'presence or aurora [sic] about you'.[27] McDermott's findings from his investigations of some 100 individuals who had completed at least 22 years of army ser-vice uphold the view that, while some ex-servicemen 'suffer' as a result of their military experiences, the 'great majority' do not and, after leaving the armed forces, go on to lead 'successful civilian lives'.[28] A more complete picture of the returned veteran, therefore, would include success, strength and competence, even 'mystique', alongside threat and victimhood.

---

[22] Waller, *The Veteran Comes Back*, 13.
[23] Shay, *Odysseus in America*, 154.
[24] Citing René Girard, Simon Parkes makes the case for the 'Broken Soldier' as scapegoat, a figure who, purged of the contamination of violence, becomes the means through which society is also purged ('Wooden Legs and Tales of Sorrow Done: The Literary Broken Soldier of the late Eighteenth Century', *Journal for Eighteenth-Century Studies* 26.2 (June 2013), 191–207: 201).
[25] McMullin, 'Integration or Separation?' 397, 399, 399.
[26] McDermott, 'Old Soldiers Never Die', 46, 146.
[27] Ibid., 198.
[28] Ibid., 7, 14.

Indeed, the auratic veteran, the figure of inexplicable 'presence', points to the far end of the spectrum of veteran constructions from the threat and the victim: the not-necessarily-more-helpful figure of the veteran as hero.[29] In this guise, as Graham Dawson forcefully illustrates in *Soldier Heroes* (1994), the veteran becomes 'a quintessential figure of masculinity', drawn on in the gendering of the nation and exploited to promote military recruitment and popular support for waging war.[30]

This spectrum of constructions – from delinquent to superhuman – is a vivid indication of the social uncertainty that surrounds the veteran. It also reveals the extent to which the figure is subject to social construction, as different parties, who may be more or less sympathetic to someone returned from war, experiment with what is publicly acceptable. Illustrating this, David Gerber (focusing on the United States) has traced the treatment of one particular category of ex-serviceman – the disabled veteran. In the 'distant past', Gerber notes, when conceptions of disability were based on 'inchoate combinations of religion, humanitarianism, superstition, and psychic terror', many disabled veterans were 'pauperized, roleless, and utterly dependent', even as they were 'lionized' as 'heroes'.[31] But, by the time of the First World War, according to Joanna Bourke, there was a 'sentimental sense' that the disabled soldier was 'not less but more of a man'.[32] Gerber argues that, following a century of medical advances, the 'visibility' of disabled veterans increased in the twentieth century and, with it, the 'ability to *see* them', to have a greater understanding of what it is to live with disability.[33] At the same time, he suggests, chivalric ideas of honour and bravery have been replaced by the '[p]ostheroic assumptions' associated with modern warfare: a 'peer group of behavior that valorizes the individual's ability to respond effectively in war by doing a *job* in the

---

[29] The British charity Help for Heroes, or H4H, was founded on 1 October 2007 by an ex-serviceman and his wife. See www.helpforheroes.org.uk/. I am not dealing with heroizing in this chapter but would note that the social utility of the hero was recognized by Rousseau (see M. W. Jackson, 'Rousseau's Discourse on Heroes and Heroism', *Proceedings of the American Philosophical Society* 133.3 (1989), 434–46). The psychoanalyst Elizabeth Goren reiterates that 'how the image of the hero evolves over time tells us more about the psyche of the society at any given moment than about the individual or group identified as the hero' ('Society's Use of the Hero Following a National Trauma', *American Journal of Psychoanalysis* 67.1 (2007), 37–52: 37).

[30] Graham Dawson, *Soldier Heroes: British Adventure, Empire, and the Imagining of Masculinities* (London: Routledge, 1994), 1.

[31] David. A Gerber, 'Introduction: Finding Disabled Veterans in History', *Disabled Veterans in History*, ed. David A. Gerber (Ann Arbor, MI: The University of Michigan Press, 2000), 1–51, 4, 2.

[32] Joanna Bourke, *Dismembering the Male. Men's Bodies, Britain and the Great War* (London: Reaktion, 1996), 58.

[33] Gerber, 'Introduction', 2.

face of fear, which is acknowledged to be inevitable'.[34] In these terms, the disabled veteran is neither a hero nor a charity case but an ex-professional contractually entitled to compensation for work-related injuries.

But stereotypes die hard. While most ex-servicemen reject any notion that they are 'not fully "civilianised"', McDermott comments, it is clear that 'full disengagement' from military society is 'only ever partially achieved'.[35] The former soldier 'remains different in the way that he or she associates with others in civilian society'.[36] Audible in the suggestion that veterans are not fully 'civilianized' is the suspicion that they are not fully civilized. The status of the *xenos* endures. In the texts explored in this chapter by Miller, Ashton, Balchin, Priestley and Henriques, it is often (though not always) the standard preconceptions and assumptions about veteran behaviour that inform the figure's literary functioning. Enigmatic, auratic, irritating, the veteran-as-*xenos* offers a rich figurative resource for airing social concerns. And so, the veteran comes to serve as a gauge for a community's attitudes towards those who are different, those who are vulnerable, those who are threatening and even those who pose problems because they exceed normal standards of fortitude, strength and bravery.

Unsurprisingly, such disruptive figures put certain notions of hospitality under pressure. Kant's ideas about hospitality, as set out in 'To Perpetual Peace', derive, as Genevieve Lloyd demonstrates, from ancient Greek concepts of world citizenry and the beginnings of the rule of law.[37] They are inextricably entwined with his thoughts about cosmopolitanism. As Peter Melville notes, Kant's views developed in the context of the French Revolution's 'destabilizing impact on the integrity of the borders [...] organizing Western Europe':[38] during the Revolution and the global wars that arose from it, such borders were crossed, weakened, redefined and undermined by the mass movement of refugees, armies, displaced persons and homecoming veterans. Kant sought to impose order on the chaos. Proceeding from the premise of a 'common right to the face of the earth,

---

[34] Ibid., 5.

[35] Jim McDermott, 'Struggling on Civvy Street', *Public Service Review: Transport, Local Government and the Regions* 8 (2009), unpaginated.

[36] Ibid.

[37] Genevieve Lloyd, 'Providence as Progress: Kant's Variations on a Tale of Origins', *Kant's Idea for a Universal History with a Cosmopolitan Aim: A Critical Guide*, ed. Amélie Oksenberg Rorty and James Schmidt (Cambridge: Cambridge University Press, 2009), 200–15: 214, 200, 201. For the argument that Kant's views are in fact '*estranged*' from Enlightenment philosophemes such as reason and rationality', see Peter Melville, *Romantic Hospitality and the Resistance of Accommodation* (Waterloo, ON: Wilfred Laurier University Press, 2007), 12 (original emphasis).

[38] Melville, *Romantic Hospitality*, 12.

which belongs to human beings generally', he posited a principle of 'universal hospitality', which would underlie 'the right of a foreigner not to be treated with hostility because he has arrived on the land of another'.[39] The rights and duties are reciprocal, however. Reflecting the linguistic continuity between 'guest' and host',[40] Kant also imposed obligations of hospitality upon the visitor: entry can be refused to guests with violent or colonising intentions.[41] But so long as the guest 'behaves peaceably where he is', he should not be treated 'with hostility'.[42] Kant is not very specific here about what would constitute hospitable behaviour in an *individual*, though the concept is clearly not solely a state matter: looser collections of persons such as 'the inhabitants of sea coasts' and 'the inhabitants of deserts' are also mentioned.[43] What individual hospitable behaviour would look like can be inferred, however, from the second categorical imperative, formulated in *Groundwork of the Metaphysics of Morals* (*Grundlegung zur Metaphysik der Sitten*) (1785): '*act that you use humanity, in your own person as well as in the person of any other, always at the same time as an end, never merely as a means*'.[44] Further advice is contained in Kant's description of an ideal dinner-party in *Anthropology from a Pragmatic Point of View* (*Anthopologie in pragmatischer Hinsicht*) (1798), in which hospitality comprises benevolence towards others, disciplined disagreement and mutual respect.[45]

Kant's formulations of cosmopolitanism and hospitality find a twentieth- and twenty-first-century successor in Jürgen Habermas's concepts of the public sphere and communicative action and his more recent work on political theory. Habermas's publications, from *The Structural Transformation of the Public Sphere* (*Strukturwandel der Öffentlichkeit*) (1962) to *The Crisis of the European Union* (*Zur Verfassung Europas*) (2011), have stressed the role of reason in co-ordinating action through human speech exchanges.

---

[39] Immanuel Kant, *Practical Philosophy*, trans. and ed. Mary J. Gregor, *The Cambridge Edition of the Works of Immanuel Kant* (Cambridge: Cambridge University Press, 1999), 328–9 [8.358].

[40] In Latin, *hospes* means both host and guest.

[41] The obligations of hospitality imposed on the visitor are mentioned by Coleridge in his introductory note to 'The Rime of the Ancient Mariner' (1800): reaching a 'cold country' the Mariner is said to have killed a sea-bird 'in contempt of the laws of hospitality' (*Poetical Works II: Poems (Variorum Text): Part I*, ed. J. C. C. Mays, 16.3/16 vols, *The Collected Works of Samuel Taylor Coleridge* (Princeton, NJ: Princeton University Press, 2001), 509).

[42] Kant, *Practical Philosophy*, 329 [8.358].

[43] Ibid., 329 [8.358].

[44] Ibid., 329 [8.358], original emphasis.

[45] Immanuel Kant, *Anthropology from a Pragmatic Point of View* (*Die Anthropologie in pragmatischer Hinsicht*) [1796–7], trans. and ed. Robert B. Louden, *The Cambridge Edition of the Works of Immanuel Kant* (Cambridge: Cambridge University Press, 2006), 178–82, 278–82.

He writes: '[t]he goal of coming to an understanding is to bring about an agreement that terminates in the intersubjective mutuality of reciprocal understanding, shared knowledge, mutual trust, and accord with one another'.[46] Such accord depends upon having a 'performative attitude', a Shaftesburian 'taking up the perspective of the other'.[47] Habermas's 'ideal speech situation', the inception of which he dated to the coffee-houses of the seventeenth century, is one of Kantian hospitality: reciprocity and mutual respect.[48] On a more macro-political level, Habermas has noted the capacity of democratic constitutions 'to cover even the conditions for overstepping [their] own boundaries', the conditions being that the 'transgressing resistance' be justified within 'the spirit and wording of the constitution' and have a 'nonviolent appeal'.[49] This is another iteration of mutual hospitality – the host anticipates and accommodates the guest's dissidence, the guest takes advantage of the proffered vehicles of dissent – which promises 'solidarity and a nondiscriminating inclusion' and protects all equally in their 'individuality and otherness'.[50] Habermas has acknowledged that Kant's precise formulations have been out-stripped by mass warfare and globalization. Writing explicitly on 'To Perpetual Peace' in *The Inclusion of the Other* (*Die Einbeziehung des Anderen*) (1996), he cites 'the mass mobilization of recruits inflamed by nationalist passions' (exactly the phenomenon of the *levée en masse*, with its incitement to the entire French population 'to preach the hatred of kings and the unity of the Republic');[51] the channelling by 'accelerating capitalist industrialization' of foreign policy into 'violent imperialism'; and the transformation of the bourgeois public sphere into 'a semantically degenerated public sphere dominated by the electronic mass media and pervaded by images and virtual realities'.[52] Nonetheless, Habermas finds a way to preserve Kantian

---

[46] Jürgen Habermas, *Communication and the Evolution of Society* (*Sprachpragmatik und Philosophie; Zur Rekonstruktion des historischen Materialismus*) [1976], trans. Thomas McCarthy (London: Heinemann, 1979), 3.

[47] Jürgen Habermas, *Postmetaphysical Thinking: Philosophical Essays* (*Nachmetaphysisches Denken: Philosophische Aufsätze*) [1988], trans. William Mark Hohengarten (Cambridge, MA: The MIT Press, 1994), 24, 189.

[48] Ibid., 27–32.

[49] Giovanna Borradori, *Philosophy in a Time of Terror: Dialogues with Jürgen Habermas and Jacques Derrida* (Chicago: The University of Chicago Press, 1994), 41, 42.

[50] Ibid., 42.

[51] Quoted in Ute Frevert, 'War', *A Companion to Nineteenth-Century Europe: 1789–1914*, ed. Stefan Berger (Oxford: Blackwell Reference Online, 2006), unpaginated.

[52] Jürgen Habermas, *The Inclusion of the Other: Studies in Political Theory* (*Die Einbeziehung des Anderen: Studien zur politischen Theorie*) [1988], trans. Ciaran Cronin, ed. Ciaran Cronin and Pablo de Greiff (Cambridge, MA: The MIT Press, 1989), 72, 173, 176.

cosmopolitan hospitality by relocating it in a supra-national legal order that protects human rights.[53]

In the weeks after 9/11, both Habermas and Jacques Derrida visited New York City and (separately) discussed Kant (among other things) with the philosopher Giovanna Borradori.[54] In his remarks on Kantian and Habermasian hospitality across a variety of publications, Derrida keeps its *conditional* nature at the forefront of the discussion.[55] As Derrida characterizes it, this conditionality derives from the paradoxical nature of hospitality that inheres in the etyma of the word itself: *hostis* effects a 'strange crossing between enemy and host' and *potis* 'unites the semantics of power, mastery, and despotic sovereignty'.[56] The presence of 'the master of the household' ensures that hospitality is inevitably conditional, since the host's '*being-oneself in one's own home*' precludes the same state in the guest.[57] Translated to a geopolitical level, this means that state-sponsored hospitality is 'always under surveillance, parsimonious and protective of its sovereignty'.[58] If Kant and Habermas's ideas of conditional hospitality depend upon a juridical order (and that, in turn, upon a reasoned, social contract-based view of the polity), Derrida's alternative notion of unconditional or 'absolute' hospitality 'commands a break with hospitality by right, with law or justice as rights'.[59] Though acknowledging the impossibility of unconditional hospitality (at least etymologically), Derrida nonetheless hypothesizes what it might entail: 'the arriving of the other who could come at any moment without asking my opinion and who could come with the best or worst of intentions [...] an invasion by the worst'.[60] In the novels about to be discussed, the veteran-as-*xenos* tests conditional

[53] Ibid., 201.
[54] The non-face-to-face colloquy is recorded in Borradori, *Philosophy in a Time of Terror*. Derrida's remarks to Borradori develop the thinking he expounded in a series of seminars on hospitality in Paris in January 1996 and in subsequent venues.
[55] Kant's 'Third Definitive Article for Perpetual Peace' is explicitly conditional: 'Cosmopolitan right shall be limited to conditions of universal *hospitality*' (*Practical Philosophy*, 328 [8.358], original emphasis).
[56] Jacques Derrida, 'Hostipitality', trans. Barry Stocker and Morlock Forbes, *Angelaki* 5.3 (2000), 3–18: 13. Derrida is citing Émile Benveniste, *Indo-European Language and Society* (*Le Vocabulaire des institutions indo-européennes*) [1969], trans. Elizabeth Palmer (London: Faber and Faber, 1973), 72.
[57] Derrida, 'Hostipitality', 4.
[58] Borradori, *Philosophy in a Time of Terror*, 128.
[59] Jacques Derrida and Anne Dufourmantelle, *Of Hospitality: Anne Dufourmantelle Invites Jacques Derrida to Respond* (Stanford, CA: Stanford University Press, 2000), 25. Derrida leaves the nature of this extra-juridical realm undefined: 'unconditional hospitality is transcendent with regard to the political, the juridical, perhaps even to the ethical' (Borradori, *Philosophy in a Time of Terror*, 129).
[60] Derrida, 'Hostipitality', 17, n17.

hospitality to its limits, exploring what happens when individuals and communities confront the 'invasion by the worst'.

### Imposture: Betty Miller, *On the Side of the Angels* (1945)

A cluster of works of fiction from the 1940s – Betty Miller's *On the Side of the Angels* (1945), Denton Welch's short story 'Brave and Cruel' (1948) and Elizabeth Taylor's *A Wreath of Roses* (1949) – explore the construction of social identity, and the social construction of identity, through characters who impersonate veterans. In this section, I concentrate on Miller's novel *On the Side of the Angels*, which sets veteran imposture within a set of (gendered) performances in a small community and suggests that these performances reveal qualities of competitiveness and aggression that are among the root causes of war. Imposture is a special case of dissonance between the individual and the community: its revelation raises questions about the hospitality that has been proffered and engenders both personal and communal self-scrutiny in Miller's novel.

In a note to a friend, the author John Verney, Miller remarked that what 'fascinated' her during the Second World War was 'the astonishing effect on quite ordinary civilians of army life'.[61] 'No sooner had they donned uniforms,' she wrote, 'than these men (and women too) who in everyday life were respectable God-fearing citizens became – under the influence of a *very* peculiar CO[62] quite unrecognizable.'[63] The significance of uniform is underscored in a crucial early scene in *On the Side of the Angels* in which a character, Andrew Peirse, is uncharacteristically *out* of uniform, in a pair of grey flannels and a white shirt that seem to his fiancée, Claudia Abbott, 'unfamiliar after so much khaki' (39).[64] In this scene, Andrew tells Claudia that he is out of khaki for good – he has been invalided out of the army – and a country walk becomes the occasion for the testing of a postwar social identity.

The disability that excludes Andrew from the army is not in the category of the heroic wound: pneumonia has left him with a 'groggy heart'

---

[61] Quoted in Sarah Miller, 'Introduction', *On the Side of the Angels* by Betty Miller (London: Capuchin Classics, 2012), 11–23: 18.

[62] Commanding Officer.

[63] Quoted in Sarah Miller, 'Introduction', 18.

[64] Betty Miller, *On the Side of the Angels* [1945] (London: Capuchin Classis, 2012). Page references are given in the text. On the significance of uniforms in the novel, see Victoria Stewart, 'Masculinity, Masquerade and the Second World War: Betty Miller's *On the Side of the Angels*', *Conflict, Nationhood and Corporeality in Modern Literature: Bodies-at-War*, ed. Petra Rau (Basingstoke: Palgrave Macmillan, 2010), 124–42.

and this, in the eyes of the military, renders him 'Damaged goods' (42). Andrew comments: 'They don't go in for salvage sales, for remnants in the army, why should they? So they've boarded me out, returned me to civil life, C. O. D.[65] [...] And here I am, *mens sana in corpore C3*.[66] At your service, Claudia, bowler hat and all' (42). The language of salvage, of remnants, is that of waste matter, and waste is here associated with civilian status ('bowler hat and all'). As the conversation progresses, Andrew also begins to dissociate himself from fitness to marry, simultaneously under-mining his own masculinity and sexual competence. 'No nice normal girl wants to be tied for life to a crock,' he informs her (44). To go through with their marriage would not be 'fair exchange', he insists, 'and I don't feel inclined to rob you, Claudia' (45). His vision of marriage as 'exchange' is on a par with his sense of himself as goods-for-cash; his value, in his own eyes, has depreciated – feeling socially useless, he positions himself as *xenos* within the community.

For her part, Claudia, though a civilian, apprehends the scene in terms of military strategy. As Andrew looks at her with a 'queer triumphant expression in his face', she feels 'a new defensive reaction' (41). She perceives that what he now has to acknowledge is 'not weakness but a source of secret strength' (42). Illness, 'like a strategic withdrawal, a falling back on prepared positions', offers him 'undeniable advantages' (43): he is protecting 'not me, not himself – but his own invalidism' (44). That inval-idism, in future, 'perhaps is to be the dominant thing' (44). Immediately, the Andrew she has known 'vanishe[s]' and in his place sits an 'incalcul-able stranger, whose acquaintance she would have to make slowly, warily' (44). The dialogue not only reveals the role played by military fitness in constructing masculine identity but also exposes a sense of civilian society as both sick and unfit-for-purpose because it hypocritically valorizes mili-tary service while remaining ignorant of its realities. 'You've got to have a war to show where people's real values lie,' argues Andrew. 'A war turns us inside out, shows the lining: pacifists become war-mongers, intellectuals worship the man with the tommy-gun' (47). In other words, war uncovers mass peacetime imposture. And at the same time, the scene reveals the powerful threat ('secret strength', 'undeniable advantages') of the 'incalcul-able stranger' or *xenos* who refuses to behave hospitably.

---

[65] Cash on delivery.
[66] 'A healthy mind in a C3 body'. The fitness grade C3 meant that an individual was fit only for home service and sedentary work.

One of those who the war has turned inside out is Claudia's brother-in-law Colin Carmichael. A doctor in peacetime, Colin is now Captain Carmichael, a member of the Royal Army Medical Corps, sitting in judgement on the fitness to fight of other men at the newly established War Office Selection Board at the local hospital. As Claudia observes, the war has given Colin 'a heaven-sent opportunity' of living as he's 'always wanted to live and never quite dared to' (51). 'You don't believe that the pre-war Colin was the real one – was the whole story – do you?' she asks her sister, Honor, Colin's wife, 'the natty little small-town doctor, lifting his hat to the old ladies?' (51). 'Natty', 'little', 'small', deferent, and elsewhere a 'little bantam cock [...] dapper' (35): if Colin's physical slightness has undermined his masculinity in peacetime, in wartime he compensates through such props as his uniform and a long-ago rugger injury, 'appearing to attach to that once fractured humerus of his a significance so disproportionate as to be almost mystical' (68). In Honor's view, his new military role gives Colin 'a new sense of freedom and irresponsibility'; the anonymity conferred by his uniform renders him 'masked, and, being masked privileged, in a sort of carnival spirit, to conduct himself in a manner wholly alien to his normal way of life' (118). The references to the carnivalesque and to 'irresponsibility' hint that his new guise licenses Colin himself to behave with some inhospitality himself.

While Andrew embraces invalidity and Colin joyfully masculinizes himself, a third performance is taking place. The new Military Testing Officer, Captain Neil Herriot – the veteran impostor – is *über*-militarized, *über*-masculine: not just a soldier but a Commando who has 'seen a lot of active service, been on most of the big raids'.[67] Miller – sometimes comically – emphasizes the contrast between Herriot's physical largeness and strength and Colin's diminutiveness and weakness: Colin stands there, 'uncertain, biting at his frail moustache' while Herriot looks down at him 'from his great height' (70), and the pair are compared by Rita the barmaid to 'Mutt and Jeff' (71).[68] At the hospital sports day, the scene is set for a competition between the two that will result in Colin's mortification. Colin is duly humiliated – his body is revealed to public view as flawed and attenuated ('His legs were rather bleached-looking; the calves small and knotty [...] he looked less like an athlete stripped for action than a bather coming down, unwilling, to the water's edge' (104)) and his own son is embarrassed by his failure to win the

---

[67] For the significance of Herriot's Commando rank, see Stewart, 'Masculinity, Masquerade and the Second World War'.

[68] From the American comic strip (1907–82) by Bud Fisher. Mutt was extremely tall, Jeff equally short.

race – but Herriot is also found wanting as he proves unable to compete due to a ricked ankle. Later in the day, Honor notices that Herriot is not limping and mentions the fact to Colin: the incident makes 'a queer disturbing impression' on both of them (119). The moment is important as it is one in which the dual nature of the impostor is fleetingly visible. It is disturbing – in a way that the revelation that Colin is not, after all, an excellent sportsman is not disturbing – because Herriot's dissimulation has been publicly colluded in, not least by Honor, Colin and Claudia. What disturbs Honor and Colin is the sudden perception that, in terms of Kantian and Habermasian reciprocity, Herriot may not have kept his side of the bargain.

After Herriot has been unmasked as a 'respectable middle-aged man', a 'small-town bank manager', a 'dutiful husband' and 'affectionate father' (247) (a domesticating, emasculating set of descriptors in the context), Andrew's Freudian-based diagnosis[69] applies a notion of communal interpretation to the phenomenon of mass imposture:

> It's an illustration of the things we really want and expect. We create a fiction out of our own desires. The fiction in this case happened to be the Commando hero: the killer, tough, unscrupulous; outside the bounds of ordinary convention. A fiction so attractive to the law-abiding that we chose in its favour to ignore the reality: the fact that a Commando is a Commando precisely because he can be relied upon to conduct himself in a manner not less, but infinitely more disciplined and responsible than that of the average citizen.

> (246)

Herriot's deception – a false claim of identity – constitutes a significant act of inhospitality towards his host community. In turn, the community's collusion in his imposture – a 'fairy-tale we ourselves helped to create' (248) – could be criticized as excessively hospitable, a potentially self-harmful, if understandable, collective misjudgement. The outcome demonstrates the risks inherent in Derrida's unconditional hospitality. But the point goes beyond a single act of deception. In Andrew's remarks, Miller suggests that imposture is practised not only by the obvious counterfeit but by other members of the community most of the time. Barred from a military persona, Andrew perceives the extent to which social roles (military roles particularly, but not exclusively) are a form of 'escapism' (his own 'ununiformed' (56), un-constructed identity is visible in his 'gaunt, vein-laced arm that the sun could not brown' (39): his body refuses to assume that key sign of veterancy – tanning). Uniforms make the point

---

[69] See Stewart, 'Masculinity, Masquerade and the Second World War', 126.

visually and metaphorically, but other, 'ununiformed' personae – spouse, parent, teacher (Claudia, whose profession is the last, is 'in some doubt as to where camouflage ended and the field of her own spontaneous nature began' (30)) – have the same ontological basis.

In his Foreword to the 2012 Capuchin Classics edition of *On the Side of the Angels*, Miller's son, the opera director Jonathan Miller, describes how the novel has shaped his various productions of *Così Fan Tutte*. 'Under the influence of her book,' Jonathan Miller writes, 'it became increasingly apparent to me that Mozart's work was about identity rather than fidelity and about the dangers of pretending to be someone other than your previous self.'[70] *Così Fan Tutte* concerns veteran imposture, as two officers disguise themselves and successfully attempt to seduce each other's fiancées. But, in a sense, *all* returning veterans are impostors as all are, to some extent, required to play the part of the person who left home. Endorsing Jonathan Miller's perception, Betty Miller further suggests that imposture is a common way of being, a way of being that is 'so costive', moreover, that it needs 'a regular dose of high explosive' to blast it away (293). Deception constipates communal functioning, that is. In the next novel discussed, Helen Ashton's *The Captain Comes Home*, ascertaining identity is again a tricky issue. Mutual hospitality is put under pressure as another small village debates what to do with a homecoming soldier who is both a deeply familiar figure and a disturbing stranger.

## The Veteran on Trial: Helen Ashton, *The Captain Comes Home* (1947)

In *The Captain Comes Home*, the question troubling everyone is as simple to state as it is ontologically complex: is the person who has come back from war the same as the one who went away? The veteran is the perfect figure via which to explore ideas regarding the persistence and stability of the self, ideas discussed and finessed in the age of mass warfare by, among others, Locke, Hume, Kant, Nietzsche, William James and Henri Bergson. A former soldier, the veteran is, inescapably, no longer what he was, and so has a built-in *has-been-ness*. Coming home, he is both known and expected and unknown and unexpected and so blurs the distinction between return and arrival,[71] between the one who comes back and the one who comes

---

[70] Jonathan Miller, 'Foreword', *On the Side of the Angels*, by Betty Miller (London: Capuchin Classics, 2012) 9–10: 10.

[71] This is similar to, but essentially distinct from, Derrida's distinction between the *revenant* (that which 'is going to come') and the *arrivant* (that which 'has not yet arrived') (*Specters of Marx: The State of the Debt, the Work of Mourning and the New International* (*Spectres de Marx: L'État de la dette, le travail du deuil et la nouvelle Internationale*) [1993], trans. Peggy Kamuf

newly. In a state of indefinite transit (returning to civilian life, he is also leaving the home that was the military), he constantly poses the question 'who am I *now?*' It is an unsettling question, a threatening question, as well as (potentially) a liberating question. In *The Captain Comes Home*, it is not only for the individual concerned to answer, but for the community as a whole.

Missing for four years, Captain Johnny Crowe is presumed dead and his wife has remarried, to a civilian who has 'done very well for himself in the changing conditions of wartime' (71)[72] – a 'not unheard-of case', according to a contemporary review.[73] But from 1941 to 1945, Crowe has been hidden on a remote island off Greece, suffering from a leg wound and living in a cave. His war experience, in other words, is not conventionally heroic, but neither does he fit the Prodigal Son paradigm. On his return to his native village of Lambscot, rather than being welcomed, honoured and rewarded, he is feared, abused, rejected and, finally, put on trial.

Helen Ashton herself served as a nurse with the Voluntary Aid Detachment in the First World War, thereby acquiring a version of veteran status and observing at first hand the effects of armed combat. Born in 1891, the daughter of a judge, Ashton went on to qualify as a doctor after the war, turning to writing after her marriage to a barrister in 1927.[74] *The Captain Comes Home*, which draws on both medical and legal expertise, is

---

(New York: Routledge, 1994), 245 n39). John D. Caputo, alluding to (*inter alia*) Derrida's critique of Fukuyama's *The End of History and the Last Man* (1992) in *Specters of Marx*, notes that the 'sails of deconstruction strain toward what is coming, are bent by the winds of *l'avenir*, by the promise of the in-coming, of the *in-venire*, of the wholly other, *tout autre, l'invention de l'autre*' (*The Prayers and Tears of Jacques Derrida: Religion without Religion* (Bloomington, IN: Indian University Press, 1997), XXIII). 'The one who is coming, the just one [what Derrida envisages is messianic], the *tout autre* [...] must always function as a breach of the present', Caputo continues (XIV). Derrida's point in *Specters of Marx* is historiographical but his language is that of missing persons. Casting the 'event' as 'the foreigner itself', he speaks of an hospitable attitude towards the future that would 'leave an empty place' 'in memory of the hope' of what is to come (82). The breach – which may literally be marked by an empty place at the table when someone has gone off to war – is necessary because 'nothing and no one would arrive otherwise' (82): return/ arrival is predicated upon departure/absence. It endures even after the return/arrival of the veteran – Caputo comments vis-à-vis deconstruction that, 'if the messiah ever showed up, in the flesh [...] the one question we would have for him is "when will you come?"' (XIV) – keeping the present open to the 'new' and the 'impossible' (XIV). In *The Captain Comes Home*, in addition to emphasizing Johnny Crowe's lack of marital viability, Phyllis's remarriage removes her from the open, risky state-of-being that is maintaining the empty place at the table or an hospitable attitude towards the future.

72  Helen Ashton, *The Captain Comes Home* (London: Collins, 1947). Page references are given in the text.
73  Ruby Millar, 'Home Is the Soldier', *Times Literary Supplement* (16 August 1947), 413.
74  Anonymous, 'Helen Ashton, M.B., B.S.', *British Medical Journal* (12 July 1958), 110.

a rendition of Sophocles' *Philoctetes*.[75] Sophocles, another veteran (of the Athenian campaign against Samos), wrote the drama, which is set in the Trojan War, during the Peloponnesian War. The genesis of the story is that Apollo has given Heracles a bow that never misses its mark. In unbearable agony from the poisoned Shirt of Nessus, Heracles gives the bow to Philoctetes in return for lighting his death pyre and Philoctetes takes it with him when he sets off for Troy with Agamemnon and Menelaus. They stop off at the island of Chrysè to make a sacrifice to the local deity, where, walking on holy ground, Philoctetes is bitten on the foot by a snake. The wound becomes infected, suppurating and malodorous, and Philoctetes' comrades are unable to bear his presence among them: 'He filled the entire camp with savage and ill-omened cries, shouting and screaming.'[76] They take him to Lemnos – Odysseus is among the most vociferous to call for his abandonment – and leave him 'without a share of anything in life, far from all others [...] pitiable in his pain and hunger'.[77] After ten years, motivated by a prophecy that the Greeks can only win with the help of Philoctetes and his enchanted bow, Odysseus returns to Lemnos. He brings with him the young Neoptolemus (whose necessity to victory has also been decreed by the gods): the idea is that the youth, who Philoctetes does not know, will persuade him to return with them to Troy. The usefulness of a wounded warrior is therefore recognized, and he is (ultimately) recuperated, but not before, to use Gerber's searing words regarding disabled veterans, he has suffered 'repulsion, stigmatization, humiliation, bitterness, and loss of self-regard'.[78]

Ashton alludes to the *Philoctetes* framework explicitly in her novel: '[l]ike Philoctetes', Johnny has been left on a Greek island with a 'poisoned foot' for years (118). But, with his 'red gold hair' (137), Johnny is also Neoptolemus, also known as Pyrrhus on account of his red hair (πύρρος (purrhos) means 'red'). Neoptolemus is the son of Achilles and Deidamia, who met when Achilles was disguised as a girl in Deidamia's father's court.

---

[75] Theater of War's Ajax and Philoctetes Program now presents Sophocles' *Philoctetes* and *Ajax* to veteran and civilian audiences, aiming 'to de-stigmatize psychological injury, increase awareness of post-deployment psychological health issues, disseminate information regarding available resources, and foster greater family, community, and troop resilience': http://theaterofwar.com/projects/theater-of-war/overview. *Philoctetes* is discussed further in Chapter 4.

[76] Sophocles, *Antigone. The Women of Trachis. Philoctetes. Oedipus at Colonus*, trans. and ed. Hugh Lloyd-Jones, Loeb Classical Library (Cambridge, MA: Harvard University Press, 2014), 256–6, ll. 9–10.

[77] Ibid., 274–5, ll. 182–4.

[78] David A. Gerber, 'Heroes and Misfits: The Troubled Social Reintegration of Disabled Veterans of World War II in *The Best Years of Our Lives*', *Disabled Veterans in History*, ed. David A. Gerber (Ann Arbor, MI: University of Michigan Press, 2000), 70–95: 73.

Deidamia corresponds to Johnny's lost mother – 'a red-haired piece [...]
with long legs and a big mouth and green eyes' (52) – while Achilles' cross-
dressing resonates with the novel's play with constructions of masculinity.
Mrs Pye, the housekeeper who has brought Johnny up, has some affinities
with Achilles' mother, Thetis, agonized by her son's departure for war; her
surname also echoes 'Pyrrhus'.[79]

   Central to Philoctetes' story are questions regarding the proper treatment
and valuation of incapacitated warriors: the suppurating, malodorous foot
figures both the disgrace of a society's failure to recognize and recompense
its ex-servicemen and the festering potential for violence on the part of
such veterans.[80] But there is more to the myth than the politics of veteran relief. In *The Wound and the Bow* (1941), Edmund Wilson compares
Philoctetes with another of Sophocles' protagonists – Oedipus: both are
'accursed', 'pariahs'.[81] Yet, somehow, both are also 'sacred persons who
have acquired superhuman powers, and who are destined to be purged of
their guilt'.[82] Ashton's complex re-working of her classical sources retains
the paradox of the outcast/superhuman – accommodating it to a rural
English setting – and also highlights the interwoven gender implications
encapsulated in the oedipal story of a warrior who is too wounded to fight
but whose assistance is nevertheless indispensable to victory in battle and
must be requested by a younger, physically stronger man.

   *The Captain Comes Home* renders the conduct of Johnny/Philoctetes
primarily a communal matter, maximizing the dissonance of conflicting
expectations and putting them to definitive judgement in a trial. As in
the *Odyssey*, the dissonance begins long before the veteran's homecoming.
The Greek who has saved Johnny's life and taken him to the cave has

---

[79] In addition to petitioning a complex network of classical sources, Ashton also makes astonishing
   textual play with birds' names. The following characters all have birds' names or bird-related
   names: the Crowes, the Mavises, the Francolins, Joe Starling, Colonel Heron, Camilla Shearwater,
   George Lark, Farmer Woodcock, Mary Dove, Cassandra Nightingale, Laura Craik, Bob Finch,
   Edward Bullfinch, Albert Bunting, Tom Wheeler (wheel-bird), James Swift, Dr Siskin, Mrs Drake,
   Inspector Plover, Robin Fowler, Mrs Twitcher. Phyllis's new husband is Bob Slater: appropriately, a
   slater is a bird-dog. Similarly, Constable Roper's surname denotes 'A person who uses a lasso to catch
   an animal' ('roper, n.', 2 (*Oxford English Dictionary* (Oxford University Press), online edition).
[80] In a letter to *The Nation* seven years after American troops had been withdrawn, a Vietnam veteran,
   Ron Faust, wrote: 'We're not home yet, not as long as the rest of this country refuses to *let* us come
   home; that is, not until it faces up to what *we* did as a nation in Vietnam. We will "finally come
   home" on the day we can look other Americans in the eye and see there the confession: "Yes, we did
   this terrible thing *together*"' ('Vets: "Not Home Yet"', *The Nation* 235.21 (18 December 1982), 642).
[81] Edmund Wilson, *The Wound and the Bow: Seven Studies in Literature* [1941] (London: Methuen,
   1961), 284.
[82] Ibid., 284.

certain assumptions concerning the reception that will ultimately greet him: ' "When you come back from the war," said Yanni, "every shepherd will give you a lamb out of his own fold, so that you may have a flock of your own. You will build yourself a house and plant vines and olive trees; you will marry a young wife and all your sons will be soldiers" ' (14). Here, veterancy is envisaged as prompting beneficent hospitality on the part of the receiving community – gratitude, respect, reward and honour that will result in the homecomer's prosperity, sexual satisfaction, fecundity and proud procreation of future warriors. Johnny contests this vision, remarking that he thinks his wife will have remarried. 'No girl will look at a sick man with only one foot,' he groans (15), associating masculinity and marital eligibility with physical wholeness. In Lambscot, meanwhile, the news that Johnny has been found meets with a mixed reception. For many, his quasi-resurrection from the dead is excessive, tmetic. Anne Mavis tells Admiral Francolin, Johnny's father-in-law, 'I'm afraid I've brought some news that's going to give you rather a shock' (43). The Admiral blinks 'as if a stunning blow just missed him' (44). Dinah Mavis 'startle[s] everyone' by 'sitting bolt upright' and 'gasping out', as though she has 'received a blow over the heart' (36). Johnny's (ex-)wife Phyllis's reaction to the news is also explosive, her face changing 'as if under some violent emotion', expressing 'a kind of helpless rage' (78). 'You told me he was dead,' she complains (78). This is tmesis on a metaphysical level as well as on a social and textual level and Phyllis 'shudder[s] with fright' as a consequence (79). These reactions mark considerable anxiety in the community: Lambscot has closed over Johnny's disappearance, and his return will, at best, cause significant disruption to village life.

As Johnny's return becomes imminent, concerns about the impact of the *xenos* grow as the villagers anticipate – and fear – deep change: 'He was like a young prince. [...] Oh! deary me! what will he be like now?' (55); 'I reckon we shall hardly know him' (86). The young Dinah Mavis, who adores Johnny, reveals her anxieties in her query, 'Mother, when Johnny comes back [...] Will he look just the same?' (56–7). Her underlying concern might be that ontological conundrum of whether, when Johnny comes back, he will *be* – or be allowed to be – just the same, but the fact that Dinah couches the question in terms of physical appearance is telling. What Johnny looks like – a clue to the threat he poses to the community as a former warrior – will, to a great extent, determine his reception and placement in Lambscot. And these will decided by the receiving community rather than by the homecomer himself.

Dinah's mother can only provide a non-committal 'Darling, I don't know; I hope so' (57) to her question. The fluidity of his identity only increases the otherness of the *xenos* and when Johnny at last returns to Lambscot, having spent some weeks in hospital, the village's hopes and fears are in a febrile state. Incrementally, Ashton creates a picture of a lost identity, a Johnny-less Johnny, who can be written over by the villagers jointly and severally. It is hugely significant that 'Nobody [sees] him at first' (99): the identity-less figure is invisible to the community, 'shadowy' (134), a 'stranger' (134).[83] Canon Crowe, his grandfather, thinks of him as a 'fabulous and possibly alarming monster' (104): '[t]he boy's so changed, I feel I scarcely know him,' he confesses, 'he isn't the same being' (175). Qualitative transform-ation is ontologically troubling as it suggests the possibility of multiple persons in the same body: no wonder the Canon reaches for the realm of fable to make sense of it. Johnny himself expresses a missing subjectivity that involves forgetfulness and confusion: 'I can't remember anything' (95), 'It's all a muddle in my mind' (96). He experiences 'a feeling of horrible emptiness and lightness, as if I were a scrap of paper and the wind could blow me away' (188). The scrap of paper image underlines the fragility, negligibility and impermanence of his identity, encapsulating the idea that Johnny is now a *tabula rasa* for everyone to write on. It also conveys a sense of something on the point of being exhausted and discarded, as though, at any moment, the village might cease to have any use for him and cast him aside as waste matter, to be blown away by the wind. While Lambscot decides what to make of, or do with, Johnny, his social identity remains suspended until the outcome of the trial.[84]

---

[83] Cf. Andrew Cowan's novel *Worthless Men* (London: Sceptre, 2013) in which a returning First World War veteran, Walter Barley, cannot be seen or heard by the inhabitants of his home town. They 'hurry on by, as if he isn't there' (11).

[84] An illuminating parallel with Johnny Crowe is the real-life sixteenth-century case of Martin Guerre, explored in the film *Le Retour de Martin Guerre*, dir. Daniel Vigne (1982) and by Natalie Zemon Davis in her influential book *The Return of Martin Guerre* (Cambridge, MA: Harvard University Press, 1983). As Zemon Davis reconstructs it, available means of identification were severely strained when a person claiming to be Martin Guerre returned to the Languedoc village of Artigat after eight years away in the wars. '[I]n a time without photographs, with few portraits, without tape recorders, without fingerprinting, without identity cards, without birth certificates, with parish records still irregular if kept at all – how did one establish a person's identity beyond doubt?' asks Zemon Davis (63). The villagers could test 'Martin's' memory (though there was always the pos-sibility that he had been coached), ask witnesses to identify him and 'hope they were accurate and truthful', consider special marks on his face and body (this would require witnesses who had known the 'earlier person'), look to see whether he resembled other members of the family or check his handwriting (if he and the earlier person could both write) (63). Importantly, the process of identifying the *xenos* was public, collaborative, a working through of dissenting views until a con-sensus was reached. 'Martin', that is, was not just a matter of common acceptance but a communal

A word is in order here about veterancy and masculinity. Military service constructs and depends upon models of masculinity in which strength, physical prowess, courage, leadership, violence and mental toughness are valorized and male bonding is strongly promoted.[85] Return to civilian status may alter the significance of these qualities and compromise the models of masculinity that have been absorbed. Sexual drives are also affected by war experience, as commentators have noted from the eighteenth century. 'When [soldiers] are [...] prevented from mixing with the innocent and estimable part of the softer sex, and when all the other circumstances attendant upon such confinement are taken into consideration,' declared the radical orator and writer John Thelwall in 1795, 'we cannot but dread the production of a degree of ferocity which they would never otherwise know.'[86] Similar dread can easily take hold of the community – its denizens

---

enterprise. Commenting further on the ontological implications of the story, Stephen Greenblatt argues that the trial that ensued seemed 'to confirm a principle essential to the constitution of the Freudian subject: the real Martin Guerre cannot be definitively robbed of his identity, even when he has apparently abandoned it and even when its superficial signs have been successfully mimicked by a cunning impostor' ('Psychoanalysis and Renaissance Culture', *Literary Theory/Renaissance Texts*, ed. Patricia Parker and David Quint (Baltimore, MD: The Johns Hopkins University Press, 1986), 210–24: 215, 212). But, Greenblatt continues, the sixteenth century did not see it like this: no one invoked Martin's 'biological individuality or his soul or his infancy' (215, 212). At issue was 'not Martin Guerre as subject but Martin Guerre as object', his identity 'the *product* of the relations, material objects, and judgments exposed in the case rather than the *producer* of these relations, objects, and judgments' (215, 212). When *The Captain Comes Home* was written, identity was scientifically easier to establish. Nonetheless, the community of Lambscot still has an active role in determining who 'Johnny' shall be, constructing him, that is, as object in Greenblatt's terms.

[85] Susan M. Hartmann, 'Prescriptions for Penelope: Literature on Women's Obligations to Returning World War II Veterans', *Women's Studies* 5.3 (January 1978), 223–39: 224.

[86] John Thelwall, 'The Lecture "On Barracks and Fortifications; with Sketches of the Character and Treatment of the British Soldiery." Delivered Wednesday, 10 June 1795 (Issue 19)', *The Tribune, A Periodical Publication Consisting Chiefly of the Political Lectures of J. Thelwall* (London: printed for the author, 1795), 85–110: 100; quoted in Gillian Russell, *The Theatres of War: Performance, Politics, and Society, 1793–1815* (Oxford: The Clarendon Press, 1995), 49; see also Dawson, *Soldier Heroes*, passim. In a similar vein, David Erskine, 11th Earl of Buchan, in a 1793 pamphlet arguing against the maintenance of a standing army, noted: 'Doomed by their situation to a state of celibacy, though they have voluntarily given up the essential rights of *freemen*, yet it is not in their power to divest themselves of the feelings and passions of mere *men*; "Nature will prevail." – It is not from the *Soldier* that we can expect the impetus of Passion to be subjected to the controul of Reason; and thus we see them exposed, and in a great degree driven to gratify the instincts of nature at the expence of innocence and virtue. In towns where they are quartered for any length of time, how many parents and masters of families experience the most affecting, and even afflicting inconveniences? while the poor, unhappy objects of seduction, become too often miserable for life' (David Steuart Erskine Buchan, *Letters on the Impolicy of a Standing Army in Time of Peace, and on the Unconstitutional and Illegal Measure of Barracks: With a Post[S]cript Illustrative of the Real Constitutional Mode of Defence for this Island; Containing Also a Short Review of the Effects which are Produced by a Standing Army on Morality, Population and Labour* (London: printed for D. J. Eaton, 1793), 83–4, original emphasis). On veteran homecoming and sexual dysfunction, see further James Campbell, 'Coming Home: Difference and Reconciliation in Narratives of Return to the "World" ', The United States

and its authorities – to which an ex-soldier returns. With extra potential for constituting a threat, a veteran makes communal and personal decisions about the hospitality that will be offered all the more difficult.

In *The Captain Comes Home*, the collective appraisal process begins when the doctor at the hospital for 'nerve cases' (87) where Johnny has been kept for several weeks tells his grandfather, 'I'm recommending him for discharge; he's not going to be any more use as a soldier, you know' (91). His military usefulness officially terminated, Johnny is already treated as a form of waste matter (note the other senses of 'discharge'); the question now becomes what, if any, his future use will be. Ashton emphasizes the depletion of his youth and virility: 'He had been a tall strong young man when he was first taken [to the cave]; by the end of the time he had become a walking skeleton, so dried and salted by long hardship and sickness that his bones were ready to stick through his skin. His red-gold hair straggled down over his forehead' (17). Johnny's atrophied physique makes him seem ghostly (he has been legally presumed dead). This seam of imagery continues: he is variously described as 'an immensely tall red-haired skeleton of a man' (30), 'an old ghost' (99), a 'corpse' (101). These descriptors lend themselves to a reading in terms of Freud's theories of the uncanny and the return of the repressed, but here it is more pertinent to note how they position Johnny as other, outside social conventions, external to the group, and, in particular, as a weak, unhealthy individual.[87] (He is also

---

and Viet Nam from War to Peace: Papers from an Interdisciplinary Conference on Reconciliation, ed. Robert M. Slabey (Jefferson, NC: McFarland, 1996), 198–207.

[87] In his 1919 essay 'Das Unheimliche' ('The Uncanny'), written in response to the psychiatrist Ernst Jentsch's study, 'Über die Psychologie des Unheimlichen' ('On the Psychology of the Uncanny'), Freud famously noted that the word 'heimlich' has two opposing meanings: 'belonging to the house, not strange, familiar, tame, intimate, comfortable, homely' and '[c]oncealed, kept from sight, so that others do not get to know about it, withheld from others' (*An Infantile Neurosis and Other Works*, ed. James Strachey in collaboration with Anna Freud, assisted by Alix Strachey and Alan Tyson (London: The Hogarth Press / Institute of Psycho-Analysis, 1955), 219–52: 222, 223). Curiously, the latter meaning coincides with the antonym of 'heimlich', 'unheimlich': 'eerie, weird, arousing gruesome fear' – or uncanny (224). Freud continued: '[W]e can understand why linguistic usage has extended das Heimliche into its opposite, das Unheimliche; for this uncanny is in reality nothing new or alien, but something which is familiar and old-established in the mind and which has become alienated from it only by the process of repression. This reference to the factor of repression enables us, furthermore, to understand Schelling's definition of the uncanny as something which ought to have remained hidden but has come to light' (241). A Freudian reading would render a returning/arriving veteran an unheimlicher Heimkehrer (an uncanny homecomer), a ghostly revenant at once familiar and strange, figuring something repressed, both wanted and feared. Ghostly veterans appear in Ellen Wood's Indian Mutiny tale 'A Mysterious Visitor' (1857) and Rhoda Broughton's story 'Poor Pretty Bobby' (1873). In Elizabeth Gaskell's *Sylvia's Lovers* (1863), the reappearance of Charley Kinraid, presumed dead, occurs in a chapter titled 'The Apparition'. These spectral revenants have been given Freudian interpretations: see, for example, Nick Freeman, 'Sensational Ghosts, Ghostly Sensations', *Women's Writing* 20.2 (2013) (Special Issue: Beyond

called a 'wild man' (30) and a 'madman' (34), both descriptors placing him beyond the norms of civilization and sanity.)

In Lambscot, more than one villager holds the view that his disabilities disqualify Johnny from a full, procreative role in the community (as noted, Johnny himself anticipates this view in Greece: 'No girl will look at a sick man with only one foot'). This view is cast in terms of retrospective justifications of Phyllis's remarriage. 'Phyllis is being very sensible, Doctor, if you ask me,' says Mrs Drake. 'Poor Johnny doesn't sound as if he'd be much of a husband for her, a nervous wreck, from all you tell me, who's got months of hospital treatment ahead of him and will probably never be much good for anything again' (84). Mrs Lark agrees (using the same word as Andrew Peirse in *On the Side of the Angels*): 'you wouldn't want her tied to a crock' (85). For this body-reading community, physical and mental damage is equated with marital (that is, sexual) inadequacy and hence damaged masculinity. It is noteworthy that Johnny is variously described as 'like a child' (94), 'as bewildered and terrified as an animal in a trap' (94), 'a wary, terrified animal' (103), 'a cornered, frightened animal' (103), all descriptions suggestive of smallness, fear and vulnerability – the very opposite of sexual maturity. Having lost his wife Phyllis, he is paired with Dinah Mavis, but Dinah is too young for this to be a sexual relationship and she herself is described in the same diminutive, vulnerable terms as Johnny: 'a young, nervous animal' (105), 'a small, considering bird aware of danger' (106), 'an excited little dog' (215). At the end of the novel, no role as a sexual being is envisaged in Johnny's future: only partially hospitable, Lambscot will reabsorb him, but only in an emasculated – and hence non-threatening – state.

A key scene in the village's communal and corporeal assessment of Johnny takes place in the police cell. Inspector Plover and Constable Roper notice that Johnny has scribbled his name in two or three places on the wall, 'as if he were trying to establish his own identity' (168):

'*Withered*,' was put down once or twice; then he had made a fresh start and written plainly, '*O, wither'd is the garland of the war, The soldier's pole is fallen*,' setting the two lines under one another. Then he had gone away and put in another place, much lower down, '*Nothing left remarkable beneath the visiting*

Braddon: Re-assessing Female Sensationalists), 186–201, and Patsy Stoneman, *Elizabeth Gaskell*, 2nd ed. (Manchester: Manchester University Press, 2006), 99, 100. A contemporary review of *The Captain Comes Home* contained the comment, 'I am unhappy about that disfigured and crippled man who [...] pushes into the foreground from heaven knows what shady region of the mind: there is more in this than meets the eye' (D. S. Savage, 'Fiction', *Spectator* (25 July 1947), 122).

*moon*'; and then he had scratched it all over with a light impatient maze of pencil scribbling, so that it was hardly legible.

(168, original emphasis)

In this explicit attempt to establish his identity, Johnny has turned to Shakespeare's *Antony and Cleopatra*, citing the lines spoken by Cleopatra immediately after Antony's death (4.15.64–5, 67–8). It is an attempt to borrow a persona, to associate himself with the veteran Antony by means of textual proximity.[88] A few lines earlier, on the point of death, Antony has begged Cleopatra to disregard his present state – 'The miserable change now at my end / Lament nor sorrow at' (4.15.51–2) – and there is a sense that Johnny, too, is struggling to identify with his current diminution. The repeated inscription of '*withered*' is at once an attempt to come to terms with his situation through multiple iterations of its reality, a comment on his relationship with Phyllis, a sense of his own depleted masculinity (the 'fallen pole', like Philoctetes' wounded foot, is an image of impotence) and a crisis that goes to the heart of Johnny's selfhood: this brilliant scholar is finding it difficult to recollect a familiar text. '*Withered*' also recalls Enobarbus' description of Cleopatra – 'Age cannot wither her, nor custom stale / Her infinite variety' (2.2.245–6) – a line echoed in Laurence Binyon's well-known war poem 'For the Fallen' (1914), a text that urges due appreciation of those fallen in battle.[89] These intertexts resonate poignantly with Johnny's own specific circumstances, particularly as Cleopatra's grief and devotion make a stark contrast with the actions of the shallow Phyllis. Johnny's erasure of the quotations is telling: he is unable to face the writing on the wall.

The debate as to Johnny's future in Lambscot comes to a head in the trial. This takes place because he has assaulted Phyllis's new husband, Bob Slater, during the VE Day celebrations. Johnny's arrival at the VE Day dance emphasizes his status as *xenos*: people become aware of 'a tall and dreadfully pale young man with a lock of red gold hair loose on his forehead', who stands 'like a reproachful ghost', 'unsmiling, contemptuous and haggard', 'pale as death' (137). He is 'recognized' – that is, known – as 'the lost captain who had been given up for dead, but had come back from the other side of the grave and had scarcely as yet found himself a place among the living' (137), a fearful revenant who lacks proper 'place' and evokes terror ('I'd be

---

[88] There is also a possible etymological link between Johnny Crowe and Antony. A few lines earlier in this scene, Cleopatra laments that 'The crown o' the earth doth melt' (4.15.63). The Latin for 'crown', *corona*, is the same as the Greek for crow, κορωνίς (coronis).

[89] 'Age shall not wither them, nor the years condemn' (Laurence Binyon, 'For the Fallen' (1914), *The Oxford Book of War Poetry*, ed. Jon Stallworthy (Oxford: Oxford University Press, 2003), 209).

frit to death to meet a chap like that after dark' (137)). After some remarkably thoughtless remarks by Phyllis, Johnny 'turn[s]' on her, telling her 'to keep off, to keep away, to let him alone' (139). Bob Slater intervenes with the words 'Leave my wife alone, you've no business to come in here and frighten her' (139), positioning Johnny as outsider, intruder, one who mistreats women. It is at this point Johnny flies at him, and injures him in the ensuing fight. Now violent, he is explicitly a threat to the public peace in Lambscot; he has become inhospitable himself – Derrida's 'invasion by the worst'.

As the village magistrates debate the case, Ashton portrays a spectrum of attitudes towards this threat. Mrs Drake is of the opinion that 'You can't have a young man like Johnny running loose about the country, thinking he can murder anybody who gets in his way, just because he's been in the army' (164–5). Another magistrate, Tom Wheeler, concurs: 'I'm afraid these young soldiers will give us a lot of trouble when they starts coming back [...] a lot of wild young chaps cramfull of good food and drink, better than many of them had ever had in their lives, all being taught how to fight and all running round looking for trouble' (165). These comments – exaggerating Johnny's conduct – make the stereotypical connection between military experience and (sexual) violence on arrival home. Wheeler is also concerned about returning soldiers' expectations: 'Before we can turn round we shall have 'em all trooping back again, hundreds and thousands of 'em, all wanting one thing or another; wives and families, jobs and houses, everything they had before and better' (165) 'Well, haven't they earned it?' retorts another magistrate, Alfred Bunting. Bunting, himself a veteran, makes a case for public gratitude towards veterans and, perhaps even more importantly, public understanding: 'I said to myself, this young chap's been off fighting for the rest of us; 'tisn't his fault that he was out of a lot of it through being wounded and in hiding. He was treated badly while he was away and it's not for me to start taking sides against him before I've heard the whole story' (165). At the trial itself, Johnny listens carefully, seeming 'as much interested as anybody in hearing what had happened' (221). 'What had happened' is shorthand for 'what people think of him' or 'who he is', for, in casting him as criminal or innocent, this is essentially what the trial will determine. The closing speech of Johnny's defence counsel goes beyond requesting a verdict of 'not guilty' to assert his ongoing worth to society. Describing him as 'a man of the highest possible character who has fought and suffered for his country, that is for you and me and everyone in this court' (250), the barrister asks the jury to let Johnny 'resume the position of responsibility and trust in his university which he gave up at his country's call, and at so much cost to himself'

(251). Johnny is more than socially 'useful' in this description: he is a brilliantly talented, unique asset to society, who has already performed great service to his community and country.

The verdict – not guilty – gives Johnny the benefit of the doubt, setting him free to return to his Oxford fellowship. It endorses a vision of social usefulness in which a damaged member of a community is recuperated from his status as delinquent and given public recognition of his talents. But it also ensures that the *xenos* is expelled from the immediate community and assigned to a life of scholarship – a species of withdrawal from the world.[90] Lambscot has protected itself even as it has validated its son. Conditional hospitality, which would have made Johnny feel at home in the village, has been eschewed. Though at one level, the Captain's trial is about what is expected of veterans and civilians, at another level, it concerns the extent to which such hospitality can cope with the marginalized and the potentially dangerous. The theme continues in the next novels to be discussed – Nigel Balchin's *Mine Own Executioner* (1945) and *A Sort of Traitors* (1949), J. B. Priestley's *Three Men in New Suits* (1945) and Robert Henriques's *The Journey Home* (1944) – with the veteran representing an ever greater threat to social order, becoming the focus of fears about nonconformity, dissent, violence and even revolution.

## Inhospitable: Nigel Balchin's *Mine Own Executioner* (1945)

Before the Second World War, Nigel Balchin, a Cambridge Natural Sciences graduate, worked for the National Institute of Industrial Psychology. He joined the War Office as a psychologist in its personnel section in 1941 and became deputy scientific adviser to the army council, attaining the rank of brigadier.[91] *Mine Own Executioner* has been accurately described

---

[90] That the community determines Johnny's future brings to mind Jerrold Seigel's interpretation of the French Revolution. Seigel identifies a revolutionary impulse to 'remake' or 'reform' or 'regenerate' individuals (*The Idea of the Self: Thought and Experience in Western Europe since the Seventeenth Century* (Cambridge: Cambridge University Press, 2005), 248–9). In the 'liberal' vision, this could be achieved 'as a spontaneous consequence of the Revolution's break with the past' – 'simply living through so great and powerful an event would transform people's sense of themselves' (249). In the 'radical or Jacobin' vision, the remaking would be by means of education, linguistic reform and propaganda, 'as well as participation in public ceremonies and rituals and, even, for the most dedicated or desperate, terror' (249). Lambscot's vision for Johnny is far less radical, but it demonstrates a similar belief in the right of the community to determine an individual's rehabilitation.

[91] Balchin also acted as a consultant to the confectioners J. S. Rowntree and Son where, among other things, he advised on how to increase the appeal of different chocolate products to consumers. He claimed 'to be largely responsible for the marketing success of the Aero and Kit Kat chocolate bars'.

as a 'popular primer on psychoanalysis'.[92] Here, though, I want to resist a psychoanalytic reading of the returned veteran, except to the extent that the notion of repressed trauma that needs to be expelled to ensure mental well-being – 'I reckon there's something there that the boy Adam's got to get out of his system' (45)[93] – resembles the veteran's own perceived position in society: a 'foreign body' whose continued presence is an irritant. The two main male protagonists – Felix Milne and Adam Lucian – have both served in the military in the Second World War. Lucian was a pilot, tortured as a prisoner of war by the Japanese in Burma; Milne, his psychoanalyst, was a gunner. This is a postwar society in which the veteran is a familiar, if not entirely trusted, figure. In the jeweller's shop from which Lucian has stolen a gold cigarette case, Milne tells the manager that the thief is a 'war case' (104): ' "Ah," said the manager, as though that made everything clear. "A war case." He wrote that down' (104). This and the manager's later comment – 'a war case. A man who is affected by his war experiences – You know what I mean?' (104) – indicates that 'a war case' is viewed with certain assumptions, fear, mystification and only limited knowledge. The adenoidal young man working at the jeweller's (medically unfit for service himself?) listens to the conversation with 'mingled horror and awe' (105). The contrast between the two cases (the war case and the cigarette case) is instructive. Milne tells Lucian's wife Mollie, 'I wanted him to talk about the case – meaning himself. So he brought me another sort of case – a gold one – and tried very hard to get me to let him talk about that instead' (107): an instance of Freudian displacement (notably Milne offers his cigarette case to his wife Patricia, too (212)). While the cigarette case is valuable in economic terms ('The case is a very valuable case [...] That's why it's made of gold' (102)) and has a functional use, it is difficult to say the same of the war case in the postwar society the novel depicts. (The image reprises the negative 'cash-on-delivery' and 'scrap of paper' self-evaluations of Andrew Peirse in *On the Side of the Angels* and Johnny Crowe in *The Captain Comes Home*.)

　　Milne proceeds to analyse Lucian in terms of traumatic repression, explaining that 'things which have been shoved out of sight haven't

---

Balchin's daughter is the child psychologist Penelope Leach (Peter Rowland, 'Balchin, Nigel Marlin (1908–1970)', *Oxford Dictionary of National Biography* (Oxford University Press, 2004), online edition).

[92]　Gill Plain, *Literature of the 1940s: War, Postwar and 'Peace'* (Edinburgh: Edinburgh University Press, 2013), 188.

[93]　Nigel Balchin, *Mine Own Executioner* [1945] (London: The Reprint Society, 1947). Page references are given in the text.

really gone' but merely 'pushed' into the sub-conscious mind. He elaborates: '[U]nfortunately they have a habit of making trouble. [...] they set up a sort of pressure – raise a sort of mental blister. It may take all sorts of forms – hysterical paralysis, or headaches, or hatred of being in a confined space – all sorts of oddities' (50). Here, Milne might be describing the stereotypical view of the veteran: a 'blister' on society, 'making trouble'. In Lucian's case, he adds that 'the root of the trouble' is 'something which happened when he was a small boy' (50). Gill Plain reads this hint of 'pre-existing susceptibility' as a 'culturally reassuring suggestion' that Lucian's breakdown – he has tried to strangle his wife – is 'not the logical outcome of war' but the product of 'exceptional circumstances', the assumption being that 'he was weak anyway'.[94] The idea of pre-combat trauma has been a contentious one as it can be invoked to diminish the liability of military and government authorities for psychiatric war casualties. Nonetheless, it seems to have psychological validity. The psychiatrist Jonathan Shay – not a person to side with the military powers-that-be against the veteran – notes that many veterans suffering from post-traumatic stress disorder also experienced rape, abuse and neglect in childhood or adolescence.[95] Shay proposes as a figure for this the wound Odysseus received from a boar in his youth: the resulting scar he bears on his thigh (the means by which Eurycleia recognizes him, and so a key part of his identity) is a reminder of the 'interconnection between childhood trauma, combat trauma and a veteran's adult character'.[96] In literary terms, this interconnection reinforces the veteran's potency as a figure of outsiderness: multiply victimized, he is feared and ostracized as victims are.

That Milne, as well as Lucian, suffers from a 'mental blister' is made clear in the novel. 'I've got a certain amount of reason for thinking there is something funny,' he tells his wife, Patricia, 'Loewe dug up quite a lot of it when I was in Vienna' (171). His identification of headaches as a symptom of buried trauma makes it noteworthy that he experiences them himself, and his most significant headache is the one that prevents him from recalling Lucian, so allowing Lucian to kill Mollie. Milne 'saw clearly for a moment through a gap in his headache and went quickly towards the door. But the throbbing veil closed again,' writes Balchin (182). The point is reiterated: 'I had a headache and I looked through my fingers and let him go' (203); 'he had stood and looked through his fingers and let Lucian go [...] He had

94  Plain, *Literature of the 1940s*, 189.
95  Shay, *Odysseus in America*, 142.
96  Ibid., 144.

a headache and that killed Mollie' (211). The language used here suggests that, in some way, Milne's vision of Lucian is restricted. When he sees 'clearly', he is able to read Lucian accurately. But clarity is achieved only in fleeting glimpses and the partiality of Milne's vision is self-imposed (he looks through his fingers). The effect resembles the moment in Miller's *On the Side of the Angels* when Neil Herriot's true identity becomes visible for an instant: there is a sense in which Lucian, too, is a double figure, aspects of whom come into view only intermittently.

Milne's treatment method is to attempt to oust the trauma with the aid of the 'truth drug' sodium pentothal.[97] Under the influence of this drug, Lucian reveals that, under torture, he divulged crucial information to the Japanese:

> Lucian's voice rose suddenly to a shriek. 'The whole bloody lot. I told them everything I knew and what I didn't know I made up. Everything. Everything the little runt asked. I poured it out. Sometimes I told him without his asking me. About locations, about 'planes, about training –' His body stiffened and rose for a moment, a taut bow between his shoulders and heels. Then he collapsed suddenly and fell back sobbing, with his head buried in his cushions.
>
> (147)

The moment is presented as climactic; the arching of Lucian's body (which, incidentally, mimics the bow with which Odysseus' masculinity is tested, as well as Philoctetes' magical weapon) suggests an exorcism. The description of an outpouring releases something else in him. Fear that he has talked too much has rendered a veteran unable to talk about his experiences.[98] But now, in Milne's words, 'the whole thing's just a story [...] like the things that happened to you at school' (149). The incident, that is, can now be repeatedly and safely retold, though the descriptor 'like the things that happened to you at school', indicating further possibilities of adolescent trauma, is a dark hint that such retellings may not be unproblematic. The fact of having betrayed his comrades reinforces the impression of Lucian as an outsider, one who has breached social trust, and this sense of incompatibility with social norms continues to be apparent in his thefts of the

---

[97] On Milne's use of this drug, see Victoria Stewart, *Narratives of Memory: British Writing of the 1940s* (Basingstoke: Palgrave Macmillan, 2006), 145–6. Gilbert Frankau's 1948 novel *Michael's Wife* also portrays scenes in which a veteran re-lives a traumatic war experience by means of narcoanalysis.

[98] There is a striking resonance with Lucian's experience later in the novel when Milne meets with a policeman after Lucian's suicide: 'Milne met his eyes and realised with a sudden shock that he mustn't talk – mustn't say things. He shook his head doubtfully and did not reply' (203). Jack Aistrop's 1949 novel *Pretend I Am A Stranger* also features a veteran muted by the subconscious realization that he has talked too much.

cigarette case and of Milne's walking stick, his lateness for appointments, his eccentric behaviour, his attempted and eventual actual murder of his wife and his suicide. In Kantian and Habermasian terms, Lucian is inhospitable to the society in which he is a 'visitor'. But equally as important – if not more important – as what Lucian divulges under the sodium pentothal is what its administration reveals about Milne.

The drug is supposed only to be given to patients 'under medical supervision' and, as Milne tells Mrs Lucian, 'not being a doctor, I can't go pushing drugs into people' (110). This comment takes the reader back to the opening scene of the novel in which, as an undergraduate at Cambridge, Milne goes to consult the 'University Lecturer in Abnormal Psychology', Dr Field, about the appropriate path to his desired career of analyst (7) (he asks Field to advise about his field). Given his limited financial resources, should he follow his two years in physiology, anatomy and chemistry by qualifying as a medical doctor or spend the equivalent time gaining experience in a psychiatric clinic? Field is in no doubt: 'If you don't qualify first you'll be a quack' (10). Milne, unconvinced, retorts, 'surely a quack is simply somebody who practises without a medical degree? It's purely a conventional difference, isn't it?' (10). Milne's choice – he goes to Vienna to work in the clinic of the lionized Dr Loewe – is the equivalent of what he terms a 'mental blister' in both the novel and his career. Having made the decision not to take a medical degree, he becomes a professional misfit: highly regarded, but always viewed with some suspicion.

Milne is as much a *xenos* as Lucian, that is.[99] Two scenes highlight his status. The first is when a doctor, Sir George Freestone, comes to inspect the clinic in which he works. Milne has been discussing the administration of mepacrine with obvious professional expertise when the following exchange occurs:

> 'But you were in the war, I take it?'
> 'Yes, I was a gunner.'
> 'A gunner?' said Freestone, frowning.
> 'Yes.'
> 'But how did you manage that? No doctor – '
> Milne said, 'I'm not a doctor.'
> 'You mean – ?'
>
> (133)

---

[99] A contemporary reviewer in the *Irish Times* caustically compared Milne with the protagonist of Balchin's earlier novel, *The Small Back Room* (1943), who, like Philoctetes, had been wounded in the foot: 'the strong implication is that if the one had a foot and the other a degree, they would be no happier' (Anonymous, 'The Analyst Analysed', *The Irish Times* (10 November 1945), 2).

The dialogue exposes Milne as both the wrong kind of veteran and the wrong kind of practitioner. His colleague, Garsten, who *is* medically qualified, comes to his assistance – 'it means we have got at least one man who knows the job from A to Z and isn't just a G. P. messing about with things he doesn't understand' (133) – but it is clear that Sir George's reaction is solidly one of mistrust and rejection. He is professionally inhospitable to Milne.

The second scene in which Milne's outsider status comes under the spotlight is during the inquest into Lucian's suicide. The exchange with the coroner goes as follows:

> 'You're a psycho-analyst or a psychiatrist or some sort of
>      consultant on mental trouble?'
> 'Yes. I'm an analyst.'
> 'You're not medically qualified?'
> 'No.'
> 'In fact you're a – a – ?'
> 'I'm a quack,' said Milne stonily.

The coroner looked at him unsmilingly. 'Well, you said it. I didn't. I was going to say a lay practitioner. Anyhow, people consult you and you treat them?'

(234)

In terms of social identity, this is a crucial moment. Like Johnny Crowe, Milne is (if not in an official sense) on trial. He is being asked to identify and define himself publicly, on oath. Though not explicitly interpellated as such, he nonetheless names himself a 'quack', a medical impostor. Here he is not so much expressing his own view – in his conversation with Dr Field, he described the possession of a medical degree as 'purely a conventional difference' and he has obtained for himself the best training in psychoanalysis available – as voicing the view society (professional and public) holds of him. Garsten again comes to his aid – 'I would certainly not presume to supervise the work of Mr. Milne, who is one of the finest clinicians in London' (240) – but the coroner's prejudices, representing those of the public, are reiterated in his summing up:

The public ought to know and – and professional men ought to know, that mental disease, or the symptoms of it, is a thing to take very seriously, or there may be tragedy, as there was here. As soon as there's the least suspicion of it – most highly qualified advice at the earliest possible moment. Only safe way. That needs to be more widely realised.

(243)

The words, albeit without naming him, cast Milne as a pretender. What is surprising is his reaction not to this but to Garsten's intervention. 'You're all the same,' he tells him outside the court. 'Some of you are good doctors and some of you are bad doctors, but you're all doctors. […] I don't believe in Wimpole Street addresses and sponge-bag trousers and a professional manner. […] And I don't believe in it any more when it plays on my side than when it plays on the other' (246). For Milne, the accoutrements of the medical profession amount to imposture, a paradoxical stance given that the authorities of that profession view him as an impostor: reciprocal inhospitability. His refusal to conform with professional standards – not because he could not meet them, but because he wished to exceed them – renders him an irritant, a 'blister'. As both veteran and quack – personally and professionally a *xenos* – he cannot be accommodated by conditional hospitality.

## Malign: Nigel Balchin's *A Sort of Traitors* (1949)

In *A Sort of Traitors*, which draws on the author's wartime experience at the Ministry of Food and department of the Scientific Adviser to the Army Council,[100] Balchin goes even further in his depiction of the veteran as a 'blister' in society, acting and being treated with inhospitality in Kantian and Habermasian terms. Captain Ivor Gates describes himself as 'one of the Irishmen who said, "We may be neutral but who are we neutral *against*?"' (138).[101] He volunteered for the army, he continues, only for the RAF to blow his arms off 'just to show how grateful they were' (138). The comment casts his war injuries as the result of an act of ingratitude, as though a gift has been met, not with appropriate acceptance and proper treatment, but with indifference and carelessness. Britain, that is, has been inhospitable to Ivor and he now responds in kind, manipulating young Marriott into betraying his country and his research institution. Balchin depicts Ivor as loathsome, inducing feelings of unease, even queasiness, like the infected flies that Marriot agrees to have feed on his arm in the interests of scientific research (Marriott, like Ivor, is, in a sense, giving up his arms for a greater cause).[102]

---

[100] Clive James, *At the Pillars of Hercules* (London: Picador, 1979), 140, 141.

[101] Nigel Balchin, *A Sort of Traitors* (London: Collins, 1949). Page references are given in the text.

[102] I can't resist quoting Clive James's description of Ivor: 'a combination of Jake in *The Sun Also Rises* and John Cleese playing an armless subaltern in a *Monty Python* sketch' (*At the Pillars of Hercules*, 149).

This veteran, then, is portrayed not as heroic but abusive, despite his great sacrifices. In a key scene involving Ivor and his girlfriend, Lucy, Balchin builds up a sense of threat as Lucy reads the body language that indicates that Ivor is working up to an emotional outburst. When Ivor complains that reading the newspaper is boring, she can see 'what is coming' but nonetheless reminds him that he can turn over the pages: 'He smiled at her brightly and said, "No. I'm afraid I've lost both my arms. The left one is gone as you see, and if you look closely you will see that this one on the right is artificial"' (28). Ivor's 'smile', as the reader is learning, is a sign of danger, while the comments, needlessly reminding Lucy of what she already knows, aggressively force her to focus on the fact of his disabil-ities. When Lucy tells Ivor that Marriott has suggested that she go to the pictures with him and 'hold hands', Ivor responds with:

> 'And what a pleasant change for you to have a hand to hold.' He waited for a moment and then said in an odd, brittle voice, 'I said, "What a pleasant change for you to have a hand to hold." That was quite a good joke. When I make as good a joke as that you might laugh. [...] Because after all,' said Ivor rather breathlessly, 'a man who's got hands – two real hands – can do a lot of things with them besides hold yours. Even in a comparatively public place like the back of a cinema, for example, he can ...' He was breathing very hard now. 'And of course you want these things, don't you, darling?' (29)

This is an emotionally violent speech, full of anger, reiterating the uncomfort-able fact of his lack of hands, attempting to manipulate reactions and induce guilt. Notably, it also carries a sexual charge, relating bodily wholeness to sexual prowess and imputing sexual desire to Lucy, desire that Ivor purports to treat as natural and acceptable ('And of course you want these things, don't you, darling?') but that tone and context turn into a form of betrayal.

The maimed Ivor is associated not only with impotence in the novel but also with a sexuality presented as nauseating. Ivor delights in drawing attention to his own disabilities, requesting assistance that involves phys-ical intimacy with him or inviting others to imagine his body, including his body in the act of having sex – to Marriott an 'unspeakable vision' (138). Putting a cigarette between Ivor's lips feels 'peculiarly unpleasant' to Marriott (114); when Ivor asks him to throw the cigarette away – 'It's a wicked waste but I can't smoke more than half, or the smoke gets in my eyes'[103] – he takes the opportunity to tell Marriott that 'sexual

---

[103] The song 'Smoke Gets in Your Eyes' was written by Jerome Kern (music) and Otto Harbach (lyrics) in 1933 for their musical *Roberta*. The sultry number concerns the authenticity of feelings of love.

competition should be open and completely rational': 'I realise that I, who am sick and damaged, can't hope to compete with you, who are fit and whole' (116). Ivor's studied helplessness, his forced intimacies, his 'caressing smile' (117), his 'horrifyingly light' body (118–19) induce in Marriott 'a queer feeling in his stomach' that reminds him of 'seasickness' (117). These traits are summed up in Ivor's 'odd, intimate, feminine smile' (166): his loathsomeness is a matter of his being neither fully human nor fully male. In this portrayal, inhospitality has become malignancy.

And this is a veteran who is violent in intention. The loss of his arms means that it is virtually impossible for Ivor to inflict physical harm – there is an armless/harmless equation, which plays on the double meaning of 'arms' – but he explicitly states his desire to hurt Lucy: 'I can't hurt her physically. Often I should if I could' (118); 'You bullying little bitch. If I had the use of my hands you'd think twice before you spoke to me like that' (161). Nonetheless, he 'give[s] her hell' (118) with his carefully calibrated psychological cruelty. The depiction of Ivor feeds in to the novel's treatment of social responsibility. Marriott, who believes that, as a scientist, he has a responsibility 'to blueprint the future of civilisation' (51), considers that Lucy's looking after Ivor is 'all wrong [...] it's sacrificing a fit, useful member of society for a – a person of no social value' (50). Viewed as an economic contributor, Ivor is, indeed, of no – or even negative – value, but his characterization forces the question of whether his social value would be seen differently if he were *nicer*. His war service may have qualified Ivor for the role of hero/victim, but Balchin ensures that, loathsome, sociopathic and traitorous as he is, such status is obliterated and this veteran is a festering sore in society. The situation has gone beyond the threat posed by the likes of Neil Herriot and Johnny Crowe; the 'worst' has invaded. Though Balchin explicitly excludes the possibility in Ivor's case, the obvious cause for concern is that ex-servicemen in such circumstances have the potential to overthrow the social order entirely. This potential is imaginatively realized in the next two texts for discussion.

### The Veteran as Demagogue: J. B. Priestley's *Three Men in New Suits* (1945) and Robert Henriques's *The Journey Home* (1944)

In 1945, J. B. Priestley published what was very nearly a call to arms. In a pamphlet entitled *Letter to a Returning Serviceman*, described by Maggie

Gale as having a 'Marxist flavour',[104] he advised the recipient – an imaginary Second World War veteran called 'Robert' – 'to be a real citizen and not a hermit in a bungalow'.[105] Basing his authority on his own combat service in the First World War – 'I spent nearly five years in the infantry, was three times a casualty, and saw the flower of my generation mown down among the barbed wire' (3) – Priestley tells Robert that, postwar, a 'citizen-soldier' is split into a 'red half' and a 'blue half' (4). The red half wants 'to re-organise society' and the blue half wants 'privacy and a domestic life' (4). 'Last time,' Priestley continues, the red half 'lost completely': the returning soldiers of 1914–18, that is, were let down by the promises of '[t]he politicians and most of the Press' (4). Now, Priestley advocates the nationalization of industry, attacks the press barons and urges the English to refuse 'once and for all to be bullied by highly organized little gangs of teetotalers, Sabbatarians, and all the unloved and the life-haters' (20). The *Letter* is whimsical. But Priestley shrewdly spotted the potential for activism among returning veterans, angry, traumatized, promised much, high in expectations, used to fighting. In such terms, individually and collectively, since ancient times, have demobilized soldiers excited society's deepest fears.

Priestley explores the revolutionary potential of the demobbed at greater length in his novel *Three Men in New Suits.* The three are Alan Strete (in a blue suit), Herbert Kenford (in grey) and Eddie Mold (in brown), all returning to the village of Lambury after war service in the same battalion.[106] Alan's family own Swanford Manor, Herbert's father is a farmer, while Eddie is a former quarry worker: each, therefore, represents a particular social-economic stratum. For Alan, who has acted against class expectations by serving as a non-commissioned sergeant, rather than an officer, homecoming brings a questioning of what this 'remote place' means to him (11)[107] and a growing sense that his people 'can't survive as a class' and 'should stop trying' (164). Herbert is taken aback by civilians' self-interestedness, their ' "Damn you, I'm all right" tack' (105), and feels now that farming is too isolating: 'After a time, if you don't look out, you don't seem to care

---

[104] Maggie B. Gale, *J. B. Priestley* (London: Routledge, 2008), 22.

[105] J. B. Priestley, *Letter to a Returning Serviceman* (London: Home and Van Thal, 1945), 29. Page references are given in the text.

[106] On 'demob suits' see Alan Allport, *Demobbed: Coming Home after the Second World War* (New Haven, CT: Yale University Press, 2009), 118–21. 'Lambury', like Ashton's 'Lambscot', has connotations of innocence and sacrifice.

[107] J. B. Priestley, *Three Men in New Suits* (London: William Heinemann, 1945). Page references are given in the text.

what's happening to other people' (109). Eddie returns to a missing wife and a village that, far from expressing gratitude and understanding, is 'stale and ugly, full of slurs and jeers' (64). Lambury's inhospitability will foment reciprocal feelings on the part of all three veterans.

That returning servicemen are being let down is made explicit in the exchanges between Alan and Lord Darrald, owner of the newspaper for which his mother, Lady Strete, wants him to write. Darrald tries to persuade Alan to work for the paper so as to inform its readers about the ranks of the demobilized: 'what are they thinking, what are they talking about, what are they wanting – these fellows who are coming back now?' (86). But it becomes clear that Darrald's aim is to shape, rather than report, veterans' desires, which he summarizes as 'Dog tracks, cheap racing, plenty of football, better movies, good places to eat and drink where they can take their wives, nice holidays' (89). When Alan responds that he thinks that veterans 'want more than that stuff, you know' (89), Darrald is dismissive. His views (reminiscent of those of Tom Wheeler in *The Captain Comes Home*) are echoed by Herbert's father and brother:

> A lot of these chaps you came back with [...] think they're going to ask for this and that – fancy houses, nice easy jobs, plenty of holidays with pay, and so forth – and get 'em served on a plate. But in a few years some of 'em'll be asking where they can emigrate to, never mind whether they get fancy houses and nice easy jobs at the other end or not.
>
> (47)

The assumptions contain a fear that veterans' demands will become excessive. Darrald's strategy is pre-emptive: to smother discontent with racing, football, movies and holidays. But Alan sees more potential in the disappointed expectations and further warns that 'our chaps won't merely threaten trouble, as the last lot did in the early 'Twenties, they'll *make* it' (88, emphasis original).

As the novel closes, the three comrades, their combat experiences and friendship assuaging their class differences, are making plans of action for achieving '[n]ot what suits us best, in our little corner, but what's best for everybody' (158). But whatever they, with others, do must be 'co-operative and communal' (169). Priestley is careful to distinguish this kind of visionary action – which is essentially socialist[108] – from fascism and

---

[108] Priestley was a co-founder in 1942 of the socialist political party Common Wealth. He resigned as chairman after three months (John Baxendale, *Priestley's England: J. B. Priestley and English Culture* (Manchester: Manchester University Press, 2007), 155).

demagoguery, which only lead to 'more wars, more bloody revolutions, and probably more mad dictators' (166). Only having decided this, can they – led by Alan – approach the 'open door' of the Manor and its 'welcome glow' (170). The image is one of hospitality, though it is unclear how long the veteran activists will be able to remain hospitable to their hosts.

In Alan Strete, Priestley portrays a potential leader of veteran activism, though is careful to note the risks of demagoguery. Robert Henriques's *The Journey Home* (published in the United States as *Home Fires Burning*)[109] takes the idea of the veteran demagogue further. Henriques, who had seen service in Egypt and the Sudan from 1926 to 1933, rejoined the Royal Artillery at the start of the Second World War and rose to the rank of Colonel, serving in the Commandos, as a staff Planner at Combined Operations Headquarters and as an adviser to the American General Staff on the landings in North Africa.[110] *The Journey Home* was 'started in North Africa in May 1943', continued 'throughout the Sicilian campaign' and completed 'shortly before D-Day'.[111] As Mark Goldman points out, the novel is based on a 1944 Mass Observation survey of the same title,[112] whose authors warned that '[c]urrent negativism for the future, the *virtual collapse of the idea of inevitable progress*, is not going to be easily remedied'.[113] Like the survey, the novel is pre-emptive, opening with a scene on board a troopship returning veterans from the Mediterranean theatre. Unusually, the veteran depicted is a woman: Jane, an army nurse. Jane is placed on an equal footing with the male veterans in the novel: 'I'm […] a soldier' she thinks 'with joy' (84), and she has combat memories of '[t]he shaft of African sunlight, the blown dust, the faint cordite smell' (97).[114] The potential demogogue is her fiancé, Brigadier David Sloane, '[s]oldier, explorer, poet, author ... Elizabethan' (5), one of few 'with the gift of speech and the gift of action', a 'natural leader of men' (6). Jane's homecoming is a return to see David, who has sustained a head injury.

[109] Mark Goldman, 'Robert Henriques, *The Journey Home*', *Modern Language Stdies*, 21.1 (Winter 1991), 22–36: 22.

[110] Ibid., 22.

[111] Robert Henriques, *From a Biography of Myself: A Posthumous Selection of the Autobiographical Writings of Robert Henriques* (London: Secker and Warburg, 1969), xii; quoted in Goldman, 'Robert Henriques, *The Journey Home*', 22.

[112] Ibid., 35 n1.

[113] Anonymous, *The Journey Home: A Report Prepared by Mass-Observation for the Advertising Service Guild*, 'Change' Wartime Surveys (London: John Murray, 1944), 13. A copy of this report is among Henriques's papers at the University of Reading

[114] Robert Henriques, *The Journey Home* (London: William Heinemann, 1944). Page references are given in the text.

Henriques delays David's entry to the novel, building up the reader's anticipation and apprehension as well as Jane's (just how bad will his head injury be?) and creating expectations of a messianic figure with references to a 'vast multitude, lacking what they need, looking for a Christ' (6). Before they are reunited, Jane must visit the brain specialist who has been treating David. The doctor emphasizes the fact that David will have changed: 'A person in this state may appear to be living a new life; or he may discard a part of his old life, lose old interests' (19). Combat service has wrought qualitative change. From London, Jane travels to the village in the valley where she and David have their homes, meeting a quartet of returning ex-servicemen en route. Two scenes with these men drama-tize the significance of hospitality in the context of mass demobilization. On a crowded train, a civilian objects to the ex-soldiers' occupation of a carriage: '"You're in a civilised country now," he said, "a civilised country, see? You've got to behave, see, got to behave. You can't go on behaving like this, as if you'd bought the train. We've all a right to get ourself a seat. You can't go keeping a whole carriage. You can't do that sort of thing"' (102–3). The repeated reference to 'a civilised country' hints at the civilian's view of the veterans as barbarous, other. As a contemporary review of Henriques's novel put it, 'it is as if Penelope had turned a hard and hostile mask to greet the returning Odysseus'.[115] The civilian passenger's speech induces the following reaction in Charlie, one of the ex-servicemen: 'Charlie stood quivering, his mouth half open, his eyes contracted, his hands to his head. This was a stage closer to lunacy, the twisted grin and the far gaze. The muscles of his limbs were tensed, knees slightly bent, elbows pressed to his side, forearms raised, hands half-open. He was like a wild beast, prisoned but beyond fear' (104). The description, with its references to lunacy and savagery, resonates with the civilian's fears. The exchange is in stark con-trast to the behaviour of the veterans at Swincot, where they change trains. The platform is freezing cold – 'the spine of the world where all the winds meet' (110) – but the porter insists that the waiting room is closed for the night. The veterans break the door down, make a fire using the wooden table and invite in women and children. In the face of inhospitality – 'This is England [...] our England that they don't want to let us into' (149) – the men both exhibit hospitality, making others at home, and demonstrate group resourcefulness.

The veterans' political potential is discussed by Jane, first with David's brother Robert and finally with David himself. Robert, always less

---

[115] Lionel Hale, 'Soldiers Come Home', *The Observer* (10 December 1944), 3.

visionary and charismatic than his brother, has a new job 'talking and writing', putting forward in the press and on the radio propaganda for the government's 'National Reconstruction' (33). As he describes it to Jane, he is speaking to a 'few million men', men 'in uniform, coming back to their dreams', men 'who cry for the stars, for a new world, for dreams come true; not hoping, mind you; sure that their cry won't be answered, but yet determined to ... get something' (35). As 'the mouthpiece of *They*', Robert must 'tell those men the things that *They* says those men are to hear', 'tempt and entice' them on 'the road that *They* calls prosperity – and peace' (35). The brief is very similar to that offered to Alan Strete by Lord Darrald: not so much to meet as to shape and contain veterans' demands. Robert has more sympathy with the veteran he heard calling for 'a Soldiers' Party with their own leaders' (57)[116] and notes the revolutionary potential of all these men '[b]anded together' against 'their *They*, against the official idol, the remote, painted, grinning idol who caused a drought on their lives, tormented their women, starved their widows and orphans, kicked them across the oceans and deserts' (62). When it comes to a key radio broadcast, instead of delivering *They*'s propaganda, he speaks of *They* as 'the common foe of the common man' (185) and is cut off in mid-flow. At the end of the novel, it is David who, as expected, assumes the mantle of leadership, announcing his intention to go to London and serve the Soldiers' Party as one of a council of five and describing his vision of '[m]illions of men already organised [...] already enrolled in a great company, bound by common experience, common understanding, and a common way of thought' (207).

But this revolutionary vision is not universally appealing to the listening veterans. One of them, Ginger, protests: ' "'Ere [...] 'old on a minute. March, you said? Parades? Lining the streets? No more of that for me." He rose from the sofa, wrathful, indignant. "You know what *that* is?" he said. "You know what they called *that* – the 'Uns and the Wops? Fascism – that's what they called it! We don't want none of that 'ere" ' (208). The warning is the same as that in *Three Men in New Suits*. It is possible to interpret Ginger's concern as a wish not to be inhospitable. Quietly, the novel endorses his ideals in a series of domestic settings. As the just-quoted passage reveals, he makes his intervention when sitting on a sofa in David's grand house. The discussion has been reasoned and courteous: the veteran 'guests' have behaved with propriety. It is notable, too, that Jane invites

---

[116] Goldman notes that the 'only real new party' to emerge during the war was Priestley's Common Wealth (Goldman, 'Robert Henriques, *The Journey Home*', 35 n16).

the four soldiers to her own home – 'Beds, sheets, baths now and again I suppose. A roof ... [...] This is strange language to us, the roofless men' (122) – and that David explicitly instructs her not to come to his. David and his revolutionary ideas are inhospitable, while the veterans 'carry their home with them' (175). They are the hospitable ones, Henriques suggests, but a lack of proper welcome could easily alter all that.


## Conclusion

Postwar, the question of the hospitality that can and should be afforded to demobilized veterans is one of the highest political importance, not least because it affects future recruitment and national defence. But the novels discussed in this chapter have wider implications for the status and treatment of other displaced or marginal figures in a host society, since they reveal what communities perceive to be threatening and how they react to such perceived threats. An unnerving combination of familiarity and strangeness, the homecoming veteran in fiction raises questions regarding the endurance of the self over time and requires both self and communal ongoing definition. This strains hospitality on both sides to its limits. The *xenos* may appear to be contained, but remains a potential breach in the social order, testing capacities of respect and trust.

# CHAPTER 3

# *Problem-Solving*

## *Odyssey* 3: Scarred

On his return to Ithaca, a number of people close to Odysseus fail to recognize him on first meeting. Indeed, two of the closest, his wife Penelope and his father Laertes, demand that he *prove* that he is who he claims to be. That a returning war veteran should be challenged, tried and tested is no surprise: as discussed in the previous chapter, such trials serve not only to establish an individual's identity but also to fix his role within the social group. But for the purposes of this chapter, whose concerns are epistemological, heuristic and pedagogical, what is significant is not the nature of the identity that is constructed in these testing processes, but the questions that arise regarding different kinds of knowledge and different ways of acquiring them.

One of the proofs that Odysseus offers his doubters is a scar on his thigh, acquired when he was gored by a boar while out hunting as a boy with the sons of Autolycus (19.393f). This scar is the means by which his old wet nurse, Eurycleia, identifies him as she is washing his feet. Eurycleia not only recognizes the scar visually but also remembers the 'feel' of it as she passes her hands over her erstwhile master's legs (19.468).[1] Later, when Odysseus has revealed himself to his father and Laertes has asked for 'some definite proof to make me sure' (24.329), the scar is displayed again. On seeing it, Laertes acknowledges immediately 'that Odysseus' evidence had proved his claim' (24.326).

The scar of Odysseus has assumed paradigmatic status in the history of poetics, beginning with Aristotle citing Eurycleia's identification as the archetype for recognition by a sign on the body acquired after

---

[1] Eurycleia's account of the scar is not sufficient to convince Penelope. After all, Penelope has not seen the scar with her own eyes, and, after entertaining numbers of unwanted suitors for the past twenty years, she is cautious. Her own test, which turns on Odysseus being privy to the fact that he built their bed-post from an olive tree, is epistemologically cognate with the proof of the scar.

birth.[2] In Erich Auerbach's *Mimesis* (1953), in the introductory chapter entitled 'Odysseus' Scar', the story of the boar hunt stands for nothing less than an entire literary tradition: the Hellenistic style which, in contrast to Hebraic Old Testament narrative, 'knows only a foreground, only a uniformly illuminated, uniformly objective present'.[3] In Terence Cave's *Recognitions* (1988), in another section entitled 'Odysseus' Scar', the mark is designated, following Aristotle, 'an archetypal sign of recognition'.[4] And recognition or *anagnorisis* brings about 'a shift in ignorance to knowledge'.[5]

It is a very specific kind of knowledge. Eurycleia and Laertes reach informed belief through a process of observing physical evidence and making a logical inference from it. It is *just* possible that their inference is incorrect – it is not impossible, though it is extremely unlikely, that another person has an identical scar – but chances of this are vanishingly small and may be dismissed on a rational basis of probability. Both characters can accept that Odysseus is who he says he is because the fact that Odysseus has a scar of a certain shape on his thigh is propositional knowledge (based on earlier empirical observation) and they now see a scar of the same shape on the stranger's thigh with their own eyes and, in Eurycleia's case, feel it with her own hands. Though they are a long way from the methodologies pioneered by Francis Bacon, René Descartes and others during the scientific revolution and developed through the Enlightenment, some three millennia earlier Eurycleia and Laertes are nonetheless shown as drawing on empiricism and logic to form conclusions.

But this is not the only kind of knowledge or way of acquiring knowledge represented in the *Odyssey*. Another kind associated with the Scarred One is that encapsulated in the other epithets with which he is garlanded:[6] *polytropos* (much-turned, i.e. much-travelled), *polymetis* (of many counsels) and *polymechanos* (resourceful, inventive). This collocation of qualities indicates a wisdom concerning human nature and practical affairs comprised of the insight gained from wide travel, encounters with many

[2] Aristotle, 'Poetics', trans. Stephen Halliwell, *Aristotle. Poetics; Longinus on the Sublime; Demetrius On Style*, Loeb Classical Library (Cambridge, MA: Harvard University Press, 1995), 16.

[3] Erich Auerbach, *Mimesis: The Representation of Reality in Western Literature* (Princeton, NJ: Princeton University Press, 1953), 7.

[4] Terence Cave, *Recognitions: A Study in Poetics* (Oxford: The Clarendon Press, 1988), 39.

[5] Ibid., 1.

[6] Odysseus' alternative name 'Ulysses' ('Oulixes' in Greek) derives from the Greek word *oule* ('scar'). Jonathan Shay suggests that, in the 'scar-name' Oulixes or Ulysses, we should hear 'He who was permanently scarred in youth' (Shay, *Odysseus in America: Combat Trauma and the Trials of Homecoming* (New York: Scribner, 2002), 143).

different kinds of people and lengthy suffering. These matters comprise the self-acknowledged subject matter of the *Odyssey*, as is announced in the very first lines:

> The hero of the tale which I beg the Muse to help me tell is that resourceful man who roamed the wide world after he had sacked the holy citadel of Troy. He saw the cities of many peoples and he learnt their ways. He suffered many hardships on the high seas in his struggles to preserve his life and bring his comrades home.
>
> (1.1–5)

That Odysseus is rich in experience and suffering is insisted upon throughout the epic. 'I have had many bitter and shattering experiences in war and on the stormy seas,' he tells Calypso, as he begs to be released from Ogygia (5.223–4). Later, he describes himself to Queen Arete 'as one who has suffered much [...] I have had to live through many a long day of hardship since last I saw my friends' (7.147, 152). He rejects a sporting challenge on the grounds of having 'been through many bitter and exhausting experiences' (8.155). The variety of knowledge that such accumulated experiences give rise to is a complex amalgam of perception, assimilation, reflection and memory rather than observation-based inference. It forms the basis of further intuition or gut feeling. Odysseus acknowledges it explicitly when he says of the Cyclops, 'I knew enough of the world to see through him' (9.281–2).

In the *Odyssey*, such knowledge, dependent upon being conversant with the ways of the world, is, not surprisingly, linked to age. Aegyptius, for example, is described as being both 'bent with years and rich in wisdom' (2.15–16), while Telemachus remarks that Nestor's 'knowledge of men's ways and thoughts is unrivalled' since he has 'been king through three generations' (3.244–5). The reference to multiple generations reveals a pedagogical aspect: this is wisdom that can be handed on – a process that is dramatized in the scene in which Athene, disguised as the aged Mentor, passes the golden cup to the younger Telemachus (3.63). A parental–filial relationship is implied in such mentoring; indeed, Telemachus' acquisition of wisdom is cast in terms of his coming increasingly to resemble his father. 'In saying all you said just now,' Menelaus tells him, 'you spoke and acted with the discretion of a man of twice your years. In fact you show the sense I should have looked for in the son of such a father' (4.204–6).

This kind of 'sense' – astute, discreet, mature – is the fruit of experience, personally acquired over long years or received from elders or those more experienced. As Martin Jay points out, the word 'experience' is derived from the Latin *experientia* (trial, proof, experiment). This etymon reveals the connections not only between experience and scientific method but also between experience and that other Enlightenment achievement, empiricism. Locke's classic precept that '*Experience [...] must teach me, what Reason cannot: and 'tis by trying alone, that I can certainly know*' has a wide range of applications, from the perception of objects to self-understanding to right conduct.[7] Behind *experientia* is also the root *periculum* (danger), which gives another sense of experience as 'having survived risks and learned something from the encounter' or 'a worldliness that has left innocence behind by facing and surmounting the dangers and challenges that life may present'[8] – definitions that might have been formulated with the veteran in mind.

## *Erfahrung*

In the twentieth century, especial pains were taken by Wilhelm Dilthey, Martin Buber and Walter Benjamin, among others, to distinguish between kinds of experience, and in particular, the kinds represented by the German words *Erlebnis* and *Erfahrung*. *Erlebnis*, from the verb *leben* (to live), denotes 'immediate' or 'isolated' experience, as Benjamin put it, while *Erfahrung*, from the verb *fahren* (to travel), signifies cumulative experience 'that accompanies one to the far reaches of time'.[9] *Erlebnis* is experience in the raw, un-reflected upon, while *Erfahrung*, in a tradition that can be traced back to Plato via Kant, Hume, Locke and Augustine, encompasses both outer sense impressions and cognitive judgements about them; in Jay's words, 'a more temporally elongated notion of experience based on a learning process, an integration of discrete moments of experience into a narrative whole or an adventure'.[10] William Godwin demonstrates the idea

---

[7] John Locke, *An Essay Concerning Human Understanding* [1689], ed. Roger Woolhouse (London: Penguin, 1997), 4.12.92; quoted in Martin Jay, *Songs of Experience: Modern American and European Variations on a Universal Theme* (Berkeley, CA: University of California Press, 2004), 38. See further 36–40.

[8] Jay, *Songs of Experience*, 10. Another etymon is the Greek *pathos* (suffering).

[9] Walter Benjamin, 'On Some Motifs in Baudelaire' ('Über einige Motive bei Baudelaire') [1939], trans. Harry Zohn, *Selected Writings. Volume 4: 1938–40*, ed. Michael W. Jennings, Howard Eiland and Gary Smith (Cambridge, MA: The Belknap Press of Harvard University Press, 1999), 313–55: 317, 333, 317, 331. On *Erfahrung* and *Erlebnis*, see also the valuable discussion in Rex Ferguson, *Criminal Law and the Modernist Novel: Experience on Trial* (Cambridge: Cambridge University Press, 2013), particularly 31–7.

[10] Jay, *Songs of Experience*, 11. Paul Grimstad's description of the classical pragmatist view of experience is another helpful characterization of *Erfahrung*: 'an experimental loop of perception, actions, consequences, further perception of consequences, further action, further consequences, and so forth' (*Experience and Experimental Writing: Literary Pragmatism from Emerson to the Jameses* (Oxford: Oxford University Press, 2013), 2).

in *Caleb Williams* (1794), a novel published in the year following the *levée en masse*. As a young man, '[n]ew to the world', Caleb knows 'nothing of its affairs but what has reached me by rumour, or is recorded in books'.[11] Having been put through the mill by Ferdinando Falkland, he acquires what he calls 'the dear bought result of experience' and is no longer 'irresolute and pliable'.[12] In other words, *Erfahrung* is what you graduate with from the University of Life, aka the School of Hard Knocks.

As epistemology and as moral philosophy, *Erfahrung* has had both supporters and detractors. In a strand that can be traced back to Shaftesburian ideas of sympathy and instinctive moral discrimination, *Erfahrung* is presented as issuing in acts of loving kindness and human understanding. Dinah Morris in George Eliot's *Adam Bede* (1859) exemplifies this: 'From her girlhood upwards she had had experience among the sick and the mourning, among minds hardened and shrivelled through poverty and ignorance, and had gained the subtlest perception of the mode in which they could best be touched, and softened into willingness to receive words of spiritual consolation or warning'.[13] Dinah has learned compassion the hard way, and Eliot reiterates the point explicitly. 'I think the higher nature has to learn this comprehension [of the lower nature] […] by a good deal of hard experience,' she writes, 'often with bruises and gashes incurred in taking things up by the wrong end.'[14] Hard experience forms the narrative arc of Eliot's novels – in this sense, veteran poetics are their very foundation – and a principle to be respected in every walk of life, as when Adam confesses to his audience of local farmers, '[i]t hardly becomes so young a man as I am, to talk much about farming to you, who are most of you so much older, and are men of experience'.[15]

But others are more sceptical. In another, Christian-inflected strand reaching back to Milton's Satan as a 'weather-beaten vessel'[16] and Blake's *Songs of Innocence and of Experience* (1789), experience is viewed with distrust and fear. Trollope is an instance of a Victorian novelist for whom 'the man of the world' – the descriptor referring, in this case, to the unreliable,

[11] William Godwin, *Caleb Williams* [1794], ed. Pamela Clemit (Oxford: Oxford University Press, 2009), 167.

[12] Ibid., 279.

[13] George Eliot, *Adam Bede* [1859], ed. Stephen Gill (Oxford: Oxford University Press, 1986), 158.

[14] Ibid., 206.

[15] Ibid., 311.

[16] John Milton, *The Major Works*, ed. Stephen Orgel and Jonathan Goldberg (Oxford: Oxford University Press, 1991/2003), 401 [2.1043].

ruinous Sowerby of *Framley Parsonage* (1860) – is a byword for iniquity.[17]
Even Eliot concedes, in *Felix Holt* (1866), that experience is only as good as
the quality of its contents. 'Experience is enlightening,' she writes, 'but with
a difference. Experiments on live animals may go on for a long period, and
yet the fauna on which they are made may be limited.'[18] Carlyle's *Sartor
Resartus* (1833–4) mocks *Erfahrung* as the basis of knowledge, noting that
Professor Teufelsdröckh's method is not 'that of common school Logic,
where the truths all stand in a row, each holding by the skirts of the other'
but 'at best that of practical Reason, proceeding by large Intuition over
whole systematic groups and kingdoms'.[19] '[I]t seems […] as if it were
not Argument that had taught him, but Experience,' concludes Carlyle,
in mock outrage.[20]

There is a conservatism inherent in *Erfahrung* – as Jay notes, it can
function as 'a prudential warning against the urge to tinker or innovate
in a radical way'[21] – which is evident in its forming a generational legacy
in the *Odyssey*. (One can hear this conservatism in the timeless opinion
that young people have it easy nowadays.) Such legacies – the wisdom
of elders – came under particular attack during and after the First World
War, as a young, fighting generation turned on the older generation that
had initiated and directed the war from home. In this vein, in 1915 the
writer, linguist and philosopher C. K. Ogden savaged the conscription
campaign that had 'once more let loose upon the world that gerontocratic garrulity that seemed for a time to have been shamed into silence by
the holocausts of young men'.[22] In a BBC radio broadcast of 24 October
1932, E. M. Forster sounded another kind of warning, singling out for
approval a passage from E. M. Benson's *As We Are* (1932): 'Experience has
its dangers: it may bring wisdom, but it may also bring stiffness and cause

---

[17] Anthony Trollope, *Framley Parsonage* [1860], ed. David Skilton and Peter Miles (Oxford: Oxford University Press, 1986) 70.

[18] George Eliot, *Felix Holt* [1866], ed. Lynda Mugglestone (Oxford: Oxford University Press, 1995), 416.

[19] Thomas Carlyle, *Selected Writings*, ed. Alan Shelston (London: Penguin, 1986), 89.

[20] Ibid., 90.

[21] Jay, *Songs of Experience*, 180.

[22] C. K. Ogden, 'The One Thing Needful. A Suggestion to Members of Parliament', *The Cambridge Magazine* 5.11 (29 January 1915), 240–1. That word 'gerontocratic' summons up Eliot's 'Gerontion' (1920), the 'old man in a dry month', strangely phlegmatic at not having fought, nonetheless hinting at the unbearable nature of experience – 'After such knowledge, what forgiveness?' (T. S. Eliot, *The Poems of T. S. Eliot. Volume I: Collected and Uncollected Poems*, ed. Christopher Ricks and Jim McCue (London: Faber and Faber, 2015), 31, 32). See further Vincent Sherry, *The Great War and the Language of Modernism* (Oxford: Oxford University Press, 2003), 207–16, who quotes Ogden on 208.

hardened deposits in the mind, and its resulting inelasticity is crippling.'[23] Other critiques in the twentieth century questioned whether experience could even be accessed. According to Freud, 'memory-records' were often 'strongest and most enduring' when 'the process that left them behind never reached consciousness at all'.[24] What had not been a conscious experience in the first place, that is, often made the greatest impression on the psyche.[25] By 1958, Théodor Adorno was warning that 'the very possibility of experience is in jeopardy';[26] twenty years later, Giorgio Agamben claimed that 'the question of experience can be approached nowadays only with an acknowledgement that it is no longer accessible to us'.[27] As Jay points out, the last decades of the century saw post-structuralist attacks on experience as 'a simplistic ground of immediacy that fails to register the always already mediated nature of cultural relations and the instability of the subject who is supposedly the bearer of experiences'.[28]

The veteran – the one who has literally been through the wars, the one who has suffered and learned from his sufferings, the one who returns older and (therefore) wiser than when he went away – is the natural figurative expression of *Erfahrung*. As Jay asks, 'has there ever been as vivid a depiction of the perilous *Fahrt* in *Erfahrung* as the *Odyssey*?'[29] And the veteran of the kind of warfare inaugurated by the French Revolutionary and Napoleonic Wars is *particularly* apt to express it. For, in the striking phrase of Anders Engberg-Pedersen, '[e]pistemology suffered a concussion at Austerlitz, at Wagram, at Borodino'.[30] As Engberg-Pedersen explains, the scale and complexity of these wars, and succeeding wars in the same mould, turned them into 'a realm of radical contingency, a realm shot through with chance events, replete with errors and uncertainties'.[31] Here, where 'averages,

---

[23] E. F. Benson, *As We Are: A Modern Revue* (London: Longmans, Green, 1932), 39–40; quoted in E. M. Forster, *The BBC Talks of E. M. Forster 1929–1960: A Selected Edition*, ed. Mary Lago, Linda K. Hughes and Elizabeth Macleod Walls (Columbia, MO: University of Missouri Press, 2008), 96. I am grateful to Bárbara Gallego Larrarte for bringing this to my attention.

[24] *Beyond the Pleasure Principle (Jenseits des Lustprinzips)* [1920], trans. C. J. M. Hubback, ed. Ernest Jones (London: The Hogarth Press/The Institute for Psycho-Analysis, 1922), 27.

[25] See Ferguson, *Criminal Law and the Modernist Novel*, 33, on this point by Freud.

[26] Théodor Adorno, 'In Memory of Eichendorff' ('Zum Gedächtnis Eichendorffs') [1958], trans. Shierry Weber Nicholson, *Notes to Literature*, ed. Rolf Tiedemann (New York: Columbia University Press, 1991), 55–79: 55; quoted in Jay, *Songs of Experience*, 2.

[27] Giorgio Agamben, *Infancy and History: Essays on the Destruction of Experience (Infanzia e storia: Distruzione dell'esperienza e origine della storia)* [1979], trans. Liz Heron (London: Verso, 1993), 13; quoted in Jay, *Songs of Experience*, 2.

[28] Jay, *Songs of Experience*, 3.

[29] Ibid., 14.

[30] Anders Engberg-Pedersen, *Empire of Chance: The Napoleonic Wars and the Disorder of Things* (Cambridge, MA: Harvard University Press, 2015), 5.

[31] Ibid., 4.

hypothetical scenarios, and probable worlds' proliferated, a 'new form of praxis-oriented knowledge' was in the ascendant.[32] Trustworthy gut feeling was the key to success on this new kind of battlefield, and an experienced combatant had it in spades. Now, an important distinction needs to be made here. Being able to rely on *Erfahrung* – for this is, essentially, the quality Engberg-Pedersen is talking about – to ensure local or large-scale military success in a war is not the same as being able to make sense of one's experiences in that war during or after it. This point is crucial to Chapter 5. But for now, let us accept the veterancy/*Erfahrung* connection. Betokening it are signs of age, weather-beaten faces, bronzed complexions and tired and injured bodies: those physical changes – already noted in this book for their metaphorical potential – that are the product of suffering and time. These include the scar of Odysseus itself that, as much as it is a physical datum on which to base logical inference, is the mark of (harsh) experience.

The veteran is also a natural pedagogue. His capacity to instruct, to edify, to serve as an exemplar, has been exploited in literature from the outset of the time frame of this book. In 1797, John Foster, a shoemaker and later a private in the North Lincoln Militia, published a poem called 'The Veteran Soldier, Or The Exercise of Faith, Hope, and Patience', which explicitly refers to soldierly learning-through-experience:

> While unexperienc'd soldiers are
> To sudden fear or rashness prone,
> He's taught by long intrigues of war
> To fight when seeming hopes are gone.
>                               (5–8)[33]

Years of practice have taught this veteran *sang-froid* and the need to play the long game. These insights are in turn taught to others via what Benjamin identified in his 1936 essay 'The Storyteller' (*Der Erzähler*) – a piece to which I will constantly refer in this section – as the perfect generic form through which to transmit *Erfahrung*:

> Where we by some old warrior set,
> And list'ning to his chequer'd tales,
> We're taught at once by what he's met,
> That patient courage best avails.
>                               (1–4)

---

[32] Ibid., 68, 73.
[33] John Foster, *Poems, Chiefly on Religious Subjects* (London: publisher unknown, 1797), 11–14, ll. 1–4.

Foster converts the patience-preaching old warhorse into a parable for Christian conduct, with the result that the storytelling veteran not only passes on wisdom but *models* its passing on.[34] The figure had resonance. As Ruskin informed his audience of young soldiers at the Royal Military Academy, Woolwich, in 1866, 'the experience, the hardship, and the activity of a soldier's life render his powers of thought more accurate than those of other men'.[35] (One wonders what his listeners made of a civilian telling them that.)

What contributes to the veteran's authority, it would seem, is something akin to the process involved in pastoral retreat and return. As Terry Gifford points out, retreat into pastoral inevitably requires return – a return that 'delivers insights into the culture from which it originates'.[36] War is an unlikely pastoral retreat[37] but the pastoral model nonetheless contributes the idea of home-stayers learning from the person who has been away, the person who has had more – or, at least, different – experiences. This is, to be sure, something of a romanticized view of the veteran, and it might be objected that the militarization of a person is likelier to diminish than enhance *Erfahrung*-associated qualities such as human insight, empathy and sensitivity. As far as I can tell, real-life veterans are no more or less likely to possess these qualities than other people. But the veteran is an apt *literary* figure to depict them.

In this chapter, I chart the fortunes of *Erfahrung* as an epistemological resource, exploring literary probings of how it functions heuristically (as a mode of problem-solving) and what it implies pedagogically (how things can be taught and learned). More specifically, I investigate how *Erfahrung*, accrued through and expressed by veterancy, is put to the test in literary accounts of a certain kind of problem-solving. The problems in question are murders, and the veterans are detectives. Veterans form a small but distinguished group of fictional detectives in British litera-ture:[38] Dorothy L. Sayers's Lord Peter Wimsey, Ian Rankin's John Rebus,

---

[34] Another instance of the edifying veteran can be found in a Second World War novel – Monica Dickens's *The Happy Prisoner* (London: Michael Joseph and The Book Society, 1946) – in which a bedridden veteran becomes a sounding board for other members of the family, 'doling out wisdom from [his] bed like a Salvationist handing out tracts' (148).

[35] John Ruskin, *The Crown of Wild Olive: Three Lectures on Work, Traffic, and War* (New York: John Wiley, 1866), 119.

[36] Terry Gifford, *Pastoral* (London and New York: Routledge, 1999), 82.

[37] See Kate McLoughlin, *Authoring War: The Literary Representation of War from the* Iliad *to Iraq* (Cambridge: Cambridge University Press, 2011), ch. 3.

[38] Their overseas counterparts include Lynn Brock's Colonel Gore, Ngaio Marsh's Roderick Alleyn, Mickey Spillane's Mike Hammer, Léo Malet's Nestor Burma (revived by Patrick Pécherot), Didier

Kate Atkinson's Jackson Brodie and, most recently, Cormoran Strike, the creation of J. K. Rowling writing as 'Robert Galbraith'.[39] To these veteran characters may be added the assistant of the most famous literary detective of them all: Sherlock Holmes's confidant and chronicler, Dr Watson. In this chapter, I discuss Watson, Wimsey and Strike. What emerges is that, while *Erfahrung* enjoys an ascendancy in the period of mass warfare, it is accompanied by significant unease about its epistemological potential. But before turning to the literary veteran detectives, a more detailed look at detection and pedagogy is in order.

## Detection and Pedagogy

Given what has just been said about *Erfahrung*, it may seem counter-intuitive to speak of veteran wisdom in connection with the detective genre. After all, the epistemological approach for which detectives, literary and otherwise, are best known is deduction, or at least what is frequently labelled deduction, rather than anything experientially based. The inception and rise of detective fiction (variously dated between the end of the eighteenth and middle of the nineteenth century)[40] has widely been attributed to a desire for reason and order in a dark, violent and increasingly incomprehensible world. Dennis Porter, for example, points to 'a preoccupation with the collective violence of war, revolution, rebellion, repression, and public execution' growing alongside 'anxiety at the random, individual violence of murder, rape, abduction, burglary, and street theft' on both sides of the Channel in the decades after the French Revolution.[41] Into this mire, accurately attributing consequences to causes, vanquishing wrong-doers, stabilizing the social and epistemological status quo, stepped what Siegfried Kracauer called 'the personification of *ratio*':[42] the rationalizing, forensically minded literary detective. Critics have, accordingly, pointed out that the figure is of the same metaphysical order as 'the construction

---

Daeninckx's René Griffon, Robert B. Parker's Spenser, Ross Macdonald's Lew Archer, James Crumley's C. W. Sughrue and Milo Milodragovich and James Lee Burke's Dave Robicheaux.

[39] In this chapter, for convenience's sake, I refer to Rowling as the author of the three Cormoran Strike novels, rather than 'Galbraith'.

[40] Gertrude Stein called the detective story 'the only really modern novel form' (*Look At Me Now and Here I Am: Writings and Lectures 1911–1945*, ed. Patricia Meyerowitz (London: Peter Owen, 1967), 149, quoted in Laura Marcus, 'Detection and Literary Fiction', *The Cambridge Companion to Crime Fiction*, ed. Martin Priestman (Cambridge: Cambridge University Press, 2003), 245–68: 250).

[41] Dennis Porter, *The Pursuit of Crime: Art and Ideology in Detective Fiction* (New Haven, CT: Yale University Press, 1981), 16–17.

[42] 'Der Personifikation der ratio' (Siegfried Kracauer, *Der Detektiv-Roman: Ein philosophisches Fragment* (Frankfurt-am-Main: Suhrkamp, 1979), 86 (my translation)).

of the nation-state in Europe';[43] 'the development of modern scientific and rationalistic epistemologies';[44] the emergent 'secular and naturalistic' worldview;[45] and specific advances in philology, geology, palaeontology, archaeology and evolutionary biology.[46] The detective as embodiment of reason required matching heuristic tools; as Heather Worthington notes, pre-Enlightenment systems of identifying and controlling criminals – 'visible guilt, witnesses, confession and divine justice' – were superseded in succeeding secularized, reason-based times by a 'drive to discover hard evidence that would prove guilt beyond question'.[47]

Coincident with the first mass, global, technologically advanced wars that began at the end of the eighteenth century and start of the nineteenth were a number of developments in forensic medicine and science aimed at acquiring just such evidence. The first professor of medical jurisprudence was appointed at the University of Edinburgh in 1807; in 1832 the seminal *Medical Jurisprudence* by J. A. Paris and J. S. M. Fonblanque was published.[48] The Metropolitan Police was founded in 1829.[49] By the early twentieth century, significant advances had been made in anthropometry, statistical analysis, photography, blood-typing, fingerprinting and ballistics[50] – tools designed to establish identity through physical continuity. The detective who solves crimes using such means of forensic analysis – and this is the protagonist of 'classic' detective fiction as opposed to the epistemologically more uncertain 'metaphysical' or postmodern detective fiction[51] – naturally appears as a figure who re-imposes social order and certainty: as W. H. Auden commented in 1948, '[t]he job of the detective is to restore the state of grace in which the aesthetic

---

[43] Luc Boltanski, *Mysteries and Conspiracies: Detective Stories, Spy Novels and the Making of Modern Societies, Énigmes et complots: Une enquête à propos d'enquêtes)* [2012], trans. Catherine Porter (Cambridge: Polity Press, 2014), 19.

[44] John G. Cawelti, 'Detecting the Detective', *ANQ: A Quarterly Journal of Short Articles, Notes and Reviews* 12.3 (1999), 44–55: 49.

[45] Laurence Frank, *Victorian Detective Fiction and the Nature of Evidence: The Scientific Investigations of Poe, Dickens and Doyle* (Basingstoke: Palgrave Macmillan, 2003), 3.

[46] Frank, *Victorian Detective Fiction and the Nature of Evidence*, 4.

[47] Heather Worthington, *Key Concepts in Crime Fiction* (Basingstoke: Palgrave Macmillan, 2011), 33.

[48] Ibid., 35.

[49] Ibid., 35.

[50] Ibid., 37; Porter, *The Pursuit of Crime*, 124.

[51] On metaphysical detective fiction, see Michael Holquist, 'Whodunit and Other Questions: Metaphysical Detective Stories in Postwar Fiction', *The Poetics of Murder: Detective Fiction and Literary Theory*, ed. Glenn W. Most and William W. Stowe (New York: Harcourt Brace Jovanovich, 1983), 149–74; and Patricia Merivale, 'Postmodern and Metaphysical Detection', *A Companion to Crime Fiction*, ed. Charles J. Rzepka and Lee Horsley (Chichester: Wiley-Blackwell, 2010), 308–20.

and the ethical are one'.[52] From here, it is but a step to comparing detection to psychoanalysis – both disciplines 'share a focus on details and model of decipherment'[53] – with the detective as, variously, psychoanalyst or super-ego.[54]

But in this chapter, rather than add to readings of the literary veteran detective as a force of social or psychic order (and I note Lawrence Frank's challenge to the idea that detective fiction serves a 'bourgeois, panoptical society' on the basis that no such coherent society has ever existed),[55] I want to focus on what the figure says about kinds of knowledge and ways of knowing in the period of mass warfare. Detective fiction is host to a number of epistemologies – not for nothing did Brian McHale call it the 'epistemological genre *par excellence*'.[56] In his story 'The Murders in the Rue Morgue' (1841), Edgar Allan Poe gives the following account of the 'analyst' or detective:

> He is fond of enigmas, of conundrums, of hieroglyphics; exhibiting in his solutions of each a degree of acumen which appears to the ordinary apprehension preternatural. His results, brought about by the very soul and essence of

[52] W. H. Auden, 'The Guilty Vicarage', *Detective Fiction: A Collection of Critical Essays*, ed. Robin W. Winks (Woodstock, VT: Foul Play Press, 1980), 15–24: 21. In a similar vein, Charles Rzepka notes 'detective fiction's valorizations of rationality and law' ('What is Crime Fiction?', *A Companion to Crime Fiction*, ed. Charles J. Rzepka and Lee Horsley, 1–9: 4); Heta Pyrhönen argues that the genre 'demonstrates the importance of closure, as the conclusion represents a definitive ending, which reveals the logical, causal, and temporal connections among the events' ('Criticism and Theory', *A Companion to Crime Fiction*, ed. Charles J. Rzepka and Lee Horsley, 43–56: 50); and Luc Boltanski suggests that detection tests 'the state's claim not only to make order reign but also and especially to make intelligible and to some extent predictable the events that enter into the field of the possible' (*Mysteries and Conspiracies*, 20). Such readings lead to a sense of the fictional detective – or his creator – controlling meaning and hence social justice.

[53] Laura Marcus, *Dreams of Modernity: Psychoanalysis, Literature, Cinema* (Cambridge: Cambridge University Press, 2014), 5. On the affinities between detection and psychoanalysis, see further Robert A. Rushing, *Resisting Arrest: Detective Fiction and Popular Culture* (New York: Other Press, 2007) and Henry James Morello, 'Time and Trauma in Ricardo Piglia's *The Absent City*', *The Comparatist* 37 (2013), 219–33: 223.

[54] In his classic essay, 'Clues: Roots of an Evidential Paradigm' (1979), Carlo Ginzburg links the practices of the art critic Giovanni Morelli, Sherlock Holmes and Sigmund Freud: '[i]n each case, infinitesimal traces permit the comprehension of a deeper, otherwise unattainable reality: traces – more precisely, symptoms (in the case of Freud), clues (in the case of Sherlock Holmes), pictorial marks (in the case of Morelli)' (*Myths, Emblems, Clues* [*Miti, Emblemi, Spie*] [1986], trans. John Tedeschi and Anne C. Tedeschi (London: Hutchinson Radus, 1990), 101). Ginzburg initially sets 'evidential and conjectural disciplines', which include medicine, against 'Galilean scientism', but later comes to 'dismember' the paradigm, noting that '[i]t is one thing to analyze footprints, stars, feces, sputum, corneas, pulsations, snow-covered fields, or cigarette ashes; it is quite another to examine handwriting or paintings or conversation' (106, 118). In this chapter, I am tracing what happens when the objects of conjecture bifurcate in this way.

[55] Frank, *Victorian Detective Fiction and the Nature of Evidence*, 4, 5.

[56] Brian McHale, *Postmodern Fiction* (London: Routledge, 1987), 7.

method, have, in truth, the whole air of intuition. The faculty of re-solution is possibly much invigorated by mathematical study, and especially by that highest branch of it, which, unjustly, and merely on account of its retrograde operations, has been called, as if *par excellence*, analysis. Yet to calculate is not in itself to analyse.[57]

The fondness for enigmas, conundrums and hieroglyphics, the preternatural acumen: these are the hallmarks of the traditional (nineteenth-century) detective, magnifying glass in hand. But it is instructive that Poe refers also to 'intuition' and carefully distinguishes between 'calculation' and 'analysis'. Detection (analysis), unlike mathematical calculation, is not solely a matter of *a priori* reasoning. The process of making *a posteriori* inferences from physical data is also involved,[58] which calls for intuition and imagination. It also calls for knowing what to look for and 'retrospective logic', both of which are dependent upon memory,[59] and Frank further suggests that the detective must 'imaginatively transform' a fact or event into 'a chain of natural causes and effects'.[60] Alongside a calculative capacity, therefore, a number of qualities encompassed by *Erfahrung* play a part in modern successful crime-solving.

Indeed, *Erfahrung* inheres in criminal narratology. As Edmond Locard, one of the pioneers of forensic science, remarked, 'in every crime scene, the criminal will bring something to that scene and take something away'.[61] The story of a crime is a story of having-been-there and having-done-that: as was noted earlier of Odysseus' scar, the datum that forms the starting point for forensic analysis is also the mark of experience. And, as detective fiction developed over the nineteenth and twentieth centuries, the capacity of the detective to recognize the qualities of having-been-there and having-done-that became increasingly important.

Reliance on *Erfahrung* constitutes the second major strand in the development of detective fiction, competing with the idea of the detective as agent of social order. Here the link with what Dennis Porter calls the 'late romantic preoccupation with the nightside of the soul' comes into view,[62]

---

[57] Edgar Allan Poe, *Tales of Mystery and Imagination* (London: Dent, 1981), 37–8.
[58] Ronald Knox gives a pithy example of the epistemological range of Sherlock Holmes's methods: 'It is by observation a posteriori that he recognizes Watson's visit to the Post Office from the mud on his trousers; it is by deduction a priori that he knows he has been sending a telegram since he has seen plenty of stamps and postcards in Watson's desk' (*Essays in Satire* (New York: E. P. Dutton, 1930), 170–1).
[59] Pyrhönen, 'Criticism and Theory', 54.
[60] Frank, *Victorian Detective Fiction and the Nature of Evidence*, 157.
[61] Quoted in Worthington, *Key Concepts in Crime Fiction*, 36.
[62] Porter, *The Pursuit of Crime*, 25.

a link that proves that the genre's heritage is, as Stefano Tani points out, as much the Gothic novel as French encyclopaedism, as much *Sturm und Drang* as Kantian intellectual idealism.[63] The two strands, which might loosely be termed 'classic' and 'romantic', have both resulted in a number of celebrated representations. The 'classic' strand can be traced from Poe's Dupin and Sherlock Holmes to the forensic scientists in TV dramas such as the BBC's *Silent Witness* (1996–) and *Waking the Dead* (2000–11): scientific brilliance is the object of interest. The 'romantic' strand is manifest in Dostoevsky's Porfiry Petrovich, Dickens's Inspector Bucket, Agatha Christie's Miss Marple, Raymond Chandler's Philip Marlowe, Colin Dexter's Inspector Morse and the title character of ITV's *A Touch of Frost* (1992–2010): it foregrounds human insight, often accompanied by a certain world-weariness.

Such insight – comprising the *Erfahrung*-related qualities of imagination, intuition, memory and worldliness – is required not only of the fictional detective. It must also be exercised by the *reader*, who is attempting to solve the mystery in parallel. As Heta Pyrhönen observes, reading detective fiction involves a 'constant comparison between this particular text and similar texts held in a reader's memory'.[64] Dependent upon genre cues – it is never the butler; inconsistent behaviour is suggestive; a gun, once introduced, will inevitably be fired – as well as upon the clues of the story, the successful detective-reader draws on accumulated textual experience.[65] Though this might be true of reading in any genre, it is *particularly* true of detective fiction-reading, which is, as Robert Rushing notes, associated with 'unlimited *serial* reading'[66] – aficionados read story after story after story. But this amassed expertise is constantly under challenge as the reader progresses through a given story. As Samuel Cohen has pointed out, detective fiction is driven by Barthes' 'hermeneutic code', a form of narrative propulsion that poses questions such as 'What will happen next?

[63] Stefano Tani, *The Doomed Detective: The Contribution of the Detective Novel to Postmodern American and Italian Fiction* (Carbondale, IL: Southern Illinois University Press, 1984), 1. The dual 'classic' and 'romantic' heritage of detective fiction may also owe something to the divide between scientific method and experience that arose in English empiricism. As A. D. Nuttall remarks, it is the 'great irony of English empiricism that, through its reverence of a scientific metaphysic, it soon proved hostile to experience' (*A Common Sky: Philosophy and the Literary Imagination* (Berkeley, CA: University of California Press, 1974), 20).

[64] Pyrhönen, 'Criticism and Theory', 54.

[65] For a detailed discussion of this phenomenon, see George N. Dove, *The Reader and the Detective Story* (Bowling Green, OH: Bowling Green State University Popular Press, 1997).

[66] Rushing, *Resisting Arrest*, 3, original emphasis.

How will it end?'[67] In addition to actively considering such questions, the reader of the detective story must constantly scan for cues and clues in the light of his or her genre experience: it is never the butler, *but sometimes it is* – is this one of those instances?[68] Reading detective fiction, that is, is a process of assimilating, hypothesizing and revising. It is, in other words, a *learning* experience. Todorov called it 'a slow apprenticeship'.[69]

A number of critics have drawn further parallels between detection and scholarship in general and literary scholarship in particular. In a 1929 essay, 'The Professor and the Detective', Marjorie Nicolson, a professor at Smith College and later Columbia University, asked 'what essential difference is there between the technique of the detective tracking his quarry through Europe and that of the historian tracking his fact, the philosopher his idea, down the ages?'[70] Luc Boltanski inverts the analogy: 'the detective is indeed a scholar par excellence'.[71] For Laura Marcus, an academic setting such as that in Dorothy L. Sayer's *Gaudy Night* (1935), 'brings to the fore the concept of literary scholarship as a form of detective work',[72] and Dennis Porter suggests that that early literary detective Oedipus showed, in solving the crime of his father's death, a 'sensitivity to ambiguities and levels of meaning in verbal utterances that we expect of the literary critic'.[73] It could be added that detection has in common with a certain kind of literary criticism the habit of conferring significance from a retrospective point of view.[74]

In the literary texts discussed in this chapter, veterancy, detection and pedagogy form the three crucial elements in complex investigations into how knowledge is arrived at. If detection demonstrates the potential of veterancy in problem-solving, pedagogy – and I have in mind here not merely general edification but actual methods of teaching – reveals the

---

[67] Samuel Cohen, *After the End of History: American Fiction in the 1990s* (Iowa City: University of Iowa Press, 2009), 199, quoting Roland Barthes, *S/Z* [1970], trans. Richard Miller (New York: Hill and Wang, 1974), 18–20.

[68] Dorothy L. Sayers describes this fraught process in 'Aristotle on Detective Fiction', a lecture given on 5 March 1935: 'A is the obvious suspect. But in a detective story, the obvious suspect is always innocent. Therefore A is innocent' (*Unpopular Opinions* (London: Victor Gollancz, 1946), 187).

[69] Tzvetan Todorov, *The Poetics of Prose* (*Poétique de la prose*) [1971], trans. Richard Howard (Oxford: Basil Blackwell, 1977), 43.

[70] Marjorie Nicolson, 'The Professor and the Detective', *The Atlantic Monthly* 143.4 (April 1929), 484–93: 492.

[71] Boltanski, *Mysteries and Conspiracies*, 56.

[72] Marcus, 'Detection and Literary Fiction', 262.

[73] Porter, *The Pursuit of Crime*, 227.

[74] On the affinities between Holmesian 'backward reasoning' and T. S. Eliot's notion of 'criticism', see Vicki Mahaffey, *Modernist Literature: Challenging Fictions* (Malden, MA: Blackwell, 2007), 86–7. See, further, Porter, *The Pursuit of Crime*, 228.

(limited) extent to which such heuristic techniques can be transmitted to others. Scientific method can be taught even if individual scientific brilliance may be, as in Holmes's case, autochthonous and inimitable, but understanding of the ways of the world has to be personally, more painfully acquired. It is no coincidence that the three writers I discuss – Doyle, Sayers and Rowling – all had distinct pedagogical opinions. Two of them – Sayers and Rowling – worked as teachers. Doyle made public pronouncements on medical training; Sayers also wrote and spoke publicly about education. Their ideas play out in their literary creations, to which I now turn.

### 'The Air of a Military Man': Arthur Conan Doyle's The Sign of Four (1890)

Sherlock Holmes's first words to Dr Watson, in A Study in Scarlet (1887), are 'You have been in Afghanistan, I perceive' (1.151).[75] The remark, coming from someone he has only just met, astonishes Watson. After they have been flatmates for a while, Holmes explains the thinking behind his insight:

> The train of reasoning ran, 'Here is a gentleman of a medical type, but with the air of a military man. Clearly an army doctor, then. He has just come from the tropics, for his face is dark, and that is not the natural tint of his skin, for his wrists are fair. He has undergone hardship and sickness, as his haggard face says clearly. His left arm has been injured. He holds it in a stiff and unnatural manner. Where in the tropics could an English army doctor have seen much hardship and got his arm wounded? Clearly in Afghanistan.'
>
> (1.160, 162)

It is a classic Holmesian exposition: physical observation – body-reading[76] – is conducted at lightning speed; logical inferences are made from the observed data; alternative explanations are dismissed on the basis of probability. Such displays of forensic brilliance have led critics to term Holmes 'the archetypal rational, scientific detective',[77] a 'master scientist',[78] 'a genius in whom scientific curiosity is raised to the status of a heroic passion'.[79] In fact, there is more epistemological variety in Holmes's detection methods

---

[75] The edition of Doyle's works used is The Annotated Sherlock Holmes, ed. William S. Baring-Gould, 2 vols (London: John Murray, 1968). Volume and page numbers are given in the text.

[76] On Holmes as a reader of body language, see further Sarah Dauncey, 'Crime, Forensics, and Modern Science', A Companion to Crime Fiction, ed. Rzepka and Horsley, 164–74, and Mahaffey, Modernist Literature, 84–5.

[77] Worthington, Key Concepts in Crime Fiction, 39.

[78] Diana Barsham, Conan Doyle and the Meaning of Masculinity (Aldershot: Ashgate, 2000), 99.

[79] Auden, 'The Guilty Vicarage', 21.

than is usually given credit for: intuition, imagination, personal experience, empathy and memory are in play alongside reason and logic, and Holmes himself is not unknown to display 'kindness and skill' (1.616), not insensible to the claims of natural justice and not unaware that there is more than one side to a story.[80] But there is no doubt that the chief impression of him remains as, in his creator's words, 'an automaton, – a calculating-machine' (1.619).[81] The scene quoted above was based, according to Doyle, on one of the 'best' instances of the diagnostic method of the surgeon Joseph Bell, who taught him at the University of Edinburgh medical school.[82] (In the real-life case, Bell correctly inferred that a patient had served in the army as a non-commissioned officer in a Highland regiment stationed in Barbados and had been not long discharged.)[83] In a letter of 4 May 1892 to Bell, Doyle wrote:

> It is most certainly to you that I owe Sherlock Holmes [...] I do not think that his analytical work is in the least an exaggeration of some effects which I have seen you produce in the out-patient ward. Round the centre of deduction and inference and observation which I have heard you inculcate I have tried to go – further occasionally.[84]

The word Doyle used for Bell was 'miraculous'.[85] And the most telling image he created for Holmes, which occurs in the novella *The Sign of Four* (1890), shares this quality. Here, the detective is described as an 'enormous glow-worm', crawling along the roof in the darkness. At once non-human

---

[80] Stefano Tani perceptively notes that Holmes embodies a 'conflict' between the rational and the irrational, linking the former to positivism and the latter to decadence (*The Doomed Detective*, 17).

[81] Doyle repeated the phrase 'calculating machine' in his memoirs (*Memories and Adventures* [1924] (London: John Murray, 1930), 128). Critics have followed his lead, describing the detective as 'the archetypal rational, scientific detective' (Worthington, *Key Concepts in Crime Fiction*, 39), a 'master scientist' (Barsham, *Conan Doyle and the Meaning of Masculinity*, 99) and 'a genius in whom scientific curiosity is raised to the status of a heroic passion' (Auden, 'The Guilty Vicarage', 21). Most persuasively, Laurence Frank has read Holmes's detection in the context of nineteenth-century science outlined earlier. For Frank, Doyle, like Poe and Dickens, appropriated for his fictional detective the language and procedures of the developing sciences of biology, geology, cosmology, archaeology and palaeontology, whose objective was, in the words of William Whewell, 'to ascend from the present state of things to a more ancient condition, from which the present is derived by intelligible causes' (William Whewell, *History of the Inductive Sciences, from the Earliest to the Present Times*, 3/3 vols (London: John W. Parker, 1837), 471; quoted in Frank, *Victorian Detective Fiction and the Nature of Evidence*, 25).

[82] Doyle, *Memories and Adventures*, 33.

[83] Ibid., 33.

[84] Quoted in William S. Baring-Gould, 'Two Doctors and a Detective', *The Annotated Sherlock Holmes*, ed. Baring-Gould (London: John Murray, 1968), 1–104: 8.

[85] Doyle, *Memories and Adventures*, 33.

and eye-catching, the glow-worm evokes a pyrotechnical forensics that are as alien as they are impressive.

That Holmes's feats of detection are somehow superhuman, impenetrable to ordinary understanding, is reinforced by the detective's frequent but abortive attempts at explanation. Holmes evinces a 'didactic manner' (1.611) and certain of his comments reveal his belief that detective competence can be acquired. He remarks that the (fictional) French detective François le Villard 'has the power of observation and that of deduction. He is only wanting in knowledge; and that may come in time' (1.612). Time and experience, that is, can accumulate the body of knowledge that improves the accuracy of inference from observed data. Watson comments that in his note of gratitude to Holmes le Villard 'speaks as a pupil to his master' (1.612). But Holmes's most tested pupil is Watson himself. Holmes is constantly – famously – bidding Watson to apply his methods and is always keen to hear Watson's conclusions. Given that Watson is a highly trained 'medical man' (1.611),[86] it might be thought that he would be an adept student. He does, on occasion, perform some limited deductive diagnoses. In *The Sign of Four*, he notices that Miss Morstan is showing 'every side of intense inward agitation' (1.616). He uses his stethoscope to determine that there is nothing amiss with Thaddeus Sholto's mitral valve. He is able to infer from Bartholomew Sholto's extremely rigid corpse that death has been caused by 'some powerful vegetable alkaloid [...] some strychnine-like substance which would produce tetanus' (1.639). But, on the whole, Watson shows himself to be incapable of the same logical reasoning as Holmes. As a result, *The Sign of Four*, like the other Holmes and Watson stories, is studded with Holmesian deprecations of his student. 'This is all an insoluble mystery to me,' remarks Watson; '[o]n the contrary [...] it clears every instant,' counters Holmes (1.635). Watson thinks that the footprints in the garret 'appear to be much as other footmarks'; '[n]ot at all!' ripostes Holmes (1.644). Eventually, Watson concludes that the marks must be those of a 'savage'; '[h]ardly that,' is Holmes's crushing reply (1.654).

Watson will never be right. In both real-life detection and detective fiction, the aim of the crime-solver is to arrive at a solution. In real life, whether the solution matches the crime can only be known by those directly involved in the latter, if at all (no one has a perfect, synoptic view). In

---

[86] Watson has earned the degree of Doctor of Medicine (MD) from the University of London ('A Study in Scarlet', 1.143). The MD, a research degree, is a higher qualification than those of Bachelor of Medicine/Bachelor of Surgery, which permit the holder to practise medicine in Britain.

fiction, the crime is determined by the author, so only certain solutions can be correct. ('Crime' and 'solution' map on to what Tzvetan Todorov, in his discussion of detective fiction, calls *'fable'* [*fabula*] and *'subject'* [*sjuzhet*].)[87] Watson's inferences may be as perfectly logical and justified as Holmes's, but only Holmes's will ever be correct in the universe of the fiction. This results in a point being made repeatedly: Watson will not learn. The problem is not that Holmes is a terrible teacher or Watson a dull pupil. There is something wrong with the pedagogy itself.

In the remarks he made on education, Doyle consistently endorsed praxis. The 'weary hours' he spent studying Latin and Greek at school were of 'little use',[88] he recalled late in life, but 'the art of reading aloud', learned 'when my mother was knitting', or 'the reading of French books, learned by spelling out the captions of the Jules Verne illustrations' both stuck.[89] The medical education he received at the University of Edinburgh was 'far too oblique and not nearly practical enough for the purpose in view';[90] even Bell himself provided more in the way of spectacle than useful instruction, Doyle finding his methods difficult and 'artificial' to apply in later years.[91] The same diagnosis can be made of Watson's inability to learn from Holmes. (Doyle commented that Holmes's 'semi-scientific methods' were 'occasionally laboured and slow compared with the results of the rough-and-ready, practical man'.)[92] The pedagogical impasse in their teacher–learner relationship is the same as that in the other teacher–learner relationship in the stories – that is, the relationship between Watson-as-narrator and the reader. It is, at heart, one of genre.

As Doyle frames it, Holmes and Watson both know that the public will learn of and from Holmes via Watson. And Holmes frequently advises Watson on the generic conventions he should use for his accounts. Early in *The Sign of Four*, Watson alludes to having 'embodied' the Jefferson Hope case in a 'small brochure' with the 'somewhat fantastic title' of 'A Study in Scarlet' (1.611). Holmes is unimpressed:

> He shook his head sadly. 'I glanced over it,' said he. 'Honestly, I cannot congratulate you upon it. Detection is, or ought to be, an exact science, and should be treated in the same cold and unemotional manner. You have attempted

---

[87] Todorov, *The Poetics of Prose*, 45, original emphasis.
[88] Doyle, *Memories and Adventures*, 20.
[89] Ibid., 20–1.
[90] Ibid., 30.
[91] Ibid., 119. Doyle records that Bell took an interest in the Sherlock Holmes stories and even made suggestions, which – significantly – 'were not very practical' (33).
[92] Ibid., 133.

to tinge it with romanticism, which produces much the same effect as if you worked a love-story or an elopement into the fifth proposition of Euclid.'

'But the romance was there,' I remonstrated. 'I could not tamper with the facts.'

'Some facts should be suppressed, or at least a just sense of proportion should be observed in treating them. The only point in the case which deserved mention was the curious analytical reasoning from effects to causes by which I succeeded in unraveling it.'

(1.611)

The fifth proposition of Euclid holds that if two sides of a triangle are equal, then the angles opposite these sides will also be equal: a mathematical law from which particular instances can be deduced. In Holmes's example, Watson's generic choices regarding his case-solving have the same effect as introducing a love story into this piece of strict deductive logic. What is noticeable is that in this exchange, Watson characterizes the romantic or 'fantastic' elements as 'the facts'. Holmes, the forensic detective for whom 'the facts' are everything, does not challenge this characterization but rather recommends suppressing them. In his view, the only thing worth mentioning is 'the curious analytical reasoning from effects to causes': his generic ideal is the description of a scientific experiment.[93] But his last seven words – 'by which *I* succeeded in unraveling it' (emphasis added) – betray him. Expressing an entirely human desire to enjoy credit for a job brilliantly done, they also point to the spectacular quality of Holmes's performances. Here again is Holmes as glow-worm, miraculous and inimitable.

Of these generic instructions, Watson takes not a blind bit of notice. Instead, Watsonian narrative, as constructed by Doyle, consists of a different genre entirely, a genre that is notable both for passing on experience and for being associated with veterancy. The 'air' of the military man, understood generically, is the story.[94] In 'The Storyteller', Walter Benjamin noted that the teller of tales 'takes what he tells from experience', which can either be his own or that reported by others.[95] (Benjamin is here referring to *Erfahrung*.) In turn,

[93] Cf. Holmes's remarks to Watson in 'The Adventure of the Abbey Grange' (1897): 'Your fatal habit of looking at everything from the point of view of a story instead of as a scientific exercise has ruined what might have been an instructive and even classical series of demonstrations. You slur over work of the utmost finesse and delicacy in order to dwell upon sensational details which may excite, but cannot possibly instruct, the reader' (2.491).

[94] Trooper George in Dickens's *Bleak House* also has a 'Military air' (Charles Dickens, *Bleak House* [1852–3], ed. Stephen Gill (Oxford: Oxford University Press, 2008), 503).

[95] Walter Benjamin, 'The Storyteller' ('Der Erzähler') [1936], trans. Harry Zohn, *Selected Writings. Volume 3: 1935–38*, ed., Michael W. Jennings and Howard Eiland (Cambridge, MA: The Belknap Press of Harvard University Press, 1999), 143–66: 146. In 'Kriminalromane, auf Reisen' (1930), Benjamin described detective fiction as the perfect reading to assuage the anxieties of train travel,

he makes it the experience of those who are listening to his tale.[96] This diffusive storytelling – the transfer and ongoing dissemination of experience via narrative – results in a textual veterancy on the part of the narrative's recipients.

Watson, so frequently dismissed as dull and stolid – 'the normative, unexceptional Englishman', 'the wounded, dutiful soldier', the 'perpetual fool'[97] – is rich in *Erfahrung*. (In this he resembles his creator: Doyle, in his own words, 'sampled every kind of human experience' in a life 'dotted with adventures of all kinds'.)[98] As is narrated in *A Study in Scarlet*, Watson proceeded from his MD to training as an army surgeon and was duly attached to the Fifth Northumberland Fusiliers.[99] The second Anglo-Afghan War broke out as he travelled to join his regiment, then in India, and he therefore journeyed from Bombay to Candahar.[100] There, he was attached to the Berkshires[101] with whom he served at the battle of Maiwand.[102] These experiences are written on the 'haggard face' that is so clearly legible to Holmes (1.162) and they continue to be alluded to throughout the Holmesian canon, underwriting a heuristic approach dependent upon having undergone 'hardship and sickness', upon having been through tough life experiences and having seen others do so. In *The Sign of Four*, the shoulder injury has turned into a leg injury, and the chase after Jonathan Small becomes 'a six-mile limp for a half-pay officer with a damaged *tendo Achillis*' (1.648). This literal instance of Watson's war

---

imagining Sherlock Holmes and Watson sharing a second-class compartment in companionable silence (*Gesammelte Schriften. Band IV.1, 2. Kleine Prosa. Baudelaire-Übertragungen. Werkausgabe*, ed. Théodor W. Adorno, Gershom Scholem, Rolf Tiedemann and Hermann Schweppenhäuser (Frankfurt-am-Main: Suhrkamp, 1980), 381–2). See further Marcus, *Dreams of Modernity*, 59–63.

[96] Benjamin, 'The Storyteller', 146.

[97] Barsham, *Conan Doyle and the Meaning of Masculinity*, 2; Ronald R. Thomas, *Detective Fiction and the Rise of Forensic Science* (Cambridge: Cambridge University Press, 1999), 227; Porter, *The Pursuit of Crime*, 37.

[98] Doyle, *Memories and Adventures*, 7. In addition to his training in diagnostic reasoning as a medical doctor, Doyle briefly witnessed action as the British re-took the Sudan in 1896; served as an army doctor in Bloemfontein during the Second Boer War, publishing *The Great Boer War* in 1900; observed the breaking of the Hindenberg Line on a visit to the front during the First World War; and published the six-volume *The British Campaign in France and Flanders, 1914–1918* in 1919 (Barsham, *Conan Doyle and the Meaning of Masculinity*, 15–42). Watson also resembles another veteran of Doyle's creation – Brigadier Gerard – a Švejk-like figure with the 'thickest head' and 'stoutest heart' in Napoleon's army (Arthur Conan Doyle, *The Complete Brigadier Gerard* [1924], ed. Owen Dudley Edwards (Edinburgh: Canongate Classics, 1995), 39).

[99] William Baring-Gould points out that the 'Fifth Northumberland Fusiliers' (1.143) is an 'ambiguous reference' to the Fifth Regiment of Foot. The Northumberland Fusiliers, that is, were the Fifth Regiment of Foot ('Two Doctors and a Detective', 76).

[100] 'Bombay' and 'Candahar' are Doyle's usages (1.143).

[101] Princess Charlotte of Wales' Royal Berkshire Regiment (Baring-Gould, 'Two Doctors and a Detective', 77).

[102] The battle of Maiwand took place on 27 July 1880.

injury impeding Holmes's investigation nicely figures the generic dissonance between Watsonian veterancy and Holmesian forensics.[103]

Watson's role as Holmes's 'chronicler' (1.594) is to attempt first to assimilate
the detective's mystery-solving in a way that makes sense to him and then
to render it into something capable of being imparted to others. Facilitating
both these processes are the foibles, misunderstandings, emotions and human
interest that he introduces to what would otherwise resemble a rehearsal of
Euclid's fifth proposition. It is notable that, in *The Sign of Four*, Watson's pen-
chant for storytelling is associated, not with his medical experience (which
would have familiarized him with the genre of the case history) but with his
military veterancy. He records that, while sharing the cab with Miss Morstan:

> I endeavoured to cheer and amuse her by reminiscences of my adventures in
> Afghanistan; but, to tell the truth, I was myself so excited at our situation and so
> curious as to our destination that my stories were slightly involved. To this day
> she declares that I told her one moving anecdote as to how a musket looked into
> my tent at the dead of night, and how I fired a double-barrelled tiger cub at it.
>
> (1.622–3)

Watson here is an Othello *manqué*. His confused boasts have generic
significance, the switches taking the 'stories' into the realm of the 'fantastic', to use his earlier description of 'A Study in Scarlet'. Another generic
description is provided by Mrs Forrester:

> 'It is a romance!' cried Mrs Forrester. 'An injured lady, half a million in treasure,
> a black cannibal, and a wooden-legged ruffian. They take the place of the con-
> ventional dragon or wicked earl.'
>
> 'And two knight-errants to the rescue,' added Miss Morstan with a bright
> glance at me.
>
> (1.656)

As a 'romance' – a word, incidentally, Doyle used in relation to his own
colourful life[104] – Watson's narrative embodies and transmits the wisdom
associated with *Erfahrung*:[105] this is an account, not of forensic methods, but

---

[103] Watson also remarks, '[m]y constitution has not got over the Afghan campaign yet. I cannot afford
to throw any extra strain upon it' (1.610) and sits 'nursing [his] wounded leg': 'I had a Jezail bullet
through it some time before, and, though it did not prevent me from walking, it ached wearily
at every change of the weather' (1.611). On the discrepancy between Watson's wounds in *A Study
in Scarlet* and *The Sign of Four*, see William S. Baring-Gould, '"Your hand stole towards your old
wound …"', *The Annotated Sherlock Holmes*, ed. Baring-Gould, 606–9.

[104] 'I have had a life which, for variety and romance, could, I think, hardly be exceeded,' he wrote at
the start of his memoir *Memories and Adventures* (7).

[105] Holmes, by contrast, begins 'an act of interpretation' with 'his mind "entirely free of impressions"'
(Mahaffey, *Modernist Literature*, 85, citing *A Study in Scarlet* (1.231)).

of quest and resolution, damage and making good, dealing with setbacks, finding a significant other and overcoming the obstacles to forming a relationship with that person.[106] In this light, the crime at the centre of the novella is revealed, not as a scientific problem requiring solution, but a tale of experience – and it is worth noting, in this context, that Captain Morstan, Major Sholto and Jonathan Small are all military veterans themselves.

My point is not simply that Watson's romantic liaison with Miss Morstan is of a different narrative texture to Holmes's case-solving. Rather, the very genre of Watsonian epistemology is at odds with the Holmesian logical methodology it purports to transmit. Despite his encouragement, neither Watson nor the reader will apply Holmes's methods: they are to be wondered at, rather than emulated. The generic discordance ensures that Holmes will remain glow-worm-like: non-human but light-emitting and marvellous. Doyle himself acknowledged as much when he referred to 'what the South Americans now call "Sherlockholmitos" ' – 'clever little deductions, which often have nothing to do with the matter in hand, but impress the reader with a general sense of power'.[107] Watson's genre-of-choice – the story or romance – is an inter-personal form, apt for wide dissemination: as Sherlock's brother Mycroft Holmes comments to him in 'The Greek Interpreter' (1893), 'I hear of Sherlock everywhere since you became his chronicler' (1.594). Certainly, Watson's stories will be told and retold. But what they convey will impress, rather than instruct. The point is not so much that scientific method has been shown to be ineffective, but that its reconditeness impedes its transmission.

In the next texts for discussion, veteran epistemology enters the case-solving itself. Lord Peter Wimsey and Cormoran Strike increasingly resemble Dr Watson, rather than Sherlock Holmes, but now there enters a lingering uneasiness about its applicability which undermines *Erfahrung*-based heuristics.

### 'The Triumph of Instinct over Reason': Dorothy L. Sayers, *The Unpleasantness at the Bellona Club* (1921)

In all she said about pedagogy,[108] Dorothy L. Sayers emphasized the importance of learning to think, a process she likened to acquiring a craft. While

---

[106] Significantly, when Watson despairs of this last, he distracts himself by reading 'the latest treatise on pathology' (1.620).

[107] Doyle, *Memories and Adventures*, 126.

[108] Sayers's public talks included *The Tools of Learning*, a paper read at a vacation course in education held in Oxford in 1947, and 'The Teaching of Latin: A New Approach', given to the Association for the Reform of Latin Teaching in 1952.

modern education concentrated on '*teaching subjects*', she told students on a vacation course held in Oxford in 1947, the medieval variety concentrated on 'first *forging and learning to handle the tools of learning*'.[109] School pupils could usefully be taken through the trivium of grammar, logic and rhetoric before emerging able 'to think for themselves'.[110] 'Knowledge', she wrote elsewhere, 'does not become thought till we have made it part of our lives by relating it to our experience and acting upon it.'[111] Putting things into practice, in other words, was preferable to being told about them – a pedagogical leaning similar to Doyle's. Sayers's beliefs informed the writing of her detective fiction, which she seems to have considered as a pedagogical 'tool' – an opportunity for exercising the reason – in itself. 'Perhaps the vogue for detective stories (the genuine kind, I mean, where the reader is given all the clues and can work out the solution for himself),' she remarked during the Second World War, 'is the faint and feeble demand of the reason for something, however limited and trivial, into which it can set its teeth.'[112]

Sayers's fictional veteran detective, Lord Peter Wimsey, demonstrates how to think. He demonstrates this to other characters, to his manservant Bunter, to Harriet Vane, to Charles Parker (no mean thinkers, any of them, themselves) and to the reader – and so, as was the case with Sherlock Holmes, there is a pedagogical aspect to his detection. Wimsey's thinking is shaped by his veterancy: the First World War haunts the Wimsey canon, and Lord Peter's own veterancy is emphasized throughout. His methods of detection are as epistemologically varied as Holmes's, but there is a moment in Sayers's novel *The Unpleasantness at the Bellona Club* (1921) at which *Erfahrung* clearly overrides scientific reasoning as the means of solving the mystery. This shift in approach is directly attributed to Wimsey's veterancy.

Critics have argued that the First World War changed the detective novel, ushering in the 'golden age' of the 'clue-puzzle model'.[113] Golden

---

[109] Dorothy L. Sayers, *The Lost Tools of Learning: Paper Read at a Vacation Course in Education, Oxford 1947* (London: Methuen, 1948), 10, original emphasis. Sayers's analogy closely resembles Benjamin's description of the storyteller as a craftsman, discussed in more detail in Chapter 5.

[110] Sayers, *The Lost Tools of Learning*, 30.

[111] Dorothy L. Sayers, *Begin Here: A War-Time Essay* (London: Victor Gollancz, 1940), 19.

[112] Ibid., 119.

[113] Lee Horsley, 'From Sherlock Holmes to the Present', *A Companion to Crime Fiction*, ed. Charles J. Rzepka and Lee Horsley, 28–42: 30; Susan Rowland, 'The "Classical" Model of the Golden Age', *A Companion to Crime Fiction*, ed. Rzepka and Horsley, 117–27: 116. The term 'clue-puzzle' was coined by Stephen Knight, *Crime Fiction 1800–2000: Detection, Death, Diversity* (Basingstoke: Palgrave Macmillan, 2004), 91.

age detective fiction has been cast as 'reacting against the bloodshed of war';[114] the detective a 'new hero' for a 'traumatized landscape', seeking to 'redeem the modern world from death, war, and chaos'.[115] For Gill Plain, the genre becomes an 'arena that displays the body made safe'.[116] In this arena, the corpse, in contrast to the myriad, merged-together corpses of the First World War battlefields, is re-individualized, untimely deaths are meticulously investigated and proper funeral rites are observed: 'the fragmented, inexplicable and even unattributable corpses of war are replaced by the whole, over-explained, completely known bodies of detection'.[117] Moreover, golden age detective fiction has been associated with the ascendancy of a new approach to crime-solving. In Lee Horsley's words, the detectives of the interwar years, including Peter Wimsey, can, in their 'reliance on intuition and empathy', be seen as 'a reaction against [...] wartime endeavor'.[118] In a similar vein, Susan Rowland has argued that golden age detectives 'detect as much through connection and immersion in their suspects' worlds as they do through detachment and logical analysis of clues'.[119] These detectives are 'intuitive', gaining knowledge by 'connection, empathy or ethical feeling'.[120] Some critics have characterized this shift in approach in gendered terms. Horsley describes Wimsey, Agatha Christie's Hercule Poirot and Margery Allingham's Albert Campion as 'feminized detectives', while Rowland places 'nonrational, emotive, so-called "feminine" methods' in opposition to 'hard "masculine" rationality'.[121] But gendering competing epistemologies in this way risks obscuring the ascendancy of *Erfahrung*. Golden age literary detection need not only be read as a 'soft' 'feminine' reaction to the 'hard' 'masculine' realities of the First World War, but can also be understood as embracing an epistemological method both produced and figured – if also undermined – by combat experience.

In the Lord Peter Wimsey novels there are, as in the Sherlock Holmes canon, many epistemological approaches in play. Wimsey is, indeed, often

[114] Alison Light, *Forever England: Femininity, Literature and Conservatism Between the Wars* (London: Routledge, 1991), 74–5.
[115] Rowland, 'The "Classical" Model of the Golden Age', 120.
[116] Gill Plain, *Twentieth-Century Crime Fiction: Gender, Sexuality and the Body* (Edinburgh: Edinburgh University Press, 2001), 33.
[117] Ibid., 34.
[118] Horsley, 'From Sherlock Holmes to the Present', 32.
[119] Rowland, 'The "Classical" Model of the Golden Age', 121.
[120] Ibid., 123.
[121] Horsley, 'From Sherlock Holmes to the Present', 32; Rowland, 'The "Classical" Model of the Golden Age', 121.

likened to Holmes.[122] 'I merely proceed on the old Sherlock Holmes basis that when you have eliminated the impossible, then whatever remains, however improbable, must be true,' he claims in *Strong Poison* (1930), petitioning Holmes at his inferential best.[123] In *Gaudy Night*, a novel that explores both the absolute necessity and frequent danger of insisting on 'the truth' (the former aligned with the codes and standards of scholarship, the latter with a gentler humaneness), he comments that the mystery of the poison pen letters and acts of vandalism can be solved 'by a little straight and unprejudiced reasoning'.[124] In a telling exchange, Miss Edwards, a biologist and science tutor, insists on the importance of 'establishing scientific facts'. 'Now we have found common ground to stand on,' replies Wimsey. 'Establish the facts, no matter what comes of it.' The conversation continues as follows:

> 'On that ground, Lord Peter,' said the Warden, 'your inquisitiveness becomes a principle. And a very dangerous one.' 'But the fact that A killed B isn't necessarily the whole of the truth,' persisted Miss Barton. 'A's provocation and state of health are facts, too.'[125]

Miss Barton, the author of a book that attacks the Nazi doctrine that women should be confined to *Kinder, Küche, Kirche*,[126] complicates Wimsey's heuristic approach by insisting on the pertinence of factors which are not scientifically quantifiable. The exchange recalls that between Holmes and Watson in *The Sign of Four* quoted earlier, in which Watson remarks that 'the romance was there [...] I could not tamper with the facts' (1.611). Enlarging the definition of 'the facts', Watson and Miss Barton expose the need for an expansion of methods of detection.

In Wimsey's case – if not in Holmes's – such reminders are superfluous. Despite his academic background – he is famously an alumnus of Balliol College, Oxford – he does not so much favour academic learning as getting 'the feel of the tool',[127] as Sayers put it, through painstaking

---

[122] See also Dorothy L. Sayers, 'Dr. Watson's Christian Name: A Brief Contribution to the Exegetical Literature of Sherlock Holmes', *Queen Mary's Book for India*, ed. Cornelia Sorabji (London: G. G. Harrap, 1943), 78–82.

[123] Dorothy L. Sayers, *Strong Poison* [1926] (London: Stodder, 1968), 83. Other Holmesian comparisons include an elderly woman commenting 'Like Sherlock Holmes, I do declare' in 'The Unsolved Puzzle of the Man with No Face' (1928) (*Lord Peter Views the Body* [1928] (London: Hodder and Stoughton, 1979), 233) and the Dean in *Gaudy Night* (1935) inquiring 'What does Sherlock Holmes do now?' (*Gaudy Night* [1935] (London: Hodder and Stoughton, 1987), 374).

[124] Sayers, *Gaudy Night*, 358.

[125] Ibid., 409.

[126] Ibid., 522.

[127] Sayers, *The Lost Tools of Learning*, 8.

practice. And here the significance of his veterancy becomes apparent. The reader is constantly confronted with Wimsey's war service, not least in the 'short biography', purportedly by his uncle, Paul Austin Delagardie, which is appended to each novel. From this, the reader learns that Wimsey 'did very well in France'; earned the DSO;[128] performed some 'recklessly good intelligence work behind the German front'; and was blown up and buried in a shell-hole in 1918 (249–50).[129] These experiences are explicitly shown as enhancing Wimsey's powers of detection. In 'The Vindictive Story of the Footsteps That Ran' (1928), he notices a wire working loose on the cage the dentist keeps his mice in: ' "Built noticin' – improved by practice," said Lord Peter quietly. "Anythin' wrong leaves a kind of impression on the eye, brain trots along afterwards with the warnin'. I saw that when we came in. Only just grasped it. Can't say my mind was glued on the matter." '[130] Combat experience – 'practice' – that is, has refined his innate aptitude for observation: the ability to spot that something is 'wrong' has become an indispensable survival skill. Wimsey expands upon the point in 'The Unsolved Puzzle of the Man with No Face' (1928):

> [I]t's like the way a gunner, say, looks at a landscape where he happens to be posted. He doesn't see it as a landscape. He doesn't see it as a thing of magic beauty, full of sweeping lines and lovely colour. He sees it as so much cover, so many landmarks to aim by, so many gun-emplacements. And when the war is over and he goes back to it, he will still see it as cover and landmarks and gun-emplacements. It isn't a landscape any more. It's a war map.[131]

War alters perception irrevocably: landscapes lose their innocence, converted into systems of prospects, hazards and refuges.[132] Instinct and intuition, as well as observation, have been transformed through a process of habituation.

But of greater relevance to the present argument is the fact that Wimsey's war experiences left him 'with a bad nervous breakdown' (250). During this, according to his uncle, he 'shut everybody out of his confidence', 'adopted an impenetrable frivolity of manner and a dilettante pose' and became 'a

---

[128] Distinguished Service Order.

[129] Dorothy L. Sayers, *The Unpleasantness at the Bellona Club* [1921] (London: Hodder and Stoughton, 1977). Page numbers are given in the text. I quote from the version of the 'biography' in this novel because it is the text focused on in this section.

[130] Sayers, *Lord Peter Views the Body*, 148.

[131] Ibid., 249.

[132] On prospect-refuge theory, see Jay Appleton, *The Experience of Landscape* [1975] (Chichester: John Wiley, 1996), 163, and McLoughlin, *Authoring War*, 92–5.

complete comedian' (250). Detective work, beginning with 'the business of the Attenbury Emeralds', proved a curative distraction, but '[a]t the end of every case we had the old nightmares and shell-shock over again' (250, 251). The reader's attention is drawn to the character's symptoms throughout the Wimsey oeuvre. To give some examples: Wimsey suffers a nightmare and flashbacks in *Whose Body?* (1923); is reminded of horses screaming in burning stables in *Clouds of Witness* (1926); exhibits symptoms of trauma on finding Vera Linklater's body in *Unnatural Death* (1927); compares the crash and scream in 'The Man With Copper Fingers' (1928) with the noises of war; feels his nerves to be 'in a rotten state' in 'The Undignified Melodrama of the Bone of Contention' (1928);[133] and has another nightmare in *Busman's Honeymoon* (1937). These moments are more than period detail. They underscore the fact that Wimsey has suffered and is suffering: his detective activities may be cast as a 'distraction' from the ongoing effects of his war service,[134] but those effects inevitably crowd in. And nowhere is their epistemological significance more apparent that in *The Unpleasantness at the Bellona Club*.

The Bellona Club – a London gentleman's club – is imbued with veterancy. (Bellona was the name of an ancient Roman goddess of war).[135] In the novel's opening pages, it is described as a 'Morgue', its members as 'corpses' and a joke is made – anticipating the mystery to be solved – to the effect that a dead body would be unlikely to be noticed: 'Waiter, take away Lord Whatsisname, he's been dead two days' (5). Shellshock is a recognized state in the Bellona Club;[136] George Fentiman's 'neurasthenia' is understood and accepted by the members, with the explanation that they 'knew too much' (10). Their number includes Wimsey, who 'knew better than the old solicitor the kind of mental and physical strain George Fentiman had undergone' (18). The use of the verb 'knew' in both cases is suggestive: this is knowledge hard won in a war of whose conditions those who did not fight in it have little inkling.

---

[133] Sayers, *Lord Peter Views the Body*, 121.

[134] Dorothy L. Sayers, *Whose Body?* [1927] (London: Hodder and Stoughton, 2003), 176.

[135] Dr Penberthy's aims are, ironically, to reverse the state of veterancy: 'Has an idea, if only he could start one of these clinics for rejuvenating people, he could be a millionaire. All these giddy old goats who want their gay time over again – why, they're a perfect fortune to the man with a bit of capital and a hell of a lot of cheek' (209).

[136] George Fentiman's shellshock allows Sayers to comment on the contemporary treatment of veterans; as the character remarks: 'What's the damn good of it, Wimsey? A man goes and fights for his country, gets his inside gassed out, and loses his job, and all they give him is the privilege of marching past the Cenotaph once a year and paying four shillings in the pound income tax' (6). On the parallels between Fentiman and Sayers's husband Oswald Fleming, who suffered ill-health as a result of being gassed in the First World War, see Mitzi Brunsdale, *Dorothy L. Sayers: Solving the Mystery of Wickedness* (Oxford: Berg, 1990), 106, and Esme Miskimmins, 'Dorothy L. Sayers (1893–1957)', *A Companion to Crime Fiction*, ed. Charles J. Rzepka and Lee Horsley, 438–49: 440.

In the first half of the novel, Wimsey proceeds in Holmesian fashion, explicitly likened to Doyle's detective ('Hear you're turning into a regular Sherlock' (43); 'Even a comparative imbecile like myself can play the giddy sleuth on the amateur Moriarty' (6); 'Work it out for yourself, my dear Watson' (53)). His initial investigations involve a magnifying glass, fingerprint powder, chemical analysis and graphology – all the tools of Holmes's trade. But the following comically rendered exchange indicates that Holmesian methods are not entirely satisfactory:

> '[W]e might be able to get some sort of clue from the dust on the clothes, if any [says Wimsey] – to show us where the General spent the night. If – to take a rather unlikely example – we were to find a lot of sawdust, for instance, we might suppose that he had been visiting a carpenter. Or a dead leaf might suggest a garden or a common, or something of that sort. While a cobweb might mean a wine-cellar, or – or a potting-shed – and so on. You see?'
> 'Yes, my lord' (rather doubtfully).
>
> (52)

Pedagogically, this is revealing. Even as he purports to explain the process of forensic inference, Wimsey's hesitations underscore its potential limitations. The rather doubtful 'yes' from the General's manservant – at that moment *in statu pupillari* – emphasizes the paucity of the learning opportunity. But the Holmesian investigations continue, nonetheless. In a moment of forensic pyrotechnics worthy of Doyle's detective, Wimsey and Parker predict from their analyses of the data what will be found at the crime scene:

> 'I say we shall find a long scratch on the paint [...] where the foot of the corpse rested and stiffened in that position. [...] And as the body was in a sitting position [...] we shall, of course, find a seat inside the cabinet.'
> 'Yes, and, with luck, we may find a projecting nail or something which caught the General's trouser-leg when the body was removed.' (120–1)

Their eagerness sounds a comic note again: this is forensic detection as a larkish Boy's Own adventure. Nonetheless, examination of the scene proves their logic correct. Wimsey accordingly proposes a Holmesian *coup de théâtre*, a literal display of forensic reasoning:

> Charles, we will lay out the *pièces de conviction* on the table. The boots. The photographs. The microscopic slides showing the various specimens. The paper of notes from the library. The outer garments of the deceased. Just so. And *Oliver Twist*. Beautiful. Now, as Sherlock Holmes says, we shall look imposing enough to strike terror into the guilty breast, though armed in triple steel.
>
> (136)

Sure enough, the guilty party, when confronted with the evidence, confesses his deeds. And in a Sherlock Holmes story, this is where the plot would end, having ingeniously incorporated into the circumstances of the disposal of the body those First World War indispensables: Armistice Day, the Two Minutes' Silence and the memorial poppy. But just at this moment, precisely when Wimsey's logical, data-based conjectures are proved correct and – crucially – as if to mock them, it emerges that solution is incomplete. General Fentiman has been poisoned.[137] And this development marks the point at which Wimsey's investigations must draw on *Erfahrung*.

In the second half of the novel, the clues are not fingerprints, stains and blotting paper but the contents of a bookshelf, the execution of a painting, a recent engagement and the roughening of a voice. Taste, comportment, artistic style and emotional development assume ascendancy over the advancement of *rigor mortis*, paint samples and torn clothing. The first, 'mechanically perfect' solution (212) must give way to a second that is messier and less susceptible to measurement. In the process of arriving at it, Wimsey lets slip some remarks that explain his revised methodology. 'I'm an ordinary person, and have met women, and talked to them like ordinary human beings,' he tells Parker, adding, '[o]ne learns something' (212). Only disappointed love can explain Ann Dorland's behaviour, he informs Marjorie Phelps: '[m]y experienced eye told me as much at the first glance' (225). He speaks, in his own self-description, as 'a man of the world' (228). Experience of people and worldliness enable Wimsey to appreciate what is unquantifiable in human motivation. But, beyond this, they also make him good at handling other people.

For Wimsey, as it emerges from a number of instances, is adept at people management. He makes George Fentiman laugh, helpfully releasing tension from their conversation. He responds 'sympathetically' when Fentiman describes the humiliation of being poor (92). He skilfully extracts information from Mrs Munns. He rounds on Mr Munns when he has been tactless in front of Sheila Fentiman. Interviewing General Fentiman's nurse, he asks questions that relate to personal feelings: 'Did you like Miss Dorland?', 'Was she happy?', 'Did she cry much?' (204). And his ability to manage people is noted. '[Y]ou twist people into doing things they ought to blush for,' scolds Marjorie Phelps (163). 'Make her give it [the bottle] to you. You can. You can do anything,' urges Sheila Fentiman (191). The way is prepared for a second, definitive denouement,

---

[137] It emerges that Wimsey suspected the poisoning, since he has made a 'rather obscurely-expressed suggestion' to Sir James Lubbock to test for it (142).

this time based on hunches, inexplicable feelings, 'unsupported opinion' (213), empathy and intuition.

The key scene is Wimsey's first meeting with Miss Dorland. Via a series of careful remarks, he elicits her story by showing an empathy derived from the fact that he, like her, knows what it is to have suffered. 'You've been through it, haven't you?' he asks 'gently' (217), and, a little later, '[e]verything's pretty hateful, isn't it? [...] [s]omething's hurt you' (218). It is the legacy of his First World War experiences that allows Wimsey to make such remarks authentically; without it, he would be unable to reassure her: 'One gets over everything [...] [p]articularly if one tells somebody about it' (218). Knowledge of humanity and the ways of the world enable Wimsey to piece together the crime, while gentleness, understanding and reassurance suffuse his handling of this crucial witness.

Such qualities also shape the novel's ending. Wimsey realizes that Miss Dorland will, even if acquitted, always be 'suspect' (226). He reflects: 'the question was not one which could be conveniently settled by a brilliant flash of deductive logic, or the discovery of a blood-stained thumb-mark. It was a case for lawyers to argue – for a weighing of the emotional situation by twelve good and lawful persons' (226). Holmesian heuristics are explicitly rejected here. Resolution – as opposed to solution – will depend upon the appreciation of both ethical arguments and emotional truth by Miss Dorland's peers,[138] the outcome of deliberation, collaboration and consensus informed by life experience. Nor is Penberthy's fate determined after a forensic investigation of the facts. Instead, his military peers, Wimsey and Colonel Marchbanks, facilitate for him a way out that avoids dishonour: in many ways an act of mercy. The outcome of *The Unpleasantness at the Bellona Club* therefore seems to mark, in Wimsey's words to Bunter, 'The triumph of Instinct over Reason' (114).

Instinct is pedagogically tricky. How might the set of qualities involved in *Erfahrung*-based detection be passed on to others? As noted, Sayers, like Doyle, endorsed praxis: in another craftsman analogy, she advised 'using whatever subject [comes] handy as a piece of material on which to doodle until the use of the tool [becomes] second nature'.[139] It is important that Wimsey is an *amateur* detective – as Sayers noted to Victor Gollancz, the series was originally called 'Lord Peter Wimsey: Unprofessional Sleuth'

---

[138] Such peers could include women: the first woman served on an English jury in 1921, the year *The Unpleasantness at the Bellona Club* was published.

[139] Sayers, *The Lost Tools of Learning*, 10.

and then altered by *Pearson's Magazine* to 'Unprofessional Detective'.[140] Amateurism fosters risk-taking, experimentation, making mistakes, unorthodox methods, repeated practice: all important ways of learning, of getting the 'feel of the tool'. But these ways of learning are for individual discovery rather than external observation: the glow-worm has given way to the mentor.

And so *The Unpleasantness at the Bellona Club* commemorates the triumph of instinct over reason – until right at the very end. In the 'Post-Mortem' postscript, Wimsey makes another comment that turns all this on its head. Discussing the case with the policeman, Parker, he remarks, 'A damned unsatisfactory case, Charles. Not the kind I like. No real proof' (242). Wimsey's dissatisfaction suggests that, however successful its application to problem-solving, *Erfahrung*-based epistemology is somehow inadequate. Hard empirical proof is indispensable: for certainty and for the protection of the reputations of those wrongly suspected. The moment is a cautionary one, alerting the reader, not to the invalidity of *Erfahrung*-based problem-solving, but at least to its limitations. Similar epistemological tensions emerge in the next texts for discussion: J. K. Rowling's *The Cuckoo's Calling*, *The Silkworm* and *Career of Evil*.

## 'The Reading of Subtle Signs': J. K. Rowling, *The Cuckoo's Calling* (2013), *The Silkworm* (2014) and *Career of Evil* (2015)

In 2013, a début detective novel that had received positive, though not ecstatic, reviews and that was selling moderately well was revealed to have been written by *Harry Potter* author J. K. Rowling. Sales on amazon.com increased by 156,866 per cent in a single day.[141] *The Cuckoo's Calling* features a detective who is also a war veteran, Cormoran Strike.[142] What is more, the novel's 'first' – pseudonymous – author, 'Robert Galbraith', was also, purportedly, a veteran. Rowling gave two reasons for her pseudonym's military career. Her first motivation was to attempt to restrict the publicity given to

---

[140] Letter of 28 November 1927 (*The Letters of Dorothy L. Sayers: 1899–1936: The Making of a Detective Novelist*, ed. Barbara Reynolds (London: Hodder and Stoughton, 1995), 267).

[141] Alex Hern, 'Sales of "The Cuckoo's Calling" Surge by 150,000% After JK Rowling Revealed as Author', *New Statesman* (14 July 2013), www.newstatesman.com/2013/07/sales-cuckoos-calling-surge-150000-after-jk-rowling-revealed-author.

[142] Recalling the bird imagery in Helen Ashton's *The Captain Comes Home*, the name 'Cormoran Strike' has avian echoes (cormorant, shrike), which recur in the first name of Robin Ellacott and in the nickname ('Cuckoo') of Lula Landry. Katy Waldman also notes the bird allusions in 'Private "I"', *Slate* (16 July 2013), www.slate.com/articles/arts/books/2013/07/the_cuckoo_s_calling_by_j_k_rowling_or_robert_galbraith_reviewed.html.

the work. A former military policeman now working in the civilian security sector, Galbraith had 'a solid excuse not to appear in public or provide a photograph'.[143] Galbraith, like Rowling, would not be publicly 'known'. Rowling's second reason for giving Galbraith a military background was to provide a 'plausible' excuse for his familiarity with the procedures of the army detective branch.[144]

In inventing Galbraith as the inventor of Strike, Rowling created a veteran to create a veteran. Galbraith was, according to the biographical note on the dust jacket of the first edition of *The Cuckoo's Calling*, a civilian security expert who had previously worked with the Royal Military Police and its Special Investigation Branch (SIB).[145] On the Robert Galbraith website, in reply to the self-posed 'frequently asked question' 'why did you choose for the author to have a military background?', Rowling explains, '[i]t was the easiest and most plausible reason for Robert to know how the Special Investigation Branch operates and investigates'.[146] An author must be credible, this implies, and credibility comes from personal experience (in this case, experience and military veterancy are literally the same). More specifically, the remark indicates that, for Rowling, personal experience is the most credible source of *knowledge*: after all, information about the SIB could also have been gleaned from books or interviews.[147] When the true author of *The Cuckoo's Calling* became known, a number of commentators expressed similar epistemological assumptions. By now, however, they were wondering at the fact that no one had previously questioned ex-military policeman Robert Galbraith's familiarity with luxury hand-bags. 'After all,' asked Michiko Kakutani in the *New York Times*, 'how many former military men are more adept writing about high fashion – describing a "clinging poison-green" Cavalli dress, vintage Ossie Clark confections and "fabby handbags" with custom-printed "detachable silk linings" – than they are about their hero's war experiences in Afghanistan or his training in forensics?'[148] When Rowling was revealed as the author, this no longer

---

[143] J.K.Rowling,'FrequentlyAskedQuestions',www.robert-galbraith.com/#frequentlyAskedQuestions.

[144] Ibid.

[145] J. K. Rowling, *The Cuckoo's Calling* [2013] (London: Sphere Books, 2014). Page numbers are given in the text.

[146] www.robert-galbraith.com/#frequentlyAskedQuestions.

[147] In the 'Acknowledgements' to *Career of Evil*, Rowling thanks 'MP, who enabled me to make a fascinating visit to 35 Section SIB (UK) RMP in Edinburgh Castle', revealing that the scenes set in this office – as well as other details – are based on this first-hand experience.

[148] Michiko Kakutani, 'A Murder Is Solved, a Sleuth Is Born', *New York Times* (17 July 2013), www.nytimes.com/2013/07/18/books/in-j-k-rowlings-cuckoos-calling-model-dies-but-why .html?pagewanted=all&_r=1&.

appeared to be a difficulty. (Rowling herself satirizes these notions in *The Silkworm* when a character comments that 'With the invention of the internet, any subliterate cretin can be Michiko Kakutani' (502).)[149]

A former teacher[150] and the inventor of that esteemed educational establishment, Hogwarts School of Witchcraft and Wizardry, Rowling has demonstrated her interest in pedagogy as well as epistemology. In the commencement speech she gave at Harvard in 2008, she spoke of the 'fringe benefits of failure', among which she included the suggestion that '[t]he knowledge that you have emerged wiser and stronger from setbacks means that you are, ever after, secure in your ability to survive'.[151] She also mentioned 'the importance of imagination', which, in its 'most transformative and revelatory capacity', 'enables us to empathise with humans whose experiences we have never shared'.[152] I don't mean to suggest that these remarks constitute an educational philosophy. But I would note Rowling's impassioned belief in the value of learning from experience and the capacity to imagine ourselves in others' places.

*The Cuckoo's Calling* explores experience and imagination (a by-product of *Erfahrung*) as the basis of knowledge. *Erfahrung* is, as in *The Sign of Four* and *The Unpleasantness at the Bellona Club*, expressed as veterancy. Cormoran Strike has seen service in Kenya, Angola and, most recently, Afghanistan, where half his right leg was blown off (the geographical and physiological locations of his injury link him to Dr Watson). Strike explicitly likens himself to Odysseus via Tennyson's Ulysses, and the Odysseus connection is also discernable in the fact that he has had a 'complicated, peripatetic childhood' (21) – the psychological equivalent of Odysseus' boyhood wounding by the boar. If this wound is central to Odysseus' identity, the means by which others recognize him on his return to Ithaca, Strike's disordered childhood informs his adult behaviour. 'Fascinated by the smooth workings of other children's homes', he has 'from his most extreme youth [...] needed to investigate, to know for sure, to winkle the truth out of the smallest conundrums' (53). Extensive detail is given to reinforce the fact that Strike is a former serviceman. He sleeps on a camp bed and eats Pot Noodles because they remind him 'of the fare he used to carry in his ration pack' through a 'deep-rooted association between

---

[149] J. K. Rowling, *The Silkworm* (London: Sphere Books, 2014). Page numbers are given in the text.
[150] Lindsey Fraser, *An Interview with J. K. Rowling* (London: Mammoth, 2000), 23, 25.
[151] J. K. Rowling, 'Very Good Lives: The Fringe Benefits of Failure, and the Importance of Imagination', http://news.harvard.edu/gazette/story/2008/06/text-of-j-k-rowling-speech/.
[152] Ibid.

quickly heated and rehydrated food and makeshift dwelling places' (49). His default modus operandi is a 'familiarly soldierly state of doing what needed to be done, without question or complaint' (49). He has smelled 'many times' the 'sweet and unmistakable smell of human brains': '[y]ou never forgot' (90). Habit, repetition, instinct and memory emerge as the cornerstones of Strike's thought and behaviour.

Nonetheless, Rowling also endows Strike with some forensic abilities. This is, to some degree, a nod to traditional generic expectations, but it also serves to put pressure on *Erfahrung*-based methodologies. Compared to Sherlock Holmes (237) – albeit ironically – Strike is noted as possessing 'an exceptionally accurate memory' and an 'incurable habit of thoroughness' (23, 93). He has been 'trained to investigate to a high and rigorous standard', arranging facts 'rigorously and precisely' (32, 33).[153] But, notably, this rigorous training has also taught him to 'allow the witness to tell their story in their own way': the ensuing 'gush of impression and recollection' must be 'harvested' for 'revealed details' and 'apparent inconsequentialities' that will 'later prove invaluable nuggets of evidence' (32–3). In a revealing passage, Rowling writes: 'Strike was used to playing archaeologist among the ruins of people's traumatised memories; he had made himself the confidant of thugs; he had bullied the terrified, baited the dangerous and laid traps for the cunning' (93). Strike has a range of methods of elicitation, that is, from digging to reassurance to intimidation to ambush (the military flavour of these methods is unmistakable). His most conspicuous skill is being able to listen to people and judge the sincerity of their discourse. The way that the driver Kolovas-Jones launches into his story tells Strike that he has 'rehearsed it' (98). He senses that only part of Tansy Bestigui's account rings with 'authenticity', an authenticity that shines 'a garish light on the fakery with which she garnished it' (156). Bryony Radford, a 'highly unreliable witness', 'suggestive and mendacious', nevertheless tells him 'much more than she knew' (315). He watches and listens for signs that the model Ciara Porter is 'lying or exaggerating' but the words come, 'to all appearances, frankly' (322). He 'intuit[s]' that Evan Duffield is 'lying' (345). And Strike evinces further skills of personal interaction. In questioning the porter Derrick Wilson, he asks 'simple, deft questions', focusing on what Wilson had 'felt, touched, seen and heard at each step of his way' (282). As a consequence, Wilson's 'body language' starts to

---

[153] Some critics took the hint. Charles Finch, for example, described Strike as a 'private detective with a brilliant mind' ('The Master Is Back in "The Cuckoo's Calling"', *USA Today* (16 July 2013), www.usatoday.com/story/life/books/2013/07/24/the-cuckoos-calling/2581907/).

'change' as he begins to 'enact the way he had held the door jambs, leaning into rooms, casting a rapid look around' (282). Strike is able to read both the verbal and the physical language, exhibiting a high degree of empathy. Empathy is evident, too, in his imaginative connection with the dead Lula Landry: 'feeling' her behind her written words, looking at the last thing she looked upon in life and sensing himself to be 'strangely close' to her (280). Strike's ability to understand other people, the languages of their words and bodies, their lies, evasions and elaborations, is explicitly linked to his experiences. Rowling writes: 'Strike's strange, nomadic childhood, with its constant uprootings and graftings on to motley groups of children and teenagers, had forged in him an advanced set of social skills; he knew how to fit in, to make people laugh, to render himself acceptable to almost anyone' (217). The exigencies of non-belonging – an Odyssean itinerary – have forged these 'social skills': a set of tools refined through suffering. Significantly, Rowling places the second part of the novel beneath the epigraph of Virgil's *Non ignara mali miseris succurrere disco*,[154] which she translates as 'No stranger to trouble myself, I am learning to care for the unhappy' (56).

*Erfahrung*, the yield of veterancy, is in large part the key to Strike's solution of the crime of Lula Landry's murder, allowing him to appraise witnesses, intuit 'truth' and sense motives. Noticeably, as the novel progresses, Strike's veterancy also seems to increase, in the sense that his stump – visual and somatic reminder of his military experience – becomes more and more painful. His recent weight gain puts an 'additional load' on his prosthesis, causing 'chafing' and 'the shadow of a limp' (42). The gel liner becomes 'an inadequate cushion against pain' as the scar tissue is 'inflamed and over-warm'; the friction between the stump and the prosthesis is 'more painful with every step' (52, 215, 211). Falling downstairs towards the end of the novel, he lands with 'an excruciating, fiery pain in both the joint and the end of his stump, as though it was freshly severed, as though the scar tissue was still healing' (413). Strike is not only in pain: he is in pain that is constantly increasing. As the pain intensifies, and as though in direct relation to it, his empathy and intuition lead him to the solution of the mystery. His prosthesis, visible sign of his veterancy, is what finally stops the killer in his tracks.

Yet *Erfahrung* as the basis of knowledge is ultimately inadequate. In the final scene before the Epilogue, Strike confronts Bristow with his guilt. The scene takes the classic form of the denouement of golden age detection: Strike

---

[154] *Aeneid* 1.630. These are the words with which Dido welcomes the veteran Aeneas.

tells Bristow the story, or *sjuzhet*, of the *fabula* of his wrong-doing. Bristow's tactic is to insist that empirical proof must link *sjuzhet* to *fabula*, a link that Strike acknowledges will be necessary to secure Bristow's conviction and that he therefore proceeds to establish with reference to incontrovertible physical data such as CCTV footage, the unique design of a hoodie and droplets of water on the stairs. Notably, Bristow characterizes the epistemological point in terms of genre. Using a cognate of the word that Doyle deploys to characterize Watson's accounts, he tells Strike, 'You ought to give up detecting and try fantasy writing [...] Total fantasy' (522, 525). Forensic proof, this implies, is anathema to the *Erfahrung*-based form of the story. If experience, as Rowling suggested in her choice of career for her protagonist, is both the actual source and the acceptable explanation for knowledge, that knowledge is painfully and imperfectly gained.

By 2014, 'Robert Galbraith' had become 'Robert Galbraith Limited'. The second novel in the series, *The Silkworm*, concerns the murder of a novelist, Owen Quine. Strike appears still very much the grizzled veteran, his jaw 'grimy with stubble', 'bruise-coloured shadows' around his dark eyes (5). His stump continues to cause him trouble: he slips on shiny floors, has problems on public transport, falls over and is unable to pursue runaway suspects. The pain increases as he delves deeper into the mystery, creating an ever closer relationship between his veterancy and his detection; the point at which he is driven by pain to buy a new walking stick matches his growing dependency on his assistant, Robin.

As in the previous novel, Strike's methodology is primarily *Erfahrung*-based: he follows hunches, relies on his gut feelings about people (his judgement of Leonora Quine is correct from the outset), sympathizes with the underdog, listens carefully. In this novel, his 'instinct for the strange, the dangerous, the suspicious' (190) is again repeatedly linked with his military experience, specifically the moment at which he sensed an 'imminent explosion' in Afghanistan (163). The incident has led Detective Inspector Richard Anstis, the fellow soldier whose life Strike saved in the explosion and now the policeman in charge of the case, to give him the nickname 'Mystic Bob'. As his investigations bring him closer to the killer, Strike has the same feeling of foreboding that he had in an armoured vehicle in Afghanistan:

> Much as he had disliked the Mystic Bob tag with which Anstis had saddled him, Strike had a sense of approaching danger now, almost as strongly as when he had known, without question, that the Viking was about to blow up around him. Intuition, they called it, but Strike knew it to be the reading of subtle signs, the subconscious joining of dots.
>
> (512)

Intuition, or instinct, is an awareness that is the product of experience, a skilled way of 'reading' developed through having read similar 'subtle signs'.

The word 'reading' is significant, as solving Quine's murder turns out to depend on skilled reading – not just of body language and people's emotions, but specifically of a literary manuscript. Though Strike couches his perception of 'whodunnit' in instinctive terms – ' "Look," he said, suddenly serious. "I don't know what to tell you except I can feel it. *I can smell it*" ' (478) – what has in fact led him to the murder is the realization that Quine's novel contains 'a foreign voice' (552). 'The more I've talked to people who knew Quine,' he notes, 'the clearer it's become that the book everyone's read bears only a vague resemblance to the one he claimed to be writing' (550). Detection has literally turned into literary criticism – and vice versa; indeed, the murder is described as 'elaborate, strange, sadistic […] grotesque' and '*literary*' (186, my emphasis). In Strike's view, Anstis, 'an efficient recognizer of patterns, a reliable pursuer of the obvious' (186), lacks both the 'wit and the imagination' to appreciate a solution that appears 'incredible' (464): in other words, he is not a good enough *reader*.

That detection is equated with reading challenges the novel's actual reader, who must also perform *Erfahrung*-based problem-solving, sifting clues from red herrings through familiarity with generic conventions, the particular idiosyncrasies of the Cormoran Strike series[155] and the relationship between *fabula* and *sjuzhet* in this particular novel. Rowling slyly sets traps to undermine excessive self-confidence on the part of the reader in this regard. To give one example of this: Strike's friend Nick mentions at a dinner party that he is a gastroenterologist (139). Given that the murder involves the removal of the victim's intestines and given that gastroenterology is a specialized and specific job as well as a noticeable word, it seems a reasonable assumption that Nick's expertise will be called upon. Instead, it is Nick's father's occupation as a cabbie that proves significant. Another example occurs when, fairly early in the novel, a character, Elizabeth Tassel, says that it is a pity that a bite once administered to Quine by her Doberman did not prove fatal (71). Real murderers – at least, real fictional murderers – never tell investigators that they wish the victim dead, but generic conventions are there to be subverted. The remark creates a moment of

---

[155] As *Harry Potter* readers know, Rowling's holistic conception and composition of the series rewards textual veterancy and the signs are that the Cormoran Strike series – unfinished as I write – will function in the same way. On 14 March 2017, Rowling confirmed on Twitter that the fourth book in the series will be called *Lethal White*. No release date has been given as this book goes into press.

uncertainty in the reader, an anxiety about the epistemological robustness of textual veterancy. Exposing the limitations of readerly expertise in this way allows Rowling a small triumph: after all, the reactions to the first, pseudonymous Strike novel demonstrated that 'the book everyone's read' became a different text when its true author was revealed.

Strike's ability to read – his ability to read situations, that is – is also shown to be fallible. As an accident looms as his assistant, Robin Ellacott, is driving him to Devon, he shouts 'BRAKE!', because 'that was what he had done last time to try to stave off death' (311). His judgement is precisely wrong: Robin instead presses the accelerator and remarks later, 'You realise that if I'd braked, we'd have skidded right into the tanker' (312). The scene continues: ' "Yeah," said Strike, and he laughed too. "Dunno why I said that," he lied' (312). Here Strike conceals the link with the incident in Afghanistan, when his 'reading' of 'subtle signs' produced a correct reaction. The lesson of this, second, road incident is clear: experience cannot necessarily be relied upon.

This near accident is important pedagogically. Learning, as a theme, is focused in *The Silkworm* on the developing career of Strike's assistant, Robin Ellacott. Robin has, in Strike's words, 'a lot of aptitude' (336) for detection (he sees in her 'what he possessed himself' (338)), which is enhanced as she gains experience. There is an expectation, shared by both of them, that she will 'learn on the job' (336); that is, by observing and imitating Strike in a mentor–mentee relationship. But, as the near miss on the road to Devon shows, this transmission of experience-derived expertise is only partly successful. Notably, Robin describes herself as Strike's 'Watson'. Strike is Sherlockian in the sense of being superhuman: named after a Cornish giant (39), he is capable of seeming to fill 'twice as much space as he had just seconds before' (16). Robin's fiancé's view of him is that he is 'attention-seeking and arrogant' (28), and, to an extent, like the miraculous glow-worm Holmes, Strike is to be marvelled at, rather than emulated. It is made clear that Robin's detective skills will be improved, not by the imparting of the benefit of Strike's experience, but through professional courses in counter-surveillance ('[s]o next time you pull a bag of dog shit out of a bin no one notices you're doing it' (572)) and books like *Investigative Interviewing: Psychology and Practice* (174).

Strike arrives at the crime's solution through a combination of such professional investigative techniques and *Erfahrung*-based skilled reading. Immediately, though, the solution – 'incontrovertibly correct, unassailably right [...] perfect, snug and solid' (426) – is presented as deficient: '[t]he problem was that he could not yet see how to prove it' (462). Robin's reaction is the same: 'it's all ... opinion [...] There's no *physical* evidence at all'

(476). Indeed, Strike must arrange for corroborative proof to be found: this is necessary to convince the police and to secure a safe conviction. It is worth noting that, in the denouement of this novel, the accused murderer dismisses Strike's *sjuzhet* both on the basis of its genre ('Sick fantasist' (561) – that 'fantasy' word again) and also on the basis of his veterancy: 'He was badly hurt in Afghanistan [...] I think he's shell-shocked [...] He needs help' (556). *Erfahrung*-based insight without physical proof, that is, is mere storytelling. The epistemological conclusion of the novel (like the conclusion of *The Cuckoo's Calling*) is the same as that of *The Unpleasantness at the Bellona Club*: knowledge based upon experience, worldliness, accrued wisdom and imaginative empathy is worth having but insufficiently robust.

*Career of Evil* (2015), the third in the Cormoran Strike series, keeps the detective's veterancy – in the form of his missing leg – in central view. Strike's stump continues to be 'stiff' (185) and 'sore' (56) and he is 'feeling the pain' in it when the identity of the culprit dawns on him (423).[156] But in this novel, the implications of his veterancy form the killer's motive, as is made clear by the delivery of a severed leg to Robin. In the following passage, Robin hypothesizes how the severed limb might influence a reading of Strike's own absent leg:

> 'He's making clear reference to your injury,' Robin said. 'What does your missing leg mean to him?'
> 'Christ knows,' said Strike [...].
> 'Heroism,' said Robin.
> Strike snorted.
> 'There's nothing heroic about being in the wrong place at the wrong time.'
> 'You're a decorated veteran.'
> 'I wasn't decorated for being blown up. That happened before.'
> [...]
>
> 'Your injury's a legacy of war. It represents bravery, adversity overcome. Your amputation's mentioned every single time they talk about you in the press. I think – for him – it's tied up with fame and achievement and – and honour. He's trying to denigrate your injury, to tie it to something horrible, divert the public's perception away from you as hero towards you as a man in receipt of part of a dismembered girl. He wants to cause you trouble, yes, but he wants to diminish you in the process. He's somebody who wants what you've got, who wants recognition and importance.'
>
> (211)

---

[156] J. K. Rowling, *Career of Evil* (London: Sphere Books, 2015). Page numbers are given in the text.

If the missing leg means 'heroism', it also means experience, and this is another novel in which the solution comes to the veteran detective as he mulls over his mistakes. But, again, unease surrounds *Erfahrung*-based heuristics and pedagogy.

In this novel, the serial killer is also a veteran and the idea of a 'career' now also encompasses growing skill, gained through experience, in inflicting violent death. While the killer is intent upon destroying Strike's post-army detective career, Robin is entertaining doubts about her own career as a private investigator. Though she is beginning to build up experience – she is 'experienced enough, now, to know that there were usually nuggets of truth to be sifted from even the most obvious dross' (198) – she is not yet confident enough to rely on it, and she assumes that Strike shares her concerns. 'You obviously don't think my counter-surveillance abilities are up to much', she complains to him (24). If Robin's skills improve with professional training in counter-surveillance and in self-defence, the latter from a 'brilliant', ex-army female instructor (419), it is less clear that she learns from Strike. Indeed, she is fired because she 'won't take instruction' (450). Learning on the job – through experience – is not as efficacious as it might be. The same is true of the reader's learning process. In this third book of the series, Rowling releases a detail from Robin's backstory: that at university she was raped. To Robin's frustration, the result of simply 'being in the wrong stairwell at the wrong time, seven years previously' (note the echo of Strike's 'being in the wrong place at the wrong time' in Afghanistan) has given her what she assumes to be a 'permanent handicap' in Strike's eyes (302). But Strike is not the only one thrown by the rape. The reader, too, who now understands Robin's history, realizes that his or her reading of the previous two novels requires revision in the light of this new information. Textual veterancy, that is, has been put under pressure, and the result is to induce a readerly hypervigilance, a constant wary wondering about what is and what is not connected. Experience, it seems, is not as reliable as might have been thought.

## Conclusion

In applying an experientially based epistemology to murders, the veteran detective proves that there are more ways to solve a problem than the forensic reasoning descended from the scientific revolution. Already, the figure is chafing at the constraints of certain received methodologies. But the examples we have looked at also reveal the limits of *Erfahrung*-based epistemology in its turn. Wisdom in the ways of the world – possessed par excellence by the veteran such as Wimsey and Strike – makes a heuristically useful but ultimately shaky contribution. Sayers's and Rowling's creations are, like Watson and unlike Holmes, mistake prone: their detection proceeds hesitantly (Holmes is a smooth operator), spasmodically (Holmes moves unerringly) and with anguish (Holmes is more troubled by enforced leisure than by anything his investigations turn up). Ultimately, both concede the importance of forensic proof. What they show in the course of their detective activities is that *Erfahrung* is epistemologically messy: what is known will be known painfully, contingently and imperfectly. The final chapter casts further doubt on even that imperfect version of knowledge. But before then, in Chapter 4, I trace further incursions into reason-based behaviour in the impolite form of talking too much.

CHAPTER 4

# *Telling Tales*

## *Odyssey* 4: Storyteller

After hearing Odysseus' stories of his adventures, King Alcinous begs him to continue: 'Tell me more of your marvellous doings. I could hold out till the blessed dawn, if only you could bring yourself to stay in this hall and continue the tale of your misfortunes' (11.374–6). Civilians expect and, often, desire veterans to tell war stories. Indeed, the encounter with the person returned from war is the *locus classicus* of dialogic communication: 'What happened to you?' 'This … '. The figure of the storytelling former serviceman is a familiar one in literature and culture, from Othello's boasts about his 'hair-breadth 'scapes' (1.3.138) to Uncle Albert's tales that begin 'During the war … ' in the BBC comedy series *Only Fools and Horses* (1984–2003)[1] – an opening gambit that always provokes much groaning and rolling of eyes on the part of his listeners. The *Odyssey* is replete with the tellings and re-tellings of stories by veterans. When Alcinous, having heard Odysseus' accounts of his adventures to date, demands further stories, Odysseus obliges with yet more tales, now describing the fate of his companions in Hades. Like the first,[2] this round of storytelling leaves the audience so spellbound that 'not a sound' is heard throughout the 'shadowy hall' (13.1–2). His listeners' silence indicates a range of affects: wonder, awe, admiration, fascination, disbelief, horror, sadness, sympathy, chastened edification.

Such is the demonstrated power of stories in the *Odyssey*: these are telling tales. But, at the same time, it becomes apparent in the epic that veteran storytelling is, in certain respects, problematic. 'What memories the name of Troy brings back!' remarks Nestor as he begins to relate exploits of the war to the young Telemachus who is visiting him for news of his

---

[1] The series began in 1981 but Uncle Albert only featured from 1984.
[2] Cf. *Odyssey*, 11.333–4.

father (3.103). Though his words suggest that he relishes the opportunity to recount the events of the conflict, Nestor manages only a brief over-view before seeming to quail at the task, informing Telemachus: 'There is no man on earth who could unfold to you the whole disastrous tale, not though you sat and questioned him for half a dozen years, by which time your patience would be gone, and you yourself would be home' (3.114–17).[3] The telling of war stories – or, at least, this particular war story – is impossible, because the matter is excessive. (A similar idea is detectable in Alcinous' demand for more war stories: all that has happened to Odysseus is still insufficient to sate his desire to hear of battle.) And, as Nestor indicates, war stories can be flat out boring, the exhausted listener on his way home before the teller has even finished. This tendency gives rise to the sense of the war story as the tale of woe, the burdensome, often self-pitying narrative of one who has been 'in the wars' – that is, sub-ject to any kind of misfortune.[4] The propensity is remarked upon several

---

[3] A cynical interpretation of Nestor's words would be to take them as the staking of a claim to owner-ship. In this vein, William Broyles informs the readers of his memoir of service in Vietnam that the purpose of the war story that all soldiers tell is 'not to enlighten but to exclude': 'Its message is not its content but to put the listener in his place. I suffered, I was there. You were not' (William Broyles, *Brothers in Arms: A Journey from War to Peace* (New York: Alfred A. Knopf, 1986), 196). I am grateful to Rosemary Pearce for this reference. 'I suffered, I was there' alludes to Walt Whitman's 'Song of Myself': 'I am the man, I suffer'd, I was there'. Ironically, Whitman was a non-combatant.

[4] 'War, n.1', 1.c, 'to have been in the wars (colloq.), to show marks of injury or traces of rough usage' (*Oxford English Dictionary* (Oxford University Press), online edition). In his version of Sophocles' *Philoctetes*, *The Cure at Troy*, first performed in 1990, Seamus Heaney refers to:

> People so deep into
> Their own self-pity, self-pity buoys them up.
> People so staunch and true, they're fixated,
> Shining with self-regard like polished stones.
> And their whole life spent admiring themselves
> For their own long-suffering.
> Licking their wounds
> And flashing them around like decorations.

(*Cure at Troy: A Version of Sophocles' Philoctetes* (New York: Farrar, Straus and Giroux, 1991), 1–2). Such behaviour is seen as a barrier to (re)constructive negotiation. Quoting André Gide's *Philoctète* (1898) – 'I took to telling the story of my sufferings, and if the phrase was very beautiful, I was by so much consoled' – Edmund Wilson draws a parallel between Gide and Philoctetes, the former suffering from a 'psychological disorder' that made him 'ill-regarded by his fellows'; the latter 'the victim of a malodorous disease which renders him abhorrent to society' (quoted and trans. in *The Wound and the Bow: Seven Studies in Literature* [1941] (London: Methuen, 1961), 258, 259, 263). But, as Gide and Sophocles both show, in telling the story of his suffering, Philoctetes has also become 'the master of a superhuman art which everybody has to respect and which the normal man finds he needs' (263). In consequence, Wilson points out, the idea arises 'that genius and disease, like strength and mutilation, may be inextricably bound up together' (259). The bow requires the wound. The subject of this chapter is the bow becoming one with the wound; the discourse that, like the lesion, merely swells and suppurates, becoming repellent and edifying no

times in Homer's epic. 'It would be a wearisome business to tell you all I have been through from first to last,' Odysseus advises Arete (7.241–2). Having related the stories of his adventures to Alcinous' court, he reaches the moment at which he arrived at Calypso's island – the point at which his recital began. 'But why go again through all this?' he asks. 'Only yesterday I told you and your noble consort the whole story here in your house, and it goes against the grain with me to repeat a tale already plainly told' (12.450–3). A number of anxieties emerge in relation to veteran storytelling: the potential for boredom and irritation; the dangers of repetition; difficulties in sating the audience's demands; the inability to do justice to the subject matter; even the impossibility of knowing when a tale will (finally) have been told.

Imbued with such anxieties, the veteran story is apt to convey concerns surrounding communication more broadly. The subject of this chapter is veteran genres that are in different ways surplus to requirements: unsolicited or unwanted accounts; tales that are repeated too many times or go on too long; discourses that go beyond their purported subject matter or take exaggeration as a stylistic principle or surpass the interest or attention span of their audiences/readers. Distended discourses have long associations with armed conflict, from the classic battlefield vaunt and taunt to the piece of propaganda.[5] Not necessarily empty words, these inflationary micro-genres can do useful work: boosting self-esteem and morale in others, undermining the enemy and creating a preferred version of events. But as a model for communication more broadly, the over-abundant utterance can express an unease apparently at odds with the confidence implied by its grandiloquence.

---

one. In Sophocles' play – which is very much concerned with words, their emptiness and the trust, if any, that can be placed in them – the paradigmatic figure for this kind of utterance is Thersites (notably mistaken for Odysseus) who is 'never content to speak once and for all, even when no one wishes to let him talk' (*Antigone: The Women of Trachis. Philoctetes. Oedipus at Colunus*, trans. and ed. Hugh Lloyd-Jones, Loeb Classical Library (Cambridge, MA: Harvard University Press, 2014), 289–99, ll. 442–4). Cf. Telemachus in the *Menelaiad* in John Barth's *Lost in the Funhouse* (New York: Anchor Books, 1968) stating himself 'willing to have his cloak clutched and listen all night to the tale How You Lost Your Navigator, Wandered Seven Years, Came Ashore at Pharos, Waylaid Eidothea, Tackled Proteus, Learned to Reach Greece by Sailing up the Nile, and Made Love to Your Wife, the most beautiful woman I've ever seen, After an Abstinence of Eighteen Years' (132). In Barth's *Menelaiad*, endless, self-reflexive, layered veteran storytelling reaches its postmodernist high-point.

5  On the vaunt, see Poulheria Kyriakou, 'Warrior Vaunts in the "Iliad"', *Rheinisches Museum für Philologie* 144.3/4 (2001), 250–77, and on the taunt, see A. L. Keith, 'The Taunt in Homer and Vergil', *The Classical Journal* 19.9 (1924), 554–60. As Othello's boasts to Desdemona indicate, there is a sexual nature to the vaunt, which has a further amplificatory effect.

## Talking Too Much

Veterans tell war stories for any number of reasons: to satisfy the expectations of comrades and civilians; for catharsis; to set the record straight; to cover up the truth; to memorialize; to forget; to shock; to entertain; to focus attention; to distract attention … the list could go on. And the age of mass warfare reinforced the connection between veterancy and storytelling; indeed, made veteran identity and existence foundational upon it and so produced in excess a figure apt to convey its own excesses. As is explained in the Appendix, the system for providing relief for ex-soldiers and sailors of the French Revolutionary and Napoleonic Wars, overseen by the Royal Hospital, Chelsea, required would-be veteran pensioners to prove that they had come from active service, demonstrate incapacity and present themselves in their native parishes to receive monies granted to them. In other words, the veteran had to deliver – verbally, visually and by documentary proof – at a certain place and time a certain kind of story. Veterans were and are both natural and officially interpellated raconteurs and, as literary texts reveal, their tales are enjoyed and celebrated by civilians. Susanna Blamire's 'Stoklewath; or, The Cumbrian Village' (c.1780), for example, contains a scene in which a returned soldier's narratives are proactively elicited, welcomed and heard with attention and interest:

> 'Welcome, old soldier, welcome from the wars!
> Honour the man, my lads, seam'd o'er with scars!
> Come give's thy hand, and bring the t'other can,
> And tell us all thou'st done, and seen, my man.'
> Now expectation stares in every eye,
> The jaw falls down, and every soul draws nigh,
> With ear turn'd up, and head held all awry.
>
> (ll. 499–505)[6]

---

[6] Susanna Blamire, 'Stoklewath; or, The Cumbrian Village', *British Women Poets of the Romantic Era: An Anthology*, ed. Paula R. Feldman (Baltimore, MD: The Johns Hopkins University Press, 2000), 115–47: 129. Paula R. Feldman suggests that Blamire was inspired by the 'tales of sea voyages' and 'stories of war' told by her Naval surgeon brother William on visits home ('Susanna Blamire (1747–1794)', *British Women Poets of the Romantic Era*, ed. Feldman, 103–5: 103), while Christopher Hugh Maycock proposes that Blamire's veteran is based on her brother-in-law Thomas Graeme, who fought in the Seven Years War (*A Passionate Poet: Susanna Blamire, 1747–94* (Penzance: Hypatia, 2003), 32). 'Stoklewath' has been compared to Oliver Goldsmith's *The Deserted Village* (1770), which features a similar scene:

> The broken soldier, kindly bade to say,
> Sat by his [a clergyman's] fire, and talk'd the night away;
> Wept o'er his wounds, or tales of sorrow done,
> Shoulder'd his crutch, and show'd how fields were won.

The auditor in Rudyard Kipling's short story 'A Conference of the Powers' (1890) is similarly agog. This piece depicts a renowned author both humbled and admiring on hearing the accounts that three young soldiers give of their experiences in India and Burma. The story concludes with the professional 'golden talker' transformed into an eager listener demanding 'more tales – more tales!'[7]

But, as much as they celebrate it, literary texts of the age of mass warfare reveal uncomfortable aspects to veteran storytelling. Pacificus' 'Effects of War' (1793) refers to 'the tale, / The mournful tale that [the veteran] is doom'd to tell' (ll. 44–5).[8] The accounts are (necessarily) doleful, and 'doom'd' implies a miserable inevitability to the act of narration. John Foster's 'The Veteran Soldier' (1797) presents an 'old warrior' recounting 'chequer'd tales' (ll. 1, 2):[9] 'chequer'd' suggests not only a narrative composed of diverse experiences but hints at a degree of waywardness in both the content and the telling. The speaker in Joseph Badworth's 'Half-Pay' (1794) notes that an old soldier 'faithful tell'st thy story thrice a day' (l. 76).[10] Repetitive recounting may well be a sign of faithfulness but it might also indicate a certain obsessive anxiety. 'We doze in listless languor, when the veteran fights his battles over again,' complained one reviewer in the *Edinburgh Review* in 1816,[11] summing up civilian feeling about the veteran who tells his story again and again and again.

The full-blown version of the over-talking veteran can be viewed in two Second World War works of fiction, both of which feature the figure encountered in Chapter 2 – the veteran impostor. In Denton Welch's short story 'Brave and Cruel' (1948), the individual holding himself out as a veteran, Micki Beaumont, tells 'the most thrilling stories' (457) involving 'the most astonishing things' (471) about his supposed fighter-pilot career.[12]

---

(*Selected Writings of Oliver Goldsmith*, ed. John Lucas (Manchester: Carcanet, 1988/2003), 51–62: 55). See, for example, Robert A. Aubin, *Topographical Poetry in XVIII-Century England* (New York: Modern Language Association of America, 1936), 179.

7   Rudyard Kipling, *Many Inventions* (London: Macmillan, 1913), 23–42: 26, 41.

8   Pacificus, 'Effects of War', *The Cambridge Intelligencer* (16 November 1793); quoted in Betty T. Bennett, ed., *British War Poetry in the Age of Romanticism: 1793–1815* (New York: Garland, 1976), 97.

9   John Foster, *Poems, Chiefly on Religious Subjects* (London: publisher unknown, 1797), 11.

10  Jos[eph] Badworth, 'Half-Pay', *The Gentleman's Magazine* 64 (December 1794), 1129; quoted in Bennett, ed., *British War Poetry in the Age of Romanticism*, 134.

11  Anonymous, 'Art III: *Der Krieg der Tyroler Landleute im Jahre* 1809 von J. L. S. Bartholdy', *Edinburgh Review* 27.53 (1816), 67–86; quoted in Neil Ramsey, *The Military Memoir and Romantic Literary Culture, 1780–1835* (Farnham: Ashgate, 2011), 50.

12  Denton Welch, *Fragments of a Life Story: The Collected Short Stories of Denton Welch* (Harmondsworth: Penguin, 1987), 457, 471. Page references are given in the text.

His flights of fancy grow ever more fantastic, and the other characters soon remark the sheer quantity of his tales. 'Oh, he's told me *so* much,' says Julia Bellingley, adding '[i]n his confusion he contradicts himself too' (471). Micki tells and re-tells his stories, layering variation upon variation:

> he could not help making stories up and acting them; it was in his blood. Then he said the stories ran away with him, so that he couldn't control his behaviour. He was sometimes amazed at his own inventions; but he was in their power. All this time he was gesticulating, talking very fast, just as he does when he gets excited. He went on and on, until he had to be stopped.
>
> (505)

In this description, Micki simultaneously accounts for and enacts over-talking. His storytelling performance exceeds what his auditors can accept and they cease to credit him ('I don't believe he's ever even been up in an aeroplane,' comments the narrator, literally and figuratively bringing him down to earth (486)) and then withhold their attention from him. In Elizabeth Taylor's novel *A Wreath of Roses* (1949), another veteran impostor is associated with fecund, even nightmarish tale telling. Richard Elton is introduced as writing a book 'about the war' (5). 'What experiences did you have?' Camilla Hill feels 'obliged' to ask him, 'What were you? What did you do?' (6). Her inquiries elicit incredible tales from Elton: 'Dropped by moonlight half-way across France', 'Sat between Gestapo men in trains', 'passwords, disguises, swallowing bits of paper, hiding others in currant buns' (6). These details are the clichés of sensational war literature: Elton openly admits that it was all 'so much like the books I read as a boy'[13] and grows 'excited, as if he were listening to this story, not telling it' (6). The tales are simulacra, surface stories with no basis in reality, and Elton's storytelling becomes dangerous mythomania. 'Unreadable' is Camilla's private opinion of how his book will turn out. The 'unreadability' will not so much be due to its being distressing or even boring, but because his fabrications go beyond what can comfortably be consumed. These impostor-veterans telling outlandish tales are a literary magnification of the possibilities inherent in genuine veteran recounting. As these examples from across the time frame of this book demonstrate, veteran storytelling has as many negative associations as it does positive: it can over-satiate an audience to the point of alienation.

---

[13] This is a point at which Victoria Stewart's observation that 'Taylor asks how, in the context of the developing and solidifying mythologies of war, individual experiences can be held separate from cultural inscription' (*Narratives of Memory: British Writing of the 1940s* (Basingstoke: Palgrave Macmillan, 2006), 158) is particularly pertinent.

Veteran storytelling gone bad – repeated, over-long, unwanted, pre-posterous tales – lends itself easily to psychological and psychoanalytical interpretations. One could add nuance, for example, to the idea put forward by, among others, Cathy Caruth, Jonathan Shay and Lawrence Tritle, that talking or telling is psychologically cathartic and otherwise curative.[14] Shay, a psychiatrist who works with Vietnam veterans suffering from post-traumatic stress disorder (PTSD), argues that psychological recovery from such trauma – insofar as it is possible – depends upon its 'communalization': the retelling of experience so that it is 'under-stood, remembered and retold'.[15] Tritle, himself a veteran, notes that re-experiencing traumatic experiences through re-telling has been shown to stimulate the production of neuro-hormones with psycho-active tran-quilizing properties.[16] Discussing storytelling specifically, Judith Herman observes that: ' "[T]he action of telling a story" in the safety of a protected relationship can actually produce a change in the abnormal processing of the traumatic memory. [...] The *physioneurosis* induced by terror can apparently be reversed through the use of words.'[17] The veteran who talks too much adds a further pathological twist to this model, and one could speculate as to the psychological impulses behind repetition, protraction and the imposition of unwanted tales on reluctant audiences. But in this chapter, rather than offer psychological or psychoanalytical interpretations, I focus on aesthetics and epistemology.

Placing the unwanted, lengthy, multiply reiterated, unedifying story in its stylistic and epistemological contexts in the age of mass warfare involves probing the 'tension' that has been identified between a 'nostalgia

[14] Caruth's arguments are discussed in the section on 'The Ancient Mariner' below.

[15] Jonathan Shay, *Achilles in Vietnam: Combat Trauma and the Undoing of Character* (New York: Simon and Schuster Touchstone, 1995), 4, 55, 188–92; *Odysseus in America: Combat Trauma and the Trials of Homecoming* (New York: Scribner, 2002), 244).

[16] Lawrence A. Tritle, *From Melos to My Lai: War and Survival* (New York: Routledge, 2000), 69. Shay's and Tritle's work are discussed in Kate McLoughlin, *Martha Gellhorn: The War Writer in the Field and in the Text* (Manchester: Manchester University Press, 2007), 64.

[17] Judith Lewis Herman, *Trauma and Recovery* (London: HarperCollins, 1992), 183, original emphasis. Cf. Freud's point that psychically distressed people 'can give the physician plenty of coherent infor-mation about this or that period of their lives; but it is sure to be followed by another period as to which their communications run dry, leaving gaps unfilled, and riddles unanswered' ('Fragment of an Analysis of a Case of Hysteria' (1905 [1901])' ('Traum und Hysterie'), '*A Case of Hysteria*', *Three Essays on Sexuality' and Other Works*, ed. James Strachey in collaboration with Anna Freud, assisted by Alix Strachey and Alan Tyson (London: Vintage, 2001), 7–122: 16). On the idea that illness 'amounts at least in part to suffering from an incoherent story or an inadequate narrative account of oneself', see Steve Marcus, *Freud and the Culture of Psychoanalysis: Studies in the Transition from Victorian Humanism to Modernity* (Boston: George Allen and Unwin, 1984), 61. On writing and rewriting the self into being, see Finn Fordham, *I Do I Undo I Redo: The Textual Genesis of Modernist Selves in Hopkins, Yeats, Conrad, Forster, Joyce, and Woolf* (Oxford: Oxford University Press, 2010).

for ancient eloquence' and 'an emerging ideology of polite style' in mid-eighteenth-century Britain.[18] At first glance, excessive utterances might seem to have more in common with eloquence, given that, like the latter, they can come across to listeners as torrential.[19] But the resemblance stops there. Droning on incessantly is no *copia verborum*.[20] If eloquence is 'swelled' – Hume's word – by rhetorical amplification, the long, frankly boring tale is inflated by nothing more than its teller's lack of consideration for his audience.[21] For talking too much is *rude*. Unlike eloquence, which sympathetically tries to move the listener, it is disrespectful to its audience; it is, in the thinking we encountered in Chapter 2, *inhospitable*. But it is not only these things. The lengthy, unsolicited, unwanted discourse forms, alongside but distinct from rhetorically framed eloquence, a mode of utterance at odds with the politeness whose manner is restraint, precision and transparency. That such qualities were espoused by the Royal Society (founded 1660) further linked them to 'the experimental ideal' and 'procedural rigor'.[22] Anything other than the 'close, naked, natural way of speaking' that Thomas Sprat described in his 1667 history of the Society, would cast 'mists and uncertainties' on knowledge.[23] Politeness was not just a style, then; it was also a way of thinking. In consequence, talking too much subverts Enlightenment ideals of both hospitality and reason. In the terms of the twentieth- and twenty-first-century conceptualizations of the issue by Jürgen Habermas, Karl-Otto Aptel and others (conceptualizations that fall under the general rubric of discourse ethics), an over-talker lacks 'communicative competence', undermines the egalitarian nature of ideal

---

[18] Adam Potkay, *The Fate of Eloquence in the Age of Hume* (Ithaca, NY: Cornell University Press, 1994), 1.

[19] The word 'torrential' and its cognates crop up in a number of mid-eighteenth-century accounts of eloquence: in *Liberty* (1735–6), James Thomson describes ancient oratory as 'a clear Torrent close, or else diffus'd / A broad majestic Stream' (*Liberty, The Castle of Indolence and Other Poems*, ed. James Sambrook (Oxford: Oxford University Press, 1986), 64 [2.253–4]); Hume twice mentions a 'torrent' of eloquence in his essay 'Of Eloquence' (1742, 1793) (*Essays and Treatises on Several Subjects* (London: A. Millar, 1758), 103, 106); quoted in Potkay, *The Fate of Eloquence*, 33, 47.

[20] Cf. Quintilian's distinction between eloquent ('facundus') and loquacious ('loquax') (*Institutio Oratoria* 4.2.2; *The Orator's Education*, trans. Donald Russell, *Loeb Classical Library* (Cambridge, MA: Harvard University Press, 2001), 218–19), and, further, on the fault of perissologia (4.2.43–4, 241–3).

[21] Hume commented that figures like prosopopoeia 'serve to give an idea of the style of ancient eloquence, where such swelling expressions were not rejected as wholly monstrous and gigantic' (Hume, *Essays and Treatises*, 103); quoted in Potkay, *The Fate of Eloquence*, 74.

[22] Potkay, *The Fate of Eloquence*, 4.

[23] Thomas Sprat, *The History of the Royal Society of London, for the Improving of Natural Knowledge* (London: J. Martyn and T. Allestry, 1667), 113, 112; quoted in Potkay, *The Fate of Eloquence*, 52, 53.

speech situations, nullifies validity claims to truthfulness (in other words, lacks credibility) and so thwarts the very possibility of rational communicative action.[24]

I begin my exploration of over-abundant discourse in this chapter with an analysis of an anonymous poem of 1804, 'The Soldier's Return', illustrating how a tale that is intended to be explicatory, justificatory and palliative in the context of a veteran's homecoming is charged with a discomfiting 'feign'd' quality. Unsolicited, it fails to prepare its audience for the truth. I then consider a text voiced by one who, though not strictly a war veteran, nonetheless shares defining veteran traits: Samuel Taylor Coleridge's 'The Rime of the Ancient Mariner' (1797–1834). In this poem, the recounting of traumatic experiences is excessive, the telling is neither curative for the teller nor edifying for the listener (at least, the tale's contents are unedifying, although the *spectacle* of its telling famously leaves its witness/auditor sadder and wiser): the ensuing model of communication is that of an infinitely repeatable but ultimately incomprehensible narrative. The final text for discussion is Henry Green's Second World War novel *Back* (1946). This work does not feature veteran tale-telling per se, but, in the discourse surrounding the return of an ex-combatant, a single word – 'rose' – is used to such an extent that it is drained of signification. Talking about talking too much, this chapter proposes that over-telling or excessive signifying on the part of veterans provokes and dramatizes misgivings about the capacities of rational discourse, which are among the prime concerns of modernity.

## 'My Feign'd Story': Anon, 'The Soldier's Return' (1804)

In April 1804, *The Scots Magazine* published an anonymous ballad, 'The Soldier's Return'.[25] Voiced by a homecoming soldier in the first person

---

[24] Jürgen Habermas, 'Towards a Theory of Communicative Competence', *Inquiry* 13.1 (1970), 360–75: 367, 371; *Communication and the Evolution of Society* (*Sprachpragmatik und Philosophie; Zur Rekonstruktion des historischen Materialismus*) [1976], trans. Thomas McCarthy (London: Heinemann, 1979), 2–3, 63.

[25] Anonymous, 'The Soldier's Return', *The Scots Magazine* LXVI (April 1804), 297; quoted in Bennett, ed., *British War Poetry in the Age of Romanticism*, 322–4. The poem is also available online at www.rc.umd.edu/editions/warpoetry/1804/1804_7.html. Given the obscurity of the poem, I quote it, in segments, in its entirety. Line numbers are given in the text. Simon Bainbridge suggests that 'The Soldier's Return' 'reads like a rewriting' of Robert Merry's 'The Wounded Soldier' (discussed in Chapter 1) (*British Poetry and the Revolutionary and Napoleonic Wars: Visions of Conflict* (Oxford: Oxford University Press, 2003), 43). In rewriting Merry's ending with a positive spin, 'The Soldier's Return' inverts the anti-Pitt politics of the former.

singular, the poem opens with a common concern: that those waiting at home will have given up the returning combatant for dead:

> The wars for many a month were o'er,
>     E'er I could reach my native shed;
> My friends ne'er hop'd to see me more,
>     But wept for me as for the dead.
>
> (ll. 1–4)

Lines 3 and 4 are a projection: the soldier, whose name is Harry, is picturing his friends weeping over his death *before* he reaches home to witness the fact. In his imagination, his friends have declared him dead, even – in some sense – killed him. Arriving at his family's cottage, Harry, like so many homecoming veterans before and since, does not enter immediately but spends a considerable interval looking through the window to a well-illuminated interior:

> As I drew nigh, the cottage blaz'd;
>     The ev'ning fire was clear and bright;
> And through the window long I gaz'd,
>     And saw each friend with dear delight.

Within is a tableau of waiting attitudes:

> My father in his corner sat,
>     My mother drew her useful thread,
> My brothers strove to make them chat,
>     My sisters bak'd the household bread:
>
> And Jean oft whisper'd to a friend,
>     That still let fall a silent tear:
> But soon my Jessy's grief shall end –
>     She little thinks her Harry's near.
>
> My mother saw her catching sighs,
>     And hid her face behind the rock;
> While tears swam round in all their eyes,
>     And not a single word was spoke.
>
> (ll. 9–12)

Absence permeates this scene of cosy domesticity, registered in the signs of grief for the missing one. The manifestation of this grief is distinctive for its lack of verbal articulation: in place of words are 'silent tears', 'sighs', 'whispers' and a general disinclination to talk. Absence, the opposite of return, has bred the opposite of narrative: 'not a single word was spoke'. Into this silent space, the travelling ex-soldier must bring self-identification and explanation.

The reception anxiety involved in veteran homecoming discussed in Chapter 2 now becomes acute in Harry. How can he enter the scene? How, that is, can he re-integrate himself into the society he left to go to war?

> What could I do? – If in I went,
> > Surprize might chill each tender heart;
> Some story, then, I must invent,
> > And act the poor maim'd soldier's part.
>
> (ll. 13–16)

Fearing that he will cause emotional and even physical harm if he reveals himself immediately to his family ('Surprize might chill each tender heart'), Harry decides to unfold his identity gradually to alleviate the shock of his reappearance – protraction is built in to the process. In his judgement, telling a tale is key to successful entry and re-integration ('Some story, then, I must invent') and the invented story is that of another veteran. The tale, that is, adds veterancy to veterancy; already, it is showing signs of inflation. The tale itself is barely reported – just a line gives the gist – but its performance, which supplements verbal delivery with physical dissimulation, is described as follows:

> I drew a bandage o'er my face,
> > And crooked up a lying knee,
> And found that e'en in that blest place
> > Not one dear friend knew ought of me.
>
> I ventur'd in – Tray wagg'd his tail,
> > And fawn'd – and to my mother ran:
> 'Come here,' they cry'd; 'what can he ail!'
> > While my feign'd story I began.
>
> I chang'd my voice to that of age,
> > 'A poor old soldier lodgings crave:'
> The very name their loves engage –
> > 'A soldier! aye, the best we have.'
>
> (ll. 17–28)

The presentation of the 'feign'd story' is noteworthy. It includes many of the generic motifs of real-life pension petitions. Acting 'the poor maim'd soldier's part', wearing a 'bandage', 'crook[ing] up' his knee, speaking in 'the voice [...] of age', Harry draws attention both to the sacrifices his assumed persona has made in battle and to his ongoing disabilities. But this tale is not so much aimed at persuading the military authorities to grant relief as allowing a soldier to infiltrate an intimate milieu. It must function as a discursive bridge between the world of combat and the domestic circle. Constructing such a bridge is fraught with difficulties. Once in the army, as the American sociologist Willard Waller noted with reference to the Second World War, the civilian-turned-soldier is 'shut off from the main currents of communication characteristic of civilian life'.[26] The military is an 'intense world', 'replete with meaning': its abbreviations alone are 'almost sufficient' to make its speech 'incomprehensible to the civilian'.[27] Common ground must be sought. Hence, in 'The Soldier's Return', the recently-demilitarized Harry draws on a repertoire of widely understood and familiar attributes – the bandaged face, the injured knee, the homeless old soldier – to create a physical and verbal narrative that will palliate the family and improve his chances of acceptance.

Harry's performance is successful insofar as no one except the family dog, Tray, recognizes him in his assumed persona (this echoes the scene in Homer in which Odysseus is recognized by Argus the hound (*Odyssey*, 17.291–304)).[28] But even though the human members of the family fail to recognize the visitor, the descriptor 'soldier' prompts the kind of hospitality discussed in Chapter 2:

> My father then drew in a seat,
>    'You're welcome,' with a sigh, he said:
> My mother fry'd her best hung meat,
>    And curds and cheese the table spread.
>                     (ll. 29–32)

Safely welcomed with conspicuous hospitality, Harry now offers a further, ontologically complex narrative in which, in the persona of an aged veteran, he announces the news of his own continued existence:

> 'I had a son,' my father sigh'd,
>    'A soldier, too; but he is gone!'
> 'Have you heard from him?' I reply'd;
>    'I left behind me many a one: –

---

[26] Willard Waller, *The Veteran Comes Back* (New York: Dryden Press, 1944), 25.
[27] Ibid., 26, 29.
[28] 'Tray' might be an echo of 'Troy'.

'And many a message I have brought
　　'To families I cannot find;
'Long for John Goodman's have I sought,
　　'To tell them Hall's not far behind.'

'O! does he live?' my father cry'd,
　　My mother did not stay to speak;
My Jessy now I silent ey'd,
　　Who throbb'd as if her heart would break.

'He lives indeed! – this 'kerchief see,
　　'At parting his dear Jessy gave;
'He sent it her, with love, by me,
　　'To shew he yet escapes the grave.'
　　　　　　　　　　　　　　(ll. 33–48)

*Two* narratives are in play here: the 'feign'd story' of the aged veteran and, in the voice of that veteran, the news of Harry. Having tried to ensure that his family can withstand the shock (although the incrementally released information seems to have a similar effect on Jessy's heart as the feared 'surprize' of l. 14), Harry proceeds to his revelation, removing the bandage from his face in a *coup de théâtre*. His audience's reactions are, despite the preparation, extreme:

An arrow, darting from a bow,
　　Could not more quick the token reach:
The patch from off my face I drew,
　　And gave my voice its well-known speech.

'My Jessy, dear!' I softly said:
　　She gaz'd, and answer'd with a sigh:
My sisters look'd as half-afraid;
　　My mother fainted quite for joy.

My father danced round his son;
　　My brothers shook my hand away;
My mother said, Her glass might run,
　　She car'd not now how soon that day.

'Hout, woman!' cry'd my father dear,
　　'A wedding first I'm sure we'll have:
'I warrant we'll live this hundred year –
　　'Nay, may be, lass, escape the grave.'
　　　　　　　　　　　　　　(ll. 49–64)

What is described here is a set of miniature deaths and resurrections: Jessy's sigh or expiration and the mother's fainting and statement that she no longer cares how soon she dies are counterpointed by her recovery, the father's dancing, the brothers' vigorous hand-shaking and the father's looking forward to a wedding, to living a hundred years and even to escaping the grave altogether. The family's reactions in these stanzas, then, reprise the soldier's own return to life, a return which the telling of a tale has facilitated. But despite the positive outcome, Harry's story raises a number of concerns regarding veterancy and communication.

The adjectives used in respect of his tale – 'feign'd', 'invent[ed]' – merit pause. Though the etymology of 'story' links it to factual history, 'to tell a story' has also come colloquially to mean 'to tell a lie'.[29] Harry's story of being an aged, wounded veteran is a lie, a lie told corporeally as well as verbally (note his 'lying knee'). A link between veterancy and lying is established by Homer: as Athene wryly observes, 'Odysseus the arch-deceiver, with his craving for intrigue, does not propose even in his own country to drop his sharp practice and the lying tales that he loves from the bottom of his heart' (*Odyssey*, 13.293–5). In *Odysseus in America* (2002), Jonathan Shay argues that Odysseus' *dolos* or guile has been acquired through veterancy: the '[s]trengths, skills, and capacities acquired during prolonged combat' include 'cunning', 'the arts of deception', 'the arts of the "mind fuck"' and the 'capacity to lie fluently and convincingly'.[30] Disguising intentions is a key element of military tactics, but deception is also part of day-to-day getting by. Shay cites Robert Graves's reference to his 'Army habit of commandeering anything of uncertain ownership that [he] found lying about; also a difficulty in telling the truth'.[31] As this indicates, lying is an habituated practice, directed towards self-preservation whether among comrades or foes. Dissembling can also be a means of dealing with trauma. As Judith Herman explains, 'the conflict between the will to deny horrible events and the will to proclaim them aloud' is a 'central dialectic'.[32] In consequence, she goes on: 'People who have survived atrocities often tell their stories in a highly emotional, contradictory, and fragmented manner which undermines their credibility and thereby serves the twin

---

[29] 'Story, n.', I.7a (*Oxford English Dictionary* (Oxford University Press), online edition). This usage dates from 1648.
[30] Shay, *Odysseus in America*, 6, 21.
[31] Robert Graves, *Good-Bye to All That* [1929] (New York: Anchor, 1957), 287; quoted in Shay, *Odysseus in America*, 32.
[32] Herman, *Trauma and Recovery*, 2.

imperatives of truth-telling and secrecy.'[33] In addition to these factors, there is another incentive for the war veteran to lie: the sheer magnitude of the task of encapsulating his experiences. There is a temptation to '*surrender* in the face of representing war', to 'capitulate' to strong, well-established prior paradigms, and to produce, as a result, accounts that are more faithful to an audience's preconceptions than to actual experience.[34] In 'The Soldier's Return', Harry makes a surrender of this sort as he draws on the standard repertoire of veteran motifs. It gains him entry to the domestic milieu: his story of the aged, infirm veteran is familiar to his audience ('The very name their loves engage – "A soldier! aye, the best we have"') and elicits a reaction of welcome.

The veteran lie is explicable and justifiable, then, but it is also excessive, irrational and impolite. This is not a moral judgement but an aesthetic and epistemological assessment. Harry, it should be remembered, is not obliged to tell his story. But his instinct in the face of his anxieties concerning reception and reintegration is not to tell the plain truth but to concoct an excessive fiction. (The fiction is, as already noted, an exaggeration of his own circumstances: the old, wounded veteran he performs is a more veterated version of himself.) Rational discourse, it would seem, has been discarded as inadequate to the circumstances. Politeness, with its epistemological roots in empiricism, has been eschewed: deception, even when perpetrated with the best intentions, lacks respect. Centred around an unsolicited and misleading pretence, 'The Soldier's Return' questions the capacity of transparent, reasoned utterance to deal, at least on the individual and familial level, with the effects of mass warfare.

The gratuitous nature of Harry's storytelling in 'The Soldier's Return' strikes a further note of caution. It is not, after all, a great conceptual or generic step from the unsolicited story to the unwanted story. If the instigation of Harry's 'feign'd story' receives a warm welcome, equally or more prevalent responses to veterans' tales are, as we have seen, indifference, exasperation, boredom, resentment, rage, rejection, antipathy, avoidance. The anthropologist (and Second World War veteran) Jack Goody has argued that the personal narrative or 'relational account' requires 'the suspension not of disbelief but of discourse, at least in the sense of interplay'.[35] Active

---

[33] Ibid., 2.

[34] Kate McLoughlin, *Authoring War: The Literary Representation of War from the* Iliad *to* Iraq (Cambridge: Cambridge University Press, 2011), 5–6.

[35] Jack Goody, 'The Time of Telling and the Telling of Time in Written and Oral Cultures', *Chronotypes: The Construction of Time*, ed. John Bender and David D. Wellbery (Stanford, CA: Stanford University Press, 1991), 77–96: 81.

interlocutors must become passive listeners, that is, but, Goody continues, 'such is the nature of interaction that we rarely get the chance to finish our account':[36] 'Unless we impose ourselves upon our fellows and run the risk of becoming "bores," the story often remains incompletely told, partly because its telling demands not so much an attention others are unwilling to give as an inaction they are unwilling to undergo.'[37] Harry is not a bore, but some storytelling veterans can be. And there is something in the nature of storytelling that tends towards proliferation. In 1793, eleven years before the publication of 'The Soldier's Return', the writer and scholar Isaac D'Israeli noted this tendency in his work on a particular species of story, *A Dissertation on Anecdotes*. The anecdote, D'Israeli remarked, is a 'literary luxury', to be read with 'voluptuous delight'.[38] Deliciously moreish, anecdotes 'recall others of a kindred nature: one suggests another' and the pile accumulates.[39] 'More tales – more tales!' But, like any delicacy, stories can also become sating. This is particularly the case with those that are in some respect surplus, whether in length, quantity, repetitiousness, concatenation with other tales or through being unwanted by their recipients. They go beyond rich creative plenitude to intolerable overload, wearying the auditor/reader to the point of exhaustion (in the senses both of extreme fatigue and of being emptied out). The most famous – or infamous – of such tales is the one told by Coleridge's quasi-veteran, the Ancient Mariner.

## On Speaking On: Coleridge's 'The Rime of the Ancient Mariner' (1797–1834)

In works written in the years leading up to the composition of 'The Rime of the Ancient Mariner' and during its subsequent revision, Coleridge showed consistent interest in discourses that are unattended to or difficult to engage with or that otherwise elicit negative reactions. In 'Ode to the Departing Year' (1796),[40] for example (a poem Coleridge never finished revising and that he reported readers finding 'a rant of turgid obscurity'),[41] the speaker in the first strophe informs the 'Spirit who sweepest the wild

---

[36] Ibid., 81.
[37] Ibid., 81.
[38] Isaac D'Israeli, *A Dissertation on Anecdotes* (London: C. and G. Kearsley and J. Murray, 1793), 2.
[39] Ibid., 3.
[40] Samuel Taylor Coleridge, *Poetical Works I: Poems (Reading Text): Part 1*, ed. J. C. C. Mays, 16:I:1/16 vols, *The Collected Works of Samuel Taylor Coleridge* (Princeton, NJ: Princeton University Press, 2001), 302–11.
[41] Ibid., 302.

Harp of Time' that 'It is most hard, with an untroubled Ear / Thy dark inwoven Harmonies to hear!' (ll. 1–3). The image contains the senses both that historic harmonies are difficult to detect and painful to bear in the present moment. Another troubled reaction greets the account of the departing year in the first antistrophe: 'Thou storied'st thy sad Hours! Silence ensued, / Deep Silence o'er the ethereal Multitude' (ll. 78–9). The scene evoked here presents a powerful response to undesired or unassimilable information: silence on the part of the recipients. The unfinished 'Christabel' (1798, 1800) contains a similar moment in the lines describing the church bell that tolls 'a warning Knell, / Which not a Soul can choose but hear / From Bratha Head to Wyn'dermere' (ll. 342–4).[42] The sound, unwanted but unavoidable, resonates with other instances in the poem involving problematic utterances and their reception: refusal to listen (ll. 564–71) and inability to speak (ll. 473–4). In 'Dejection: An Ode' (1802), another multiply reiterated work, lines evoking a storm in which the wind, addressed variously as a musician, actor and poet, brings harrowing news are followed by reference to a silencing 'pause', a silence that is itself soon superimposed with the sound of a little girl screaming to make herself heard:

> Mad Lutanist! who in this month of show'rs,
> Of dark brown gardens, and of peeping flow'rs,
> Mak'st Devils' yule, with worse than wint'ry song,
> The blossoms, buds, and tim'rous leaves among.
>     Thou Actor, perfect in all tragic sounds!
> Thou mighty Poet, e'en to Frenzy bold!
>         What tell'st thou now about?
>       'Tis of the Rushing of an Host in rout,
>     With groans, of trampled men, with smarting wounds –
> At once they groan with pain, and shudder with the cold!
> But hush! there is a pause of deepest silence!
>     And all that noise, as of a rushing crowd,
> With groans, and tremulous shudderings – all is over –
>     It tells another tale, with sounds less deep and loud!
>         A tale of less affright,
>         And tempered with delight,
> [...]
>         'Tis of a little child

[42] Ibid., 477–504.

Upon a lonesome wild,
Not far from home, but she hath lost her way:
And now moans low in bitter grief and fear,
And now screams loud, and hopes to make her mother hear.

(ll.104–119, 121–5)[43]

As a tale-teller, the wind is exorbitant ('e'en to frenzy bold'), bringing, like a veteran (or, in Mary Favret's reading, 'a mighty journalist'),[44] accounts of war and its aftermath. The 'pause of deepest silence' stems the sonic deluge, only for another story to begin, a 'tale of less affright'. Yet this story, too, becomes aurally and emotionally difficult to tolerate as the lost child begins to scream. Entwined with the anxieties about his personal creativity that Coleridge expresses in the poem ('A stifled, drowsy, unimpassion'd grief, / Which finds no natural outlet' (ll. 22–3)) is a concern about public discourses – specifically information about war – which are both overwhelming and capable of being overwhelmed.

Such concern is also evident in two of the lectures Coleridge gave in the mid-1790s – 'On the Present War' and 'On the Slave Trade' – and in the poem 'Fears in Solitude' (1798). 'On the Present War', a version of one or two public lectures given in Bristol in February 1795[45] and published in *Conciones ad Populum* (1795), states as an opening principle that 'In the disclosal of Opinion, it is our duty to consider the character of those, to whom we address ourselves, their situations, and probable degree of knowledge' (51).[46] Maximum communicative efficiency is the aim, in other words, always keeping in mind that 'when the prejudices of a man are strong, the most over-powering Evidence becomes weak' (52). Indeed, it is possible that, for such a prejudiced listener, some 'unmeaning Term' can acquire 'almost a mechanical power over his frame' (52). In such cases, efforts at persuasion are fruitless: 'the shuddering Bigot flings the door of Argument in your face, and excludes all Parley' (53). In a lecture that powerfully conveys his loathing of the excesses of both the American and the French Revolutionary Wars,

---

[43] Samuel Taylor Coleridge, *Poetical Works I: Poems (Reading Text): Part 2*, ed. J. C. C. Mays, 16:I:2/ 16 vols, *The Collected Works of Samuel Taylor Coleridge* (Princeton, NJ: Princeton University Press, 2001), 695–702.

[44] Mary Favret, *War at a Distance: Romanticism and the Making of Modern Warfare* (Princeton, NJ: Princeton University Press, 2010), 120.

[45] Samuel Taylor Coleridge, *Lectures 1795 on Politics and Religion*, ed. Lewis Patton and Peter Mann, 1/ 16 vols, *The Collected Works of Samuel Taylor Coleridge* (Princeton, NJ: Princeton University Press, 2001), 22.

[46] Ibid., 51–74. Page numbers are given in the text.

Coleridge at once and contradictorily expresses minimal confidence in the easily swayed masses, endorses rational persuasion and is both admiring of and appalled by the power of rhetoric. Edmund Burke is praised as a 'Hercules Furens of Oratory', while the speeches of the Prime Minister, William Pitt the Younger, are decried as 'Harangues! – Mystery concealing Meanness, as steam-clouds invelope a dunghill' (63). The steam-clouds suggest insubstantial inflation (though the use of 'hot air' to mean 'empty or boastful talk' did not enter the English language until 1873),[47] an image extended a line later: 'His speeches, which seemed so swoln with meaning, alas! what did they mean?' (63). The signification of Pitt's remarks is in inverse proportion to their ballooning quantity. In his lecture 'On the Slave Trade', given a few months later in Bristol and published in *The Watchman* on 25 March 1796,[48] Coleridge expresses similar concerns regarding the impressionableness of the public and the insidious effects of political oratory. Facts regarding the slave trade have been 'pressed' on the people 'even to satiety' (133), but at the same time anti-Abolitionist arguments have been 'the cosmetics with which our parliamentary orators have endeavoured to conceal the deformities of a commerce, which is blotched all over with one leprosy of evil' (136). There are two, opposing anxieties regarding excessive utterance here: that audiences may be overloaded to the point of ceasing to listen (a late-eighteenth-century version of compassion fatigue) and that rhetorical distortion ('cosmetics') may nonetheless be effective.

But it is in 'Fears in Solitude: Written in April 1798, During the Alarm of an Invasion' that Coleridge is most explicit about his anxieties concerning inflationary talking.[49] The poem contains a number of instances in which certain utterances are overwhelmed by others. The 'sweet words / Of Christian promises, words that even yet / Might stem destruction were they wisely preached' are 'muttered o'er' (ll. 64–7); indeed, the requirement for Nonconformists and Roman Catholics to swear the Oaths of Allegiance and Supremacy imposed by the Test and Corporation Acts[50] has had the effect that 'the very name of God / Sounds like a juggler's charm' (ll. 81–2). The proliferation of 'Courts, Committees, Institutions, / Associations and Societies' has created a bombastic-sounding 'vain,

---

[47] 'Hot air, n.', 2 (*Oxford English Dictionary* (Oxford University Press), online edition).

[48] Samuel Taylor Coleridge, *The Watchman*, ed. Lewis Patton, 2/16 vols, *The Collected Works of Samuel Taylor Coleridge* (Princeton, NJ: Princeton University Press, 1970), 13–40. Page numbers are given in the text.

[49] Coleridge, *Poetical Works I: Poems (Reading Text)*, 468–76.

[50] Ibid., 472n.

speech-mouthing, speech-reporting Guild, / One BENEFIT-CLUB for mutual flattery' (ll. 56–9). And, in dangerous ignorance, the public has 'loved / To swell the war-whoop' (l. 90), an image of the discursive turgidity that results when war is regarded merely 'as a thing to talk of' (l. 96). In an extended critical passage, Coleridge then describes the vain eloquence of those who fail to connect what they read of armed conflict in the newspapers with its reality:

> Boys and girls,
> And women, that would groan to see a child
> Pull off an insect's leg, all read of war,
> The best amusement for our morning meal!
> The poor wretch, who has learnt his only prayers
> From curses, who knows scarcely words enough
> To ask a blessing from his Heavenly Father,
> Becomes a fluent phraseman, absolute
> And technical in victories and defeats,
> And all our dainty terms for fratricide;
> Terms which we trundle smoothly o'er our tongues
> Like mere abstractions, empty sounds to which
> We join no feeling and attach no form!
> As if the soldier died without a wound;
> As if the fibres of this godlike frame
> Were gored without a pang; as if the wretch,
> Who fell in battle, doing bloody deeds,
> Passed off to Heaven, translated and not killed.
>
> (ll. 105–22)

'Fluent phrase[s]', 'dainty terms', 'mere abstractions', 'empty sounds': the lines themselves swell with synonyms for vacant yet proliferating utterances. Angrily, the poet questions what might befall the nation if 'all-avenging Providence' should 'make us know / The meaning of our words' (ll. 126–8); that is, provide a referent in suffering to what are, at present, meaningless terms. The threat itself is conceptualized as overpowering, inflated discourse: 'the vaunts' of the 'vengeful enemy' that may 'roar' like a 'gust' (ll. 199–201). Counterpointing the hullaballoo, at the beginning and end of the poem is the *locus amoenus* of a 'silent dell' (ll. 2, 229), a small, green place where the poet takes refuge from the noise of war and from the dilating sounds of ill-informed debate.

'Fears in Solitude', with its central idea that over-talking is not merely vain but actually potentially dangerous, sits incongruously with Coleridge's own reputation for loquaciousness.[51] To listen to Coleridge talk was to feel you were drowning. The illustrator David Scott reported that '[t]he moment he [Coleridge] is seated [...] he begins to talk, and on it goes, flowing and full, almost without even what might be called paragraphic division, and leaving colloquy out of the question entirely'.[52] The writer John Sterling, a long-standing intellectual associate of the poet, recalled, in terms that are themselves by no means laconic:

> Nothing could be more copious than his talk; and furthermore it was always, vir-
> tually or literally, of the nature of a monologue; suffering no interruption [...] It
> was talk not flowing any-whither like a river, but spreading every-whither in inex-
> tricable currents and regurgitations like a lake or sea [...] So that, most times, you
> felt [...] swamped near to drowning in this tide of ingenious vocables, spreading
> out boundless as if to submerge the world.[53]

The image conveys torrential talking that over-flows the listener to the point of submerging any response. Coleridge's auditors, like the speaker in 'Fears in Solitude', must have craved the haven of a silent (dry) place. The composition of 'The Rime of the Ancient Mariner', then, took place in verbally deluged years,[54] the poet both contributing to the sea of words and conscious of the danger of drowning.

In 'The Rime', Coleridge produced a piece of creative writing that questions the very nature and purpose of creativity even as it models creativity's delightful and terrifying capacity to run on and on and on. Strictly speaking, its logorrhoeic protagonist is not a war veteran (at least, the poem does not list combat among his experiences),[55] though he is an ex-seaman, an armed killer, has seen mass death and, like Odysseus, is

---

[51] Seamus Perry notes the 'obvious parallel' between the 'wonderfully talkative' Coleridge and the Ancient Mariner ('The Talker', *The Cambridge Companion to Coleridge*, ed. Lucy Newlyn (Cambridge: Cambridge University Press, 2002), 103–25: 112, 105).

[52] Quoted in ibid., 109.

[53] Thomas Carlyle, *The Life of John Sterling*, 11/30 vols, *The Works of Thomas Carlyle in Thirty Volumes: Centenary Edition* (London: Chapman and Hall, 1897), 55.

[54] On the composition history of the poem, see Coleridge, *Poetical Works I: Poems (Reading Text)*, 365–8.

[55] Alan Bewell argues that the Ancient Mariner has been 'traumatized' by 'colonial experience', suggesting that he is implicated in the slave trade. For Bewell, the 'epidemiological cost of colonialism returns in the form of "tropical invalids" who wander through the landscape as vagrants or frightening pariahs' (*Romanticism and Colonial Disease* (Baltimore, MD: The Johns Hopkins University Press, 1999), 100, 101). Joel Faflak agrees that the Ancient Mariner has suffered 'trauma' (*Romantic Psychoanalysis: The Burden of the Mystery* Albany, NY: State University of New York Press, 2008), 8). Neither, however, suggest combat experience on the Ancient Mariner's part. In this context, it is worth noting that Coleridge himself was what J. R. Watson describes as a 'hopeless dragoon' from 1793–4 (*Romanticism and War: A Study of British Romantic Period Writers and the Napoleonic Wars* (Basingstoke: Palgrave Macmillan, 2003), 5).

unsure on homecoming of the reality of his 'own countrée' (467).[56] His epithet, 'ancient', connotes not only advanced age (and, therefore, substantial life experience) but also, from the Latin *ante* ('former, previous'), the quality of anteriority.[57] Indeed, the first line of the poem – 'It is an ancient Mariner' – firmly and yet wholly ambiguously founds his present identity on his past occupation. 'It is a no-longer-a-Mariner' or 'It is a not-a-Mariner' would be logical equivalents. Who, or what, is someone when he or she is no longer who, or what, he or she once was?[58] 'Mariner' is an identity that has out-lasted or over-lived its applicability, in a manner similar to that in which the Ancient Mariner over-tells his story. 'Ancient Mariner', therefore, comprises veterancy both in the sense of being older and of being *former*.[59]

The Ancient Mariner certainly bears the physical signs of veterancy. His beard is 'long', 'grey' and 'hoar' (3, 619), he is 'lank' and 'brown' (226), his hand is 'skinny' (9, 225, 229): these are marks of age, harsh experience and suffering. It is with this 'skinny hand' that the Ancient Mariner literally grabs the Wedding Guest's attention in an opening that dramatizes an insistence that veterancy must be attended to in the form of storytelling. In what has been described as the 'locus classicus in all discussions of orality in the period',[60] Hugh Blair's *Lectures on Rhetoric and Belles Lettres* (1783),

---

56 Coleridge, *Poetical Works I: Poems (Reading Text)*, 365–419. Cf. *Odyssey* 13.185–249. The version of 'The Rime of the Ancient Mariner' used is that which Coleridge published in *Sibylline Leaves* (1817) and in all subsequent editions of his poetry. Line numbers are given in the text. Piero Boitani points out another resemblance between the Ancient Mariner and Odysseus: both are 'borne back to their homeland in their sleep, the ship manned by others' (*The Shadow of Ulysses: Figures of a Myth* (*L'Ombre di Ulisse: Figure di un Mito*) [1992], trans. Anita Wilson (Oxford: The Clarendon Press, 1994), 79).

57 'Ancient, adj. and n.1', 1, 5 (*Oxford English Dictionary* (Oxford University Press), online edition). There is evidence that 'ancient' and 'veteran' were used synonymously in the period, as in an advert for Smollett's *The Expedition of Humphrey Clinker*: 'the veteran Admiral Balderick and other ancient friends' (Anonymous, 'Rowlandson's Edition of Smollet's [sic] Novels', *Diary or Woodfall's Register* (14 February 1793) (Gale-Cengage 17th–18th Century Burney Newspaper Collection)). But 'veteran' could also simply mean 'old' (cf. its use to describe an 87-year-old great-grandfather in Anonymous, 'Further Extracts from the New Edition of Pratt's Gleanings, Etc.: State of Methodism in Catholic Countries; and the Wakes or Fairs of Germany', *St. James's Chronicle or the British Evening Post* (Gale-Cengage 17th–18th Century Burney Newspaper Collection).

58 This reminds me of being puzzled, as a child, by Paddington Bear's Aunt Lucy entering a Home for Retired Bears. What was she, I wondered, if she had retired from being a bear?

59 Cf. 'The man was once a mariner, as the word "ancient" implies in its sense of "former." He was singled out by nothing but his suffering' (David Bromwich, *Disowned by Memory: Wordsworth's Poetry of the 1790s* (Chicago: The University of Chicago Press, 1998), 114). I refer to the character as the 'Ancient Mariner' rather than simply the 'Mariner' throughout to preserve the sense that he is a no-longer-a-Mariner.

60 Lucy Newlyn, *Reading, Writing, and Romanticism: The Anxiety of Reception* (Oxford: Oxford University Press, 2000), 63.

read by both Coleridge and Wordsworth in 1798,[61] there is the following description of the rhetorical role of hands:

> In the motions made with the hands, consist the chief part of gesture in Speaking. [...] Warm emotions demand the motion of both hands corresponding together. But whether one gesticulates with one or with both hands, it is an important rule, that all his motions should be free and easy. Narrow and straitened movements are generally ungraceful; for which reason, motions made with the hands are directed to proceed from the shoulder rather than from the elbow. [...] Oblique motions are, in general, the most graceful. Too sudden and nimble motions should be likewise avoided.[62]

In the light of this, the Ancient Mariner's frenzied grasping of the Wedding Guest can be read either as a piece of hyper-rhetoric, heralding the over-talking that will ensue, or, simply, as a highly impolite action. The reaction is an immediate rejection – ' "Hold off! unhand me, grey-beard loon!" ' (11) – notably undermining the credibility that might be conferred by veterancy ('grey-beard') with an imputation of irrationality ('loon'). The hand is quickly 'dropt' (12), an inverted precursor of the Ancient Mariner's later assertion that 'This body dropt not down' (231). This assertion is made to reassure the Wedding Guest that the Ancient Mariner is no ghost and his utterances can accordingly be relied upon; the 'dropt' hand is therefore an early hint of communicative problems. (The importance of hand/arm to communication is reinforced when the Ancient Mariner is forced to bite his own arm in order to lubricate his parched mouth with blood so as to be able to alert his fellow-sailors to the passing ship (160–1).)

Undeterred by his interlocutor's reluctance, the Ancient Mariner proceeds to talk. Ostensibly, given all the marks of veterancy, this would promise to be an encounter in which, following Benjamin's model of *Erfahrung*, experience would be handed, edifyingly, on. That the communication is urgent is made clear. The Wedding Guest is no minor attendee of the nuptials, but 'next of kin': he is waylaid en route to a highly important, unrepeatable – unmissable, that is – social occasion. But he stands 'still' (14). Indeed, held by the Ancient Mariner's 'glittering eye' (3, 228), 'he cannot choose but hear' (18, 40).[63] But even if the listening is enforced, it might be expected that this intense, urgent encounter would be salutary.

---

[61] Duncan Wu, *Wordsworth's Reading 1770–1799* (Cambridge: Cambridge University Press, 1993), 16.

[62] Hugh Blair, *Lectures on Rhetoric and Belles Lettres* [1783], 2/2 vols (London: A. Strahan and T. Cadell, 1783), 221n. On the connection between hands and veterancy, see, further, Chapter 5.

[63] On mesmerism in Coleridge, see Faflak, *Romantic Psychoanalysis*, ch. 3.

Certainly, what ensues is extraordinary. The Ancient Mariner's utterances
are not conventional talking: they are excessive talk, over-talking, talk-
passing-talk. This is the war story to out-war-story all war stories. Twice,
the reader is told the Ancient Mariner 'spake on' (19, 29) and the pre-
position gives a sense of perpetuity to the action: in fact, he speaks on and
on and on and on. For his part, his auditor is the most reluctant auditor in
the history of storytelling. The Wedding Guest is so desirous *not* to listen
to the Ancient Mariner, indeed, that he actually beats his breasts – twice –
so anguished is he (31, 37). He makes only one intervention that could
be regarded as encouragement to the Ancient Mariner to proceed (the
question in lines 79–81); otherwise, his few spoken responses convey that,
forced to listen against his will, he is in a state of absolute consternation
(224–5, 345).

Extraordinary it may be, but whether the exchange is edifying is more
doubtful. Certainly, for his part, the Ancient Mariner derives no solace
(or, in modern parlance, 'closure') from making his revelations: indeed, he
is under a compulsion forever to repeat his story.[64] The 'woful agony' that
'forced' him to tell his tale for the first time regularly but unpredictably
revisits him, dissipating only when it has been related again:

> Since then, at an uncertain hour,
> That agony returns:
> And till my ghastly tale is told,
> This heart within me burns.
>
> (578–81)

The Ancient Mariner casts his compulsion as the need to 'pass' from land
to land (586) until he sees 'the man that must hear me: To him my tale
I teach' (590). 'Teach' seems here to mean something other than 'instruct',
'impart' or 'inform': what the Ancient Mariner does is closer to the early
signification of the verb, 'to show, present or offer to view'.[65] As he passes
by, that is, he exhibits his story but does not pass it on: glow-worm rather
than mentor, in the terms of the previous chapter. So much is evident in
the Wedding Guest's reaction: he listens 'like a three years' child' (l. 15).
The effect of the Ancient Mariner's tale is to put the Wedding Guest, not in

---

[64] Cf. 'There never was a first time the Mariner recited his Rime. From the outset, the tale was a
repetition – of the experience itself, which the Mariner relives as he retells it, of the words in
which he retells it, and of other words, with which Coleridge and Wordsworth had been telling or
trying to tell each other tales during the last half-dozen years' (Susan Eilenberg, *Strange Power of
Speech: Wordsworth, Coleridge, and Literary Possession* (Oxford: Oxford University Press, 1992), 43).
[65] 'Teach, v.', 1 (*Oxford English Dictionary* (Oxford University Press), online edition).

a state of rational comprehension, but in a state of wondering, terrified disbelief. At the end of the poem, he is described as 'stunned' (622), 'of sense forlorn' (623): his reason is in abeyance. Though he rises the following day 'A sadder and a wiser man' (624), it is not clear what this sadness and wisdom consist of. The 'sadness' may simply be pity; the 'wisdom' might be no more than a resolution not to fall for such extreme buttonholing in future. In any event, rather than resulting from the contents of the Ancient Mariner's recital – its Christian moral (somewhat reductively) summed up in lines 610–17 – both sadness and wisdom arise from the outer spectacle of his distress.

Certainly, the contents of the Ancient Mariner's utterance pose epistemological difficulties. The subject of his story is outside human experience, being either novel ('We were the first that ever burst / Into that silent sea' (105–6)) or supernatural (the 'wondrous' cold (51); the burning water; the Polar Spirit and its fellow-daemon; the 'spectre-bark' (l202); Death and Life-in-Death playing dice; the 'seraph-man' standing on the body of each dead sailor (490); the ship's preternatural speed while the Ancient Mariner is in his trance). Such phenomena are not the stuff of empirical reality but of vision, revelation or symbol. Within the poem, the person relating them is met with fear and incredulity. The Hermit, who likes nothing better than a good chinwag with veterans ('He loves to talk with marineres / That come from a far countree' (517–18)), crosses himself, the Pilot shrieks and falls down in a fit and the Pilot's boy 'doth crazy go' (565) on encountering him. Real-life readers, encountering the tale as it appeared in *Lyrical Ballads* (1798), reacted with similar stunned incomprehension (one can only feel for those sailors who bought it, reportedly assuming from the poem's title that the collection was a naval song-book).[66] Charles Burney called it 'the strangest story of a cock and a bull that we ever saw on paper [...] a rhapsody of unintelligible wildness and incoherence, of which we do not recognise the drift, unless the joke lies in depriving the wedding guest of his share of the feast'.[67] In George Eliot's *Adam Bede* (1859), set in 1799, it appears as a curious period detail: Captain Donnithorne owns it is 'a strange, striking thing', but confesses he 'can hardly make head or tail of it as a story'.[68] Though Wordsworth kept it in the second

[66] Samuel Taylor Coleridge, *Table Talk II*, ed. Carl Woodring, 14/16 vols, *The Collected Works of Samuel Taylor Coleridge* (Princeton, NJ: Princeton University Press, 1990), 375.

[67] Charles Burney, '*Lyrical Ballads*, with a Few Other Poems', *The Monthly Review* 29 (June 1799), 202–10: 204; quoted in Jerome McGann, 'The Meaning of the Ancient Mariner', *Critical Inquiry* 8.1 (Autumn 1981), 35–67: 36.

[68] George Eliot, *Adam Bede*, ed. Stephen Gill (Harmondsworth; Penguin, 1985), 109.

(1800) edition of *Lyrical Ballads*, its archaisms having been removed, he included among its 'great defects' 'that the principal person has no distinct character, either in his profession of Mariner, or as a human being who having been long under the controul of supernatural impressions might be supposed himself to partake of something supernatural'[69] – a criticism that suggests at once that the Ancient Mariner is too fantastical and not fantastical enough. Coleridge himself did not disagree. His own word for the poem was 'incomprehensible'.[70] This extended incomprehensibility, this surpassing loquacity, has been conceptualized in psychological, ontological and what might be termed theologico-bibliographical frameworks. I will outline each of these before suggesting what the significance of the Ancient Mariner's tale-telling might be in terms of aesthetics and epistemology.

The idea of storytelling as psychologically curative has already been touched on earlier in this chapter. More specifically, Cathy Caruth has argued that, after Freud,[71] trauma is locatable in the way that 'its very unassimilated nature – the way it was precisely *not known* in the first instance – returns to haunt the survivor later on'.[72] The fact that direct experience is somehow missing becomes the basis of the repetition of the trauma in/by the traumatized person in the form of the 'wound that

[69] William Wordsworth, *Lyrical Ballads and Other Poems, 1797–1800*, ed. James Butler and Karen Green, *The Cornell Wordsworth* (Ithaca, NY: Cornell University Press, 1992), 791.

[70] In *Biographia Literaria* (1817), Coleridge recounts an 'anecdote' in which an 'amateur performer' asked a common friend to be introduced to him (Coleridge) but hesitated when the introduction was granted on the grounds that he (the performer) was the author of a 'confounded severe epigram' on 'The Rime of the Ancient Mariner'. This surprised Coleridge because the epigram in question 'proved to be one which I had myself some time before written and inserted in the *Morning Post*':

> To the author of the Ancient Mariner.
> Your poem must eternal be,
> Dear sir! it cannot fail,
> For 'tis incomprehensible
> And without head or tail.

(*Biographica Literaria I*, ed. James Engell and W. Jackson Bate, 7/16 vols, *The Collected Works of Samuel Taylor Coleridge* (Pricneton: Princeton University Press, 1983), 28). The editorial note states that Coleridge's four lines were published in the *Morning Post* on 24 January 1800 but addressed, not 'to the author of the Ancient Mariner' but to Henry James Pye. Coleridge 'may have invented the story' (ibid., 28 n1).

[71] In *Beyond the Pleasure Principle* (1922), Freud set out the idea that that 'memory-records' are often 'strongest and most enduring' when 'the process that left them behind never reached consciousness at all' (*Beyond the Pleasure Principle* (*Jenseits des Lustprinzips*) [1920], trans. C. J. M. Hubback, ed. Ernest Jones, *The International Psycho-Analytical Library* (London: The Hogarth Press/The Institute for Psycho-Analysis, 1922), 27).

[72] Cathy Caruth, *Unclaimed Experience: Trauma, Narrative, and History* (Baltimore, MD: The Johns Hopkins University Press, 1996), 4.

cries out'.[73] Sarah Cole remarks that Caruth's outcrying wound 'returns a fundamental productivity to the sufferer, in the form of his/her urgent storytelling',[74] but in the Caruthian model, it is not so much that the survivor speaks as that the trauma *tells itself*. This notion gives scope for aligning the Ancient Mariner's marvellous tale with what, after Kristeva,[75] has been termed the 'semiotic'. In Elizabeth Grosz's words, the semiotic, like the repressed, 'can return in / as irruptions within the symbolic'.[76] These irruptions represent 'the symbolization or representation of hitherto unspeakable or unintelligible phenomena, instances on the borders of the meaningful'.[77] The Ancient Mariner's utterances might be characterized as semiotic, not insofar as they are syntactically orderly and, indeed, cast in strict metrical and verse form, but insofar as they constitute an irruption in the social order (they disrupt the attending of a wedding) and, in epistemological terms, consist of vision and mystery rather than reason and logic.

Judith Herman broadly concurs with Caruth's analysis, characterizing a survivor's initial account of the traumatic event as 'repetitious, stereotyped, and emotionless'.[78] Herman notes that the trauma story 'in its untransformed state' has been described as a 'prenarrative' that 'does not develop or progress in time'.[79] But, after 'many repetitions', a moment arrives in which the telling of the trauma story 'no longer arouses quite such intense feeling' but simply becomes 'a part of the survivor's experience'.[80] Boring not only other people with one's tale but actually boring oneself with it is a measure of mental well-being. If these literary-diagnostic frameworks are applied to 'The Rime of the Ancient Mariner', the protagonist's compulsive storytelling becomes a more-or-less instinctive form of psychic defence; talking (and there could be no such thing as *over*-talking) understood as a Freudian-based remedy offering healing through the recovery and mastery of a repressed traumatic event through narrative.[81] Hence, storytelling

---

[73] Ibid., 4.

[74] Sarah Cole, 'The Poetry of Pain', *The Oxford Handbook of British and Irish War Poetry*, ed. Tim Kendall (Oxford: Oxford University Press, 2007), 483–503: 484.

[75] See Julia Kristeva, *Revolution in Poetic Language* (*La Révolution du langage poétique*) [1974], trans. Leon S. Roudiez (New York: Columbia University Press, 1984), 68.

[76] Elizabeth Grosz, *Jacques Lacan: A Feminist Introduction* (New York: Routledge, 1990), 152.

[77] Ibid., 153.

[78] Herman, *Trauma and Recovery*, 175.

[79] Ibid., 175.

[80] Ibid., 175.

[81] The so-called talking cure, and the Freudian/Caruthian model on which it is based has been questioned by psychiatrists. Richard J. McNally, for example, writes: 'As with all extremely negative emotional events, stress hormones interacting with an activated amygdala enhance the hippocampus's capacity to establish vivid, relatively durable memories of the experience – or at least

abates the 'woful agony' that periodically assails him. The problem is that the 'cure' would, at best, be a work-in-progress: as 'The Rime' ends, the Ancient Mariner has disappeared from view, but there is no reason to assume that this latest iteration of the tale has induced distress-alleviating habituation in him. The 'woful agony' may yet reappear. Far from constituting a means of psychic re-integration, a putting-back-together of self, his narrative is a process that, never ending, never confers relief.

In an ontologically inflected reading that overlaps in part with these psychological models, Seamus Perry argues that 'like *Heart of Darkness*', 'The Rime of the Ancient Mariner' is 'not about a disastrous voyage but about an old tar, years later, *retelling the story* of a disastrous voyage'.[82] Form is content, that is, but the Ancient Mariner's obsessive re-telling is more than simply 'polishing an anecdote': rather, 'it is an attempt repeatedly to make sense, to convince himself of his shaky grasp of the telling events'.[83] The 'genius of the piece' lies in 'its showing how passionate and driven may be the desire to gather one's experience into an intelligible thesis'.[84] The Ancient Mariner finds (self-)meaning through narrative. In a later essay (not discussing 'The Rime') Perry introduces a related epistemological concept: Richard Rorty's distinction between 'therapeutic', 'edifying' philosophies and 'constructive', 'systematic' ones, the former 'aiming at continuing a conversation rather than at discovering truth'.[85] Coleridge, Perry notes in this later piece, has often been read as 'following an edifying route of "anti-rationalism" and purposefully proceeding "on a disorderly, miscellaneous fashion"',[86] and, in a similar way, the utterances of the verbose Ancient Mariner might be thought to exemplify the exploratory, therapeutic open mode of ongoing conversation. But Perry insists that,

---

its salient, central features. High levels of emotional stress enhance explicit, declarative memory for the trauma itself; they do not impair it. When people with PTSD recall traumatic events, recollection is accompanied by emotional arousal that creates the illusion of reliving the event. None of these reactions requires any special "trauma" mechanisms in the brain; the mechanisms of intense emotional encoding and retrieval suffice to explain traumatic memory as well as memory for other emotionally intense experiences' (*Remembering Trauma* (Cambridge, MA; The Belknap Press of Harvard University Press, 2003), 276). McNally does not explicitly address the point as to whether the 'enhanced' traumatic memory he describes is accompanied by similarly enhanced articulacy or notable prolixity, but their presence is not a notable feature in his account.

[82] Seamus Perry, *Coleridge and the Uses of Division* (Oxford: Oxford University Press, 1999), 287, original emphasis.

[83] Ibid., 287.

[84] Ibid., 287.

[85] Perry, 'The Talker', 117, citing Richard Rorty, *Philosophy and the Mirror of Nature* (Oxford: Blackwell, 1980), 5, 373.

[86] Perry, 'The Talker', 117, citing Kathleen M. Wheeler, *Romanticism, Pragmatism and Deconstruction* (Oxford: Basil Blackwell, 1993), XI, 16.

far from endorsing 'anti-systematic thinking', Coleridge 'espouses vehemently the opposing values of unity, wholeness and system'.[87] Accordingly, the Ancient Mariner's verbal torrent might be thought of as a 'single purposeful flow' – Sterling's 'spreading every-whither' sea transformed into a swift, all-encompassing current – in which, in 'Platonic connectedness', 'digressiveness is redeemed'.[88]

In this model, profusion is unity, verbosity inter-relatedness (albeit, in Perry's words, in 'monomaniacal form, unifying as a form of dementia').[89] And in a third interpretative framework, this time a theologico-bibliographical one, Jerome McGann offers a reading of 'The Rime' in which meaning is again the product of accumulation, of quantity. Coleridge, it will be remembered, himself described the poem as 'incomprehensible'. In *Biographia Literaria* (1817), explaining the genesis of *Lyrical Ballads*, he explained what 'incomprehensible' might consist of. In the poems he was to contribute to the volume:

> [I]ncidents and agents were to be, in part at least, supernatural, and the excellence aimed at was to consist in the interesting of the affections by the dramatic truth of such emotions, as would naturally accompany such situations, supposing them real. And real in this sense they have been to every human being who, from whatever source of delusion, has at any time believed himself under supernatural agency. [...] In this idea originated the plan of the 'Lyrical Ballads'; in which it was agreed, that my endeavours should be directed to persons and characters supernatural, or at least Romantic; yet so as to transfer from our inward nature a human interest and a semblance of truth sufficient to procure for these shadows of imagination that willing suspension of disbelief for the moment, which constitutes poetic faith. [...] With this view I wrote the 'Ancient Mariner'.[90]

Here, Coleridge suggests a 'reality' to supernatural situations; at least, that is, a 'reality' deriving from 'whatever source of delusion' the person experiencing them may be under. To credit such 'reality' requires 'poetic faith', a faith with much in common with religious faith. McGann's reading of 'The Rime of the Ancient Mariner' ascribes a bibliographical quality to Coleridgean faith. Drawing on the work of Elinor Shaffer, he argues

---

[87] Perry, 'The Talker', 117.

[88] Ibid., 118, 121.

[89] Perry, *Coleridge and the Uses of Division*, 287.

[90] Samuel Taylor Coleridge, *Biographia Literaria II*, ed. James Engell and W. Jackson Bate, 7/16 vols, *The Collected Works of Samuel Taylor Coleridge* (Princeton, NJ: Princeton University Press, 1983), 6–7.

that Coleridge's following of the Higher Critical approaches of figures such as Christian Gottlob Heyne, Johann David Michaelis, Alexander Geddes, Gotthold Ephraim Lessing, Johann Gottfried Herder and Johann Gottfried Eichhorn led him to espouse a 'mythological hermeneutics'.[91] Shaffer explains further:

> Coleridge's argument reflects a long struggle of the new criticism with the idea that an eye-witness account must be of special value. If, by their own critical endeavour, it became clear that none of the Gospels was an eye-witness account, the status of the 'event' therein recounted must, on the old view, be diminished, its credibility undermined; but if there are no such privileged accounts, if all event is interpretation, then the Gospels need not suffer. Indeed, as we shall see, their value as literature is increased. For Coleridge, 'event' and 'mystery' must be expressed with equal delicacy, obliquity, and restraint. The miracle becomes the paradigm of reported historical event; the historical events reported by eye-witnesses represent instantaneous mythmaking.[92]

According to this line of thought, textual evolution (which, in the case of the Bible, involved 'accretion and interpolation over an extended period of time')[93] is at once a witnessing, an act of faith and the occasion for further acts of faith – and, McGann argues, Coleridge's views on the Bible were 'merely paradigmatic of his views on all literary texts'.[94] The textual evolution of 'The Rime of the Ancient Mariner' becomes not merely an exercise in clarification but a process with 'symbolic value and meaning, that is, a religious, a Christian, and ultimately a redemptive meaning'.[95] By extension (an extension not made by McGann), a similar argument could be made in respect of the Ancient Mariner's repetition of his tale. Multiple reiterations distance the story from its origins (whatever the epistemological status of such origins may be) and, in their very numerousness, represent a de-privileging of any single version. Excessive telling, a verbal palimpsest, models cumulative truth. The problem with this theologico-bibliographical interpretation lies in the fact that the Ancient Mariner's tale – so far as it can be discerned – never varies. What the 'woful agony' induces him to tell and re-tell is the same story: not so much a verbal palimpsest, with all that implies about a complex layering of diverse texts, as

[91] McGann, 'The Meaning of the Ancient Mariner', 44.
[92] Elinor Shaffer, 'Kubla Khan' and the Fall of Jerusalem (Cambridge: Cambridge University Press, 1975), 46–7.
[93] McGann, 'The Meaning of the Ancient Mariner', 48.
[94] Ibid., 57.
[95] Ibid., 60.

the accumulation of like on like. Such unvarying repetition in fact works counter to an understanding of accreted meaning based on models of textual criticism and book history.

These psychological, ontological and theologico-bibliographical interpretative frameworks have in common an emphasis on significance produced by plurality. Prolixity equals meaningfulness. But here I would like to propose that the Ancient Mariner's imposed, unwanted, lengthy tale forms, rather, a model of communication in which a discursive excess results in diminished signification. The marks of veterancy, in this case, accompany an account of phenomena beyond the experience they could render credible. The Ancient Mariner's telling of his story, its contents beyond comprehension, is the spectacle of a monologue:[96] what occurs is a passing by rather than a handing on. The story will be repeated ad infinitum: not by an edified Wedding Guest to the further edification of future listeners, but by the Ancient Mariner to other reluctant auditors. For the Ancient Mariner's never-ending story runs a different course from both the affect of rhetorically charged eloquence and the persuasiveness of rational communication. Those who encounter him may pity his distress, but none of them will be either moved or convinced. In making this argument, I do not dispute that Coleridge 'espouses vehemently' the values of 'unity, wholeness and system'.[97] My point is not that the Ancient Mariner's discourse is 'anti-systematic'; it is that it is *rude*. It severely inconveniences a stranger and, in doing so, it disrupts an important social ritual. It doesn't just demonstrate the inadequacy of polite, reason-based discourse, it completely overwhelms it. From this torrential outpouring, I move on from the late eighteenth century to consider a post-Second World War novel in which excess again proves that more is less.

### 'Rose after rose after rose': Henry Green, *Back* (1946)

Henry Green's sixth novel, *Back* (1946), has been widely interpreted as a commentary on the post-Second World War social and economic uncertainty that greeted those 'back' from the fighting, and, just as widely, as a study in trauma and repression (what is held, or refuses to remain, 'back'). Representing the former critical tendency, David Deeming calls the novel

---

[96] Arthur Frank's term for the kind of story that brooks no discussion or interpretation is 'monological' (*Letting Stories Breathe: A Socio-Narratology* (Chicago: The University of Chicago Press, 2010), 35).

[97] Perry, 'The Talker', 117.

'Green's most brilliant study in social alienation',[98] while Laura Doan finds it expressive of 'that historical juncture where a displaced British society passively watched the disintegration of the old order against the uncertain creation of the new'.[99] In psychological and psychoanalytical readings, Gerard Barrett describes the novel as the 1940s' 'finest representation of a condition that has only recently acquired a name', that is, post-traumatic stress disorder,[100] and Stephen A. Shapiro notes that one of the work's 'central concerns' is 'the way the present returns to the past, the way the unconscious gets back at consciousness'.[101] Siting trauma in the context of social behaviour, Kristine Miller suggests that, by 'juxtaposing physical and emotional trauma and questioning dominant political and sexual discourses', *Back* represents the wounded soldier 'as a sign of the instability of postwar gender roles'.[102] Green himself endorsed these critical propensities. 'The truth is that the present times are an absolute gift to the novelist,' he wrote in a letter of 14 March 1945 to Rosamund Lehmann, 'I see *everything* crumbling & growing all round me.'[103] But he also stated, simply, 'It's all about a man whose nerves are very bad.'[104] In this section, while not ignoring the novel's social and psychological motivations and implications, I will explore what *Back* and its veteran protagonist have to say about communication and, specifically, about how meaning is produced – or not produced.

In this exploration, I hope to build on the critical thought that has accumulated in relation to the linguistic aspects of Green's writing. In fiction in the decades following high modernism, argues Lyndsey Stonebridge, it seemed as if that heteroglossic movement had resulted in 'the effort of hearing other voices' becoming 'too much'.[105] Accordingly, Green's dialogue is constructed on 'the principle that people cannot hear

---

[98] David Deeming, 'Henry Green's "The Lull" and the Postwar Demise of Green's Modernist Aesthetic', *Modern Fiction Studies* 44.4 (Winter 1998), 865–87: 883.

[99] Laura L. Doan, 'Recuperating the Postwar Moment: Green's *Back* and Bacon's *Three Studies for Figures at the Base of a Crucifixion*', *Mosaic* 23.3 (Summer 1990), 113–24: 123–4.

[100] Gerard Barrett, 'Souvenirs from France: Textual Traumatism in Henry Green's *Back*', *The Fiction of the 1940s: Stories of Survival*, ed. Rod Mengham and N. H. Reeve (Basingstoke: Palgrave, 2001), 169–84: 169.

[101] S. A. Shapiro, 'Henry Green's *Back*: The Presence of the Past', *Critique: Studies in Contemporary Fiction* 7.1 (Spring 1964), 87–96: 93.

[102] Kristine Miller, 'The War of the Roses: Sexual Politics in Henry Green's *Back*', *Modern Fiction Studies* 49.2 (Summer 2003), 228–45: 228.

[103] Quoted in Jeremy Treglown, *Romancing: The Life and Work of Henry Green* (London: Faber and Faber, 2000), 176. The letter is held in the library of King's College, Cambridge.

[104] Quoted in ibid., 176.

[105] Lyndsey Stonebridge, *The Writing of Anxiety: Imagining Wartime in Mid-Century British Culture* (Basingstoke; Palgrave Macmillan, 2007), 124.

what others are saying to them'.[106] Rod Mengham, too, drawing attention to the many instances of acronyms in *Back* (discussed further below), proposes that Britain in 1944 was 'literally *unreadable*' and, further, that 'the crucial disadvantage for returning servicemen' was 'the inability to identify and decipher the messages received'.[107] Mengham's perception that Green's novel represents the problem of legibility as 'a form of surplusage' is particularly suggestive.[108] In what follows, I will argue that *Back* models excessive signification – a proliferation of signage – and its consequent voiding, offering a depiction of veteran communication that is simultaneously growing and crumbling.[109]

Green's chief protagonist, Charley Summers (the pluralization contained in his surname is a tiny example of a repetition, in this case of a season) is a veteran returned from a prisoner of war camp where he has spent five years of the Second World War. The second sentence of the novel mentions that he has a 'peg leg' (3):[110] the first of many instances of loss resulting in replacement or doubling (or tripling or multiplying to even greater factors). In the opening scene, Summers is visiting a graveyard, a place of death but also of (vegetal) growth. His perception of his surroundings is typical of that of an ex-combatant: he 'note[s] well' the slits in the church tower, 'built for defence'; he runs his eye 'with caution' over cypress trees and between gravestones (3). The reason for this militarized awareness is soon given: 'He might have been watching for a trap, who had lost his leg in France for not noticing the gun beneath a rose' (3). Both the structure and the contents of this sentence are worth note. Though the subordinate clause is strictly grammatically correct, it nonetheless seems to lack a 'he' ('*he* who had lost his leg…'). The small syntactical quirk serves to deprive a relative pronoun ('who') of an adjacent subject pronoun. 'Who', that is, is cut adrift from the 'he' it refers to. The effect is replicated in the contents. The rose concealing the gun functions as an image of signification in which

[106] Ibid., 124. On hearing difficulties in Green, see further Rex Ferguson, 'Blind Noise and Deaf Visions: Henry Green's *Caught*, Synaesthesia and the Blitz', *Journal of Modern Literature* 33 (Fall 2009), 102–16.

[107] Rod Mengham, *The Idiom of the Time: The Writings of Henry Green* (Cambridge: Cambridge University Press, 1982), 158, original emphasis.

[108] Ibid., 172.

[109] Elizabeth Taylor's *A Wreath of Roses*, discussed briefly above, forms a fascinating intertext with *Back*, sharing its concern with empty signification and using the same word – 'rose' – to explore this. There is not space here to compare the two novels in detail; see my forthcoming 'The Literature of Tiredness', *Postwar: British Literature in Transition: Volume 3 1940–1960*, ed. Gill Plain (Cambridge: Cambridge University Press, 2018).

[110] Henry Green, *Back* [1946] (London: Harvill, 1998). Page references are given in the text.

a sign is discontinuous with its referent.[111] While a real-life rose may be no
more or less than itself (Gertrude Stein's 'Rose is a rose is a rose is a rose'),[112]
in written discourse the word 'rose' and the concept 'rose' comprise a sign
as signifier and signified respectively, the referent of which is an actual
rose.[113] Summers remembers a rose (an actual rose in the fictional world)
becoming a sign of something else (a gun). He failed correctly to read this
rose, and paid the price with his leg. On the first page of the novel, then,
the relationship between signs and their referents – and, indeed, signification more generally – has become suspect.

Immediately after this sentence comes the following sentence-long
paragraph:

> For, climbing around and up these trees of mourning, was rose after rose after
> rose, while, here and there, the spray over-burdened by the mass of flower, a live
> wreath lay fallen on a wreath of stone, or in a box in marble colder than this day, or
> onto frosted paper blooms which, under glass, marked each bed of earth wherein
> the dear departed encouraged life above in the green grass, the cypresses and in
> those roses gay and bright which, as still as this dark afternoon, stared at whosoever
> looked, or hung their heads to droop, to grow stained, to die when their turn came.
>
> (3)

Here is a profusion of roses (they are climbing up or rising; they rose): both
the flowers in the fiction and the word 'rose' in the prose. This is, indeed,
an 'over-burdening' of roses, threatening to make the stem on which they
all depend collapse and so turn them into their own wreaths, or, reading
them in metaphorical terms, to overload the system of signification and
turn signs into dead signs. These roses repeat themselves. A naturally
occurring wreath of actual roses lies on a wreath of stone roses, another on
a wreath of paper blooms: the roses are both alive and inanimate, real and
artificial. In further complex layering, the artificial paper roses on which
the real, fallen roses are superimposed mark the graves in which remains
are fertilizing another generation of real, overhead roses that will, in their
turn, die, casting further wreaths upon those in the glass boxes. The roses

---

[111] Mengham brilliantly notes that 'beneath a rose' or *sub rosa* means 'in secret, secretly' (*The Idiom of the Time*, 172, 166).

[112] The line, which Stein modified through a number of works, appeared originally in the 1913 poem 'Sacred Emily' (Gertrude Stein, *Geography and Plays* (Madison, WI: University of Wisconsin Press, 1993), 178–88: 187). Mengham comments that *Back*'s 'ambition would be to eternalize the formula' devised by Stein (*The Idiom of the Time*, 170).

[113] I am using 'sign' and 'referent' here in the sense suggested by Ferdinand de Saussure, *Course in General Linguistics* (*Cours de linguistique générale*) [1916], trans. Roy Harris (London: Duckworth, 1983), 65f.

are perpetuating themselves in a circularity that is again reminiscent of Stein's 'Rose is a rose is a rose'. In Stein's phrase, the sign 'rose' has become self-referential, repeated in a persistent but ultimately ineffectual attempt to produce meaning (like an actual rose, the proposition that a rose is a rose does not add or subtract anything). In a similar way, Green's roses are, as signs, at once proliferating and atrophying – growing and crumbling – spreading profusely only to become the inanimate roses of paper and stone.

Almost immediately, *Back* introduces another rose: 'But he came now to visit because someone he loved, a woman, who, above all at night, had been in his feelings when he was behind barbed wire, had been put here while he was away, and her name, of all names, was Rose' (4). In this sentence, which is long – though not among Green's longest – 'name' is repeated, as is 'Rose', the word that has already been repeated multiple times. This Rose is also associated with death and with profuse growth. Summers imagines the briar roots 'pushing down to the red hair of which she had been so proud and fond' (5), her body as 'food for worms' (6), her 'great red hair, still growing, a sort of moist bower for worms' (6): a nightmarish fecundity. In another image of signification, he sees 'sharp letters, cut in marble beyond a bunch of live roses' and realizes that this is where his former sweetheart must be buried 'for the letters spelled Rose' (10). In a literalization of Stein's 'Rose is a rose is a rose is a rose', actual, live roses lie on top of the sign for roses and beneath this sign lies another referent, but this time a dead one: Rose the woman. Now the sign 'rose' must do double signifying duty, producing an excess of meaning. At the same time, there is also an excess of signs: both the live roses and the word cut in the marble refer to (memorialize) the dead woman beneath. Signs and referents are both confused and confusing. Contributing to the confusion is a further play on the meaning of 'rose': a resurrection motif that recurs throughout the novel and that I will pick up later.

The opening sequence models the profusion of R/roses in the novel. It should again be noted that *Back* is not, and does not contain, a veteran's story that is multiply reiterated or that refuses to end. Nor is it the case that the veteran protagonist over-talks. Indeed, Summers exhibits the opposing tendency, having difficulties in expressing himself. Something has happened in France that he knows 'as he value[s] his reason' that he 'must always shut out' (183). Green writes: 'He clapped his hands down tight over his ears. He concentrated on not ever remembering. On keeping himself dead empty' (183). The deadness and emptiness refer as much to the capacity to engage in meaningful communication as to emotional memory. Later, the reader is told that 'the nausea, which had recently begun to spread in [Summers'] stomach whenever prison camps were mentioned, drove all else out of his head' (15). Voided of data (dead empty), he responds to his interlocutor in a way that reveals both verbally and in terms of volume his inability to engage in signifying practices: ' "Rather not speak of it," he replied, indistinctly' (15). (In Habermasian terms, he doesn't even aspire to communicative competence.) In a variation on these instances of vacant communication, Summers is shown 'forever asking himself things he could seldom answer' (5). In the opening scene, he wonders 'what he could say' if a village gossip were to see him – to his mind, incongruously – in the graveyard, but is unable to provide himself with a reply. In another key moment, his landlady, Mrs Frazier, warns him against talking to himself: ' "Mr Summers, you want to watch out. Not at your age. Why," she said, "your voice rose," and again, as this word came through, he not even experienced guilt. "You spoke loud," she said. "Take care, you can do that when you get to my age, but for a young man like you, well ..." ' (32). Talking to oneself – particularly when no answer is forthcoming – is another example of circular signification. The point is made subtly in the phrase 'your voice rose', which juxtaposes the means of speech with the worn-out word 'rose' as copulates: in some sense, Summers' voice *is* R/rose, but R/rose has been emptied of signification. Mrs Frazier's warning is, furthermore, a reminder of the social constraints on Summers' discourses. Elsewhere, he is described as having 'a sort of block in his stomach, which, in the ordinary way, seemed to stand between him and free speech' (22): the phrasing makes 'speech' a political, as much as a somatic, psychological and emotional, phenomenon. The paradox is that Summers' reticence is linked to excess. Diagnosing Mrs Grant's amnesia, the doctor comments, 'I've a number of cases like that, now. Comes from the bombing. [...] the nervous system rejects what is surplus to its immediate requirement' (154). The same is true of Summers' traumatized and hence self-voiding memory, with the result that he volunteers little ('he sat back, having talked too much for him' (36)). Instead, the signifying surplus is displaced to the discourses that surround him.

In consequence, *Back* is a novel of repetitions and multiplications. On the formal level, Doan has noted its ABA structure (Summers' return / his 'lapse into delusion and madness' / his recovery), the outer wings of the triptych each forming a version of coming 'back'.[114] The text is thickened with parallel intertexts. As Marius Hentea has observed, Summers passes a

---

[114] Doan, 'Recuperating the Postwar Moment', 116.

second-hand bookseller's window and notices a set of the works of Rhoda Broughton (52). Surprisingly, the title that catches his eye is not 'one of Broughton's more popular works, *Red as a Rose Is She* [1870]' but *Cometh Up as a Flower* (1867)[115] (the title is a synonym of 'rose' as a past-tense verb). Hentea points out that *Cometh Up as a Flower,* like *Back,* has an opening sequence set in a graveyard, and, moreover, shares certain plot developments with another *Back* intertext – the *Souvenirs de la marquise de Créquy,* a twelve-page passage that is inserted into *Back* supposedly as a 'translation' in a journal, which James Phillips sends to Summers because it seems 'so close' to the latter's situation (87).[116] Published in Paris between 1834 and 1836, the purportedly autobiographical *Souvenirs* were early denounced as a fake.[117] Green made two long translations of passages from them, the first published in the December 1944 issue of *Horizon,* the second in *Back*: 'there could be no doubt', writes Hentea, 'that he was working with a forgery'.[118] The *Souvenirs* have two, opposing, implications in terms of meaning production. Paralleling the plot of *Back* in the overlap between the delusions of Summers and those of Septimanie de Richelieu, they add an extra – excessive – layer to that narrative. At the same time, their status as a forgery sabotages it. Gerard Barrett argues that, by 'planting' the earlier translation in *Horizon,* Green ensured that 'the most fantastic and hallucinatory aspect of *Back*' would have 'an oblique, historical validity',[119] and yet this 'validity' is hypertextual (dependent upon an external text) and therefore both produced by and productive of meaning that proliferates beyond the novel. Mengham suggests that the 'central gap' that the *Souvenirs* make in the text of *Back* is 'an image of writing as schizophrenia': '[w]hen everything is written over [...] the lengths to which it is possible to go in covering up tracks are theoretic-ally limitless'.[120] The *Souvenirs* both reinforce and undermine the fiction of *Back*: replicative, they once again model signification that is circular and so ultimately empty.

*Back* proceeds on this replicatory principle. Summers' prosthesis has already been mentioned: described both as an 'aluminium leg' (20) and as a 'wooden leg' (5), it is as though he has two false limbs, and it/they finds/

---

[115] Marius Hentea, 'Fictional Doubles in Henry Green's *Back*', *The Review of English Studies* 61.251 (September 2010), 614–26: 620 n31.

[116] Ibid., 610 n31. The extra 'l' in the surname 'Phillips' is another tiny example of surplusage.

[117] Ibid., 617–18.

[118] Ibid., 610.

[119] Barrett, 'Souvenirs from France', 180.

[120] Mengham, *The Idiom of the Time,* 172.

find another parallel in Middlewitch's 'chromium plated arm' (20). Hentea notes the 1:1 principle of the filing system Summers establishes in his office (36)[121] in which cross-indexed entries refer back to each other. This filing system has kept Summers 'sane' (35), no doubt because it is a means of controlling the proliferation of meaning even as it involves an over-production of signs. Coincidences, another form of parallelism, are rife in the work – 'Once you start on coincidence why there's no end to those things,' remarks Mrs Frazier (30). Middlewitch, for example, knows Rose's parents and is both a former lodger of Mrs Frazier's and Nancy's neighbour.[122] There are a number of doublings. The toddler Ridley connotes fecundity and proliferation ('riddling'): Summers is 'taken up by a need to see the child a second time', a reiteration that will allow him:

> to search in the shape of the bones of its face for an echo of Rose, to drag this out from the line of its full cheeks to see if he could find a memory of Rose laughing there, and even to look deep in Ridley's eyes as through a mirror, and catch the small of himself by which to detect, if he could, a likeness, a something, however false, to tell him he was a father, that Rose lived again, by his agency, in their son. (10)

There are plural Roses in this passage, the dead Rose who is potentially discernible in Ridley's bone structure and cheeks; and, in a beautifully complex construction, a Rose resurrected via the image of Summers in Ridley's pupils, an image that, if he detects in it a likeness to the boy, will allow Summers to know that Rose lives again in their son 'by his agency'. In yet another resurrection, Mrs Grant thinks that Summers is her brother, John, killed in the First World War: she sings out ' "John, John," twice'. It is not clear whether this means that the name is said two or four times in all but, in either event, the re-naming is in excess of the apparent referent.

The most important resurrection is that of Rose herself, whom Summers confuses with her half-sister, Nancy Whitmore (there is both blankness and excess in the name).[123] On first seeing Nancy, he reacts with shock: 'He looked. He sagged. Then something went inside. It was as though the frightful starts his heart was giving had burst a vein. He pitched forward in a dead faint, because there she stood alive, so close that he could touch, and

---

[121] Hentea, 'Fictional Doubles in Henry Green's *Back*', 622.

[122] See Andrew Gibson, 'Henry Green as Experimental Novelist', *Studies in the Novel* 16.2 (Summer 1984), 197–212: 207.

[123] Nancy has black hair (45) unlike Rose, whose hair is red (5, 6). Nancy is darker than Rose as a consequence of this, but, as her surname, 'Whitmore', suggests, also paler (more white). In these tiny details, Nancy appears to be, not just another version of Rose, but further plural versions.

breathing, the dead spit, the living image herself, Rose in person' (43). The shock is excessive, and this Rose, too, is excessive: it is as though there are multiple Roses – the 'dead spit' and the 'living image'.[124] The conversations between Summers and Nancy repeat the word 'R/rose' further, asserting it, questioning it, straining it, undermining it. The novel teems with Roses. Summers 'denies' her three times (10, 23, 146), giving her a Christ-like quality: she refuses to die but keeps rising, 're-flowering' (35). Nancy is affronted when Summers brings Rose's husband to her flat: 'Think of it. Him that's met his wife naked in bed with him, and you bring him along to me. Oh it's not proper' (83). Her fear is that she replicates Rose, and so her own naked body will be familiar to him: her reaction hypostasizes another Rose (later Summers accuses her of being a bigamist, doubling her husbands). Dot Miller cruelly repeats Rose's name – 'It's Rose, Rose she's called, isn't it Rose?' (107) – and Summers has to leave the room in case he vomits. His physiological urge bespeaks his emotional distress, but there is also a sense of an excess of signs, which requires purgation. 'R/rose' multiplies and multiplies so that Summers, trying to escape the sign, keeps coming upon it: 'He fled Rose, yet every place he went she rose up before him' (52).[125]

Proliferating in this way, 'R/rose' empties itself out, ceases to be a sign with meaning.[126] It comes to resemble the many acronyms in the novel ('Everything's initials these days', sighs Mr Grant (16)): a surplusage of letters that, since they are impenetrable, also marks a diminution of communication.[127] The acronyms find a physical form in the letters Summers scissors from old letters from Rose to paste together as a message that he can have compared with Nancy's handwriting. Though the intention

---

[124] 'Dead spit' derives from 'spitting image', itself a corruption of 'splitting image' ('splitting, adj.', 5 (*Oxford English Dictionary* (Oxford University Press), online edition), the exact likeness formed when something is split in two.

[125] In a sense, the roses even extend beyond the novel – and Green's life. The collection of his previously unpublished writings, *Surviving* (1992), contains a piece Green dictated in 1964 about his childhood home, Forthampton Court: 'one beached the boat at dusk to turn and see Tewkesbury Abbey's Norman tower in Caen stone glowing rose above dying light – the Rose, darling Rose – he did not know it yet but of whom he was to write, never even having met her, written of not until after the Second War, muddled as she was, unthinking but always right, the dear Rose he would love at that time just to lose the agony of the air raids' (*Surviving: The Uncollected Writings of Henry Green*, ed. Matthew Yorke (London: Chatto and Windus, 1992), 301). The passage is extraordinarily reminiscent of *Back*.

[126] Hentea reads the profusion of 'R/roses' as expressive of Locke and Hume's 'association of ideas' ('Fictional Doubles in Henry Green's *Back*', 622). Yet Summers does not seem to be *producing* these roses so much as encountering them.

[127] Willard Waller comments that 'Army abbreviations alone are almost sufficient to make military speech incomprehensible to the civilian' (*The Veteran Comes Back*, 29).

is a doubling of signs, the message is meaningless and Summers berates himself for having 'killed' Rose's letters (118): 'R/rose', like the numerous acronyms, is reduced to so many dead letters. Unsurprisingly, Summers becomes inured to the sign: 'Each time he said her name he noted he felt nothing any more, so much so that he hardly bothered to watch himself these days' (38). This is symptomatic of an atrophying of signification: exhausted, 'R/rose' has no meaning.

The ubiquity of 'R/roses' in *Back* results, not in an equivalent proliferation of significance, but in a mass of empty or dead signs. Summers' urge to vomit after he has heard the word 'Rose' three times is indicative of a model of signification in which repetition (regurgitation, bringing something up again, *rising*) is ultimately synonymous with voiding. 'R/rose' is now incomprehensible. Veteran tale-telling, over-talking, has been displaced into a more general linguistic surplusage, equally relentless, equally unsatisfying, equally unedifying.

## Conclusion

Mass warfare – itself a phenomenon of excess – produces an over-talking figure: the veteran whose tales of war, if welcome at first, quickly become unwanted. In this chapter, I have characterized such redundant, overabundant stories, and their abstraction into linguistic surfeiting, as rude and (hence) irrational. Whether read within the framework of eighteenth-century notions of polite, reason-based discourse or within that of more recent ideas of discourse ethics, the surplusage can be taken to indicate communicative anxieties. The experiences and after-effects of mass warfare cannot easily be encompassed by the parameters allowed by rational communication, but spill over, forming a torrent of verbiage. In the next chapter, I discuss in much greater detail the epistemological nature of these communicative concerns, again as figured through veteran storytelling. Rather than manifesting themselves in over-talking, however, these concerns result in under-talking; indeed, in some cases, in not talking at all. From magniloquence to pauciloquence, then, and the end of the story.

CHAPTER 5

# The End of the Story

### Odyssey 5: –

There is nothing in the *Odyssey* like this.

In the previous chapter, we noted that war veterans habitually tell war stories. In this chapter, by contrast, we encounter three literary veterans who are conspicuous for *not* telling stories. Their creators, William Wordsworth, Rebecca West and Virginia Woolf – all civilians themselves – take participation in modern, mass, global, industrialized warfare, with its dependence for successful conduct on management of a high degree of chance, to be an experience that is incomprehensible, unassimilable and (hence) unshareable. Hence, their veterans fail to articulate what they have been through. Unfathoming, they are also unfathomable. But these literary veterans do more than signify the senselessness of the wars in which they have participated. In my reading, they are impedimenta in the project of modernity – modernity understood, after Théodor Adorno and Max Horkheimer, as the Enlightenment process of replacing myth with scientific method.[1] In other words, the end of the story is the beginning of a new kind of being modern.

The fortunes of experientially based epistemology have already been partially traced in Chapter 3. The fictional veteran detectives discussed there knew that the forensic methods bequeathed by the scientific revolution only went so far in problem-solving: hunches, gut instincts and knowledge of the ways of the world were also indispensable. Yet, a certain unease was also discernible in relation to this alternative methodology. This chapter chronicles its collapse. Unable to fathom their experiences in

---

[1] Théodor Adorno and Max Horkheimer, *Dialectic of Enlightenment* (*Dialektik der Aufklärung*) [1944], trans. John Cumming (London: Verso, 1979). As noted in the Introduction, Robert Pippin uses 'modernity' and 'the Enlightenment' 'interchangeably' (*Modernism as a Philosophical Problem: On the Dissatisfactions of European High Culture* (Oxford: Blackwell, 1991/1999), 4) but the distinction between what he is deploying these terms to signify and a later phase is important.

mass warfare and, in consequence, unfathomable to anyone else, literary veterans figure the limits of both reason and experience. The texts I discuss are Wordsworth's 'The Discharged Soldier' (1798) and that poem's later incarnation in *The Prelude* of 1805, West's *The Return of the Soldier* (1918) and Virginia Woolf's *Mrs Dalloway* (1925). But before exploring these works, we need to remind ourselves of the connections between veterancy, experience and storytelling, with reference to Walter Benjamin's 1936 essay 'The Storyteller' (*Der Erzähler*).

## Veterancy, Experience and Storytelling

In this essay, which was partly reworked from earlier pieces, 'The Handkerchief' (1932) and 'Experience and Poverty' (1933), Benjamin identifies two kinds of storyteller: the person who has come from afar and the person who stays at home.[2] The former tells stories of distant places, the latter of distant times. According to Benjamin, the storyteller 'takes what he tells from experience', which can either be his own or that reported by others.[3] In turn, he makes it the experience of those who are listening to his tale.[4] This process necessarily entails certain duties on the part of the listener or reader, the most important of which is 'to assure himself of the possibility of reproducing the story'.[5] Benjamin goes on to suggest certain factors that enhance the likelihood of this reproducibility,[6] one of which is the listener being in a 'state of relaxation'.[7] 'Boredom is the dream bird that hatches the egg of experience,' writes Benjamin, a remark that recalls the weariness that listening to war stories can induce.[8] 'Companionship' is also important: for Benjamin, a person listening to a story is 'in the company of the storyteller', and this is true of reading as much as listening.[9]

---

[2] Walter Benjamin, 'The Storyteller' ('Der Erzähler') [1936], trans. Harry Zohn, *Selected Writings. Volume 3: 1935–38*, ed., Michael W. Jennings and Howard Eiland (Cambridge, MA: The Belknap Press of Harvard University Press, 1999), 143–66: 144.

[3] Ibid., 146.

[4] Ibid., 146.

[5] Ibid., 153.

[6] Benjamin's word for 'reproduction' in 'The Storyteller' (*der Wiedergabe*) is different from that used in his essay 'The Work of Art in the Age of Mechanical Reproduction' (1935) (*die Reproduzierbarkeit*): the contrast between oral, interpersonal reproduction as opposed to mechanical reproduction is suggestive.

[7] Benjamin, 'The Storyteller', 149.

[8] Ibid., 149. Cf. 'people who are not bored cannot tell stories' (Walter Benjamin, 'The Handkerchief' ('Das Taschentuch') [1932], trans. Rodney Livingstone, *Selected Writings. Volume 2, Part 2: 1931–1934*, ed. Michael W. Jennings, Howard Eiland and Gary Smith (Cambridge, MA: The Belknap Press of Harvard University Press, 1999), 658–61: 652).

[9] Benjamin, 'The Storyteller', 156.

The 'experience' that Benjamin has in mind is expressed by the German word *Erfahrung*, which is distinct from *Erlebnis*, also translated as 'experience' in English. *Erlebnis*, it will be remembered from Chapter 3, signifies immediate, raw, often shocking experience; experience that has a high impact on the senses but is un-reflected upon. *Erfahrung*, by contrast, is the kind of experience indicated in the phrase 'to speak from experience'.[10] It is both a process and the fruit of that process, in Martin Jay's words 'a learning process over time, combining negations through unpleasant episodes as well as affirmations through positive ones', producing a 'cumulative, totalizing accretion of transmittable wisdom'.[11] In English literature, the *Erlebnis/Erfahrung* distinction becomes important in Aestheticism, whose emphasis is on the former. Walter Pater, in his famous Conclusion to *The Renaissance* (1873), remarks that 'Not the fruit of experience, but experience itself is the end',[12] and, forming an inter-textual chiasmus, the line appears in reversed form in Oscar Wilde's *The Picture of Dorian Gray* (1890) in Lord Henry Wotton's prediction of 'a new Hedonism' whose aim is to be 'experience itself, and not the fruits of experience'.[13] Small wonder Dorian Gray does not age physically.

---

[10] Benjamin was interested in both kinds of experience from the outset of his career. In an early essay, 'Experience' ('Erfahrung') (1913–14), his use of *Erlebnis* and *Erfahrung* is less dichotomized than suggested above. In this essay, he challenges the alignment of wisdom-through-experience with age and instead links *Erfahrung* with philistinism. Youth, by contrast, knows 'inexperiencable' ('unerfahrbar') truths (Walter Benjamin, 'Experience' ('Erfahrung') [1913–14], trans. Lloyd Spencer and Stefan Jost, *Selected Writings. Volume 1: 1913–1926*, ed. Marcus Bullock and Michael W. Jennings (Cambridge, MA: The Belknap Press of Harvard University Press, 1996), 3–5: 4; 'Erfahrung' [1913–14], *Gesammelte Schriften. Band II.1. Aufsätze, Essays, Vorträge*, ed. Rolf Tiedemann and Hermann Schweppenhäuser (Frankfurt-am-Main: Suhrkamp, 1977), 54–6: 55).

[11] Martin Jay, 'Experience Without A Subject: Walter Benjamin and the Novel', *New Formations* 20 (Summer 1993), 145–55: 146. On the point that there never was an originary experience, see Rebecca Comay, 'Gifts Without Presents: Economies of "Experience" in Bataille and Heidegger', *Yale French Studies* 78 (1995): 66–89: 85; Martin Jay, 'The Limits of Limit-Experience: Bataille and Foucault', *Constellations* 2.2 (1995), 155–74: 155–7.

[12] Walter Pater, *Studies in the History of the Renaissance* [1873], ed. Matthew Beaumont (Oxford: Oxford University Press, 2010), 119. Note Richard Aldington's description of a caricature of Pater as resembling 'some debilitated cavalry officer in mufti' ('Introduction', *Walter Pater: Selected Works*, ed. Richard Aldington (London: William Heinemann, 1948), 1–27: 1). Distinguishing the moment of intensity Pater describes in the 'Conclusion' from 'the imaginative circumstance of the aftermath, which is the establishing condition of decadent temporality', Vincent Sherry insists that the former is 'emphatically and categorically restorable or at least repeatable' (*Modernism and the Reinvention of Decadence* (Cambridge: Cambridge University Press, 2015), 61) and therefore has more in common with 'the fictions of integrated, synthesizing time in early romanticism' (61). But I think that Pater's moment lacks both the edification and the transmissibility of, for example, Wordsworth's spot of time: as he (Pater) says, 'analysis leaves off' (Pater, *Studies in the History of the Renaissance*, 119).

[13] Oscar Wilde, *The Picture of Dorian Gray* [1890], ed. Joseph Bristow (Oxford: Oxford University Press, 2008), 111.

Here, though, our interest is in *Erfahrung*. With its etymological associations of ageing and wearing, veterancy is, as we have noted, both a condition of, and an apt figure for, this kind of experience. Crucially, it is experience that can be transmitted to others for their edification.[14] And, again, the most natural genre for this transmission, as Benjamin points out, is the story. Benjamin paints a picture of experience passed on in a storytelling chain from generation to generation: a handing-round of wisdom consisting of knowledge once personally acquired and subsequently reflected upon.[15] And, as we saw in the previous chapter, in a tradition that reaches from Odysseus to Uncle Albert of *Only Fools and Horses*, veterans are notorious storytellers.

In commenting on 'The Storyteller' in his work *Psychoanalysis and Storytelling* (1994), Peter Brooks argues that Benjamin offers a 'nostalgic and romantic view of storytelling', one that may even be thought 'utopian and mystified'.[16] For Brooks, Benjamin's 'familial and communarian gatherings' amount to a tradition and a communicative situation that are 'clearly obsolete'.[17] Benjamin's storytelling model is an oral one, which he firmly distinguishes from the written novel. While the storyteller makes his own experience the experience of his listeners, he argues, the novelist has 'secluded himself':[18] 'The birthplace of the novel is the individual in his isolation, the individual who can no longer speak of his concerns in exemplary fashion, who himself lacks counsel and can give none.'[19] The storytelling companions have been superseded by the lone novelist and the lone novel reader, narrating aloud has given way to a genre that 'neither comes from oral tradition nor enters into it', shared wisdom has become top-down didacticism, community has become society.[20] Orality

---

[14] As noted in Chapter 3, the inter-personal nature of *Erfahrung* can be traced back to its forebear, Lockean empiricism. Locke argued that *tabula rasa* of the mind is 'furnished' by a trial-and-error process of internal ideas mediating external experience (*An Essay Concerning Human Understanding* [1689], ed. Roger Woolhouse (London: Penguin, 1997), 4.12.9, 2.1.2; quoted in Martin Jay, *Songs of Experience: Modern American and European Variations on a Universal Theme* (Berkeley, CA: University of California Press, 2004), 38, 37). This trial-and-error process is, in Jay's phrase, 'social to the hilt'; judgement is 'approximate, revisable: civil' (38).

[15] Cf. Shelley's 'A Defence of Poetry' (1821), in which the story gets the worse of a comparison with the poem: 'a story is a catalogue of detached facts, which have no other bond of connection than time, place, circumstance, cause and effect; the other is the creation of actions according to the unchangeable forms of human nature, as existing in the mind of the creator' (*The Major Works*, ed. Zachary Leader (Oxford: Oxford University Press, 2003), 674–701: 679).

[16] Peter Brooks, *Psychoanalysis and Storytelling* (Oxford: Blackwell, 1994), 83.

[17] Ibid., 76

[18] Benjamin, 'The Storyteller', 146.

[19] Ibid., 146.

[20] Ibid., 146. On the transition from community (*Gemeinschaft*) to society (*Gesellschaft*), see Ferdinand Tönnies, *Community and Society (Gemeinschaft und Gesellschaft)* [1887, 1912] (New Brunswick,

has important qualities – among them the authenticity that comes from being face-to-face and an acoustic-based ability to bind listeners into an audience-community[21] – but Benjamin's point goes beyond the oral/written divide. Brooks notes that 'what is at stake' in Benjamin's account of storytelling is often less the 'message' of the story than its 'reception': less, that is, the 'poetic' function of language than its 'phatic' and 'conative' functions.[22] 'Poetic', 'phatic' and 'conative' are terms derived from Roman Jakobson's linguistic theories,[23] and are used here by Brooks to distinguish between what might loosely be called figurative or symbolic language on the one hand ('poetic') and those elements of language governing the relations between interlocutors on the other ('phatic' and 'conative'). In 'The Storyteller' Brooks detects an effort: 'to rediscover various coordinates of narrative, in narrative voice, in the transmission of a certain "wisdom" from narrator to narratee, in the transaction or transference that takes place every time that one recounts something to someone'.[24] Benjamin, Brooks suggests, is not advocating a return to the old situations of oral storytelling, but rather the restoration – or creation – of a 'certain attitude of reading that would more closely resemble listening'.[25] This listening-reading would

---

NJ: Transaction Books, 1957/1988). This is not the place to get into discussion about the novel as a genre, but it is worth noting the nuanced balance in the form's impulses to isolation and communality as framed by Peter Boxall: 'The novel has come into being [...] in the teeth of a contradiction between the desire for collective belonging [...] and the refusal of such collective forms, the struggle towards a private or withheld or non-existent space in which the mind might encounter itself outside of the conditions determined by existing cultural forms' (*The Value of the Novel* (Cambridge: Cambridge University Press, 2015), 140). On the connections between the novel and the emerging private life of the individual separate from the public sphere, see further Michael McKeon, *The Secret History of Domesticity: Public, Private and the Division of Knowledge* (Baltimore, MD: The Johns Hopkins University Press, 2007), esp. ch. 14.

[21] 'Listening to spoken words forms hearers into a group, a true audience, just as reading written or printed texts turns individuals in on themselves' (Walter Ong, *Orality and Literacy: The Technologizing of the Word* (London: Routledge, 1982), 136). The effect might be exaggerated: the anthropologist Jack Goody shared Brooks's scepticism about the kind of cosy story-sharing conjured up by Benjamin: 'I have never seen adults gather round of an evening to tell such tales to each other' ('The Time of Telling and the Telling of Time in Written and Oral Cultures', *Chronotypes: The Construction of Time*, ed. John Bender and David E. Wellbery (Stanford, CA: Stanford University Press, 1991), 77–96: 83). On the other hand, a comment by Walter Gerard in Disraeli's *Sybil* (1845) does indicate the existence of such practices: 'I can manage a book well enough, if it be well written, and on points I care for; but I would sooner listen than read any time [...] Indeed, I should be right glad to see the minstrel and storyteller going their rounds again' (*Sybil* [1845], ed. Sheila M. Smith (Oxford: Oxford University Press, 1998), 171).

[22] Brooks, *Psychoanalysis and Storytelling*, 77.

[23] See Roman Jakobson, 'Two Types of Language and Two Types of Aphasic Disturbances', *Fundamentals of Language*, ed. Roman Jakobson and Morris Halle ('s-Gravenhage: Mouton, 1956), 53–82.

[24] Brooks, *Psychoanalysis and Storytelling*, 85.

[25] Ibid., 87

foreground 'the exchange, the transaction, even the transference' that can take place 'in the offer and the reception of a narrative'.[26]

For Brooks, taking a psychoanalytic perspective, such narrative transference has 'cognitive value', a property that explains its appeal to nineteenth-century writers attracted by its 'capacity to make a difference through the transmission of experience'.[27] Telling and receiving stories are, in this model, improving. But, in 'The Storyteller', Benjamin argues that such transactional storytelling has been attenuated by certain of the developments of modernity. 'The art of storytelling is coming to an end,' he warns. 'It is as if a capability that seemed inalienable to us, the securest among our possessions, has been taken from us: the ability to exchange experiences.'[28] The factors in this denudation are industrialization, the fragmentation of traditional communities, bourgeois individualism and the rise of mass media: in other words, the arrival of the age of mechanical reproduction. With this age has come the ascendancy of information and immediate explanation over the kind of knowledge purveyed by storytelling,[29] an ascendancy epitomized in Benjamin's assessment of the poetics of the novel. Then, in the essay's most famous passage, Benjamin comes to the prime cause of the demise of storytelling in the early twentieth century:

> Beginning with the First World War, a process became apparent which continues to this day. Wasn't it noticeable at the end of the war that men who returned from the battlefield had grown silent – not richer but poorer in communicable experience? What poured out in the flood of war books ten years later was anything but experience that can be shared orally.[30]

In Benjamin's view, this state of affairs is the outcome of four betrayals. Strategic experience has been betrayed by tactical warfare. Economic experience has been betrayed by inflation. Bodily experience has been betrayed by mechanical warfare. And moral experience has been betrayed by those in power.[31]

---

[26] Ibid., 87.

[27] Ibid., 88.

[28] Benjamin, 'The Storyteller', 143.

[29] Ibid., 147.

[30] Ibid., 143–4. This passage of 'The Storyteller' is a re-working, with very little variation, from 'Experience and Poverty', showing that Benjamin had the arguments in mind in 1933 (see 'Der Erzähler' [1936], *Gesammelte Schriften. Band II.2. Literarische und Ästhetische Essays (Forsetzung)/Ästhetische Fragmente/Vorträge und Reden/Enzyklopädieartikel/Kulturpolitische Artikel und Aufsätze*, ed. Rolf Tiedemann and Hermann Schweppenhäuser (Frankfurt-am-Main: Suhrkamp, 1977), 438–65: 439, and 'Erfahrung und Armut' [1933], *Gesammelte Schriften. Band II.1. Aufsätze, Essays, Vorträge*, ed. Rolf Tiedemann and Hermann Schweppenhäuser (Frankfurt-am-Main: Suhrkamp, 1977), 213–19: 214).

[31] Benjamin, 'The Storyteller', 144.

'Men returned from the battlefield grown silent – not richer but *poorer* in communicable experience.'[32] The line can be read as a statement about trauma-induced aphasia: indeed, Cathy Caruth claims that the soldier is 'the central and recurring image of trauma in [the twentieth] century'.[33] In a similar vein, Sarah Cole writes tellingly of a 'distraught fraternity', a band made brotherly through silence.[34] But here I want to consider its epistemological significance. Benjamin was not suggesting that the war was indescribable: the 'flood of war books' that poured out ten years later could and did describe what was horrific and shocking – *Erlebnis*, that is.[35] Civilians, too, could consume – and clearly savoured – *Erlebnis*, whether via prose descriptions such as those in Ernst Jünger's *Der Kampf als inneres Erlebnis* (1922) ('The War as Inner Experience') or graphic images such as those in his book of war photographs *Der Antlitz des Weltkrieges: Fronterlebnisse deutscher Soldaten* (1930) ('The Face of the Great War: Front Experiences of German Soldiers') or in documentary films such as *The Battle of the Somme* (1916), seen by 20 million people in Britain in the first six weeks of its release.[36] But when a historian such as Robert Tombs uses such instances as evidence that 'contemporary civilian accounts demonstrate a fairly high degree of knowledge about conditions in the trenches', the knowledge is

---

[32] In the original German: 'Hatte man nicht bei Kriegsende bemerkt, daß die Leute verstummt aus dem Felde kamen? nicht reicher – ärmer an mitteilbarer Erfahrung' ('Der Erzähler', 439).

[33] Cathy Caruth, *Unclaimed Experience. Trauma, Narrative, and History* (Baltimore, MD: Johns Hopkins University Press, 1996), 11. James Dawes writes, similarly, '[a]s war reveals, violence harms language; it imposes silence upon groups and, through trauma and injury, disables the capacity of the individual to speak effectively' (*The Language of War. Literature and Culture in the U. S. from the Civil War Through World War II* (Cambridge, MA: Harvard University Press, 2002), 2). Much has been written about the deleterious effect of the First World War on language – see Hazel Hutchison *The War That Used Up Words: American Writers and the First World War* (New Haven, CT: Yale University Press, 2015), especially the 'Introduction', for a summary. Notably, Antonio Scurati links the most famous fictional articulation of the issue, the passage beginning 'I was always embarrassed by the words sacred, glorious, and sacrifice and the expression in vain' in Ernest Hemingway's *A Farewell to Arms* [1929] (London: Vintage, 1999), 165, to a nostalgia for the classic, limited post-Westphalian warfare regulated by the *ius publicum europaeum*, which was possible to describe because it was juridically contained ('Dire addio alle armi: Forma giuridica e retorica della guerra in Schmitt e Hemingway', *Le Parole e le armi*, ed. Giorgio Mariani (Milan: Marcos y Marcos, 1999), 291–326). This legally regulated warfare is the 'war in form' described by Carl Schmitt, who locates its breakdown in the constitutional revisions effected by the French Revolution and Napoleon (*The Nomos of the Earth in the International Law of the Jus Publicum Europaeum* (*Der Nomos der Erde im Völkerrecht des Jus Publicum Europaeum*) [1950], trans. G. L. Ulmen (New York: Telos, 2006), 142).

[34] Sarah Cole, *Modernism, Male Friendship, and the First World War* (Cambridge: Cambridge University Press, 2003), 196, and see further 191–216.

[35] Benjamin's original German is 'alles andere als Erfahrung, die von Mund zu Mund geht' ('Der Erzähler', 439): literally 'completely different from experience [*Erfahrung*] that goes from mouth to mouth'.

[36] Robert Tombs, *The English and Their History* (London: Allen Lane, 2014), 625.

more likely to be the vicarious thrill of *Erlebnis* rather than the edification of *Erfahrung*.[37] The experiences of the war could be described but they could not be made sense of, that is (unlike its political, military or social history); they were resistant to comprehension and assimilation and, therefore, transmission, because it is impossible to learn and teach from experience if you don't understand that experience in the first place.[38] In Benjamin's poignant words: 'A generation that had gone to school on horse-drawn streetcars now stood under the open sky in a landscape where nothing remained unchanged but the clouds, and beneath those clouds, in a force field of destructive torrents and explosions, was the tiny, fragile human body.'[39]

No story can be told when the storyteller has nothing in his past experience with which to compare his present experience. All that remains – when it escapes pulverization – is the physically veterated body. It is an ironic body – ironic because its ostensible message is at odds with its actual message. For Benjamin insisted on the corporeal nature of storytelling: 'traces' of the storyteller 'cling' to a story in the same way that 'the handprints of the potter' – hands again – 'cling' to a 'clay vessel'.[40] But the injured/incomplete body produced by mechanized mass warfare is the sign of having no mature wisdom to hand on. Hence, the war-ravaged yet uncommunicative veteran signifies the demise of storytelling. This, I suggest, is the figure we encounter in Wordsworth's 'The Discharged Soldier'. In West's *The Return of the Soldier* and Woolf's *Mrs Dalloway*, the veteran body is even more ironic because, although it has aged over time, it is physically intact. Despite what has been endured, neither body nor voice is telling.

---

[37] Ibid., 625

[38] The Czech philosopher Jan Patočka argued the contrary: that combatants on the front line in the First World War experienced 'meaninglessness and unbearable horror', but that this, in turn, produced 'an overwhelming sense of meaningfulness' in which it is understood that 'life is not everything, that it can sacrifice itself' (*Heretical Essays in the Philosophy of History* (*Kacířské eseje o filosofii dějin*) [1975], trans. Erazim Kohák, ed. James Dodd (Chicago: Open Court, 1996), 126, 129). But Patočka cites Jünger and Teilhard de Chardin on front experience: he is describing mystical insight deriving from *Erlebnis* rather than wisdom yielded by *Erfahrung*. Furthermore, Anne Dufourmantelle aligns Patočka with the Enlightenment thesis of Adorno and Horkheimer: '*Patočka interpreted the crisis of the modern world and the decline of Europe in terms of a totalitarianism of everyday knowledge. To reason on the basis of the values of the day* [i.e. clarity, Enlightenment] *is to be prompted by the wish to define and subjugate the real solely in order to attain a quantifiable knowledge pledged to technological values*' (Jacques Derrida and Anne Dufourmantelle, *Of Hospitality: Anne Dufourmantelle Invites Jacques Derrida to Respond* (Stanford, CA: Stanford University Press, 2000), 38, 40, original emphasis).

[39] Benjamin, 'The Storyteller', 144.

[40] Ibid., 148.

## A Dropped Staff: William Wordsworth, 'The Discharged Soldier' (1798, 1805) and *The Prelude* (1805)

A war veteran first enters Wordsworth's poetry in 1798, but veteran poetics have been evident, and important, before that in his oeuvre in explorations of the significance of experience, the accessibility of the past and the resources of rural tradition. It is odd, then, that when in 'The Discharged Soldier' (all versions)[41] the speaker catches sight of something extraordinary, his immediate response is to hide behind a tree. What he sees is an 'uncouth shape' (l. 38), a figure wholly outside his experience.[42] This 'uncouth shape' is a war veteran, a soldier who 'to the tropic isles had gone' (l. 99) – a detail that tells us that he has fought in the French Revolutionary Wars in the West Indies. The speaker emerges from his arboreal refuge eventually, but this first reaction is instructive: the veteran is a consternating figure, unknowable, unassimilable – a strange man on a dark night.

The veteran's very blankness has allowed a range of critical readings. In his classic 1964 study, *Wordsworth's Poetry*, Geoffrey Hartman proposes that, like the blind London beggar (*Prelude* 7.635–49) and the Leechgatherer ('Resolution and Independence' (1807)), the Soldier is a 'borderer dwelling between life and death'.[43] Jonathan Wordsworth offers a similar idea – the veteran is 'a ghost, or as the Milton echo implies, a type of death'[44] – while Alan Bewell finds that death to be inflected by the Soldier's service in the West Indies: '[t]o the extent that the soldier is a specter, a ghost from the past, he reevokes the colonial tropics as a haunted burial ground'.[45] Celeste Langan suggests further sociological aspects to the

---

[41] *The Cornell Wordsworth*, gen. ed. Stephen Maxfield Parris, 21 vols (Ithaca, NY: Cornell University Press, 1975–2007) is used for all quotations from Wordsworth's poetical works. Line numbers are given in the text.

[42] 'Uncouth, adj. and n.', 2, 'With which one is not acquainted or familiar; unfamiliar, unaccustomed, strange' (*Oxford English Dictionary* (Oxford University Press), online edition). Note that the discovery of the veteran in 'The Discharged Soldier' is very similar to an episode in Henry Mackenzie's *The Man of Feeling* (1771). Mackenzie's protagonist, Harley, is walking along in the evening: 'when, turning round, his notice was attracted by an object, which the fixture of his eye on the spot he walked had before prevented him from observing. An old man, who from his dress seemed to have been a soldier, lay fast asleep on the ground; a knapsack rested on a stone at his right hand, while his staff and brass-hilted sword were Crossed [sic] at his left' (*The Man of Feeling* [1771], ed. Brian Vickers (Oxford: Oxford University Press, 2001), 63–4). The old soldier, Edwards, is an object of sentiment *par excellence*.

[43] Geoffrey Hartman, *Wordsworth's Poetry 1787–1814* (New Haven, CT: Yale University Press, 1964), 224–5.

[44] Jonathan Wordsworth, *The Music of Humanity: A Critical Study of Wordsworth's 'Ruined Cottage'* (New York: J. and J. Harper, 1969), 14.

[45] Alan Bewell, *Romanticism and Colonial Disease* (Baltimore, MD: The Johns Hopkins University Press, 1999), 117.

borderer: she names the soldier a vagrant and therefore, following Marx, a 'tatterdemalion', subject to 'impoverishment' and 'alienation'.[46] The similarities between the veteran's disengaged status and that of his creator (Wordsworth, still relatively youthful at 27, was by no means established in a career) have not gone unnoticed: the Discharged Soldier is, in Philip Shaw's analysis, 'a double, no less, of the rootless would-be poet, William Wordsworth'.[47] Another critical strand analyses the encounter as a communicative exchange.[48] 'Wordsworth represents the experience of war through encounter and story-telling,' remarks Simon Bainbridge[49] (although what seems to mark the episode is the *absence* of any war stories). Lucy Newlyn comments on Wordsworth's 1790s encounter poems that, '[i]n emptying his own narration of any tendency to pander to the craving for stimulation, he succeeds in turning the reader's attention from extraordinary incidents to the problem of how they are to be assimilated and understood'.[50] This permits a reading of 'The Discharged Soldier' as an exercise in anti-sensationalism. In a more recent study, considering and then discarding the possibility of Steeleian/Addisonian detached spectatorship, Shaw casts the episode as 'a lesson in fellowship' from a figure who exhibits symptoms of 'post-traumatic stress disorder'.[51]

The richness of these readings is not to be gainsaid. What is offered here has more of the character of an *un*-reading, an approach that highlights the unedifying, the indecipherable, the unabsorbable and the plain missing. This approach has affinities with those critical strands that identify the Discharged Soldier as a liminal figure and with those that attend to the communicative properties of the encounter. Rather than treat him as a

---

[46] Celeste Langan, *Romantic Vagrancy: Wordsworth and the Simulation of Freedom* (Cambridge: Cambridge University Press, 1995), 12, 141.

[47] Philip Shaw, 'Introduction', *Romantic Wars: Studies in Culture and Conflict, 1793–1822*, ed. Philip Shaw (Aldershot: Ashgate, 2000), 1–12: 7.

[48] See, for example, Michael Baron, *Language and Relationship in Wordsworth's Writing* (London: Longman, 1995); Susan Eilenberg, *Strange Power of Speech: Wordsworth, Coleridge, and Literary Possession* (Oxford: Oxford University Press, 1992); Susan Edwards Meisenhelder, *Wordsworth's Informed Reader: Structures of Experience in His Poetry* (Nashville, TN: Vanderbilt University Press, 1988); Tilottama Rajan, *The Supplement of Reading: Figures of Understanding in Romantic Theory and Practice* (Ithaca, NY: Cornell University Press, 1990); Susan J. Wolfson, *The Questioning Presence: Wordsworth, Keats, and the Interrogative Mode in Romantic Poetry* (Ithaca, NY: Cornell University Press, 1986).

[49] Simon Bainbridge, *British Poetry and the Revolutionary and Napoleonic Wars: Visions of Conflict* (Oxford: Oxford University Press, 2003).

[50] Lucy Newlyn, *Reading, Writing, and Romanticism: The Anxiety of Reception* (Oxford: Oxford University Press, 2000), 112.

[51] Philip Shaw, *Suffering and Sentiment in Romantic Military Art* (Farnham: Ashgate, 2013), 212, 214, 213.

spiritual or social borderer, though, I cast him as an epistemological stumbling block, and rather than account for communicative failure, I aim to illuminate its import. One image in particular is key to this approach: a staff that has slipped through an emaciated hand.

## *'The Discharged Soldier'*

Hiding behind a tree is an atypical reaction in Wordsworth's on-the-road canon. When, in January 1798, he began to compose what would become known as 'The Discharged Soldier',[52] he was already a veteran writer of pedestrian encounters: 'An Evening Walk' (composed 1788–9), 'Salisbury Plain' (1793–4, with revisions in 1795), 'Old Man Travelling' (1797), 'The Ruined Cottage' (1797–98) and 'The Old Cumberland Beggar' (the companion-piece to 'The Discharged Soldier', also composed from January to March 1798). In these early encounter poems Wordsworth is already establishing a revisionary aesthetic, an aesthetic most evident in 'The Ruined Cottage', whose narrative consists of multiple physical re-visitings and psychological (self-)reappraisals. Just as importantly, these early road meetings lead to edifying exchanges between articulate speakers and accomplished listeners, in which painful experiences are offered fluently and accepted with kindness (the exception is 'The Old Cumberland Beggar' in which the vagrant is represented as non-speaking, but nonetheless constitutes a walking reminder of charity already dispensed and ongoing need). The writer of 'The Discharged Soldier' believed that such effective communication has to be worked at until it becomes a habit,[53] as does its outcome, charitable giving. Avoidance of the encounter is never entertained as an option.

---

[52] The text of 'The Discharged Soldier' used is that in *Lyrical Ballads and Other Poems, 1797–1800 by William Wordsworth*, ed. James Butler and Karen Green, *The Cornell Wordsworth* (Ithaca, NY: Cornell University Press, 1992). Square brackets within quotations indicate variations given in the editorial notes. Line numbers are given in the text. For composition and publication details of 'The Discharged Soldier', see Beth Darlington, 'Two Early Texts: *A Night-Piece* and *The Discharged Soldier*', *Bicentenary Wordsworth Studies in Memory of John Alban Finch*, ed. Jonathan Wordsworth and Beth Darlington (Ithaca, NY: Cornell University Press, 1970), 425–48.

[53] Writing two years after the composition of 'The Discharged Soldier', in the Preface to *Lyrical Ballads* (1800), Wordsworth argued that 'repetition' and 'continuance' will produce 'habits of mind' allowing the possessor to 'describe objects and utter sentiments of such a nature and in such connection with each other, that the understanding of the being to whom [he] addresses [himself] [...] must necessarily be in some degree enlightened, his taste exalted, and his affections ameliorated' (*The Prose Works of William Wordsworth*, ed. W. J. B. Owen and Jane Worthington Smyser, 1/3 vols (Oxford: The Clarendon Press, 1974), 126). 'Repetition' and 'continuance' are hallmarks of (discursive) veterancy: in this view, experience is requisite to the enlightening communication of experience.

So when in 'The Discharged Soldier' a 'sudden turning of the road' presents to the speaker's view 'an uncouth shape' and he 'step[s] back into the shade / Of a thick hawthorn' (ll. 37–40), something unusual is happening. Surprise, shock, fear, self-doubt, curiosity: all may be elements of his response. What is certainly present is a need for time and privacy in which to read the singular figure, 'to mark him well, / Myself unseen' (ll. 40–1). But the concealment also involves a significant spatial re-configuring: the speaker is now off the 'public way' (l. 2) while the Soldier remains upon it.

The poem has opened with a personal endorsement of the public road: 'I love to walk / Along the public way' (ll. 1–2). This is itself unusual, in that a Nature-lover such as Wordsworth might be expected to prefer to ramble in uncultivated regions. But, at night, the public way offers something more: 'Deserted, in its silence it assumes / A character of deeper quiet-ness / Than pathless solitudes' (ll. 3–5). This, then, is a journey into deep (public) silence. And, in this context, the most notable silence is that of the nearby dormant village, with its 'silent doors' and 'silent window[s]' (ll. 73, 107), a village apparently sleepily ignorant of, or indifferent to, those who might not be safe in bed at home but in difficulties on the night road. Suggesting this, those silent windows 'Sh[i]ne to the moon with a yellow glitter' (ll. 107–8), reflecting light rather than allowing it to illuminate what is within. In slipping temporarily from the public way, the speaker at once underscores his status as a private citizen and his distance from the slumbering villagers. The Soldier, strictly no longer a public servant ('on his landing he had been dismissed' (l. 101)), is nonetheless still uniformed and, as his entitlement to relief indicates, the state's responsibility. But these identities – private citizen, public servant – are far from rigidly fixed.

Figuring their fluidity is the public way, itself not quite what it seems. In the ghastly/ghostly moonlit setting, it is quickly established as a deliques-cent and deceptive path with a 'watry surface' that makes it appear a 'silent' and 'stealing' stream.[54] (The speaker also 'steal[s]' along (l. 21), in apparent collusion with the public way.) Specious, the road/stream 'glitter[s]' in the moonlight, a verb Wordsworth elsewhere uses in relation to gathering waters

---

[54] The interchangeability of solid ground and stream seems to have been inspired by Dorothy Wordsworth's journal entry for 20 January 1798 in which she notes that 'the green paths down the hill sides' have becomes 'channels for streams' and that 'the young wheat is streaked by silver lines of water' (*Journals of Dorothy Wordsworth*, ed. Ernest de Selincourt, 1/2 vols (London: Macmillan, 1941), 1). A copy of this entry precedes the earliest draft of 'The Discharged Soldier' in Dove Cottage MS 14 (*Lyrical Ballads and Other Poems*, ed. Butler and Green, 502–3). Cf. 'The brook and road / Were fellow travellers in this gloomy pass' (*The Prelude* 7.555–6).

(*The Prelude* 5.129) and that in other lines of this poem describes the opaque windows of the village (l. 108). If the public way is visually deceptive, it is also aurally disappointing. Streams should make a noise, but this road/stream falls 'with silent lapse to join the brook / That murmured in the valley' (ll. 9–10). Silent (like the village), the road/stream is here explicitly contrasted with the murmuring brook. When the word 'murmur' next appears in the poem, it is describing the strange noises coming from the Soldier's mouth: 'From his lips, meanwhile, / There issued murmuring sounds, as if of pain / Or of uneasy thought' (ll. 68–70). The word recurs later, again describing the Soldier's oral emissions: 'from time to time / Sent forth a murmuring voice of dead complaint, / A groan scarce audible' (ll. 77–9). The non-murmuring public way and the murmuring Soldier are on different discursive planes.

Silence and murmuring are not the only components of the sound-scape. There is also the dog that barks in the night-time. This dog is the 'village mastiff' (l. 127), chained in its kennel. Concealed behind the tree, the speaker hears it bark while the Soldier is murmuring:

> Yet all the while
> The chained mastiff in his wooden house
> Was vexed, and from among the village trees,
> Howled [never ceasing].
>
> (ll. 79–82)

Some significant points of comparison arise between the dog and the veteran. The dog has shelter, but is chained; the Soldier is homeless but in thrall to nobody.[55] The Soldier is unable to emit more than an intermittent murmuring sound ('from time to time / Sent forth a murmuring voice' (ll. 77–8)); the dog maintains a loud, continual howl to express its discomfort. The first time the Soldier speaks directly in the poem, it is about the dog:

> My weakness made me loth to move, in truth
> I felt myself at ease, and much relieved,
> But that the village mastiff fretted me,
> And every second moment rang a peal
> Felt at my very heart – [I do not know
> What ail'd him, but it seemed as if the dog
> Were howling to the murmur of the stream.]
>
> (ll. 125–34)

---

[55] Cf. Celeste Langan's observation that '[i]t is the bourgeois subject, of course, who is characteristic-ally free to walk toward and away from his native home' (*Romantic Vagrancy*, 207).

Why does the dog howl at the stream (this cannot be the silent road/ stream but must be the brook murmuring in the valley)? Wordsworth's earlier suggestion is that it is 'vexed' (l. 81). If murmuring vexes the mastiff, the mastiff's howling frets the veteran. A cancelled variant contains the lines (voiced by the Soldier) 'I could have thought / His wrath was bent on me'. This discarded thought makes the situation more transparent: the Soldier believes that the village dog is angry with him, a possible transference of the anticipated attitude of the villagers. The howling dog, therefore, suggests communal disapprobation of the Soldier's murmurings.

And it is to this very village community that the speaker immediately – physically and metaphorically – 'turns' on hearing the Soldier's 'history' (ll. 104, 94). He looks to other people to help the veteran, that is: one of a number of instances in which he remains personally detached from the plight before him. His next thought is to state that they will go to the house of a labourer:

> an honest man and kind
> He will not murmur should we break his rest,
> And he will give you food, if food you need,
> And lodging for the night.
>
> (ll. 111–14)

The labourer, unlike the Soldier, unlike the brook, will not 'murmur', but this non-murmuring now betokens willing compliance, or obedience, rather than public indifference. Notably, it is obedience on the part of a working-class man; rather than accept responsibility for the rank-and-file Soldier personally and bring him to his own home, the speaker shifts the burden of relief to a member of the rural poor. Later, he offers to pay the labourer's expenses in extending this charity – 'The service if need be I will requite' (l. 153) – assuming the financial, though not the emotional or practical, burden of care.

These points about a murmuring brook, a murmuring ex-public servant, a non-murmuring labourer, a barking village dog, a public way that seems to dissolve underfoot, unrevealing windows and a strange, split-second decision to hide behind a tree are not made to support an ideological reading of 'The Discharged Soldier' in which the availability and desirability of public relief and private charity for former military personnel (with attendant concerns as to whether desert should be founded on present need or past service) would be key issues.[56] Those issues *are*

---

[56] For an analysis along these lines, see Langan, *Romantic Vagrancy*, particularly ch. 3.

important but, for present purposes, they are crucial because they form part of a complex questioning of the very possibility of assimilating and transmitting experience. This (lost) possibility is figured by a staff, fallen from an emaciated hand.

Before picking up this staff, however, there is more to say about walking and talking, the association between veterancy, travelling and storytelling borne in mind. The early lines of 'The Discharged Soldier' establish an intimate connection between 'animal delight' and 'self-possession' on the one hand and the rhythm of walking on the other (ll. 35–7). Restored 'in every pause / And every gentle movement of my frame' (ll. 34–5), the speaker is visited by 'beauteous pictures' and 'harmonious imagery' (ll. 28, 29). Walking, that is, is conducive to (and a figure for) personal well-being, mental alertness, creativity and expression. It is noteworthy, then, that the Soldier is not walking. But it is not just that he is not walking. One of the most striking things about him is his extremely long legs. These are legs so long, indeed, that they make the viewer forget about the rest of his body:

> His legs were long.
> So long and shapeless that I looked at them
> Forgetful of the body they sustained.
>
> (ll. 46–7).

The immobility of these extraordinarily long legs means that the Soldier's not-walking is not just one of a range of activities he happens not to be performing, but a salient fact. He is preternaturally still: 'fixed to his place' (l. 76), maintaining a 'fearful steadiness', even his shadow 'moved not' (ll. 76, 71, 72). In a historical context in which the time limit within which veterans had to return to their homes was prescribed, the riskiness of this halt emphasizes its curiousness.

If walking is about expressiveness, motionlessness is about its opposite. Non-functioning legs/non-functional words: the Soldier who doesn't walk barely talks. The majority of his utterances are pre-verbal noises: 'murmuring sounds', 'a murmuring voice of dead complaint', 'A groan scarce audible' (ll. 70, 78, 79). His speech, when it comes, is reported rather than direct. When he does speak directly, the effect is extremely muted. His volume is 'quiet', his air 'stately' and 'mild', his delivery 'neither slow nor eager', his demeanour 'calm', his tone one of 'weakness and indifference' (ll. 96, 97, 95, 138, 142). His own recital leaves him – no less – 'unmoved' (l. 95). In a later piece, an essay 'Upon Epitaphs' published in *The Friend* in 1810, Wordsworth was to argue that 'the writer who would excite sympathy is bound [...] to give proof that he himself has been moved'.[57] What is depicted in 'The Discharged Soldier' is oral, rather than written, communication but the point may be applied across the modalities: motionless and unmoved, the Soldier will not move anyone else.

His effect on his listener, the poem's speaker, is, unsurprisingly, underwhelming, and this is a persona who has been established as peculiarly receptive to edification. Though he walks 'with mind exhausted, worn out by toil', he is still able to derive 'Amusement' from passing objects and describes himself as 'disposed to sympathy' (ll. 17, 13, 16). His walk is revivifying. He is in complete contrast to Coleridge's Wedding Guest: he could not be in a more attentive state. After a brief attempt at phatic communication ('A short while / I held discourse on things indifferent / And casual matter' (ll. 89–91)), he cannot restrain his curiosity any longer and inquires after the Soldier's 'history' (l. 94). He resumes his probing in line 125 and again in line 135 ('I did not fail / To question him of what he had endured / From war, and battle, and the pestilence'). His demands for information are reminiscent of a Chelsea Commissioner, except that what he wants to hear is the vicarious thrill of *Erlebnis*. The Soldier cannot respond with either the raw details of *Erlebnis* or the considered yield of *Erfahrung*. Every time, his responses are wholly discouraging.

What appears to be crass insensitivity on the speaker's part merits pause. In general, Wordsworth abhorred both sensationalism and the proclivity 'to pry and pore' (l. 15).[58] In the Preface to *Lyrical Ballads* (1800), he argues that a combination of 'great national events' and the 'uniformity' of city life has produced 'a craving for extraordinary incident which the rapid communication of intelligence hourly gratifies', a 'degrading thirst after outrageous stimulation'.[59] The implication of gratification without understanding resonates with Coleridge's indictment, quoted in the previous chapter, in 'Fears in Solitude' (1798), of those who read of war in the newspapers over breakfast – 'The best amusement for our morning meal!' – 'absolute / And technical in victories and defeats' but wholly ignorant of (and unlikely to be able to withstand) war's realities (ll. 107, 111–12).[60] Wordsworth himself was not immune to the temptation to thrill to tales of war. In 'Home at Grasmere' (1800), he confesses:

[57] *The Prose Works of William Wordsworth*, ed. Owen and Smyser, 59.

[58] 'Star-gazers' (1807).

[59] *The Prose Works of William Wordsworth*, ed. Owen and Smyser, 128, 130.

[60] Samuel Taylor Coleridge, *Poetical Works I: Poems (Reading Text): Part 1*, ed. J. C. C. Mays, *The Collected Works of Samuel Taylor Coleridge*, 16:I: 1/16 vols (Princeton, NJ: Princeton University Press, 2001), 468–86.

> I cannot at this moment read a tale
> Of two brave vessels matched in deadly fight
> And fighting to the death, but I am pleased
> More than a wise Man ought to be; I wish,
> I burn, I struggle, and in soul am there.
>
> (ll. 929–33)

Wordsworth is not specific about what exactly is 'unwise' about enjoying war stories, but there are implications that (vicarious) violence is exhilarating and fiction self-transporting and therefore potentially perilous. (Three years later, he was to join the Grasmere Volunteers,[61] part of the national mobilization against the threat of French invasion.) In Book 5 of *The Prelude*, he refers specifically to veterans' tales, 'adventures [...] spun' by 'dismantled warrior[s]'. 'Dismantled' suggests that these combatants are not only divested of their uniforms, but also undone by their experiences:

> adventures endless, spun
> By the dismantled warrior in old age
> Out of the bowels of those very thoughts
> In which his youth did first extravagate –
> These spread like day, and something in the shape
> Of these will live till man shall be no more.
> Dumb yearnings, hidden appetites, are ours,
> And they must have their food.
>
> (5.524–31)

This is tale-telling out of control. Like the war stories described in the previous chapter, these are 'endless' (in inexhaustible supply, constantly rehearsed and lacking conclusion) and ever-lasting. They are proliferating narratives ('spread like day'), founded on youthful 'extravagations' in thought and 'spun' in old age; there is something specious and rampant about them. They may be nourishing ('food'), but they are addictive. They are connected with the Discharged Soldier by the word 'shape', but they are entirely what his utterances are not. Later in Book 5, Wordsworth describes the process of maturity required to resist them:

> I mean to speak
> Of that delightful time of growing youth
> When cravings for the marvellous relent,

---

[61] See Toby R. Benis, *Romanticism on the Road: The Marginal Gains of Wordsworth's Homeless* (Basingstoke: Macmillan, 2000), 83–5.

And we begin to love what we have seen;
And sober truth, experience, sympathy,
Take stronger hold of us; and words themselves
Move us with conscious pleasure.

(5.564–70)

Addiction to the marvellous (*Erlebnis*) is a sign of immaturity; personal growth involves a developing preference for 'sober truth, experience, sympathy' (*Erfahrung*), and an ability to be 'moved' by words, not in self-abandonment, but fully alert to all the implications of the pleasure being taken in them. Wordsworth's 1808 pamphlet *Concerning the Convention of Cintra* displays this kind of sober maturity and understanding of the importance of an informed viewpoint in its discussion of military matters, a discussion located at the opposite end of the tonal spectrum from that of the craver of marvels:

> All have a right to speak, and to make their voices heard, as far as they have power. For these are times, in which the conduct of military men concerns us, perhaps, more intimately than that of any other class; when the business of arms comes unhappily too near to the fire side; when the character and duties of a soldier ought to be understood by every one who values his liberty, and bears in mind how soon he may have to fight for it.[62]

In stark contrast to this is the pestering speaker of 'The Discharged Soldier'. His clearly unwanted questioning is as unconducive to productive communicative exchange as the Soldier's inarticulacy.

The encounter, then, describes a failed connection. It is not that Wordsworth equates silence with non-communication: 'The Old Cumberland Beggar' shows that a charitable response can be elicited without verbal intervention. But here discursive interchange actually grinds to a halt. The speaker gives up trying to make conversation and 'discourse [...] cease[s]' (l. 146). Rather than concluding, the poem simply ends – in a strangely subdued parting with no summative comment. This absence of communicative transaction in 'The Discharged Soldier' has been read from (often overlapping) ideological, philosophical and psychological perspectives. Critics have charged Wordsworth with failing to grasp the social and political implications of the rural poverty in which he was so interested aesthetically.[63] The Soldier has been pathologized

---

[62] *The Prose Works of William Wordsworth*, ed. Owen and Smyser, 263.
[63] See Rajan, *The Supplement of Reading*, 145, citing David Sampson, 'Wordsworth and the Poor: The Poetry of Survival', *Studies in Romanticism* 23.1 (Spring 1984), 31–59 and Robert Langbaum,

as suffering from post-traumatic stress disorder[64] and with lacking the 'propriety' that would, according to Adam Smith's arguments in *The Theory of Moral Sentiments* (1759), enable 'men to understand and sympathize with one another'.[65] The roles of sympathy, empathy, imagination, sensibility – Lockean, Shaftesburian, Smithian, Humean, Kantian and the construct of medical discourses – have been extensively discussed.[66] Wordsworth's decision not to voice descriptions of warfare through the Soldier might have been due to his own lack of personal experience of the war zone, a disinclination to introduce harsh realities into the civilian sphere or a sense that what remains undescribed has a more powerful impact on the imagination than that which is directly presented.[67] But what if the question 'why doesn't the Soldier say more about his experiences of war?' were realigned so that the inquiry is not 'what stops him?' but 'what does his reticence mean?'[68]

---

'Wordsworth's Lyrical Characterisations', *Studies in Romanticism* 21.3 (Fall 1982), 319–39; and Benis, *Romanticism on the Road*, 198, on the social threat posed by discharged soldiers.

[64] 'The past has been so traumatic that he can no longer even respond to it' (Bewell, *Romanticism and Colonial Disease*), 119.

[65] Eilenberg, *Strange Power of Speech*, 12. The discussion is in F. H. Bradley, *Appearance and Reality: A Metaphysical Essay* (Oxford: The Clarendon Press, 1897), Pt. 1.

[66] See Joel Faflak, *Romantic Psychoanalysis: The Burden of the Mystery* (Albany, NY: State University of New York Press, 2008), ch. 1; Newlyn, *Reading, Writing, and Romanticism*, 113. Note particularly Newlyn's comment that the speaker's acceptance of the admonishment contained in the Soldier's refusal of charity 'implies that he has moved on from the conventional codes of sensibility into which he had attempted to slot his uncomfortable encounter' (113). For a discussion of the growth of the 'sentimental' military memoir in the period, see Neil Ramsey, *The Military Memoir and Romantic Literary Culture, 1780–1835* (Farnham: Ashgate, 2011).

[67] See Kate McLoughlin, *Authoring War: The Literary Representation of War from the* Iliad *to* Iraq (Cambridge: Cambridge University Press, 2011), ch. 5 for a discussion of this phenomenon in war writing.

[68] Cf. David Bromwich's interpretation of 'The Old Cumberland Beggar'. For Bromwich the lack of reciprocity in the poem is striking, a lack evidenced by the representation of the Beggar as non-speaking. In his *The Theory of Moral Sentiments* (1759), Adam Smith had contended that '[t]he sentiment which most immediately and directly prompts us to reward, is gratitude' (2.1.1.2) (*The Theory of Moral Sentiments* (London: A. Millar, A. Kincaid, J. Bell, 1759), 144). Wordsworth 'hated this prudent commercial morality', suggests Bromwich, and accordingly wiped the Beggar's response to the charitable acts done to him from the scene (*Disowned by Memory: Wordsworth's Poetry of the 1790s* (Chicago: The University of Chicago Press, 1998), 40). A letter Wordsworth wrote to Charles James Fox on 14 January 1801 confirms this sentiment and also conveys how highly Wordsworth valued 'the spirit of independence' – independence, that is, from state relief – he discerned in the rural poor (*The Letters of William and Dorothy Wordsworth: The Early Years 1787–1805*, ed. Chester L. Shaver, 1/8 vols (Oxford: The Clarendon Press, 1967), 314). But the letter also states that Wordsworth's poetic purpose (in 'Michael' and 'The Brothers') is 'to show that men who do not wear fine clothes can feel deeply' (315). For present purposes, it is important to note that, as Wordsworth composed 'The Discharged Soldier', he was thinking about the relief of poverty and specifically about what prompted the habit of private charity. Though Bromwich is right that he was unconcerned with gratitude, it is not quite accurate to say that his interests lay in only one side of the charitable exchange. Affect, in 'The Old Cumberland Beggar', is a dialogic process.

Approaching the episode from this angle re-directs attention to the epistemological significance of failed communicative exchange, to what happens when tale-telling is aborted. Interpellated as a 'Stranger' (l. 86), the Soldier is outside the speaker's experience (a fact underlined by his exaggerated singularity, his above-average height and his pronounced emaciation): no wonder the speaker hides behind a tree. It might be expected that this encounter with the unknown would prove edifying. But the process goes wrong. Physically, the Soldier shouts 'veterancy'. Being 'clad in military garb' defines him obviously enough as a former member of the army, but it is the additional information that the garb is 'faded' (ll. 53–5) that encapsulates the notion of having undergone experience over time. Veterancy is also inscribed on his body, in his 'wasted' visage, his 'sunken' cheeks, his 'ghastly' mouth, his 'meagre stiffness' (ll. 49, 50, 51, 44).[69] But the veteran is strangely detached from his own veterancy. 'You might almost think / That his bones wounded him', remarks the speaker (ll. 44–5), suggesting a psycho-somatic disconnection in which parts of the body ('his bones') act transitively upon the self ('him') and are therefore distinct from it. The following lines are key to the encounter's epistemological status:

> solemn and sublime
> He might have seemed, but that in all he said
> There was a strange half-absence, and a tone
> Of weakness and indifference, as of one
> Remembering the importance of his theme
> But feeling it no longer.
>
> (ll. 139–44)

The Soldier is dissociated from his own experiences, unable to 'feel' what has happened to him, a spectator of, rather than a participant in, his past

---

[69] The similarities between the Discharged Soldier and Coleridge's Ancient Mariner are striking. The Soldier's limbs are 'long' (ll. 45, 46, 48); the Ancient Mariner is 'long and lank' (l. 226). The Soldier's arm is 'lean and wasted' (l. 86); the Ancient Mariner's is 'skinny' (ll. 9, 225, 229). There are further resonances between the two poems: the Wedding Guest, like the Soldier (ll. 52, 93), sits on a stone (l. 17); the 'strange shape' of the spectre-bark (l. 175) recalls the 'uncouth shape' of the Soldier (l. 38); the 'ghastly tale' (l. 584) recalls the Soldier's 'ghastly mouth' (l. 50); the 'noise like that of a hidden brook' (l. 369) recalls the 'murmuring' brook in the valley (l. 10); the Ancient Mariner's sense of walking 'on a lonesome road' recalls the deserted 'public way' (l. 2). But while the Soldier's hand merely describes, in 'measured gesture' (l. 88), a listless salute, the Mariner's hand literally grabs the Wedding Guest's attention. Had 'The Discharged Soldier' been included in *Lyrical Ballads*, a possibility that Beth Darlington suggests that Wordsworth was contemplating ('Two Early Texts', 428), the pair's taciturnity/verbosity would have formed a contrast in the same volume.

history.[70] It is not even the case that his experiences have been so horrific as to elicit awe and wonder, a state of affairs that would have placed them in the zone of the 'sublime'.[71] They simply mean nothing to him. If a veteran is one who, by definition, has matured through time, this veteran has become older but not wiser. His experiences have left their mark on him corporeally but he is unable to assimilate them, let alone to pass them on, whether in the form of a tale or otherwise, to this or any other interlocutor.

Wordsworth encapsulates this state of affairs in the image of an oaken traveller's staff slipping from a hand:

> Which [I suppose] from his slack hand had dropp'd,
> And such the languor of the weary man,
> Had lain till now neglected in the grass,
> But not forgotten.
>
> (ll. 117–20)

In the previous chapter, the significance of the Ancient Mariner's 'skinny hand' was touched on in the context of Hugh Blair's *Lectures on Rhetoric and Belles Lettres* (1783), which Coleridge and Wordsworth both read in 1798.[72] For Blair, it will be remembered, '[i]n the motions made with the hands, consist the chief part of gesture in Speaking'.[73] Here I would additionally note a remark that Walter Benjamin made about hands in 'The Storyteller'. In 'genuine storytelling,' Benjamin suggests, 'what is expressed gains support in a hundred ways from the work-seasoned gestures of the hand.'[74] Hands, that is, collaborate with voice to tell a story. If the Ancient Mariner's seizing of the Wedding Guest is over-rhetorical, the Discharged Soldier's 'slack hand' (which has, elsewhere in the poem, made only meagre, enervated gestures (ll. 87–9, 165–6)) is a piece of hypo-rhetoric. The staff that drops from it is not the only staff in Wordsworth's poetry. The Old Cumberland Beggar has a staff, but his is carefully 'placed' across a 'broad smooth stone' (l. 7). The eponym of 'Michael' (composed 1800) fashions a 'perfect Shepherd's Staff' (l. 193) that he gives to his son, figuring his (failed) attempt to bequeath rural traditions to the boy. Another shepherd's staff

---

[70] Cf. l. 38 of Coleridge's 'Dejection: An Ode': 'I see, not feel, how beautiful they are!' (*Poetical Works I: Poems (Reading Text)*, 695–702).

[71] See McLoughlin, *Authoring War*, chs 5 and 6 for a discussion of the sublime in the context of war representation.

[72] Duncan Wu, *Wordsworth's Reading 1770–1799* (Cambridge: Cambridge University Press, 1993), 16.

[73] Hugh Blair, *Lectures on Rhetoric and Belles Lettres* [1783], 2/2 vols (London: A. Strahan and T. Cadell, 1783), 221n.

[74] Benjamin, 'The Storyteller', 162.

saves a son's life in *The Prelude* (8.308–11). In *The Prelude*, too, the speaker and his companion cross the Alps 'staff in hand on foot' (6.341). 'We went staff in hand,' the poet recalled in 1847, 'and carrying each his needments tied up in a pocket handkerchief'.[75] A staff is a sign of wayfaring, of having come far, of the travelling that is indissociable with veterancy. The Wordsworthian staff intensifies these associations of travel and experience and adds to them connotations of the inter-generational passing-on of wisdom.[76] It is *Erfahrung* incarnate. In the case of the Discharged Soldier, his staff, like his experience, has fallen from him, slipped through his grasp.

This approach to 'The Discharged Soldier' casts the poem as a study in the failure to transmit experientially based insight. The piece, possibly intended for inclusion in *Lyrical Ballads* 1800,[77] was not placed in that dialogic community nor, in fact, ever collected in Wordsworth's lifetime: an awkward epistemological misfit among the early encounter poems. An incarnation of it would not be published until *The Prelude* of 1850, but Wordsworth worked it into the 1805 version (also unpublished in his lifetime), where the dropped staff remains but the dog that barked in the night-time vanishes.[78] In the context of *The Prelude*, this early epistemological misfit becomes something else: a counter-weight to Wordsworth's entire autobiographical enterprise.

## The Prelude *1805*

Wordsworth placed the Discharged Soldier episode at the end of Book 4 of the 1805 *Prelude*,[79] following three books in which he sets out his autobiographical project, notes the importance of mature experience (informed by Nature) to that project, establishes a model of personal and philosophical progress based on constant reflection and updating, and introduces thoughts about social ethics (picked up later in Books 9 and 10 when the

---

[75] Christopher Wordsworth, *Memoirs of William Wordsworth*, 1/2 vols (London: Edward Moxon, 1851), 14; quoted in *The Prelude 1799, 1805, 1850*, ed. Jonathan Wordsworth, M. H. Abrams and Stephen Gill (New York: W. W. Norton, 1979).

[76] Vincent Sherry picks up on the same phenomenon when he identifies an 'adverse orientation' in Decadence and Modernism running counter to the romantic cult of the child (*Modernism and the Reinvention of Decadence* (Cambridge: Cambridge University Press, 2015), 25).

[77] Darlington, 'Two Early Texts', 428.

[78] This section focuses on the 1805 *Prelude*, rather than the 1850 *Prelude*, because it is concerned with the veteran poetics of the late eighteenth and early nineteenth centuries.

[79] Book and line numbers are given in the text. References are to the 1805 version, unless otherwise stated.

subject is the French Revolution). The mood is upbeat, the talk is of new starts and the opening up of possibilities, especially creative possibilities. Here is a young man at the start of his poetic career.

The poetic vocation is announced 'to the open fields' (1.59) and the poetic enterprise will be a work of memory: a veteran project, that is (if this non-military veteran, unlike the Discharged Soldier, is capable of remembering). This will involve – from 1.55 does already involve – the creation (not for the first time)[80] of a dual, or veteran, consciousness, one side of which experiences and the other side of which comments retrospectively on the experiences, the assumption being that experiences can be learned from, the aim being to do so. While this veteran consciousness implies a certain self-detachment, this is not of the same ontological order as the Soldier hurt by his own bones, but an auto-interpretative, necessary detachment. The experiential epistemology entails a revisionary poesis that will find its fullest exposition in Book 10 ('the horse is taught his manage ...' (10.70f)) – another mental practice paradoxically beyond the capacity of the Discharged Soldier.

Travelling – most often by foot – is, again, associated with expressiveness but also, more specifically, with autobiography ('A traveller I am, / And all my tale is of myself' (3.196–7)) and the processes of memory ('travelling back among those days' (5.166)).[81] The early stages of the former are figured as a deliberation about whereabouts to walk, and where to walk to. 'Whither shall I turn?' asks the neophyte speaker (1.30), 'underneath what grove / Shall I take up my home, and what sweet stream / Shall with its murmurs lull me to my rest?' (1.12–13). No mutterings here from distressed former military personnel: this stream murmurs sweetly and soothingly. 'Home' and 'rest' signify poetic and philosophical destination: the protagonist progresses towards insight rather as a war veteran of the period might journey to his native parish for relief.

Book 4 itself opens with the speaker in a glad and noisy homecoming for his first summer vacation from Cambridge, exhibiting a veteran

---

[80] See, for example, 'An Evening Walk' and 'Salisbury Plain' and, further, Newlyn, *Reading, Writing, and Romanticism*, 304, quoting David Bromwich, *A Choice of Inheritance: Self and Community from Edmund Burke to Robert Frost* (Cambridge, MA: Harvard University Press, 1989), 207.

[81] Cf. 'Wordsworth's tourism enacts the principles of return and renewal which are embedded at the heart of his imaginative self-conception and development, in the so-called "spots of time". It also, more often than not, imposes a period of delay between having the experience and writing about it' (Nicola Trott, 'Wordsworth: The Shape of the Poetical Career', *The Cambridge Companion to Wordsworth*, ed. Stephen Gill (Cambridge: Cambridge University Press, 2003), 5–21: 16). It is worth noting that the Discharged Soldier is expected to speak without delay.

consciousness in his perception of small changes that have occurred in his absence and his recognition of familiar features.[82] One of the latter is:

> The froward brook, which, soon as he was boxed
> Within our garden, found himself at once
> As if by trick insidious and unkind,
> Stripped of his voice.
>
> (4.40–3)

Another silent stream: this time, remembering it, the speaker 'marvel[s]' that 'such an emblem' of his time at Cambridge did not immediately impel him to write a 'satire on myself' (4.50, 52, 55). The voiceless brook, that is, prompts a meta-narrative loop of veteran reflection on the speaker's own voicelessness, both when in 'enthralment' (4.54) ('boxed') at Cambridge and at the moment of seeing the stream again. The stream/voice motif is picked up later, in an episode involving another dog. This canine is a domesticated 'rough terrier of the hills' who accompanies the speaker on walks on 'the public roads at eventide' (4.86, 109). As the speaker 'sauntered, like a river murmuring / And talking to itself' (i.e. composing verse), the dog would 'jog on before' and bark whenever he met a passer-by, thus giving the speaker enough time to 'compose' himself, 'hush' his voice and 'shape' himself to give and return greeting, so as not to be taken for one 'crazed in brain' (4.110, 112, 117, 116, 117, 120). Another dog, another evening walk, another public road, more murmuring, more silence, another 'shape': the affinities with 'The Discharged Soldier' are striking. The dog's bark is, again, the voice of social norms, warning the solitary road-walker to adapt to conventional expectations. The river/road/voice nexus is, again, expressive of free(-flowing) speech and creativity. Indeed, in Book 4 as a whole, walking is a means of return/revision (4.126–7) and of restoration (4.143f), remembered as a pleasure since early youth (4.364–5), associated with veteran qualities of progress and maturity, subject and metaphor of the dual consciousness. It is into this context that Wordsworth works 'The Discharged Soldier'.

Naturally, the insertion is itself a revisionary process.[83] For present purposes, the differences worth noting are the disappearance of the village mastiff, the (slight) generalizing of the Soldier and the (slightly) increased insensitivity of the speaker. What remains – and, in the context of *The*

---

[82] Cf. 11.38–41: 'how could there fail to be / Some change, if merely hence, that years of life / Were going on, and with them loss or gain / Inevitable, sure alternative?'
[83] For a fuller account of the changes, see Darlington, 'Two Early Texts', 428–30.

*Prelude* as a whole, becomes even more salient – is the episode's strange blankness. Noting as he introduces it that his 'many wanderings' have left behind 'Remembrances not lifeless', the speaker simply proposes to 'Single one out, then pass to other themes' (4.361–3). The impression is that the reader might be interested in the story but the poet does not intend to waste much time analysing it. There is no summative comment at the end of the episode (which coincides with the end of Book 4) either; an additional two-and-a-half lines after the parting (discussed further later) provide no greater sense of conclusion.

The vanishing dog entails the loss of an important aural comparison and also, more significantly, the sense of the village's (antipathetic) attitude towards the veteran. Further evidence of the latter effect is the transformation of the 'silent doors' in 'The Discharged Soldier' (l. 73) into mere 'roofs and doors' (4.427). The effect of the omission/reduction of the community's hostility and indifference to the veteran is to give greater emphasis to the speaker's own (questionable) response to him. This shift in focus is supported by a generalizing of the Soldier's character. The omission of lines 44–5 and 55–60 removes the crucial observation that the veteran's own bones hurt him and the comment he is 'cut off / From all his kind, and more than half detached / From his own nature'. His abnormal self-detachment gone, the Soldier becomes less singular. Other changes also contribute to this transformation. The detail that he lacks gloves, a note that previously accentuated the strange bareness of his hands, is omitted. The length and leanness of his arms are less emphasized. His extraordinarily long legs are not mentioned at all. He is no longer described as a 'Stranger' (l. 86). He also loses some of the marks of veterancy. The elision of 'And with the little strength he had yet left' (l. 102) and 'And, such the languour of the weary man' (l. 108) diminishes the sense of his exhaustion. His reply to the speaker's question about his 'history' is changed from 'He told a simple fact: that he had been / A Soldier, to the tropic isles had gone' (ll. 98–9) to 'He told, in simple words, a Soldier's Tale / That in the Tropic Islands he had serv'd' (4.446–7). A 'simple fact' is now a 'Tale': artifice has entered and the (reported) utterance has become more complex (note also the substitution of 'serv'd' for 'been'). The Soldier's Tale now sounds more typical than individual (the faint echoes of the template for a Chelsea pension application might be detected). As the veteran starts slightly to fade, the speaker assumes greater prominence.

This time, the speaker's engagement with the Soldier is more pointed. He does not engage in phatic discourse (ll. 89–91 are omitted). 'I did not fail …' (l. 135) is replaced with 'Nor […] could I forbear …' (4.470): the change intensifies the sense that asking the veteran about his combat experiences is of the order of a compulsion. This speaker is marginally crasser than his earlier incarnation. He is also markedly less generous. The lines:

> behind yon wood
> A labourer dwells, an honest man and kind;
> He will not murmur should we break his rest,
> And he will give you food, if food you need,
> And lodging for the night.
>
> (ll. 110–14)

are changed to:

> Behind yon wood
> A labourer dwells, and, take it on my word,
> He will not murmur should we break his rest,
> And with ready heart will give you food
> And lodging for the night.
>
> (4.456–60)

The labourer is no longer 'honest' and 'kind' (though he now possesses a 'ready heart'), and the speaker is keener to vouch for his assistance. This time, though, he does not offer to reimburse his expenses. The result of these changes is to increase the labourer's obedience (or the speaker's assumption of his obedience), and reduce the speaker's own involvement in the provision of relief. The revised Wordsworthian persona is, then – even if only slightly – less sensitive and less personally charitable than his previous incarnation. It should be stressed that the Soldier's ability to articulate his experience has not been increased in the process of revision: the dropped staff remains as a figure of the failure to hand on experience. But the cumulative effect of the amendments – both locally at the end of Book 4 and within *The Prelude* as a whole – is to intensify the failure of *Erfahrung*-based epistemology.

Positioned at the end of Book 4, the Discharged Soldier episode is the first significant personal encounter in *The Prelude*, and the first extended narration of an actual incident. It is, then, a test case. As he approaches the turn in the road that will reveal the veteran, the speaker has been established for the reader as a confident, if sermonizing, character. He has dedicated himself to poetry. He has expressed mixed feelings about Cambridge, feeling that the place is too worldly, that he is not learning what he needs to learn there, that he is himself still immature. Now back in Grasmere, he sees the small changes that mark his months of absence and is reminded that he has not himself grown over time. He chastises himself: he is still living too trivially. He goes to a dance. Walking home from it, he has a revelation: he must be a 'dedicated spirit' (4.345). There is a real sense of his being in the very process of maturity: he has grown in some respects but there is still a long way to go. At this juncture, the intervening consciousness offers the reminiscence of meeting the Discharged Soldier. It should be transformative. Instead, the young speaker immediately fails the 'test'. There is something very schoolboyish about his nipping behind the tree to spy on the Soldier, about his eagerness to hear war stories and about his persistent attempts to elicit them. But more significant in *The Prelude* than in 'The Discharged Soldier' is the absence of any analysis of the encounter, of any self-awareness of his inadequate response, whether contemporaneously or retrospectively. As a whole, the episode, as in its earlier incarnation, remains strangely meaningless. Its new ending has the following lines added after 'And so we parted':

> Back I cast a look,
> And lingered near the door a little space,
> Then sought with quiet heart my distant home.
>
> (4.503–5)

This brief pause for reflection is reminiscent of the earlier 'time out' taken behind the tree. It yields no enlightening conclusions, the speaker's heart is not moved ('quiet') and the added reference to returning home creates an awkward, unacknowledged, contrast with the plight of the Soldier. In an earlier version of *The Prelude* (the five-Book *Prelude* of 1799), the Discharged Soldier episode was followed by a transitional passage:

> Enough of private sorrow – longest lived
> Is transient, severest doth not lack
> A mitigation in th'assured trust
> Of the grave's quiet comfort and blest home,
> Inheritance vouchsafed to man perhaps
> Alone of all that suffer on the earth.[84]

This dismissive segue ('Enough of private sorrow') connected the episode to what are lines 1–48 of the 1805 Book 5. In the 1805 version of the poem,

---

[84] Quoted from MS W in Jonathan Wordsworth, 'The Five-Book "Prelude" of Early Spring 1804', *The Journal of English and Germanic Philology* 76.1 (January 1977), 1–25: 12.

even this transition is absent, and, following the break of Book 4 closing and Book 5 opening, the speaker plunges immediately into rather weighty pronouncements, not about the plight of the poor, but, more macrocosmically about the tragedy of man's dependence on worldly things and the lack of a proper, lasting receptacle for the mind's powers. Book 5, the title of which is 'Books', goes on, after the description of the Arab with his stone and shell, to discuss educational theory and the phenomenon of the infant prodigy. It is as though the Discharged Soldier and his suffering (unlike the highly articulate Arab in 5.140–7, 5.95) have passed from the mind of the poet (and the poem) without leaving an imprint on it.

Read locally in its position at the end of Book 4, then, the Discharged Soldier lines construct the Wordsworthian persona as a young man who is deeply susceptible to new experiences, but who reacts to the veteran he encounters with marked immaturity. He is wholly unable to process the encounter, and Book 5 suggests the reason for this. In 5.466–81, the ghastliness, stiffness and spectre-like quality of the Soldier will be reprised in the Drowned Man, but the speaker is not confounded by this figure as he has come across similar things in romances and fairy tales. In contrast, there is nothing in his reading or experience which he can use to assimilate the veteran. Experience is needed to benefit from experiences. If the autobiographical poetic project is a journey towards wisdom, the Discharged Soldier episode is – in its immediate context – a cul-de-sac.

It is not until after the revisionary Book 8 that the episode begins to resonate in the speaker's maturation. In Book 6, his famous unawareness that he has just crossed the Alps implies that there is still something wanting in the epistemology of experience. But perhaps it is just that he is still young. He acknowledges as much in his admission that 'In general terms / I was a better judge of thoughts than words' (6.124–6), his imperfect understanding of the latter a consequence of the 'common inexperience of youth' (6.127) as well as too much close reading of the classics. (In fact, his reaction to the Discharged Soldier suggests that his judgement of thoughts, too, could use a little work.) He is in, as he puts it later in Book 6, an 'unripe state / Of intellect and heart' (6.470–1). In summation, at the end of the Book, he notes his reaction to what he sees of the Napoleonic Wars in Italy – Republic troops of the États Belgiques Unis about to engage with the forces of Leopold II:[85]

[85] The Prelude 1799, 1805, 1850, ed. Jonathan Wordsworth, Abrams and Gill, 224 n8.

> A stripling, scarcely of the household then
> Of social life, I looked upon these things
> As from a distance – heard, and saw, and felt,
> Was touched but with no intimate concern –
> I seemed to move among them as a bird
> Moves through the air, or as a fish
> Pursues its business in its proper element.
>
> (6.693–9)

This response to a warlike spectacle is in sharp contrast with the marvel-craving delight in violence of Book 5 and earlier works: indeed, the speaker's 'distance' is more reminiscent of the Discharged Soldier's self-detachment. But this distance is no less a product (or expression) of immaturity than the thirst for the sensational.

This immaturity continues in Book 7. In a telling recollection, the speaker describes how a school-mate – 'a cripple from the birth' (7.96) – was by chance summoned to London:

> when he returned,
> After short absence, and I first set eyes
> Upon his person, verily, though strange
> The thing may seem, I was not wholly free
> From disappointment to behold the same
> Appearance, the same body, not to find
> Some change, some beams of glory brought away
> From that new region. Much I questioned him,
> And every word he uttered, on my ears
> Fell flatter than a caged parrot's note,
> That answers unexpectedly awry,
> And mocks the prompter's listening.
>
> (7.98–109)

The boy-traveller, to the speaker's disappointment, does not bear the signs of veterancy. Nonetheless, the speaker does not forbear to question him about his experiences, but finds his replies inadequate. What is notable is that, given the revisionary aesthetic of *The Prelude*, no connection is made with the strikingly similar set of expectations and disappointing outcomes of the Discharged Soldier episode. At this point in Book 7, the older, reflective Wordsworthian persona is at least able to perceive the flaws in the younger version's response, but he does not proceed to a wider assimilation. The veteran consciousness is, even at this stage, insufficiently experienced to benefit from experience.[86]

It is only in Book 8 (reinforced in Books 11, 12 and 13) that the speaker arrives at his mature endorsement of 'intellectual' (i.e. spiritual)[87] love (13.166): a love of mankind deriving from love of or sympathy for individual people, enhanced by the context of Nature and by the power of the imagination – what Coleridge, enumerating Wordsworth's 'excellencies', called 'a union of deep and subtle thought with sensibility; a sympathy with man as man; the sympathy indeed of a contemplator, rather than a fellow-sufferer or co-mate'.[88] Book 8 is the speaker's milestone, in the sense of that word given in Hugh Blair's *Lectures on Rhetoric*.[89] Describing the distribution of a public speech into sections, Blair suggests: 'The conclusion of each head is a relief to the hearers; just as, upon a journey, the mile-stones, which are set up on the road, serve to diminish the traveller's fatigue. For we are always pleased with seeing our labour begin to lessen; and, by calculating how much remains, are stirred up to finish our task more cheerfully.'[90] At the milestone of Book 8, the speaker reviews and appraises his own personal and philosophical process. The product of a veteran consciousness, it gives the later Books the character of another fresh start after consolidation. As it happens, a 'milestone' is also mentioned in 'The Discharged Soldier' and in its revised incarnation in Book 4 of *The Prelude* (ll. 52, 93; 4.413). Here it 'prop[s]' the veteran up.[91] It is not an energizing milestone as envisaged by Blair, inducing renewed vigour from a sense of progress made and still to come (Blair's milestone has affinities with the Wordsworthian 'spot of time' (11.257), which contains 'renovating

---

[86] Cf. further encounters with beggars in 7.199f (including war veterans) and 7.610f. There is not sufficient space to analyse these episodes here: suffice it to say that, in the latter, the speaker is moving towards a more sympathetic reaction.

[87] *The Prelude 1799, 1805, 1850*, ed. Jonathan Wordsworth, Abrams and Gill, n5.

[88] Samuel Taylor Coleridge, *Biographia Literaria II*, ed. James Engell and W. Jackson Bate, *The Collected Works of Samuel Taylor Coleridge*, 7/16 vols (Princeton, NJ: Princeton University Press, 1983), 142, 150.

[89] As noted in Chapter 4, Duncan Wu suggests that Wordsworth was reading Blair's *Lectures* between 9 and 26 February 1798 (*Wordsworth's Reading*, 16); that is, contemporaneously with composing 'The Discharged Soldier'. Though it is possible that Wordsworth was familiar with the *Lectures* since his school-days, it is most likely that he was introduced to them by Coleridge (see Wu, *Wordsworth's Reading*, 16; Jonathan Wordsworth, *The Music of Humanity*, 263; and Stephen Parrish, *The Art of the Lyrical Ballads* (Cambridge, MA: Harvard University Press, 1973), 169), who borrowed volume 2 from Bristol Library between 29 January and 26 February 1798 (Wu, *Wordsworth's Reading*, 181).

[90] Blair, *Lectures on Rhetoric and Belles Lettres*, 171.

[91] Cf. an anonymous 'Elegy' published in the *Sun* on 18 January 1794: 'Propt on his sword the pensive Veteran bends, / [...] Guards the pale relics of his slaughter'd Friends' (17th–18th Century Burney Collection Newspapers).

virtue' (11.257)). Rather, like the episode itself, it figures an enervating pause that threatens always to become terminal. Book 8, by contrast, is a renovating milestone and what lies ahead is further insight.

In Book 12, the speaker refers once more to 'uncouth' beggars and the public road:

> I love a public road: few sights there are
> That please me more – such object hath the power
> O'er my imagination since the dawn
> Of childhood, when its disappearing line
> Seen daily far off, on one bare steep,
> Beyond the limits which my feet had trod,
> Was like a guide into eternity,
> At least to things unknown and without bound.
> Even something of the grandeur which invests
> The mariner who sails the roaring sea
> Through storm and darkness, early in my mind
> Surrounded too the wanderers of the earth –
> Grandeur as much, and loveliness far more.
> Awed have I been by strolling bedlamites;
> From many other uncouth vagrants, passed
> In fear, have walked with quicker step – but why
> Take note of this? When I began to inquire,
> To watch and question those I met, and held
> Familiar talk with them, the lonely roads
> Were schools to me in which I daily read
> With most delight the passions of mankind,
> There saw into the depth of human souls –
> Souls that appear to have no depth at all
> To vulgar eyes.
>
> (12.145–67)

'I love a public road' / 'I love to walk / Along the public way': the opening of 'The Discharged Soldier' (ll. 1–2) has joined up with itself. But the encounter with the 'uncouth' has been transformed. What lay beyond his experience in the speaker's youth – itself figured here as a phenomenon of veteran (mariner) experience – has now been understood and even profited from. Crucially, what has enabled this understanding and edification has been the acquisition of certain skills of maturity: watching and questioning. Wordsworth does not expand greatly on how such watching and questioning differ from the sensationalizing voyeurism and tactless interrogation applied to the Discharged Soldier, except to note that those questioned will be 'Shy, and unpractised in the strife of phrase' (12.267) and that, accordingly, sensitivity to 'the language of the heavens' (12.27) – non-verbalized communication – will be requisite. It seems that the acquisition of these skills is a work-in-progress ('If future years mature me for the task' (12.232)). They are, that is, veteran skills.

How, then, might the Discharged Soldier lines be read from the perspective of the end of *The Prelude*? The poetics and ethics to which the speaker has journeyed are, no less, lessons learned in the 'school' of roadside encounters. Led by the public way, inquiring, watching and questioning those he meets on it, he has found both his epic subject ('my theme / No other than the very heart of man / As found among the best of those who live' (12.239–41)) and his route to intellectual love: an ethics and a poetics. It might be thought, then, that the Discharged Soldier episode would be revealed, or begin to resonate, as a foundational experience. But the episode resembles the ideal road meeting, as described in Book 12, only in external aspects. There is nothing in it that suggests skilled watching or questioning. Rather than constitute a transformative moment, the incident seems to lie awkwardly in the speaker's progress: an obstruction in his path that must be bypassed. Read in its immediate context, as Book 4 ends and Book 5 begins, it demonstrates at best a bafflement on the speaker's part: he cannot process the Soldier and, while he helps him, there is nothing edifying about the encounter at the time that it takes place. Even after the milestone of Book 8 and the revelations and resolutions of Book 12, and despite *The Prelude*'s revisionary aesthetic, its potential pertinence goes unremarked. Enigmatic, the episode lies inertly beneath the speaker's progress after Book 4, in the manner of what is, in another context, called an 'under-agent' (12.272): a failure in experiential epistemology casting doubt on the autobiographical project as a whole.

## Legless and Handless: Rebecca West, *The Return of the Soldier* (1918)

I will temporarily leave Wordsworth's long-legged, lean-handed veteran by the side of the road and leap forward 120 years to Rebecca West's novel, *The Return of the Soldier*, a work with a number of Wordsworthian resonances. As this text is less well known than the others discussed in this chapter, it is worth quickly running through the plot. It is 1916 and Chris Baldry is away fighting in the First World War. His cousin Jenny (the novel's narrator) and his wife Kitty remain in the ancestral home, Baldry Court, like so many women since

Penelope in that situation. One day, there is a visitor to Baldry Court, a visitor whose lower-class station Kitty so disdains that she goes down to greet her in 'last year's fashion' (23).[92] The visitor, a Mrs Margaret Grey, has news of Chris – again this disgusts Kitty, who thinks she is a fraud. It seems that Chris and Margaret had a love affair fifteen years previously in 1901 – five years before he got married to Kitty – and he has now written personal letters to her, one of which she produces. Confirmation of what Margaret says comes from an unimpeachable source – Chris's cousin, Frank 'who is in the Church' (40) (a triple authoritativeness is conferred here by the name, the gender and the occupation): Chris has shell shock and has lost his memory of everything that has happened since 1901.

Chris returns to Baldry Court. He recognizes his cousin Jenny but not his wife Kitty, and he is desperate to see Margaret. They are reunited and spend idyllic times together. But Kitty wants him to be 'cured'. This is achieved when Margaret reminds Chris of the death of his son Oliver in 1911. The novel ends with Jenny and Kitty watching Chris walk back to the house from the woods where Margaret has reminded him of his son by showing him the child's jersey and ball. He wears 'a dreadful decent smile' and walks 'with the soldier's hard tread upon the heel' (187). Kitty sucks in her breath 'with satisfaction': ' "He's cured!" she whispered slowly. "He's cured!" ' (188)

As is the case with Wordsworth's 'Discharged Soldier', the majority of critical responses to this novel have interpreted the plight of the returned, amnesiac soldier Chris Baldry in psychological or psychoanalytical terms.[93] Without disputing the insights of these readings, what I want to concentrate on here are the related epistemological themes of age, wisdom and storytelling. Chris has suffered – is suffering – from a striking temporal reversion. Physically, he bears the signs of age (though not the signs of battle – he has not been physically wounded): on seeing him again, his

---

[92] Rebecca West, *The Return of the Soldier* [1918] (London: Virago, 1980, 1990). Page numbers are given in the text.

[93] See, for example, Misha Kavka, 'Men in (Shell-)Shock: Masculinity, Trauma, and Psychoanalysis in Rebecca West's *The Return of the Soldier*', *Studies in Twentieth Century Literature* 22 (1998), 151–71; Susan Varney, 'Oedipus and the Modernist Aesthetic: Reconceiving the Social in Rebecca West's *The Return of the Soldier*', *Naming the Father: Legacies, Genealogies, and Explorations of Fatherhood in Modern and Contemporary Literature*, ed. Eva Paulino Bueno, Terry Caesar and William Hummel (Lanham, MD: Lexington, 2000), 253–75; Wyatt Bonikowski, 'The Return of the Soldier Brings Death Home', *Modern Fiction Studies* 51.3 (Fall 2005), 513–35; and Steve Pinkerton, 'Trauma and Cure in Rebecca West's *The Return of the Soldier*', *Journal of Modern Literature* 32.1 (Fall 2008), 1–12. West is on record as having read William James, Freud, Ernest Jones, Karl Abraham, Sándor Ferenczi, Jung, Adler, Rank, W. H. Rivers and others but protested strongly against psychoanalytical readings of the novel (Rebecca West, 'On "The Return of the Soldier" ', *The Yale University Library Gazette* 57 (1983), 66–70: 68).

cousin Jenny, 'crie[s] out' because she notices that his hair is 'of three colours now – brown and gold and silver' (50) and when he takes the boat out on the lake, the effect is disconcerting because '[i]t was a boy's sport' and it was 'dreadful' to see him 'turn a middle-aged face as he brought the boat inshore' (89). But mentally he is back in 1901, fifteen years younger.

This is, in one of the novel's senses of the phrase, 'the return of the soldier': Chris's return to a time in his past when he was on the cusp of sexual experience[94] and about to take on adult responsibilities towards the family business from his father. Shell shock (and rather than inquire further into that term here, I will accept it as West offers it (29))[95] has removed from him the combat experience that could have been expected to have a maturing effect. The fact that he bears no visible war wounds attesting to such experience reinforces the point. But Chris is not so much rejuvenated as de-aged, de-veteranized, living backwards through time, shedding rather than gaining experience. (This gives fresh illumination to Benjamin's description 'not richer but *poorer* in communicable experience', going beyond the idea that the war conferred *no* communicable experience to the suggestion that it actually removed it.) In a telling image, as Chris prepares to tell Jenny about his affair with Margaret, he 'laugh[s]' like a 'happy swimmer' (70). The word 'swimmer' echoes Rupert Brooke's sonnet, 'Peace' (1914):[96]

> Now, God be thanked Who has matched us with His hour,
> And caught our youth, and wakened us from sleeping,
> With hand made sure, clear eye, and sharpened power,
> To turn, as swimmers into cleanness leaping,
> Glad from a world grown old and cold and weary.[97]

If Brooke's swimmers are 'glad' to leap into what seemed in August 1914 like the 'cleanness' of a purging war (a plunge that is more reminiscent of the instant gratification of *Erlebnis* than the pondered-on yield of *Erfahrung*), Chris is, as it were, swimming happily in the opposite direction: the 'brown

---

[94] Though the description is elliptical, it seems that he had just lost his virginity to Margaret: 'He seized the hand she flung upwards and gathered her into his arms. They were so for long while the great bird's wings beat above them. Afterwards she pulled at his hand' (83).

[95] Cf. 'It is certainly the case that characters such as Septimus Smith and Christopher Baldry do not provide us with the authentic voice of the war-shocked veteran: this is shell shock as perceived and interpreted by the outsider' (Fiona Reid, *Broken Men: Shell Shock, Treatment and Recovery in Britain, 1914–1930* (London: Continuum, 2010), 73).

[96] Debra Rae Cohen also picks up the echo (*Remapping the Home Front: Locating Citizenship in British Women's Great War Fiction* (Boston: Northeastern University Press, 2002), 76).

[97] Rupert Brooke, *The Collected Poems of Rupert Brooke* (New York: Dodd, Mead, 1925), 7.

rottenness of No Man's Land' (24) has been washed off him, and with it the 'soldierly knowledge' (147) accumulated through his war experiences.[98]

His wife Kitty, meanwhile, has been frozen in time. Her name and her appearance are both suggestive of a little girl: '[H]er golden hair was all about her shoulders and [...] she wore over her frock a little silken jacket trimmed with rosebuds' (11). 'Nobody has ever been cross' with Kitty; she tosses her head 'like a child' (38). She does not seem, that is, to have reached full sexual maturity. Indeed, she is figured in terms of coldness, whiteness, virginity: dressed 'like a bride' for dinner, with an 'appearance of serene virginity'; 'cold as moonlight, as virginity'; the lights on her satin gown 'like cleft ice'; 'her face and hands and bosom shining like the snow' (55, 57, 56).[99] Resembling the ornament she has recently acquired – 'a white naked nymph' crouching over a black bowl, 'eternally innocent' (117) – Kitty encapsulates a pre-pubescent femininity, locked in time. According to Jenny, this nymphean femininity – inexperienced, immature – has shaped Chris's conception of women: 'Exquisite we were according to our equipment; unflushed by appetite or passion, even noble passion; our small heads bent intently on the black waters of life; and he had known none other than us' (118). The word 'unflushed' – not red – is particularly noteworthy given the ensuing descriptions of Margaret (discussed below). With such an idea of women, thinks Jenny, 'a man could not help but wince at Margaret' (118). Her prediction, though wrong, is logical: the pre-pubescent nymph would seem to have a natural affinity with the un-veteran.

The true veteran in the novel is Margaret, who has suffered and aged through time. Her name has changed, through marriage, to 'Grey', but unlike that other fictional Gray – Dorian – she shows the processes of senescence.[100] Her hat is 'sticky', her boots 'muddy' (it is as though it is she, rather than the 'happy swimmer' Chris, who bears the clinging

---

[98] West's portrayal of Chris is strikingly similar to her characterization of Henry James, published two years before *The Return of the Soldier*. James had, in West's view, an 'odd lack of the historic sense': 'He did not know whether the Franco-Prussian War was horrible or not, because he had been out of Europe when it raged' (Rebecca West, *Henry James* (London: Nisbet, 1916), 61) – it is as though Chris has similarly 'missed' the First World War and is therefore unable to judge it. West also remarked that James failed to appreciate 'that the wine of experience always makes a raw draught when it has just been trodden out from bruised grapes by the pitiless feet of men, that it must be subject to time before it acquires suavity' (27–8). The distinction is that between *Erfahrung* and *Erlebnis*: James, and Chris, are drinking of the 'raw draught'.

[99] Though the description is concluded with a reference to 'the white fire of [her] jewels giving a passion to the spectacle', this is an oddly chilly 'passion', its effect that of 'a deep refreshment' (58) rather than of arousal.

[100] Sherry also notices the Grey/Gray homophone (*Modernism and the Reinvention of Decadence*, 152).

traces of the 'brown rottenness of No Man's Land'). Margaret is associated
with redness: the colour of sexual arousal but also the colour of use and
age. Her house is part of a creeping 'red suburban stain' (22), her hand is
'seamed and red' (24). When Jenny visits her at home, she confesses that
she is 'very tired' and 'hot': 'I've been baking' (94). The signs of time,
age and work are indelible on Margaret, who, in Jenny's perception, is
'seamed and scored and ravaged by squalid circumstances' (90). If the
nymphean Kitty is subject to the temporal arrestation of one of Keats's
'marble [...] maidens',[101] Margaret is Wordsworth's Margaret, the soldier's
wife of 'The Ruined Cottage' (1797–8). The link with Margaret of 'The
Ruined Cottage' is made explicit by the phrase 'red stain': as mentioned,
Margaret Grey's house is situated in a 'red suburban stain', while the door
of Wordsworthian Margaret's cottage is 'With dull red stains discoloured'
(l. 332). Like Margaret Grey, Wordsworth's Margaret shows the visible evidence of time and age on her body: 'Her face was pale and thin, her figure
too / Was changed' (ll. 338–9). And there is yet another Wordsworthian
resonance.[102] In Margaret Grey's two homes – Monkey Island Inn and
the suburban house in Wealdstone[103] – there hangs a picture of a view
of Tintern Abbey (84, 93). The picture makes the connection to a poem
about the process and experience of maturity in which an older and wiser
homecomer repudiates the epistemology of 'thoughtless youth' (l. 91). The
Wordsworthian intertexts emphasize the accumulation of associations
between the character Margaret Grey and time, age and experience.

The relationship between Chris and Margaret in the novel seems to take
place outside time, or, to use West's term, in 'eternity'.[104] It does not appear
to be a relationship of mature sexuality; rather, the perception of women
inculcated in Chris by his age, gender and class has led him, in 1901, to
treat Margaret like a forerunner of Kitty's nymph. In the Greek Temple
on Monkey Island, he literally puts her on a pedestal as he lifts her into

---

[101] John Keats, 'Ode on a Grecian Urn' (*The Major Works*, ed. Elizabeth Cook (Oxford: Oxford
University Press, 2001), 288–9: 289, l. 42).
[102] Nicole Rizzuto also draws attention to this allusion ('Towards an Ethics of Witnessing: Traumatic
Testimony in Rebecca West's *The Return of the Soldier*', *College Literature* 39.4 (Fall 2012), 7–33: 21–4).
[103] 'Wealdstone' also carries veteran connotations in the homophone 'wield stone' and the sound
'weal'. The former sounds like an act of combat, the latter is the mark left by a lash. In contrast,
'Monkey Island' might denote a venue for youthful japes. The inn on Monkey Island resonates with
the tavern on the shore of Windermere in Wordsworth's *The Prelude* 2.138–44.
[104] 'I perceived clearly that the ecstatic woman lifting her eyes and her hands to the benediction of love
was Margaret as she existed in eternity; but this was Margaret as she existed in time, as the fifteen
years between Monkey Island and this damp day in Ladysmith Road had irreparably made her'
(99–100). Incidentally, the reference to 'Ladysmith Road', which evokes the Siege of Ladysmith

'a niche above the altar': 'A strong stream of moonlight rushed upon her there; by its light he could not tell if her hair was white as silver or yellow as gold, and again he was filled with exultation because he knew that it would not have mattered if it had been white. His love was changeless' (85–6). What is noticeable in this description is that the colours of Margaret's hair – white/silver/yellow/gold – resemble the colours in the returned Chris's hair, as perceived by Jenny ('brown and gold and silver'). The premature greying or silvering of hair takes the youthful Margaret out of time so that, in the various temporal switches of the novel, she is old at the same time as young, just as the returned Chris is young at the same time as old. In 1916, their relationship resembles that of mother and son. In one scene, Chris lies next to her 'like a sleeping child' (142); in her final appearance, she is seen 'mothering something' (186). Though Jenny's perception, when Chris collapses into Margaret's arms, is of 'the movement of one carrying a wounded man from under fire' (122), the tableau also strongly resembles a pietà, with Margaret as *mater dolorosa* and Chris his near-namesake, Christ.

Notably, what 'cures' Chris (188) – what reverses the temporal trend and returns him to adulthood (another sense of the 'return of the soldier' that is, in turn, essential to the final 'return of the soldier' to the battlefield) – is the reminder of the death of his son, Oliver. There is a strong sense, indeed, in which the returned Chris has merged with Oliver, who was, with his chivalric/martial name and rocking-horse, a child in warrior-guise.[105] It is as though the reiterated death of the actual child brings about the death of the de-aged Chris. With his 'cure', come the reminder and resumption of his responsibilities: to the family business, to his gender, class and estate; to the childlike Kitty; and, most ominously, to the war. The restored Chris is now 'every inch a soldier' (188). The point is made figuratively by West in terms of gait, a motif that recurs through the novel. Jenny remembers Chris as a young man possessing 'the loveliness of the spry foal' (104), a loveliness that is called to mind when Chris runs over the lawns into the arms of Margaret: 'How her near presence had been known by Chris I do not understand, but there he was, running across the lawn as night after night I had seen him in my dreams running across No Man's Land' (122). If Chris is not 'cured', Jenny reflects, instead of running lithely

during the Second Boer War, reinforces Margaret's veteran status: she is what Ladysmith has 'made her'.

[105] Oliver is a knight in the medieval French *chansons de geste*, especially *La Chanson de Roland*. The death of Oliver Baldry and Kitty's inability to have another child resonate with the 'denial of

he will 'walk for ever queer and small like a dwarf' (182). A dwarf is another figure of restricted growth: a physical version of the un-veteran. But when the 'cure' has been effected, Chris walks 'not loose limbed like a boy, as he had done that very afternoon, but with the soldier's hard tread upon the heel' (188). The soldier has marched back, banishing the boy.

As critics have noted, the returned amnesiac veteran creates narratological quirks and articulates an understanding of trauma as a revenant phenomenon.[106] But here I would like to make another suggestion: that the de-veteranizing of Chris is synonymous with the removal of his capacity for storytelling. This is, after all, a character who has just returned from two years of fighting in the First World War. Yet the only person who offers any description of the war – indeed, of Chris's past at all – is Jenny. The First World War appears in the novel solely through her dreams and imaginings.[107] Jenny, like Margaret, has aged through time, becoming a quasi-veteran. 'Jenny the woman' is explicitly separated from 'Jenny the girl', and, on Chris's return, she feels 'shame' that she is 'thirty-five instead of twenty' (61–2, 50). But Jenny's knowledge of the First World War has been gleaned from 'war-films' (13–14). Her vision of it is consequently artificial, composed of and conveyed by a few standard, even clichéd, images: 'barbed-wire entanglements', 'booming noise', 'splashes of fire', 'wails for water' and the 'brown rottenness of No Man's Land' (86, 13, 24). Jenny's is an attenuated, derivative version of First World War veterancy, and the representation of the conflict projected through her is similarly derivative. It is eminently possible to read this situation as symptomatic of the problems of witnessing, including the right to bear witness for those who witness.[108] But, again, I would propose a reading with an epistemological framework.

The classic homecoming veteran scenario is the recognition scene, involving the soldier returned so altered by experience that he is initially unrecognizable. This is what happens in the *Odyssey*. In *The Return of the Soldier*, the scenario is varied: Chris is physically recognizable but there is a psychological dissonance – his wife and cousin cannot recognize his mental state. When he is returned to his 1916 self, he also comes to recognition

---

futurity' that Vincent Sherry associates with opposing tendencies in Decadence and Modernism to the romantic cult of the child (*Modernism and the Reinvention of Decadence*, 25).

[106] See, for example, Pinkerton, 'Trauma and Cure in Rebecca West's *The Return of the Soldier*'.

[107] Cf. 'Like a traumatized soldier, Jenny is plagued by nightmares of war' (Bonikowski, 'The Return of the Soldier Brings Death Home', 522).

[108] See Margaret Higonnet, 'Authenticity and Art in Trauma Narratives of World War I', *Modernism/ Modernity* 9.1 (January 2002), 91–107; Trudi Tate, *Modernism, History and the First World*

himself: of his marriage, house, history and responsibilities. None of these are unproblematic. In Chapter 3, I quoted Terence Cave's observation that classic Aristotelian recognition (*anagnorisis*) 'brings about a shift in ignorance to knowledge'.[109] From this premise, Cave traces the diffusion of the family recognition scene into plots concerning the recovery of knowledge. West's *anagnorizes* are more troubling. The initial recognition of the homecomer is imperfect – he is not what he seems – and the final recovery of knowledge is disquieting: it is knowledge that will send a man back to the field of slaughter. The recuperation and passing on of knowledge have been vitiated, the past devalued.

The implications for storytelling are given figurative expression in Jenny's dream of wounded veterans: 'We were all of us in a barn one night, and a shell came along. My pal sang out, "*Help me, old man, I've got no legs!*" and I had to answer, "*I can't, old man, I've got no hands!*"' (14). The significance of hands in the novel has already received critical attention,[110] but here I would again recall Benjamin's remark in 'The Storyteller' that 'what is expressed gains support in a hundred ways from the work-seasoned gestures of the hand'.[111] Without hands, the second veteran of Jenny's dream is impaired in his ability to hand on stories, while his comrade, lacking legs, is precluded from the wayfaring upon which storytelling also depends. Here, then, is the storyteller produced by the First World War: the effectively de-veteranized veteran, legless and handless (this ironizes the 'hand made sure' of Brooke's sonnet 'Peace'),[112] unable to pass on experience, the figure of a collapsing epistemology. In Virginia Woolf's *Mrs Dalloway*, this figure appears *in extremis*.

### 'No mud on him': Virginia Woolf, *Mrs Dalloway* (1925)

Our third literary veteran is the most famous and most discussed First World War veteran in modernist literature – Virginia Woolf's Septimus Warren Smith, from her 1925 novel *Mrs Dalloway*. Like Wordsworth's and West's veterans, Septimus has been extensively explored from

*War* (Manchester: Manchester University Press, 1998), 19; and Rizzuto, 'Towards an Ethics of Witnessing', 8.

[109] Terence Cave, *Recognitions: A Study in Poetics* (Oxford: The Clarendon Press, 1988), 1, 28.

[110] See Marina Mackay, 'The Lunacy of Men, the Idiocy of Women: Woolf, West, and War', *NWSA Journal* 15.3 (Autumn 2003), 124–44: 133–4.

[111] Benjamin, 'The Storyteller', 162.

[112] In Jenny's nightly dreams, a cinematic reel of Chris 'running across the brown rottenness of No-Man's-Land', she sees him 'starting back' because 'he trod upon a hand' (24): the useless, detached hand impedes the runner in a never-ending loop. Cf. Alcinous' comment to the still-unrevealed Odysseus: 'nothing makes a man so famous for life as what he can do with his hands and feet' (8.148–9).

psychological and psychoanalytical perspectives.[113] But, again, my intention is to realign the discussion to consider, not the cause, but the meaning of his non-communication.

Septimus, despite being an 'eternal sufferer' (22),[114] is a veteran who is completely unable to speak from experience. There is evidence that, earlier in the war, he could communicate with his sergeant, Evans: they 'share', 'fight', 'quarrel' and 'growl good-temperedly' at each other (73). He could also communicate with his wife-to-be Lucrezia: '[a]nything, anything in the whole world [...] she would tell him, and he understood at once' (124). But now, in 1924, he talks only to himself and to the dead, uttering 'hard, cruel, wicked things' (55). In a grotesque version of Benjamin's companionable storyteller, he is intensely conscious of the importance of passing on acquired knowledge, but the knowledge is fantastical, the interlocutors equally so:

> [H]e, Septimus, was alone, called forth in advance of the mass of men to hear the truth, to learn the meaning, which now at last, after all the toils of civilization – Greeks, Romans, Shakespeare, Darwin, and now himself – was to be given whole to ... 'To whom?' he asked aloud. 'To the Prime Minister,' the voices which rustled above his head replied. The supreme secret must be told to the Cabinet; first that trees are alive; next there is no crime; next love, universal love, he muttered, gasping, trembling, painfully drawing out these profound truths which needed, so deep were they, so difficult, an immense effort to speak out.
>
> (57)

The 'profound truths' are chimeras; they are, even so, not fluently exchanged but 'painfully draw[n] out' by 'immense effort'. Moments later, 'hard, white, imperishable words' fall 'like shells' from Septimus's mouth, but these turn out to be not pearls of wisdom for mutually edifying

---

[113] See, for example, Sue Thomas, 'Virginia Woolf's Septimus Smith and Contemporary Perceptions of Shell Shock', *English Language Notes* 25.2 (1987), 49–57; Elizabeth Abel, *Virginia Woolf and the Fictions of Psychoanalysis* (Chicago: The University of Chicago Press, 1989); Karen deMeester, 'Trauma and Recovery in Virginia Woolf's *Mrs Dalloway*', *Modern Fiction Studies* 44.3 (1998), 649–73; Karen Levenback, *Virginia Woolf and the Great War* (Syracuse, NY: Syracuse University Press, 1999); and Roberta Rubenstein, ' "I Meant Nothing by the Lighthouse": Virginia Woolf's Poetics of Negation', *Journal of Modern Literature* 31.4 (Sumer 2008), 36–53. On Woolf and the First World War, see further the essays in Mark Hussey, ed., *Virginia Woolf and War: Fiction, Reality, and Myth* (Syracuse, NY: Syracuse University Press, 1991) and Karen V. Kukil, *Woolf in the Real World. Selected Papers From the Thirteenth International Conference on Virginia Woolf* (Clemson, SC: Clemson University Digital Press, 2005).

[114] Virginia Woolf, *Mrs Dalloway* [1925], ed. David Bradshaw (Oxford: Oxford University Press, 2000, 2009). Page numbers are given in the text.

circulation but inscrutable phenomena that fly 'to attach themselves to their places in [...] an immortal ode to Time' (59). As the words uselessly, uncontrollably fall and fly, Septimus sees his dead comrade, Evans, walking towards him: extraordinarily, 'no mud [is] on him; no wounds; he [is] not changed' (59). Here in this vision is the de-veteranized veteran: the reversal of the war's effects on his body figures the absence of knowledge gained from experience.

As isolated from communicative exchange is Septimus's wife Rezia, cut off from her Italian family, determined to conceal the 'failure' of his aberrant behaviour, unable to tell anyone, 'not even Septimus', that he is 'not Septimus now' (13, 20). There are moments when Rezia's desperation almost forces her to cry out for help to strangers, 'to butchers' boys and women' (20); yet at the same time, she fears that '[p]eople must notice; people must see' (13). Her terror makes Rezia adept in directing and re-directing people's attention away from Septimus's comportment and from her own suffering. And she directs Septimus's attention, too, in attempts to distract him from his visions and so normalize his behaviour; this is on medical advice from Dr Holmes who has 'told her to make her husband (who had nothing whatever seriously the matter with him but was a little out of sorts) take an interest in things outside himself' (18). Rezia is constantly bidding Septimus to 'look' (18, 20–1): instead of engaging in discursive interaction, the couple is reduced to physical deixis and glances at scenes and objects. But rather than participate even in this limited shared perception, Septimus closes his eyes: 'he would see no more' (19).

In an exemplary moment, Rezia spreads her hand before them both: 'Look! Her wedding ring slipped – she had grown so thin. It was she who suffered – but she had nobody to tell' (20). His reaction – separated from her action by some forty pages and so emphasizing the discursive and emotional disconnect between them – baffles her: 'What then had happened – why had he gone, then, why, when she sat by him, did he start, frown at her, move away, and point at her hand, take her hand, look at it terrified?' (57) Septimus, for his part, has misinterpreted the gesture: 'He dropped her hand. Their marriage was over, he thought, with agony, with relief. The rope was cut; he mounted; he was free [...] (since his wife had thrown away her wedding ring; since she had left him)' (57). The incident epitomizes the complete communicative failure between the two. What is notable for present purposes is that this is, again, figured by a hand. I have already twice cited Benjamin's remark that 'in genuine storytelling, what is expressed gains support in a hundred ways from the work-seasoned gestures of the hand'.[115] The gesture made by Rezia's hand not only fails to support what she is expressing but produces an unintended meaning. Note, too, that this is the hand of someone who has grown thin through suffering (there are echoes here again of Wordsworth's 'pale and thin' Margaret of 'The Ruined Cottage'). Rezia herself shows the physical evidence of veterancy, but, like her war veteran husband, she has no wisdom to impart.

'In most narrative fiction and drama until modern times,' writes Cave, 'anagnorisis has been total, in the sense that it reveals all that the characters want or need to know; the desire for knowledge is ostensibly set to rest.'[116] But modernist anagnorizes have included a 'sub-category of imperfect recognitions' or instances, like that in *Waiting for Godot*, 'in which an expected recognition wholly fails to materialize'.[117] The failure of recognition makes the point that knowledge is being neither recovered nor handed on. *Mrs Dalloway* demonstrates as much in a catalogue of non-communication and misunderstood gestures, spreading from the desperate attempts at inter-change by Septimus and Rezia to the community at large. Even in what should be a forum for companionable storytelling – Mrs Dalloway's party – the news of Septimus's death, offered by Lady Bradshaw as a social excuse, functions only to make Clarissa think of the self-serving nature of communal interaction, and its easy foundering.

## Unfathoming and Unfathomable

In each of the three texts, a returning war veteran – injured, traumatized, unable properly to articulate what has happened – figures a radical undermining of the possibility of profiting from experience. Unfathoming, each is also unfathomable. The knowledge that is absent is not only the content of conscious recall but also emotional and somatic understanding (see later on their explicit lack of *feeling*). But Wordsworth's Soldier discharged from the French Revolutionary Wars suggests that the crisis in communicable experience that Benjamin tied to the First World War has a longer history. In fact, Benjamin's 'vagueness in providing a chronology' for the decline of *Erfahrung* has been noted by critics,[118] and many of the factors to which he attributed it came into being with the Industrial Revolution. His

---

[115] Walter Benjamin, 'The Storyteller', 162.
[116] Cave, *Recognitions*, 233.
[117] Ibid., 233.
[118] Jay, *Songs of Experience*, 343.

horror at the First World War was due, in part, to the devastating impact of the weapons technology it drew on;[119] the French Revolutionary and Napoleonic Wars, too, were notable for their physical attrition, as well as being huge in geographical reach and extended over time. As noted in the Introduction, Anders Engberg-Pederson has recently drawn attention to the epistemological impact of these wars, proposing that their 'magnitude and character' gave rise to 'a conception of war as a world unto itself in which the usual understanding of time, space, and knowledge [was] profoundly reconfigured': '[o]n the battlefield epistemic conditions came to be regarded not only as inherently deficient; the fundamental state of knowledge was seen as contingent'.[120] 'Faced with a probabilistic complexity that neither Euler nor Newton would be able to handle', Engberg-Pedersen writes, the commander in the French Revolutionary and Napoleonic Wars was obliged to resort to 'the subconscious operations of the mind in order to perform the probability calculus.'[121] Military success, tactical and strategic, was a matter of taking an educated guess, in other words, and, as was noted in Chapter 3, in such conditions *Erfahrung* flourished. Engberg-Pedersen makes a plausible case for the value of experience for both the individual fighter and the high command. But achieving military success is not the same as making sense of what one has been through. The 'new epistemic order' that Engberg-Pedersen describes turns battle into a form of gambling on an extended scale, repeated life-or-death encounters with chance.[122] The French Revolutionary and Napoleonic Wars, in his words, marked 'a caesura in history, both from a military and an epistemological point of view'.[123] As I commented in the Introduction, fighting in those

[119] In an essay of 1925, 'Weapons of Tomorrow', Benjamin wrote starkly of the horrors of chemical warfare, describing the toxic gases that played a part in the war as a 'truly breathtaking hazard' ('ein wahrhaft atemraubender Hasard' ('Die Waffen von Morgen: Schlachten mit Chlorazetophenol, Diphenylaminchlorasin und Dichloräthylsulfid' [1925], *Gesammelte Schriften. Band IV.1, 2. Kleine Prosa. Baudelaire-Übertragungen. Werkausgabe*, ed. Théodor W. Adorno, Gershom Scholem and Rolf Tiedemann and Hermann Schweppenhäuser (Frankfurt-am-Main: Suhrkamp, 1980), 473–6: 473 (my translation)). 'Imperialist war', he said later in 'The Work of Art in the Age of Mechanical Reproduction' ('Das Kunstwerk im Zeitalter seiner technischen Reproduzierbarkeit') (1935–6), 'is an uprising on the part of technology', which 'demands repayment' in ' "human material" ' for the ' "natural material" ' that society has denied it (trans. Edmund Jephcott and Harry Zohn, *Selected Writings. Volume 3: 1935–38*, ed. Michael W. Jennings and Howard Eiland (Cambridge, MA: The Belknap Press of Harvard University Press, 1999), 101–33: 121–22).
[120] Anders Engberg-Pedersen, *Empire of Chance: The Napoleonic Wars and the Disorder of Things* (Cambridge, MA: Harvard University Press, 2015), 38, 4. Engberg-Pedersen is, strictly, referring to the Napoleonic Wars but his points can be applied to their earlier incarnation.
[121] Ibid., 78.
[122] Ibid., 68.
[123] Ibid., 51.

wars was not the same as fighting in the First World War, but the experience of the individual soldier in the 1790s, as in the 1910s, was an unprecedented state of radical and terrifying uncertainty.

As a result these wars – and the wars of a similar kind in the nineteenth, twentieth and twenty-first centuries – defied assimilation and transmission as traditional wisdom. And this is what Wordsworth, West and Woolf's literary imaginations seized upon, taking the veteran of modern, mass, industrialized warfare as a prime exemplar of the person who cannot make sense of his experiences and who cannot, therefore, be made sense of by others. But in deploying this figure, the three writers, I suggest, were saying more than the obvious '(this) war is senseless'. There are two local contexts in which I think their creations can be understood – one at the end of the eighteenth century, the other at the beginning of the twentieth. But there is also a wider context that is, in my view, more illuminating. Let me sketch the two local frameworks before looking at the wider picture.

Wordsworth, for his part, created his Discharged Soldier at the end of a century in which the overlapping cultures of sympathy and sensibility had flourished.[124] Dr Johnson's 1755 Dictionary defined 'to sympathize' as 'to feel with another; to feel in consequence of what another feels; to feel mutually'.[125] In *The Theory of Moral Sentiments*, Adam Smith agreed. Judging others, wrote Smith, necessitated 'changing places in fancy' with the person we are judging: 'we enter as it were into his body, and become in some measure the same person with him'.[126] Sympathy, in its turn, was part of the repertoire of sensibility, which also included a distrust of 'unaided reason', an 'elevation of the passions', a 'new faith in the natural goodness of mankind'.[127] These elements, Inger Brodey notes, were accompanied by 'a growing distrust of the referential and communicative powers of language', with words no longer considered 'the trustworthy allies of either reason or emotion'.[128] There is ample potential for the exercise of sensibility in the encounter described in 'The Discharged Soldier': here is an untalkative figure exhibiting visible signs of pathos, a ripe recipient for an act of imaginative sympathy.

---

[124] Discussing painting, Philip Shaw argues that images of wounded veterans in the period allude to 'an older, representational tradition' in which 'a heightened attention to the sufferings of others' predates the Steeleian/Addisonian formation of 'the distanced, bounded spectator' (*Suffering and Sentiment in Romantic Military Art* (Farnham: Ashgate, 2013), 18).

[125] Samuel Johnson, *A Dictionary of the English Language* [1755] (London: Time Books, 1983).

[126] Smith, *The Theory of Moral Sentiments*, 3.

[127] Inger S. B. Brodey, 'On Pre-Romanticism or Sensibility: Defining Ambivalences', *A Companion to European Romanticism*, ed. Michael Ferber (London: Blackwell, 2005), 10–28: 13.

[128] Ibid., 13.

Not a bit of it. The Soldier's taciturnity disappoints and finally silences his interlocutor. The speaker looks long and hard at the Soldier ('Long time I scann'd him' (l. 67)), notes the visual signs of his suffering and initially feels 'fear and sorrow' (l. 68). But as they walk together, these reactions change to 'ill-suppress'd astonishment' (l. 123) – a state of being stunned or stupefied.[129] Significantly, once the speaker understands that the Soldier is making his way home (presumably to collect his pension), his immediate thought is to turn to the nearby village for assistance. Help from that quarter being unavailable, the speaker suggests instead that a labourer living close by, 'an honest man and kind' (l. 111), will provide food and shelter to the Soldier for the night, and that, subsequently, the Soldier should not hesitate 'at the door of cottage or of inn' to 'Demand the succour which his state required' (ll. 167, 168). Handing the responsibility of care to others, the speaker reveals his sympathy for the Soldier's plight to be, at best, limited. Two minds have failed to meet.

Concern about such failure was also current when West and Woolf were writing. In his studies of the philosopher F. H. Bradley, for example, T. S. Eliot pondered the problem of solipsism – the idea that one's self is all that can be known and believed.[130] Like Wordsworth, Eliot used windows to convey his thoughts poetically: in 'The Love Song of J. Alfred Prufrock' (1915), the speaker passes 'lonely men in shirt-sleeves, leaning out of windows' (l. 72), each cut off from the others.[131] If Wordsworth's opaque windows suggest inscrutability and indifference (we can't see into each other), Eliot's signify isolation (we can't see what others are seeing). Despite the subtle difference, the larger concerns remain the same: minds don't meet, knowledge is unshareable. In *The Waste Land* (1922), Eliot

---

[129] See '† Astone | astun, v.' (*Oxford English Dictionary* (Oxford University Press), online edition).

[130] In *Appearance and Reality: A Metaphysical Essay* (Oxford: The Clarendon Press, 1897), discussing whether each individual's (sense of) reality is part of a 'fuller totality', Bradley wrote: 'Because I cannot spread out my window until all is transparent, and all windows disappear, this does not justify me in insisting on my window-frame's rigidity. For that frame has, as such, no existence in reality, but only in our impotence [...] The one Reality is what comes directly to my feeling through this window for a moment; and this, also and again, is the only Reality. But we must not turn the first "is" into "is nothing at all but," and the second "is" into "is all of." There is no objection against the disappearance of limited transparencies in an all-embracing clearness' (223–4). Bradley imagines windows joining up, allowing the possibility that an individual's (sense of) reality is only one part of a 'fuller totality'. In his doctoral thesis, published in 1964, Eliot accepted Bradley's all-embracing clearness: 'we feel obscurely an identity between the experience of other centres [roughly, "selves"] and our own. And it is this identity which gradually shapes into a public world' (*Knowledge and Experience in the Philosophy of F. H. Bradley* (London: Faber and Faber, 1964), 143).

[131] Quotations from T. S. Eliot's poetry are from *The Poems of T. S. Eliot. Volume I: Collected and Uncollected Poems*, ed. Christopher Ricks and Jim McCue (London: Faber and Faber, 2015). Line numbers are given in the text.

states it again. Here, the problem is articulated by a woman, bad with nerves, who pesters – of all people – an unresponsive war veteran:

> Speak to me. Why do you never speak? Speak.
> What are you thinking of? What thinking? What?
> I never know what you are thinking. Think.
>
>                                    (ll. 112–14)

Eliot's editors note that the passage echoes lines in Conrad's *The End of the Tether* (1902) ('Why don't you speak? [...] What does it mean? [...] What's going on in that head of yours?'); in Conrad Aiken's *The Jig of Forslin* (1916) ('What are you thinking?'); and in Aldous Huxley's poem 'Sympathy' (1920) (' "Tell me, tell me, what are you thinking of?" ').[132] The questions are anxious, persistent. They sound plaintively in a wider literary context that was accumulating techniques – free indirect discourse, stream-of-consciousness, impressionism – whereby contents of others' minds *could* be accessed.

But in West's and Woolf's novels, the minds of the veterans remain, for different reasons, unreachable, both for the other characters and for the reader. As already noted, in *The Return of the Soldier*, the only means by which the experiences Chris Baldry might have had in the First World War are accessible are via the ersatz dreams and imaginings of Jenny. Unable to remember what happened to him, it seems that Chris also, like the Discharged Soldier, 'feel[s] it no longer' – he has no haptic or motor memories of the war like those that prompt him to fall down recently installed stairs at his home, for instance. Notably, the 'tall arched' windows of Baldry Court have been 'shroud[ed]' with 'heavy blue blinds' for the duration as a precaution against Zeppelin bombing (10, 55): the blacked out windows again accompany layers of incomprehension. In *Mrs Dalloway*, the reader is led into Septimus's mind by means of free indirect discourse, but finds there only unintelligible wanderings. Six times, the reader is told that Septimus 'could not feel' (74, 75). His suicide takes the form of flinging himself through a window.

Such are the local contexts, briefly sketched, in which Wordsworth, West and Woolf wrote into being their unfathoming and unfathomable veterans. But there is, as I have indicated, a wider context still. My argument is that the three authors created characters who are at odds with the project of the Enlightenment, understood as the eradication of myth

---

[132] *The Poems of T. S. Eliot*, ed. Ricks and McCue, 632.

and substitution for it of rational scientific method.[133] This argument takes as its starting point the classic work of Théodor Adorno and Max Horkheimer, *Dialectic of Enlightenment* (1944). In this account, 'myth is already enlightenment' and 'enlightenment reverts to mythology'.[134] Myth itself arose from early attempts to make sense of the world (this kind of explanatory myth resembles *Erfahrung*-produced story). The 'program of the Enlightenment' was 'the disenchantments of the world': the 'dissolution of myths and the substitution of knowledge for fancy'.[135] Like myth, enlightenment too attempts to make sense of the world. But 'making sense of' is a form of mastery, and it becomes all-consuming.[136] The 'dutiful child of modern civilization' is 'possessed by a fear of departing from the very act of perception' that 'the dominant conventions of science, commerce and politics' have 'already molded'.[137] Demanding total allegiance to its method and its findings, enlightenment is eventually 'totalitarian'.[138] (This species of totalitarian, or fascist, myth, can be distinguished from *Erfahrung*-produced story because it is imposed from above rather than collectively formed.)[139] Adorno and Horkheimer's is, in many ways, a problematic view of the Enlightenment that risks obscuring its very real and multitudinous technological and civic achievements – a point that they accepted and that another Frankfurt School philosopher, Jürgen Habermas, insisted upon.[140]

---

[133] Yuval Noah Harari advances a similar argument, proposing that the veteran of modern warfare is a 'flesh-witness' whose participation in the 'extreme bodily conditions' of battle is, thanks to Sensationist and Romantic philosophy, a 'visceral authority' that supersedes 'the rationalist authority of logical thinking' and 'the scientific authority of objective eye-witnessing' of the Enlightenment (*The Ultimate Experience: Battlefield Revelations and the Making of Modern War Culture, 1450–2000* (Basingstoke: Palgrave Macmillan, 2008), 7). But even 'flesh-witnessing' is unreliable, as figured by the physically unimpaired bodies of Chris Baldry, Septimus Warren Smith and Sergeant Evans.

[134] Adorno and Horkheimer, *Dialectic of Enlightenment*, xvi.

[135] Ibid., 3.

[136] In his Preface to 'Alastor' (1816), Shelley likened the quest for knowledge to an adventurous youth who 'drinks deep of the fountains of knowledge, and is still insatiate' (*The Major Works*, ed. Leader, 92).

[137] Adorno and Horkheimer, *Dialectic of Enlightenment*, xiv.

[138] Ibid., 6.

[139] Benjamin recognized this phenomenon, noting that recent philosophical attempts 'to grasp "true" experience' had invoked myth: Dilthey's *Das Erlebnis und die Dichtung* (1906) (*Experience and Poetry*) was an early example of such attempts 'which culminate with Klages and Jung, who made common cause with fascism' ('On Some Motifs in Baudelaire' ('Über einige Motive bei Baudelaire') [1939], trans. Harry Zohn, *Selected Writings. Volume 4: 1938–40*, ed. Michael W. Jennings, Howard Eiland and Gary Smith (Cambridge, MA: The Belknap Press of Harvard University Press, 1999), 313–55: 314). I am grateful to Lyndsey Stonebridge for this point.

[140] 'We have no doubt [...] that freedom in society is inseparable from enlightenment thinking' (Adorno and Horkheimer, *Dialectic of Enlightenment*, xvi). Habermas, whose career has been devoted to understanding the mechanisms of rational communication, particularly noted 'the

But this acknowledgement can co-exist with the view that 'enlightenment brings new and seemingly irreversible forms of domination', a view shared by, among others, Martin Heidegger and Georges Bataille.[141]

As noted in the Introduction, Adorno and Horkheimer use a home-coming veteran – Odysseus – to illustrate their thesis. They quote from the French historian Gustave Glotz's description of Odysseus in Ithaca to characterize the state of enlightenment:

> [A 'proprietor like Odysseus'] manages from a distance a numerous, carefully gradated staff of cowherds, shepherds, swineherds and servants. In the evening, when he has seen from his castle that the countryside is illumined by a thousand fires, he can compose himself for sleep with a quiet mind: he knows that his upright servants are keeping watch lest wild animals approach, and to chase thieves from the preserves which they are there to protect.[142]

In Adorno and Horkheimer's allegorical reading, Odysseus' adventures during his return from war become the scientific advances of the Enlightenment, culminating in a state in which, back home in Ithaca and in full control of his estates and servants, he can sleep easily. The contrast between the 'quiet mind' of this returned veteran and the troubled psyches of the Discharged Soldier, Chris Baldry and Septimus Warren Smith is striking. Where do they fit in this account of the progress of Enlightenment?

There are two possible answers. The first is that they embody its inevitable outcome. In defining the relentless movement of the Enlightenment towards masterful knowledge, Adorno and Horkheimer write: 'The unification of intellectual functions by means of which domination over the senses is achieved, the resignation of thought to the rise of unanimity, means the impoverishment of thought and of experience: the separation of both areas leaves both impaired.'[143] That concept of 'impoverishment' chimes directly with Benjamin's haunting evocation of men 'returned from

---

universalistic foundations of law' produced by Enlightenment modernity. He described *Dialectic of Enlightenment* as Adorno and Horkheimer's 'blackest book' (*The Philosophical Discourse of Modernity: Twelve Lectures* (*Der philosophische Diskurs der Moderne: Zwölf Vorlesungen*) [1985], trans. Frederick G. Lawrence (Cambridge, MA: The MIT Press, 1985), 113, 106). Another narrative could certainly be told about the veteran of mass warfare as a catalyst in a different kind of enlightenment – the development of welfare, from the early modern provision of relief for disabled former soldiers to the post-Second World War welfare state.

[141] See Comay, 'Gifts without Presents', 69.

[142] Gustave Glotz, *Histoire Grecque* (Paris: Presses Universitaires de France, 1939), 140; quoted in Adorno and Horkheimer, *Dialectic of Enlightenment*, 14.

[143] Adorno and Horkheimer, *Dialectic of Enlightenment*, 36.

the battlefield grown silent – not richer but *poorer* in communicable experience'.[144] Mass, industrial warfare is the Enlightenment's apotheosis – and the silent, war-ravaged veteran is what that apotheosis looks like.[145] Adorno and Horkheimer intimate as much when they remark on the 'ability to slip through, to survive one's own ruin, which has superseded tragedy', giving as an example 'the sad pliability of the soldier returning home, unaffected by war' (that 'unaffected' presumably means physically unscathed).[146]

The second, alternative answer to the question of where Wordsworth, West and Woolf's veterans fit in the progress of the Enlightenment is that they obstruct it. In some small way, these figures of unknowing resist the Enlightenment's relentless onward surge – and, again, this is why the *Odyssey* is, finally, irrelevant.[147] Not being able to make sense of something – whether by dint of experience or reason – is, after all, the opposite tendency to that of knowing and mastering the world. And, as Adorno and Horkheimer note, while '[e]loquent discourse' is 'the law of Homeric escape'[148] – that is, the language of scientific method – '[r]eticence in narrative' is the means by which 'the semblance of freedom glimmers'.[149] Seen in this light – and, of the two, this is the construction I prefer, if only because there is something potentially positive in the resistance – the non-communication of the Discharged Soldier, Chris Baldry

---

[144] Adorno and Horkheimer's original German is: 'Die Vereinheitlichung der intellektuellen Funktion, kraft welcher die Herrschaft über die Sinne sich vollzieht, die Resignation des Denkens zur Herstellung von Einstimmigkeit, bedeutet Verarmung des Denkens so gut wie der Erfahrung' (*Dialektik Der Aufklärung: Philosophische Fragmente* (Frankfurt-am-Main: S. Fischer, 1988), 42). Cf. 'Hatte man nicht bei Kriegsende bemerkt, daß die Leute verstummt aus dem Felde kamen? nicht reicher – ärmer an mitteilbarer Erfahrung' (Benjamin, 'Der Erzähler', 439).

[145] Another image, not obviously war-wearied though expressive of the unfathomable, would be Caspar David Friedrich's *Wanderer Above the Sea of Fog* (*c*.1818), who peers into a nebulous abyss. Some art historians believe the Wanderer to be a portrait of a Napoleonic War veteran – Colonel Friedrich Gotthard von Brincken of the Saxon infantry (see, for example, Joseph Leo Koerner, *Caspar David Friedrich and the Subject of Landscape* (London: Reaktion, 2009), 210). In a further articulation of the idea, Ian Watt described the prisoner of war as 'not so much a person as an extreme case of a more general modern condition – the powerlessness of the individual caught in the grip of vast collective purposes; in the end what he does makes little difference, and he knows it' (*Essays on Conrad* (Cambridge: Cambridge University Press, 2000), 218; quoted in Marina Mackay, 'The Wartime Rise of *The Rise of the Novel*', *Representations* 119.1 (2012), 119–43: 127).

[146] Adorno and Horkheimer, *Dialectic of Enlightenment*, 124.

[147] I am aware that there are other, earlier philosophical notions of the unknowable – Plato's ideal forms, Kant's noumena, Locke's nominal essences – but this late modern unknowing has special significance in its historical context. 'Unknowing' is the adjective given to the phenomenon I am describing by Philip Weinstein in *Unknowing: The Work of Modernist Fiction* (Ithaca, NY: Cornell University Press, 2005).

[148] Adorno and Horkheimer, *Dialectic of Enlightenment*, 78.

[149] Ibid., 79.

and Septimus Warren Smith is a refusal to acquiesce in the domination of the Enlightenment and so represents an even later phase of modernity.

'Refusal' might not be the best word: there is no sense that any of the three have any choice in their unfathoming and unfathomableness. Nor is their condition presented as enviable. There is no Lotos-Eater-like willingness or even desire to remain in ignorance here. The three veterans are consistently met with consternation – the onlooker may feel sadness or sorrow, yes, but not empathy, sympathy or imaginative involvement. And, in consequence, a certain unease is transferred to the circumstances of their creation, for what is the writing of poetry and fiction if not an act of imaginative understanding, on the part of both author and reader? Stupefaction marks the death of the empathy on which writing creatively depends.

At least, it does according to a certain way of thinking about the relationship between literature and its readers. The idea that the former has the improving function of enlarging the latter's capacity for empathy has a long history;[150] the opposing view has a history at least as long.[151] Both sides of the argument work from the premise that the desired effect on the reader is the kind of understanding that comes from imagining oneself in another person's shoes: proponents say that reading works of literature facilitates this, objectors say that it doesn't and/or can't. But there is another way of considering the issue, which Judith Butler proposes as she analyses the refusal of Catherine Sloper, heroine of *Washington Square*, to explain why she chooses to reject her suitor. Denied elucidatory motives, the reader, Butler suggests, is brought to 'understand the limits of judgment and to cease judging, paradoxically, in the name of ethics'.[152] 'To cease judging,'

---

[150] In a section of his *Elements of Criticism* (1762) called 'Emotions Caused by Fiction', Henry Home, Lord Kames, noted the 'extensive influence which language hath over the heart; an influence, which, more than any other means, strengthens the bond of society, and attracts individuals from their private system to perform acts of generosity and benevolence' (*Elements of Criticism* [1762], ed. Peter Jones, vol. 1/2 (Indianapolis, IN: Liberty Fund, 2005), 74); quoted in Suzanne Keen, *Empathy and the Novel* (Oxford: Oxford University Press, 2014), 45). Keen traces the 'literary career of empathy' from the early eighteenth century through the Romantics and Victorians to its major proponent at the end of the twentieth century, Martha Nussbaum, whose works include *Poetic Justice* (1995), *Cultivating Humanity* (1997) and *Love's Knowledge* (1990).

[151] This history would stretch from Plato's distrust of poets in Books 2 and 10 of the *Republic* to views that literature-spawned sympathy is at best condescending and at worst a poor substitute for political action (see Raymond Williams, *Culture and Society 1780–1950* (London: Chatto and Windus, 1958), 109) to post-cognitive turn critics such as Suzanne Keen, who finds 'the case for altruism stemming from novel reading inconclusive at best and nearly always exaggerated in favor of the beneficial effects of novel reading' (*Empathy and the Novel*, vii).

[152] Judith Butler, 'Values of Difficulty', *Just Being Difficult: Academic Writing in the Public Arena*, ed. Jonathan Culler and Kevin Lamb (Stanford, CA: Stanford University Press, 2003), 199–215: 208.

remarks Dorothy Hale, glossing Butler, is 'to cease trying to understand Catherine' and, instead, 'to "care" for her as other'.[153] The three veterans we have encountered in this chapter prompt a similar thought – that *not knowing*, or recognizing the limits of knowledge, is the basis of an ethical attitude, not so different from the old ideas of hospitality discussed in Chapter 2,[154] which 'cares' for the other without trying to understand him or her. Inculcating this attitude will require something other than story-telling – but more on that in the Conclusion. For now, this is where the story ends – in an exhausted man propped by the roadside on a moonlit night, an infantilized amnesiac and a hallucinatory suicide.

[153] Dorothy J. Hale, 'Aesthetics and the New Ethics: Theorizing the Novel in the Twenty-First Century', *PMLA* 124.3 (May 2009), 896–905: 901. The word 'care' is quoted from Martha Nussbaum (see, for example, Nussbaum's *Love's Knowledge: Essays on Philosophy and Literature* (New York: Oxford University Press, 1990), 300).

[154] 'Writings on hospitality through the ages are unanimous in their insistence on its altruism. Socrates defined hospitality, in its purest form, as the willingness to entertain strangers without even asking their name. In Roman law, the "jus hospitii" was based on the assumed brotherhood of all men, and anticipated the teachings of Christ by recognising in every stranger (irrespective of rank) the need to be greeted, fed, and housed' (Lucy Newlyn, 'The Wordsworths' Poetics of Hospitality', *Essays in Criticism* 66.1 (2016), 1–28: 13).

# Conclusion
## Can the Veteran Speak?

At the end of the last chapter, we were left with three non-storytelling veterans, figures who are inarticulate about what they have been through. These veterans, I argued, express a double unknowing: the individual cannot fathom his experiences in mass warfare and, in turn, cannot be fathomed by others. All that remains is an uncommunicative returnee who is the object of consternation and pity rather than sympathy and imaginative understanding on the part of the onlooker. In this Conclusion, I want to discuss some of the consequences – political, epistemological, ethical and aesthetic – of this double unfathomability.

Why should it matter if the veteran doesn't speak? The world might happily be spared some tedious war stories. In Daniel Anselme's *On Leave* (1957), an exchange between a veteran of the First World War and a veteran of the Algerian War shows that, even among ex-combatants, the tale of war is dreaded and barely tolerated: '"Just because we are in uniform does not give you an excuse to recite your military memoirs [...] When you come across a sewerman wearing an oilcloth cap, do you bore him to death with the history of your shit?"'[1] But the fact is that non-communication is politically limiting. Henri Lefebvre thought that preserving the details of everyday life was important because it was one of the last shared experiences. He wrote: 'Without an (illusory) representation or a (true) knowledge of social totality, without a participation in the social totality [...] no specific group has any status or certainty. It feels it has no place. It lacks confidence in itself, in its own vitality. Its everyday experience breaks down into interindividual, socially contingent relations.'[2] Uncommunicable experience precludes participation in the

---

[1] Daniel Anselme, *On Leave* (*La Permission*) [1957], trans. David Bellos (London: Penguin, 2014), 13.

[2] Henri Lefebvre, *Critique of Everyday Life: The One Volume Edition* (*Critique de la vie quotidienne*) [1947–81], trans. John Moore (London: Verso, 2014), 475. For an illuminating account of this point, see Jen Hui Bon Hoa, 'Totality and the Common: Henri Lefebvre and Maurice Blanchot on Everyday Life', *Cultural Critique* 88 (Fall 2014), 54–78.

whole and the ensuing lack of engagement translates into a lack of political action.[3] Instead of collectivity, there is atomization. Jürgen Habermas was describing the same phenomenon when he contrasted 'everyday communicative praxis'[4] – the underpinning of a public sphere capable of rationalized action – with the lack of mutual understanding fostered by increasing specialization that, in his view, was the product of late modernity. A similar model – anthropological and historiographical this time – comes by way of Claude Lévi-Strauss and François Hartog. Lévi-Strauss distinguished between 'hot' and 'cold' societies, the former seeking 'to annul the possible effects of historical factors', the latter motivated by 'an avid need for change'.[5] To these, Hartog adds a third historiographical regime: presentism, which, in his view, dates from the fall of the Berlin wall and the collapse of the Soviet Union.[6] Matthew Taunton, in turn, links Hartog's presentism to the efforts of various Modernist writers to convey 'experience in the raw', without it being 'organized through the lens of ideas'.[7] What is heard is the voice of *Erlebnis*, rather than *Erfahrung*, and the future inflection necessary to political action is absent. This voice, as Taunton points out, is paratactic – disconnected – while the voice of *Erfahrung* is hypotactic, revealing temporal connections. And this brings us to Marxist ideas about writing and reading: Georg Lukács's recommendation of 'narration' that will 'always present a connection, disclose causes and propose consequences',[8] for instance. The consensus is that sharing experience – experience with a temporal aspect, that is – is a process of empowerment. The theorists just cited are concerned with civilian life, but their points hold good for military service. Indeed, they assume a

---

[3] Cf. 'Experience may also be made available for others through a process of post facto recounting, a kind of secondary elaboration in the Freudian sense, which turns it into a meaningful narrative. When shared, such reconstructions and recountings of experience can become the stuff of group identities, as the so-called consciousness-raising exercises of feminists showed. When thwarted, they may lead to the traumatic blockage that has been called unclaimed experience' (Martin Jay, *Songs of Experience: Modern American and European Variations on a Universal Theme* (Berkeley, CA: University of California Press, 2004), 7).

[4] Jürgen Habermas, *The Philosophical Discourse of Modernity: Twelve Lectures (Der philosophische Diskurs der Moderne: Zwölf Vorlesungen)* [1985], trans. Frederick G. Lawrence (Cambridge, MA: The MIT Press, 1985), 201.

[5] Claude Lévi-Strauss, *The Savage Mind (La Pensée sauvage)* [1962], translator unknown (London: Weidenfeld and Nicolson, 1966), 233–4.

[6] François Hartog, *Régimes d'historicité: présentisme et expériences du temps* (Paris: Seuil, 2003), passim.

[7] Matthew Taunton, ' "The Radiant Future": The Bolshevik Revolution in Modernist Temporality', conference paper, British Association of Modernist Studies Annual Conference: Modernism Now, Senate House, London (28 June 2014). I am grateful to Matthew Taunton for giving me a copy of his paper to read.

[8] Georg Lukács, *Essays on Realism (Essays über Realismus)* [1948], trans. David Fernbach, ed. Rodney Livingstone (London: Lawrence and Wishart, 1980), 54.

greater urgency. When those silenced are war veterans, armed conflict has precluded the eventuality of its being protested.

At this point, politics look to epistemology and the ethics of aesthetics. For the silenced veteran brings to mind another silenced figure: the subaltern, as theorized by Gayatri Chakravorty Spivak. Spivak derives her subaltern from Antonio Gramsci's *Quaderni del Carcere* (*Prison Notebooks*) (1929–35) in which the word refers to '[n]on-hegemonic groups or classes'.[9] Gramsci is alert, though, to the narrower military meaning of the term, placing 'subaltern officers' between 'NCOs' (non-commissioned officers) and 'senior officers' (in the British Army, this would mean Second Lieutenants and Lieutenants).[10] Spivak's subaltern, though, is no Lieutenant, but a lower-class woman of the colonized third world.[11] In a tautology that I am not the first to notice,[12] the defining attribute of this version of subalternity is the condition of being silenced. 'Can the Subaltern Speak?' asks the title of Spivak's much-revised, veteran essay, and it invites the response: 'if she could, she wouldn't be a subaltern'. But subalternity does not end in tautology: the silence matters. The question – for scholars, for readers – is what to do with it.

Dipesh Chakrabarty, one of the founders of the Subaltern Studies Collective, discusses this question as a specific historiographical problem. The rebellion of the Santal (a tribe of people indigenous to Terai of Nepal and India) against the British in 1855 was explained by the Santal themselves 'in supernatural terms'.[13] How can the academic historian both take the Santal's views seriously and confer on them 'agency or subjecthood in their own history', Chakrabarty asks.[14] Rejecting the impulses either to anthropologize or to historicize the tribespeople, he concludes that there is 'no third voice' that can assimilate the voices of the Santal and of the

[9] Geoffrey Nowell Smith and Quintin Hoare, 'Preface', Antonio Gramsci, *Selections from the Prison Notebooks* (London: Lawrence and Wishart, 1971), IX–XV: XIV.

[10] Antonio Gramsci, *Selections from the Prison Notebooks* (*Quaderni del Carcere*) [1948], trans. Geoffrey Nowell Smith and Quintin Hoare (London: Lawrence and Wishart, 1971), 13n. I am grateful to Lt-Col. Chris Keeble for confirming my understanding of the ranks.

[11] In fact, Spivak's example, Bubaneswari Bhaduri, is not of the subaltern class (see Rajeswari Sunder Rajan, 'Death and the Subaltern', *Can the Subaltern Speak?: Reflections on the History of an Idea*, ed. Rosalind C. Morris (New York: Columbia University Press, 2010), 117–38: 120).

[12] Rosalind C. Morris, 'Introduction', *Can the Subaltern Speak?*, ed. Morris, 1–18: 8; Sunder Rajan, 'Death and the Subaltern', 123.

[13] Dipesh Chakrabarty, *Provincializing Europe: Postcolonial Thought and Historical Difference* (Princeton, NJ: Princeton University Press, 2000), 102. Chakrabarty refers to a preceding discussion of the issue in Ranajit Guha, 'The Prose of Counter-Insurgency', *Subaltern Studies* II, ed. Ranajit Guha (Delhi: Oxford University Press, 1983), 1–42.

[14] Chakrabarty, *Provincializing Europe*, 103.

academy-trained historian.[15] Instead, 'we have to stay with both'.[16] The verb 'stay' is significant: it suggests a kind of 'being with', located in an atemporal present, and it turns the Santal and the historian (no matter the period in which the latter is writing) into 'contemporaries'.[17] Chakrabarty is asking for the same methodology that Rita Felski does in her description of actor-network theory: 'temporal interdependency without telos'[18] – and the time-travelling veteran fits it to a T. The methodology has an in-built ethics – epistemological egalitarianism – but Chakrabarty goes further in proposing historiography as a guide to living. For his final recommendation is to take the Santal's beliefs as 'a principle for life open today to one who ha[s] faith'.[19]

For those who lack such faith, the equivalent is not easy to see. It lies, I think, in Spivak and Butler's meld of literary theory and ethics. Spivak resists the temptations both to enable the subaltern to speak (a move for which she criticizes Foucault and Deleuze) and to speak for the subaltern, noting that, in both cases, the utterance would not bypass 'the problem of representation'.[20] Instead she performs a kind of specialized listening – uncovering and directing attention to the not-said, showing rather than telling. Butler's similar suggestion is to 'understand the limits of judgment and to cease judging, paradoxically, in the name of ethics'.[21]

The military veterans we have encountered in this book are worlds away from Spivak's subaltern. But, like her, they are silenced. Spivak and Butler offer a way of responding to their silences: noticing them, registering them and, above all, listening to them. Listening as a critical approach is relatively under-developed, but a 1976 essay by Roland Barthes gives some useful pointers. Barthes identifies three kinds of listening: being 'alert', in the manner of a wolf listening for the sound of its prey or a hare for the sounds of its hunter; 'deciphering', as in decoding heard signs; and 'taking soundings', a kind of deep listening – Barthes calls it

---

[15] Ibid., 108.
[16] Ibid., 108.
[17] Ibid., 109.
[18] Rita Felski, 'Context Stinks!', *New Literary History* 42.4 (Autumn 2011), 573–91: 579.
[19] Chakrabarty, *Provincializing Europe*, 108.
[20] Gayatri Chakravorty Spivak, 'Can the Subaltern Speak?', *Marxism and the Interpretation of Culture*, ed. Cary Nelson and Lawrence Grossberg (Urbana, IL: University of Illinois Press, 1988), 271–313: 283. Spivak is referring to Michel Foucault and Gilles Deleuze, 'Intellectuals and Power: A Conversation between Michel Foucault and Gilles Deleuze' (*Les Intellectuels et le pouvoir*) [1972], trans. Donald F. Bouchard and Sherry Simon, *Language, Counter-Memory, Practice: Selected Essays and Interviews*, ed. Michel Foucault (Ithaca, NY: Cornell University Press, 1977): 205–17.
[21] Judith Butler, 'Values of Difficulty', *Just Being Difficult: Academic Writing in the Public Arena*, ed. Jonathan Culler and Kevin Lamb (Stanford, CA: Stanford University Press, 2003), 199–215: 208.

'modern listening' – which is attuned to 'the implicit, the indirect, the supplementary, the delayed'.[22] The last of these, as Barthes acknowledges, resembles the kind of listening performed in psychoanalysis,[23] but I think it can be re-characterized in literary-theoretical, non-therapeutic terms. Angela Leighton, who discusses Barthes's essay, does just this when she writes: '[U]nderstanding literature might come precisely from detaching the churn, the errancy of language, from the drive to make sense, and thus of course to confront a different sort of sense. To replace the idea of understanding with the idea of listening might then be to accept that what literature offers is not something understood; it is something listened to.'[24] The circularity – listening to rather than understanding literature is to accept that what literature offers is not understood but listened to – makes the point: deep critical listening does not convert the not-said into knowledge. It is an act of attention, not explication; a hermeneutics of acceptance, not suspicion. It cares without comprehending, plumbs without fathoming.

I realize that this is dangerous ground. In 2016, Oxford Dictionaries selected as their Word of the Year 'post-truth', which they define as 'relating to or denoting circumstances in which objective facts are less influential in shaping public opinion than appeals to emotion and personal belief'.[25] One could weep. I cannot emphasize too strongly that my exploration of a way of reading that is alert to and caring of the ineffable in no way detracts from my belief in the democratic importance of verifiable facts, evidentially based argument and responsible reporting – not least because all those things help ensure that the wars that produce the veterans of the future will be entered into only when the arguments for and against have been fully substantiated and understood. Yet so too will attending to the not-said.

The remainder of this Conclusion explores such a critical approach in relation to two final literary war veterans: Archie Jones and Samad Iqbal, the protagonists of Zadie Smith's 2000 novel, *White Teeth*. Neither is a sub-altern in strict military terms nor in the precise sense intended by Spivak. Archie, a native-born white British man, was a sapper in the Second World

---

[22] Roland Barthes, 'Listening' ('Écoute') [1977], trans. Richard Howard, *The Responsibility of Forms: Critical Essays on Music, Art, and Representation* (Oxford: Basil Blackwell, 1986), 245–60: 245, 250, 258.

[23] Ibid., 258.

[24] Angela Leighton, 'Thresholds of Attention: On Listening in Literature', *Thinking on Thresholds: The Poetics of Transitive Spaces*, ed. Subha Mukherji (London: Anthem, 2011), 199–212: 206.

[25] https://en.oxforddictionaries.com/word-of-the-year-2016.

War (a rank below subaltern). Samad, an Indian man from West Bengal, a Muslim and an immigrant to Britain, was a Captain (a rank above subaltern).[26] But their military ranks and their ethnicities are not the factors that make Spivak's reading of subalternity applicable. What does so is their *veterancy.* The methodology variously modelled by Spivak, Barthes and Leighton allows us to think about the following question: how can we listen out for, and to, veterans' silences?

## Listen: Zadie Smith, *White Teeth* (2000)

In *White Teeth*, whenever Archie or Samad mention the Second World War, they are swiftly told to shut up. In Archie's thoughts about this, it comes to mean that people are uninterested in the experience in his life that sets him apart:

> He and Samad, old Sam, Sammy-boy, they had a few tales to tell, mind, Archie even had a bit of shrapnel in the leg for anyone who cared to see it – but nobody did. No one wanted to talk about *that* any more. It was like a club-foot, or a disfiguring mole. It was like nose hair. People looked away. If someone said to Archie, *What have you done in life, then*, or *What's your biggest memory*, well God help him if he mentioned the war; eyes glazed over, fingers tapped, everybody offered to buy the next round. No one really wanted to know.[27]
>
> (12, original emphasis)

The *main thing about Archie* goes unnoticed. But there are even more discouraging reactions. When, in the summer of 1955, Archie looks for work as a war correspondent in Fleet Street, he is told, '*We would require something other than merely having fought in a war, Mr Jones. War experience isn't really relevant*' (13, original emphasis). The last relevance of war experience – knowing about war – is here brushed aside. Archie reflects: 'And that was it, wasn't it. There was no relevance in the war – not in '55, even

---

[26] Samad has been read as a subaltern: Jennifer Gustar, for example, argues that he is 'emasculated by a racialized discourse in an ethnocentric culture that often treats him as subaltern' ('*The Tempest* in an English Teapot: Colonialism and the Measure of a Man in Zadie Smith's *White Teeth*', *Changing English: An International Journal of English Teaching* 17.4 (2010), 333–43: 335). However, bearing in mind Spivak's injunction that '[s]imply by being postcolonial or the member of an ethnic minority, we are not "subaltern"' ('Can the Subaltern Speak?' (2010), 65) and, further, that the term should not be applied simply to those 'not getting a piece of the pie' (Leon de Kock, 'Interview with Gayatri Chakravorty Spivak: New Nation Writers Conference in South Africa', *ARIEL: A Review of International English Literature* 23.3 (1992), 29–47: 45), I am refraining from conferring the description on him.

[27] Zadie Smith, *White Teeth* (London: Hamish Hamilton, 2000). Page references are given in the text.

less now in '74. Nothing he did *then* mattered *now*. The skills you learnt were, in the modern parlance, not relevant, *not transferable* (13, original emphasis). Alsana, who, as an immigrant Bangladeshi woman, has the best claim of all to Spivakian subalternity,[28] is particularly impatient of the stories told by those 'old warhorse big mouths' Archie and her husband (195). When Archie sets out the benefits of veterancy – '"you can't beat experience, can you? I mean, you two, you're young women still, in a way. Whereas we, I mean, we are, like, wells of experience the children can use, you know, when they feel the need. We're like encyclopaedias"' (209) – she simply calls him a fool. '"Don't you know you're left behind like carriage and horses, like candlewax? Don't you know to them you're old and smelly like yesterday's fishnchip paper?"' (209). For Alsana, both Archie's and Samad's belief in the value of their experiences amounts to no more than a pathetic unawareness of their inadequate masculinity, poor parenting skills, social uselessness and lack of relevance to the younger generation.

If Archie is a thwarted storyteller, Samad is the 'Ancient Mariner' (50). Unlike Archie, Samad thought ahead during the Second World War, active in his efforts towards prospective retrospection. In Greece, aware that the war has officially ended, he gathers his nondescript battalion around him and begins to march up the mountain 'in search of a war he could one day tell his grandchildren about, as his great-grandfather's exploits had been told to him' (94). The artificiality of the exercise – this is a hyperreal offensive, undertaken solely to be talked about, not even taking place within the war proper – underscores the worthlessness of what is to be handed on. In passing, it also undermines the validity of his great-grandfather's exploits. These are regularly recounted in the 'much neglected, 100-year-old, mildewed yarn of Mangal Pande' (85), a byword in the novel for boringness and irrelevancy. The deeds of the 'great hero of the Indian Mutiny' have been reduced, through the over-telling, to, in the words of Abdul-Mickey, Muslim Arab owner of an Irish pool-house, 'that Mangy Pandy whateverthefuckitis [...] Who shot who, and who hung who, my grandad ruled the Pakis or whateverthefuckitwas, as if any poor fucker gives a flying fuck' (161). Certainly Millat doesn't. Scornfully dismissing his father, he might have mentioned his insistence on the traditional values and behaviour of Bengal, but what he actually focuses on, comparing Marcus Chalfen favourably to Samad, are his war stories: 'he's not like

---

[28] Alsana stops speaking directly to Samad for eight years when he sends Magid to Bangladesh, but this is an act of power.

Samad or Mangal Pande; he didn't get a war, he never saw action, he hasn't got any analogies or anecdotes' (449).

Samad speaks all right (Archie, stung by the criticism, mostly obeys the command to shut up), but is so ridiculed, insulted and emphatically not listened to that he might as well not bother. Figuring this, both men have the same bodily damage as the silenced war veterans in Chapter 5.[29] Archie has a 'funny leg' (70) as the result of a bullet wound, while Samad's right hand is 'a broken thing, grey-skinned and unmoving, dead in every way bar the blood that ran through it' (10): both by now familiar marks of the inability to pass on experience. Samad's wrist having been shot through during the war, his hand has become a mortmain, the dead hand of history. Refusing to have it amputated – 'Every bit of my body comes from Allah. Every bit will return to him' (77) – he lives with the wounds of history on a daily basis, though unable to turn them to his or anyone else's benefit.

But in this novel about 'the century of strangers, brown, yellow and white [...] the century of the great immigrant experiment' (281), past experience is not so easily written off. Here the veteran and the immigrant – both *xenoi*, both bearers of the past – coalesce; here, too, begins the work of listening to the silences. *White Teeth* illustrates its points about roots with imagery of root canals, benefiting from the notable complexity of that bodily system. Containing dental pulp, the root canal is the part of the root that brings nourishment to the tooth, but it is also prone to decay. Both the sustaining and pain-inducing properties of roots are felt simultaneously by the immigrant (as by the veteran): as Kathleen O'Grady put it in conversation with Smith, each of the characters in *White Teeth* comes with an 'elaborate lineage – personal, familial and cultural' that 'both enables and disables' them.[30]

*White Teeth* makes clear that roots can be enriching and stabilizing, as they are in Smith's description of Clara as being '*from* somewhere': 'She had *roots*' (23, original emphasis). Other characters, more distanced from their origins, feel less well-anchored: Samad speaks of 'giv[ing] up the *very idea* of belonging' while Millat experiences 'an ever present anger and hurt, the feeling of belonging nowhere that comes to people who belong everywhere' (233, original emphasis). But more often, the novel comes across roots that

---

[29] Archie's first wife, an Italian whose mind 'is gone' (11), is reminiscent of both Septimus and Lucrezia Warren Smith.

[30] Kathleen O'Grady, 'White Teeth: An Interview with Author Zadie Smith', *Atlantis: A Women's Studies Journal/Revue d'Études sur les Femmes* 27.1 (2002), 105–11: 105.

decay and cause pain. What Smith said in an interview – 'The whole kind of 60s, 70s, liberation ethic that you will be released by knowing your roots, that you will discover yourself [...] it's partly true, but your roots come with baggage. And the baggage isn't always fun'[31] – is played out in *White Teeth* as other characters attempt to shake off history's dead hand. 'Too much bloody history,' says Shiva, Samad's Hindu colleague in the Indian restaurant, as he dishes up Chicken Bhuna (126) – a packed image that contains and conceals a colonizing history – while Irie marvels at the idea that there could exist fathers 'who dealt in the present, who didn't drag ancient history around like a chain and ball' (281). She admires the Chalfens because:

> They open a door and all they've got behind it is a bathroom or a lounge. Just neutral spaces. And not this endless maze of present rooms and past rooms and the things said in them years ago and everybody's old historical shit all over the place. [...] And every single fucking day is not this huge battle between who they are and who they should be, what they were and what they will be. [...] As far as they're concerned, *it's the past*.
>
> (440, original emphasis)

The speech may be naïve given the Chalfens' history as Jews (in contrast, when Alsana, Clara and Nina meet Sol Jozefowicz, it strikes all three women 'the way history will, embarrassingly, without warning, like a blush' what 'the ex-park-keeper's experience might have been' (69)), but it points to a desire to found identity outside history.

At the end of the novel, such rootless identity seems to have a chance of being realized, if only in the escape of the FutureMouse©, a creature that holds out the 'tantalizing promise' of a 'new phase in human history' in which 'we are not victims of the random but instead directors and arbitrators of our own fate' (370). The mouse scurries away over Archie's hand and 'through the hands of those who wished to pin it down' (461). Yet the mouse's chances of making a real getaway from history's mortmain are zero, given that it has been genetically programmed to develop in a specific way. Archie's envoi to the creature, which forms the novel's ending – '*Go on my son!*' (462) – encapsulates the point. 'Go on' is the utterance of a father willing to let his offspring make its own way, a hope for a future-inflected existence in which the grey and grasping hands of the past are shaken off. 'My son', with all its paternal investment, immediately undercuts all that.

---

[31] Quoted in ibid., 106.

Ineluctable it may be,[32] but hard listening is still required if the past is to be heard. How might a Spivakian listening work? *White Teeth* is an exuberant, noisy novel and so the silences are difficult to detect. They lie, as Smith puts it, in such matter as 'whispered asides; lost conversations; medals and photographs; lists and certificates, yellowing paper bearing the faint imprint of brown dates' (72). And in an injured foot and a broken hand that are more than they seem. Samad's wound was inflicted when the gun of a 'bastard Sikh' (77) went off in a trench – it is the visual mark of a complex, colonial history that placed a Bengali Muslim on the side of a Sikh, both fighting for the British. Entwined in that history is Samad's own story, unlistened-to, drowned out even by his own tale-telling: biology student at Delhi University, member of the 9th North Bengal Mounted Rifles and the Bengal flying corps, 'erudite', 'handsome', 'so precious his mother kept him in from the sun's rays, sent him to the best tutors and covered him in linseed oil twice a day' (96). What is not heard is what he would wish to be displayed on a large, white placard to wear in the Indian restaurant in which he works (50):

---

I AM NOT A WAITER. I HAVE BEEN A STUDENT, A SCIENTIST, A SOLDIER, MY WIFE IS CALLED ALSANA, WE LIVE IN EAST LONDON BUT WE WOULD LIKE TO MOVE NORTH. I AM A MUSLIM BUT ALLAH HAS FORSAKEN ME OR I HAVE FORSAKEN ALLAH, I'M NOT SURE. I HAVE A FRIEND — ARCHIE — AND OTHERS. I AM FORTY-NINE BUT WOMEN STILL TURN IN THE STREET. SOMETIMES.

---

This is Samad's silenced history, unappreciated by those who see him – in the words of his own son, Millat – as a 'faulty, broken, stupid, one-handed waiter of a man' (432), a description that comes to Millat's mind even as he reads the name Iqbal written in blood and stone in Trafalgar Square. The scratched name beneath the seat is a permanent if hard-to-see record of his father, a small but standing retort to Sir Henry Havelock, who so mercilessly quashed the Indian Mutiny and whose statue is across the square.

---

[32] Cf. Smith's comment in an interview: 'I think you can have historical traumas. The second [sic] World War is an obvious example. I can't think of a book by a peer of mine [...] which doesn't include some holocaust reference. I just can't think of one, of any book of any significance that doesn't have that. Even if it is deeply sublimated it is impossible to escape. Feels like it is impossible to escape' (quoted in ibid., 106). The feeling is expressed in the doomed flight of the FutureMouse©.

In Archie's case, silence seems to cover nothing much worth writing home about: newspaper boy, failed war correspondent, husband (twice), father, designer of ways to fold paper. The list is enlivened by his also having been an Olympic track cyclist, his appearance omitted from the records by a 'sloppy secretary' (13). But Archie is an extraordinary keeper of silence – the silence concealing what actually happened during his encounter with Dr Marc-Pierre Perret that night when Samad sent him off to shoot the doctor on the mountain outside Athens. The silence lies (in both senses) throughout the novel, Archie's leg injury maintaining the deceit, until Archie recognizes the bloody tears wept by Dr Perret – the un-concealable tears of genetically inherited diabetic retinopathy – and Samad recognizes them too:

> *Captain Samad Miah*, who has just stepped soundlessly through the modern door with its silent mechanism; *Captain Samad Miah* [...] who realizes that he has been lied to by his only friend in the world for fifty years. That the corner-stone of their friendship was made of nothing more firm than marshmallow and soap bubbles. That there is far, far more to Archibald Jones than he had ever imagined.
>
> (454–5, original emphasis)

Samad's younger self steps silently through a silent door – a revenant veteran – to register for the first time his friend's long silence and with it the true meaning of the shot he heard ring out fifty years before and the true meaning of Archie's leg wound. This is applied veteran poetics: Samad has, at last, listened to what has not been said.

But look what happens next: 'And then, with a certain horrid glee, he [Samad] gets to the fundamental truth of it, the anagnorisis: *This incident alone will keep us two old boys going for the next forty years*. It is the story to end all stories' (455, original emphasis). Immediately, the knowledge becomes in Samad's mind 'the story to end all stories' – to end the story of his thwarted hopes for his career, even to end the story of Mangal Pande. The story he tells of Archie's silence will itself be silencing, obscuring certain details and other points of view. A critical deep listening, by contrast, would resist the temptation to convert silence into story. Instead, having registered the silence, it would let it linger, in a spirit at once awed, admiring and amused.

# Appendix
## The Veteran in National Life and Culture

England began systematically to look after her former soldiers in 1593.[1] The Act for the Necessary Relief of Soldiers and Mariners passed in that year gave each parish in the kingdom a weekly sum 'towards the relief of sick, hurt, maimed soldiers and mariners'[2] – a scheme that has been called Europe's 'first state system of benefits for the rank-and-file disabled'.[3] Money was awarded, however, not on the basis of 'disability per se' but of 'service to the nation'.[4] One of the Act's earliest beneficiaries was one Richard Jennyns who had fought in Normandy on a campaign led by Queen Elizabeth I's then favourite, Robert Devereux, Earl of Essex. On 30 June 1594, Essex wrote to the Chester Justices of the Peace in support of Jennyns's pension application. He is 'by a wound receaved of thenemie in that service, maymed of his Right hande', Essex told the Justices, and 'thereby sorely [?] disabled in his body'.[5] Unable to continue in military service, Jennyns has been obliged to fall back on his own resources 'to the great ympairing of his estate'. The authorities were impressed: on 10 July they granted Jennyns a yearly stipend.[6] In addition to admiring a ten-day turnaround that puts the benefits system of our own day to shame, we can note the various strategies of persuasion at work in Jennyns's case: service for

---

[1] As Patricia Lin points out, relief schemes based on contributions from military personnel had existed for over 200 years before this ('Extending Her Arms: Military Families and the Transformation of the British State, 1793–1815', unpublished PhD thesis (University of California Berkeley, 1997), 63).

[2] 35 Eliz I c. 4.

[3] Geoffrey Hudson, 'Arguing Disability: Ex-Servicemen's Own Stories in Early Modern England, 1590–1790', *Medicine, Madness and Social History: Essays in Honour of Roy Porter*, ed. Roberta Bivins and John V. Pickstone (Basingstoke: Palgrave Macmillan, 2007), 105–17: 106.

[4] Lin, 'Extending Her Arms', 64. See also Geoffrey Hudson, 'Disabled Veterans and the State in Early Modern England', *Disabled Veterans in History*, ed. David A. Gerber (Ann Arbor, MI: The University of Michigan Press, 2000), 117–44: 119.

[5] F2 D36: 1594, Chester Record Office, Chester, UK.

[6] J. H. E. Bennett and J. C. Dewhurst, eds, *Quarter Sessions Records, with other Records of the Justices of the Peace for the County Palatine of Chester 1559–1760* (place of publication unknown: publisher unknown, 1940), 45. The amount of the stipend granted to Jennyns is unknown.

the nation, physical disability, exhaustion of personal financial resources – all underwritten by a member of the nobility. Unlike the 'impotent poor', a veteran like Jennyns '*merited* relief'.[7]

By the time of the Restoration, petitioning veterans began to cite other grounds for relief: poverty, their incapacity to work, their inability to support dependents, the fact that they had done everything they could to avoid reliance on public funds (this is also implied in Essex's letter),[8] and – after the Restoration and where possible – their allegiance to the Crown.[9] In Hudson's words, 'need replaced disability in recent conflict' as the basis for awarding pensions.[10] After the Restoration, state provision for disabled veterans was expanded, catering not only for the veterans of the English Civil Wars (18,000 men were demobilized in 1647),[11] but also those of the campaign to take and hold Tangier (1661–84) and the Anglo-Dutch Wars (1652–4, 1665–7, 1672–4).[12] In 1681, following the model of the Hôtel Royale des Invalides established in Paris in 1670 by Louis XIV, Charles II authorized the foundation of Chelsea Hospital, 'for the relief of such land soldiers as are, or shall be, lame or infirm in ye service of the crown'.[13] Funded by compulsory donations from soldiers' wages, Chelsea provided accommodation for a limited number of incapacitated veterans ('in-pensioners'), imposing on them army-like uniforms, ranks and rules[14] (it has been described as wielding

---

[7] Hudson, 'Disabled Veterans and the State in Early Modern England', 120.

[8] On veterans of the Parliamentary side see David Appleby, 'Veteran Politics in Restoration England, 1660–1670', *The Seventeenth Century* 28.3 (September 2013), 323–42, and Joyce Malcolm, 'Charles II and the Reconstruction of Royal Power', *The Historical Journal* 35.2 (1992), 307–30.

[9] Hudson, 'Arguing Disability', 107.

[10] Ibid., 107.

[11] Appleby, 'Veteran Politics in Restoration England', 326. On the post-Civil Wars demobilization and contemporary fears of social disturbance, see further Malcolm, 'Charles II and the Reconstruction of Royal Power' and Mark Stoyle, '"Memories of the Maimed": The Testimony of Charles I's Former Soldiers, 1660–1730', *History* 88.290 (April 2003), 204–26.

[12] Lin, 'Extending Her Arms', 164.

[13] Quoted in C. G. T. Dean, *The Royal Hospital, Chelsea* (London: Hutchinson, 1950), 23. On the Royal Hospital, Chelsea, see further Thomas Faulkner, *An Historical and Descriptive Account of the Royal Hospital, and the Royal Military Asylum, at Chelsea* (London: publisher unknown, 1805); Anonymous, 'Chelsea, Part IV: The Royal Hospital: History of the Foundation', *Survey of London*, ed. Walter Godfrey (1927) (British History Online); Joanna Innes, 'The Domestic Face of the Military-Fiscal State: Government and Society in Eighteenth-Century Britain', *An Imperial State at War: Britain from 1689–1815*, ed. Lawrence Stone (London: Routledge, 1994), 96–127: 110–11; Lin, 'Extending Her Arms'; and Hudson, 'Disabled Veterans and the State in Early Modern England', 117–44. The Royal Hospital for Seamen at Greenwich was Chelsea's naval counterpart. See further John Cooke, *An Historical Account of the Royal Hospital for Seamen at Greenwich* (London: publisher unknown, 1789) and Edward Walford, 'Greenwich: The Hospital for Seamen', *Old and New London* (London: publisher unknown, 1878) (British History Online). On the treatment of veterans in eighteenth century, see Innes, 'The Domestic Face of the Military-Fiscal State', 108–17.

[14] Hudson, 'Disabled Veterans and the State in Early Modern England', 126.

Foucauldian 'microphysics of power').[15] Demand for accommodation soon outstripped supply so, from the mid-eighteenth century, the institution also administered the provision of financial assistance to 'out-pensioners'.[16] By 1750, out-pensioners numbered over 8,000; in the 1760s, 14,000, and by the end of the American Revolutionary War, 20,000 – all supported at the rate of five pence a day.[17] By the nineteenth century Chelsea had become a 'tourist attraction', its pensioners 'living exhibits'[18] – Thomas Hardy visited on more than one occasion.[19] Chelsea in-pensioners had acquired their still-current status of national treasures, but out-pensioners and veterans the institution did not support were viewed with greater distrust.[20]

If the war veteran was a well-established figure in national life by the late eighteenth century, the French Revolutionary Wars of 1792 to 1802 and the Napoleonic Wars of 1803 to 1815 – 'one peculiarly pervasive and long-drawn out conflict', in the words of Linda Colley[21] – ramped up the scale.[22] It was a new age of mass warfare, inaugurated by the French *levée en masse* (mass conscription) decreed on 23 August 1793,[23] and costing

---

[15] Ibid., 126.

[16] Lin, 'Extending Her Arms', 65.

[17] Innes, 'The Domestic Face of the Military-Fiscal State', 111.

[18] J. W. M. Hichberger, *Images of the Army: The Military in British Art, 1815–1914* (Manchester: Manchester University Press, 1988), 142.

[19] Veterans fascinated Hardy. The Napoleonic Wars in particular engaged his imagination – his grandfather had been a Volunteer and 'lay in Weymouth with his company from time to time waiting for Bonaparte who never came' – and on hearing news of the outbreak of the Franco-Prussian War in 1870, his reaction was 'to go to a service at Chelsea Hospital and look at the tattered banners mended with netting, and talk to the old asthmatic and crippled men, many of whom in the hospital at that date had fought at Waterloo and some in the Peninsula' (Thomas Hardy, *The Life and Work of Thomas Hardy*, ed. Michael Millgate (London: Macmillan, 1984), 17, 81). He went again on Waterloo Day in 1875 (the sixtieth anniversary of the battle) and on 27 October 1878. On the first occasion, he listened to a Waterloo veteran called John Bentley describe 'his experiences of that memorable day' (81). (Bentley is also mentioned in a note in *The Dynasts* (1908): 'One of the many Waterloo men known to the writer in his youth, John Bentley of the Fusilier Guards, used to declare that he lay down on the ground in such weariness that when food was brought him he could not eat it, and slept till next morning on an empty stomach. He died at Chelsea Hospital, 187-, aged eighty six' (Thomas Hardy, *The Dynasts: An Epic-Drama of the War with Napoleon* [1908] (London: Macmillan, 1965), 518n)). On the second occasion, he met a 'deaf' and 'palsied' pensioner who had served under Sir John Moore in the Peninsular War. 'It was extraordinary to talk and shake hands with a man who had shared in that terrible winter march to Coruna, and had seen Moore face to face,' Hardy remarked (*The Life and Work of Thomas Hardy*, 127).

[20] See Hichberger, 140–2.

[21] Linda Colley, *Britons: Forging the Nation 1707–1837* [1992] (New Haven, CT: Yale University Press, 2009), 2.

[22] The French Revolutionary Wars began in 1792; the Revolutionary regime declared war on Britain on 1 February 1793. In 1803, Britain declared war on France, now led by Napoleon Bonaparte, and war lasted until his defeat at the Battle of Waterloo in 1815.

[23] Gillian Russell, *The Theatres of War: Performance, Politics, and Society, 1793–1815* (Oxford: The Clarendon Press, 1995), 4, 14.

Britain £1,500,000,000 and 315,000 lives.²⁴ The period saw nothing less than the emergence of 'a massive military machine which has only begun to be seriously dismantled since the Second World War'.²⁵ Britain became a 'country in arms'.²⁶ 'This is THE AGE OF WAR,' wrote an anonymous poet in the *Courier* on 8 November 1798, 'When ev'ry bosom swells with rage / And burns with military fame'.²⁷ Mobilization en masse had the natural outcome of producing veterans en masse. Following the Battle of Waterloo, more than a third of a million men were demobilized,²⁸ but soldiers had been coming home long before that, wounded or otherwise unfit.²⁹ State provision for these veterans was variable. Army and Navy Officers remained on half-pay.³⁰ Rank-and-file soldiers and ordinary seamen received no further financial support,³¹ unless wounded or otherwise incapacitated.

Working out the new relationship between the state and its former soldiers left its mark on the nation's cultural life. In 'The Wounded Soldier', an anonymously authored song included in *The Muse in Good Humour; or Momus's Banquet* (*c*.1795), the wars have left the eponymous veteran 'bereft of a limb and an eye'. Nonetheless, he vows: 'Should new conflicts arise and my King want support, / To the standard of honor I'll cheerful resort'.³² In 1802, in the celebrations following the Peace of Amiens, London buildings were illuminated. The display over the entrance to the Covent-Garden Theatre comprised:

> a Druid, in his magisterial capacity, bearing the Roman fasces on his arm, and presenting, as the Minister of distributive justice, a veteran soldier, bearing the standard of England, to Alfred [...] seated on a fragment of the ancient city's walls, his right hand bearing an olive branch, while with his left he presents a goblet to the soldier, as a reward for his toils.³³

²⁴ Simon Bainbridge, *British Poetry and the Revolutionary and Napoleonic Wars: Visions of Conflict* (Oxford: Oxford University Press, 2003), 6.
²⁵ Colley, *Britons*, 2.
²⁶ Mark Philp, 'Revolution', *An Oxford Companion to The Romantic Age: British Culture 1776–1832*, ed. Iain McCalman (Oxford: Oxford University Press, 1999), 17–26: 24.
²⁷ Anonymous, 'The Age of War', *Courier* (8 November 1798); quoted in Betty T. Bennett, ed., *British War Poetry in the Age of Romanticism: 1793–1815* (New York: Garland, 1976), 215.
²⁸ Colley, *Britons*, 327.
²⁹ Some 40,639 men were discharged on account of wounds or infirmity between 1794 and 1796 (Bainbridge, *British Poetry and the Revolutionary and Napoleonic Wars*, 6).
³⁰ Richard Holmes, *Redcoat: The British Soldier in the Age of Horse and Musket* (London: HarperCollins, 2001), 413.
³¹ Ibid., 416.
³² Anonymous, 'The Wounded Soldier', *The Muse in Good Humour; or Momus's Banquet: A Collection of Choice Songs, Including the Modern* (London: Printed for William Lane, 1795?), 71.
³³ Anonymous, 'Illuminations', *E. Johnson's British Gazette and Sunday Monitor* (2 May 1802), unpaginated (17th–18th Century Burney Collection Newspapers).

In tableau-form this portrays the veteran as national guardian, receiving due reward and sustenance from a peace-loving monarch.

But outside illuminated displays, Britain's modern military citizens had a number of hoops to jump through before the nation's grateful assistance was granted them. As in the Elizabethan period, would-be pensioners were obliged to prove that they had come directly from active service (a letter from a commanding officer was needed as evidence), but now they were also required to show ongoing incapacity. The National Army Museum, London, holds a petition made under this regime some time after the Battle of Albuera in 1811 by a veteran known only as E. Lynch.[34] More complex than Richard Jennyns's 1594 petition, this document, which is in the form of a letter, describes Lynch's military service over the previous fifteen years. Reaching 'Barbadoes' early in 1796, he proceeded to St Kitts, St Lucia and St Vincent, where he was present at the storming of Dorsetshire Hill[35] and shot 'through the upper part of my left leg'. Back across the Atlantic at Pamplona,[36] he 'received two balls in the left arm, which destroyed the thumb and fore finger'. The wounds 'remained open twelve months' and continued to give Lynch 'great pain at the change of Weather'. Lynch's petition is a complex narrative of need, explanation and justification: desert is now founded not only on having been incapacitated on active service but on meritorious qualities such as loyalty, usefulness and professionalism. The popular song 'Chelsea Quarters' (1802–19) suggests that such qualities are not confined to pension petitions but infiltrate war-related literature of the period as generic motifs:

> To say what foes my arm has slain
> Would dastard be a venture;
> My duty ne'er regarded pain,
> In van, or rear, or centre.
> Full oft I've drenched my sword in blood,
> And forded many waters,
> In hopes when war should cease her flood
> To fix in Chelsea Quarters.[37]

---

[34] E. Lynch, 'Copy of a Letter', London: National Army Museum, 9208–23 O/S 92, 1fr. This document is a copy, certified by Lynch, of his original letter.

[35] The British took Dorsetshire Hill in St Vincent after a battle lasting from 12 to 14 March 1795 (George Thompson, *Documentary History of the African Theatre* (Chicago: Northwestern University Press, 1998), 138) during the Second Carib War (1795–7), part of the French Revolutionary Wars.

[36] The Siege of Pamplona, Spain, lasted from 19 December 1811 to 5 January 1812, part of the Peninsular War.

[37] http://ballads.bodleian.ox.ac.uk/static/images/sheets/20000/18262.gif; quoted in Roy Palmer, ed., *The Rambling Soldier* (Gloucester: Alan Sutton, 1985), 243.

Combining an indication of possible incapacity with valuable service and martial prowess in anticipation of becoming a Chelsea in-pensioner, this stanza fulfils many of the requirements of a petition.

In this new age of mass, global warfare, the veteran was an ever more prominent figure in the life of the nation. The exploits of ex-soldiers and sailors frequently made the newspapers. In June 1793, the *Sun* ran a story about a veteran who had performed a fire-trick and nearly blown himself up in the process.[38] The *True Briton* carried an advert in August 1796 for a cricket match held between eleven men with one leg each against eleven men with one arm each at the Royal Hospital Greenwich (the outcome is unrecorded),[39] while in September 1800, the *Whitehall Evening Post* described Greenwich pensioners being 'astonished' by a leapfrog display put on by 'an athletic Duke and three elastic young women of fashion'.[40] These vignettes reveal not only an affection for veterans, but also a sense of their comic potential, potential with a long literary pedigree stretching from the *miles gloriosus* or braggart-soldier of Plautine comedy and later the *commedia dell'arte* via Shakespeare's Falstaff[41] to more recent fictional works such as *The Baffled Hero* (1746), a mock-heroic account of a pudding-eating contest between two sailors and two Chelsea pensioners; Uncle Toby in Laurence Sterne's *Tristram Shandy* (1759–67);[42] and Charles Johnstone's it-narrative *Chrysal: or, The Adventures of a Guinea* (1760), which features a veteran whose only employment 'for many years' is 'talking over the actions of his youth, and comparing them to the mistakes and losses of the present times'.[43]

If the veteran was entrenched as a stock comic figure, he was also becoming a stock figure of sentiment in the literature of the period,[44]

---

[38] Anonymous, 'Country News', *Sun* (11 June 1793), unpaginated (17th–18th Century Burney Collection Newspapers).

[39] Anonymous, 'Advertisement', *True Briton* (6 August 1796), unpaginated (17th–18th Century Burney Collection Newspapers).

[40] Anonymous, 'London', *Whitehall Evening Post* (9 September 1800), unpaginated (17th–18th Century Burney Collection Newspapers).

[41] See Kate McLoughlin, *Authoring War: The Literary Representation of War from the* Iliad *to* Iraq (Cambridge: Cambridge University Press, 2011), 179.

[42] There is insufficient space to discuss *Tristram Shandy* here, as it falls outside the period on which this book concentrates. Chapter 2 of A. D. Nuttall's *A Common Sky: Philosophy and the Literary Imagination* (Berkeley, CA: University of California Press, 1974) is a brilliant analysis of the ways in which Sterne targets 'the rock hard scientific world-pictures which Locke had codified' (51). Uncle Toby does not feature significantly in Nuttall's analysis, alas.

[43] Charles Johnstone, *Chrysal: Or, The Adventures of a Guinea. Wherein are Exhibited Views of Several Striking Scenes, With Curious and Interesting Anecdotes of the Most Noted Persons in Every Rank of Life, Whose Hands It Passed Through, in America, England, Holland, Germany and Portugal* (Dublin: Printed by Dillon Chamberlaine, in Smock-Alley, 1760), 99 (Eighteenth-Century Collections Online).

[44] On the prevalence of 'soldiers' return' poems in the period, see Simon J. White, *Robert Bloomfield, Romanticism and the Poetry of Community* (Aldershot: Ashgate, 2007), 142–4. On the literary

though 'sentimentality', as Betty T. Bennett points out, covers 'a range of emotions, from realistic benevolence to romantic titillation' when applied to the eighteenth century.[45] In W. R.'s 'The Pensioner', to take one end of the spectrum, the old veteran is an object of sentimental contempla-tion: 'Yes,' muses the narrator, 'there is still something interesting to a "man of sentiment" in the conversation of an old soldier or sailor.'[46] This notably self-centred narrator takes nothing more than having witnessed 'the joy of grief' from his encounter with an old soldier,[47] but in other cases, the veteran is a means of instruction in the proper exercise of moral feelings. 'The Wounded Soldier', a verse-letter forming part of Joseph Moser's *The Adventures of Timothy Twig* (1794), is a perfect example. The author of the letter, Miss Constantia Twig, describes to her correspondent, Miss Lucy Invoice (a name redolent of financial means as well as vocal capacity ('in voice')), being disturbed in the chestnut grove by '[a] groan […] which seem'd / The sudden burst of grief'.[48] The noise proves to come from a woman 'shriek[ing] with pain' who is supported by a soldier-husband and two children.[49] The veteran is a man 'affrighted, feeble, weak, / Lame, half bereft of life, / On crutch upheld'.[50] Constantia directs her servant to guide the family to a cottage on the estate: 'for them provide, / And sooth their wretched state'.[51] The veteran comments on this munificence:

> Disabl'd, sick, a twelve-month past,
> In England we arrived,
> War, climates, storms o'ercome at last,

representation of the veteran in the late eighteenth and early nineteenth centuries, see further Mary Favret, 'Coming Home: The Public Spaces of Romantic War', *Studies in Romanticism* 33.4 (Winter 1994), 539–48: 544; Simon Parkes, 'Home from the Wars: the Romantic Revenant-Veteran of the 1790s', unpublished PhD thesis (University of Warwick, 2009); Simon Parkes, 'Cultural Transfer, Wartime Anxiety and the *Lenore* Translations of 1796', *Romanticism* 17 (2011), 175–85; Simon Parkes, '"More Dead than Alive": The Return of Not-Orlando in Charlotte Smith's *The Old Manor House*', *European Romantic Review* 22.6 (2011), 765–84; Simon Parkes, 'Wooden Legs and Tales of Sorrow Done: The Literary Broken Soldier of the Late Eighteenth Century', *Journal for Eighteenth-Century Studies* 36.2 (June 2013), 191–207; Caroline Nielsen, 'Continuing to Serve: Representations of the Elderly Veteran Soldier in the Late Eighteenth and Early Nineteenth Centuries', *Men After War*, ed. Stephen McVeigh and Nicola Cooper (London: Routledge, 2013), 18–35; and Philip Shaw, *Suffering and Sentiment in Romantic Military Art* (Farnham: Ashgate, 2013).

[45] Betty T. Bennett, 'Introduction', *British War Poetry in the Age of Romanticism*, ed. Bennett, 1–67: 49.
[46] W. R., 'The Pensioner', *Lady's Monthly Museum* (1 April 1811), 229–32: 230.
[47] Ibid., 232.
[48] Joseph Moser, *The Adventures of Timothy Twig, Esq. in a Series of Poetical Epistles*, 1/2 vols (London: printed for B. and T. Williams, 1794), 60 (Eighteenth-Century Collections Online).
[49] Ibid., 61.
[50] Ibid., 61.
[51] Ibid., 62.

All those I had surviv'd.
In Bristole first we shelter found,
Where short report we tasted,
But illness, from my uncur'd wound,
Our slender pittance wasted.
Oblig'd by law to leave the place,
And driven from door to door,
By (mild humanity's disgrace)
The guardians of the poor.
Our settlement in Wales to gain,
We slowly travel'd on,
But found, thro' poverty and pain,
Our strength and spirits gone;
Till your benevolence reliev'd,
In the late painful hour,
A fainting wife, a father griev'd,
And babes that want, o'erpower.[52]

This speech combines testimony of service and incapacity with a narrative of having been let down by the state. But this official neglect is not emphasized: instead the poem promotes private 'benevolence'. Here, the veteran is what Simon Parkes, after a phrase in Defoe's *Memoirs of a Cavalier* (1720), calls the 'Broken Soldier': 'the smashed recipient of Sensibility's self-conscious benevolence' who allows 'those of a genteel persuasion to imagine themselves as responsible citizens of an enlightened society'.[53] The same can be said of the figures depicted in works such as Oliver Goldsmith's *The Deserted Village* (1770), Henry Mackenzie's *The Man of Feeling* (1771), Robert Anderson's 'The Soldier: A Fragment' (1798), Thomas Dermody's 'The Invalid' (1800) and Anne Bannerman's 'The Soldier' (1800). As an aesthetic exemplar, the veteran's tale has been transformed from a piece of inflationary farce into a jeremiad.

Other works of the period engaged in more radical critiques of the state's deficiencies in its care for former members of the armed forces. 'The Naval Subaltern', published in the *Star* on 30 September 1796, features one Ben Block, 'a veteran of naval renown', for whom fame is the 'only reward'.[54] Though 'year after year, in a subaltern state, / Poor Ben for his King fought and bled', he has been left in destitution, 'For the Board still

---

[52] Ibid., 63.
[53] Parkes, 'Wooden Legs and Tales of Sorrow Done', 191.
[54] Anonymous, 'The Naval Subaltern', *Star* (30 September 1796), unpaginated (17th–18th Century Burney Collection Newspapers).

neglected his merits to Crown, / As no interest he had with my Lord'.[55] This is the most explicit reference to the pension system administered by the Royal Hospitals, but other poems – 'Pacificus'' 'Effects of War' (1793); the anonymous 'The Tender's Hold, Or, Sailor's Complaint' (1794); Joseph Badworth's 'Half-Pay' (1794); John Clare's 'The Wounded Soldier', 'Poor Soldier' and 'The Disabled Soldier' (all written 1808–19); the anonymous 'The Soliloquy of a Sailor' (1814); Peter Pindar's (alias John Wolcot's) 'Ode to a Poor Soldier of Tilbury Fort' (1816); Robert Anderson's 'Poor Will' (1820) – reinforce the impression that the poorest members of society are exploited during wartime and then abandoned by the rich and powerful.

Veterans of the French Revolutionary and Napoleonic Wars continued to make appearances in literature long after the wars' conclusion, finding their way into works by Charles Dickens, William Thackeray, Elizabeth Gaskell and Thomas Hardy. They were joined, as the nineteenth century progressed, by veterans of campaigns in Afghanistan, the Crimea, India, Africa and the Middle East, featuring in works by Edward Bulwer-Lytton, Ouida, Charlotte Yonge, Wilkie Collins, Rhoda Broughton, Ellen Wood, Arthur Conan Doyle and Rudyard Kipling. In 1847, the Limited Enlistment Act reduced the length of military service and the severity of military discipline in an effort 'to remove much of the stigma attached to soldiering'.[56] This improving measure was followed, in 1870, by the 'Cardwell Reforms' – a set of military reforms steered through Parliament by the Secretary of State for War Edward Cardwell, which established a reserve force in Britain.[57] Military service now took the form of a short term with the army, followed by a commitment to serve again if required. The result was a constant stream of men re-entering civilian life: a veteran bonanza. But these returning veterans were largely left to fend for themselves and many faced destitution. Help came from voluntary sources. In 1885, an Association for Promoting the Employment in Civil Life of Reserve and Discharged Soldiers was founded. In 1896, from an outflow of 24,051 men, the Association found employment for 7,604, mostly as servants, grooms, labourers, porters and messengers. Giving a paper on the subject to the Royal United Service Institution on 3 March 1893, Commander Wallace B. McHardy, Chief Constable of Lanarkshire, lamented 'the hundreds! aye, the thousands! or ten thousands!' of 'successful and well-to-do' soldiers

[55] Ibid.

[56] See Neil Ramsey, ' "A Real English Soldier": Suffering, Manliness and Class in the Mid-Nineteenth-Century Soldiers' Tale', *Soldiering in Britain and Ireland, 1750–1850*, ed. Catriona Kennedy and Matthew McCormack (Basingstoke: Palgrave Macmillan, 2013), 137–55: 143.

[57] My information derives from Peter Reese, *Homecoming Heroes: An Account of the Reassimilation of British Military Personnel into Civilian Life* (London: Leo Cooper, 1992), ch. 4.

'lost to view' in civilian life.[58] Proposing that 'every good and deserving sol-dier' wear an approved ribbon or emblem so as to indicate his suitability for civil employment, McHardy reassured his audience that he was not referring to 'the case of the 'ne'er-do-weel': 'candidly speaking, we take no very special interest in him'.[59] An anonymous pamphlet of 1891 entitled *Soldiers' Grievances* reinforced the point: 'soldiers, as a rule, do not know what work is when they quit the colours, hence any kind of employment in civil life appears to them to be over-worked'.[60] Compare this with John Ruskin's remarks to an audience of young soldiers at the Royal Military Academy, Woolwich, in 1866, collected in *The Crown of Wild Olive* (1871): '[T]he great veteran soldiers of England are now men every way so thoughtful, so noble, and so good, that no other teaching than their knightly example, and their few words of grave and tried counsel should be either necessary for you, or even, without assurance of due modesty in the offerer, endured by you.'[61] Class difference contributes to the divergence in views here: Ruskin is talking about Officers and Warrant Officers. But the doublethink delinquent/hero perception of veterans across the ranks was as influential in the nineteenth century as in the century before.

And, like its eighteenth-century predecessor, the Victorian public loved, feared, sighed over, smiled at, defended and ignored its former soldiers. Military reforms, combined with internal 'Christianizing' of the army by its Chaplain General, the cleric, novelist and journalist George Gleig, helped popularize the image of the soldier – and hence, often, the vet-eran – as 'the very embodiment of Christian virtue', an image in place by the middle of the nineteenth century and much exploited by the Church of England.[62] But it was not all *Onward, Christian Soldiers.*[63] On 30 November 1858, the *Times* published a story involving another veteran

---

[58] Wallace B. McHardy, *A Scheme For Establishing a Royal Army Society for Each County and Great City, In Order to Improve the Status of the British Soldier on his Return to Civil Life* (London: Harrison and Sons, 3 March 1893), 2.

[59] Ibid., 4. This echoes Henry Mayhew's view in *London Labour and the London Poor*, compiled in the 1840s. Mayhew thought that the 'soldier proper', who had 'all the evidence of drill and barrack life about him', more deserving than those who had been 'ejected from the army for misconduct' and 'those with whom the military dress and bearings are pure assumptions' (*London Labour and the London Poor: Those That Will Not Work*, 4/4 vols (London: Griffin, Bone, 1862), 417).

[60] Anonymous, *Soldiers' Grievances* (London: Kegan Paul, Trench, Trübner, 1891), 19.

[61] John Ruskin, *The Crown of Wild Olive: Three Lectures on Work, Traffic, and War* (New York: John Wiley, 1866), 83.

[62] Caroline Cawthorn, 'The Soldier as Hero: Images of the Military in the Novel 1815–1860', unpub-lished DPhil thesis (University of Oxford, 2006), 16, 12. I am grateful to Dr Cawthorn for permis-sion to quote from her thesis.

[63] The lyrics to the hymn 'Onward, Christian Soldiers' were written by Sabine Baring-Gould in 1865; Arthur Sullivan composed the music in 1871.

*senex amans*, one Colonel Horne, Commanding Officer of Prince Albert's Regiment of Light Infantry, who, 'while taking his morning constitutional in the neighbourhood of Winchester', had the 'misfortune' to be 'smitten with the charms of a lady' who he encountered ' "at a stile" '.[64] The young woman's step-father, having discovered letters from the Colonel calling her 'his "own darling" ' and himself (memorably) 'her "own Horne" ', gathered together the privates of the Colonel's regiment, plied them with brandy and water and encouraged them to tell him their commanding officer's age, which they guessed to be 62. The step-father then wrote a letter to Horne and his General accusing Horne of flogging his men, whereupon Horne summoned the step-father in front of the Hampshire magistrates to answer a charge of inciting mutiny. The *Times* concluded:

> The whole affair is exquisite in its absurdities, – the irresistible old Colonel, lithe and enterprising in his age, the laughing damsel facile in flirtations, the moody father-in-law vapouring to himself of a melodramatic revenge, [...] and those delightfully characteristic soldiers, ready to drink the health of anybody who would pay for the liquor, and deciding to tell the stepfather a fiction to save themselves the trouble of finding out the fact.[65]

Plenty for everyone to enjoy, in other words, but, while relishing the story, the *Times* sounded a note of warning: 'Old gentlemen will have their follies, but it is scarcely advisable to indulge them at the head of a regiment.'[66]

Such antics aside, the association between veterancy, reliability and capability endured. Old soldiers were widely considered a better military bet than novices. On 16 July 1857, for instance, at the height of the Indian Mutiny, the *Times* recommended that veteran troops 'inured to a hot climate and the exigencies of a campaign' be deployed there from the Cape colony in South Africa.[67] A letter published in the paper two months later argued passionately that there were many 'old officers' who, 'though past the physical strength of middle age', had 'their mental vigour unimpaired and their martial fire unquenched'.[68] 'Havelock himself, remember', noted the letter-writer succinctly, 'is no chicken.'[69] The theme of the superiority of the old war-horse over the raw recruit was a particular favourite of

---

[64] Anonymous, 'An Amorous Old Gentleman is the Stock Property', *Times* (30 November 1858), 6 (The *Times* Digital Archive).

[65] Ibid., 6.

[66] Ibid., 6.

[67] Anonymous, 'The Danger of the Crisis in the North-Western', *Times* (16 July 1875), 9 (The *Times* Digital Archive).

[68] 'Old Soldiers', *Times* (25 September 1857), 10 (The *Times* Digital Archive).

[69] Ibid., 10.

Kipling's. In his short story 'The Drums of the Fore and Aft' (1888), for instance, the narrator remarks that an inexperienced young soldier, 'suddenly introduced to an enemy' who is 'always ugly, generally tall and hairy, and frequently noisy', will, if he 'looks to the right and left and sees old soldiers – men of twelve years' service, who, he knows, know what they are about' – be 'consoled' and apply his shoulder to the butt of his rifle 'with a stout heart'.[70]

From the veteran as safe pair of hands it is a short step to the veteran as an elder to be respected and venerated. This figure appears in William Lisle Bowles's poem 'The Blind Soldier and His Daughter' (1892) and in the opening, highly convoluted story of Charles Dickens's *The Seven Poor Travellers* (1854). But in Trooper George in *Bleak House* (1852–3), Dickens creates a more complex figure: 'rolling stone', 'old vagabond', prodigal, filial, incorruptible, sunny-tempered, tender, brave.[71] George has the 'sunburnt smile' and 'swarthy forehead' that denote military service overseas (Dickens does not specify the location). As seen in Chapter 1, tanned skin can figure weathered wisdom but George is more of a holy fool than an experienced hand.[72] The latter description better fits Mrs Bagnet (aka 'the old girl'), wife of the ex-artilleryman Matthew Bagnet and, having accompanied her husband on his military tours, a veteran herself. Reunited with his mother after his wrongful imprisonment, George would be a figure of pathos, were it not that his sense of propriety makes him adamantine. From here it is another short step to the veteran reprising his role as the object of sentimentality. Dickens exploits this aspect of veterancy in his *Seven Poor Travellers* story as does John Stuart Blackie in his poem 'The Old Soldier of the Gareloch Head' (1860). But for both filial piety and sentimentality, it is hard to beat Thomas Aird's poem 'The Old Soldier' (1852).

This three-part work opens with the Old Soldier using his wooden leg to poke the fire in order to give himself sufficient light for his basket-weaving, a scene that manages to combine meritorious service, personal sacrifice, need, resourcefulness, lack of self-pity, pathos, industry and virtue. His 'simple supper o'er', he reads the Bible, then smokes his pipe 'Musing on days of yore, and battles old, / And many a friend and comrade dead and

---

[70] Rudyard Kipling, *Kipling and War: From 'Tommy' to 'My Boy Jack'*, ed. Andrew Lycett (London: I. B. Tauris, 2015), 40.

[71] Charles Dickens, *Bleak House* [1852–3], ed. Stephen Gill (Oxford: Oxford University Press, 2008), 500. On Trooper George's unification of militarism and nurturing, see Holly Furneaux, *Queer Dickens: Erotics, Families, Masculinities* (Oxford: Oxford University Press, 2009), 214–22.

[72] Dickens, *Bleak House*, 500.

gone'.[73] Patient, patriotic, beloved by the local children, the 'Old Soldado' yet grieves a daughter, lost in a storm at sea.[74] This paragon of admirable yet lonely uncomplainingness established, the veteran then receives two visitors – a blind, one-armed sailor and his daughter, to whom he serves bread and honey. The sailor feels 'sudden pangs' and collapses; as he dies, he asks his daughter to let him kiss the cross she wears around her neck.[75] This the Old Soldier recognizes: it '[w]as round my daughter's neck, when in the deep / She perished from me, on that fatal night / The "Sphinx" was burnt, forth sailing from the Clyde'.[76] The sailor dies, and the birth-father and daughter, reunited, spend their days 'in peace and love'.[77] The girl will have to be a good listener, since 'all his wars the old campaigner told'.[78]

'The Old Soldier' brings together a number of themes: mistaken identity, the supernatural, storytelling. It also makes clear the veteran's isolation. Before the reunion with his daughter, the Old Soldado is notably 'dispeopled'.[79] Adulation and neglect comprised the combined public attitude faced by a great number of veterans returning from overseas service in the nineteenth century. Henry Metcalfe, born 1835 in Cumbria, enlisted at the age of 13 and served in India and South Africa. In 1857, having survived the Siege of Lucknow, he returned to Britain on a cholera-ridden ship – a voyage, which, he said in his 1858 memoirs, 'beggar[ed] description'.[80] The troops disembarked at Gravesend and took a train to Dover where there were 'no less than three military bands playing us from the station to the barracks to the old air See the Conquering Heroes Come'.[81] The streets and windows were 'beautifully decorated' with flags and banners proclaiming 'Welcome the Heroes of Lucknow – Welcome the Protectors of Women

[73] Thomas Aird, 'The Old Soldier', *Blackwood's Edinburgh Magazine* 71.436 (February 1852), 236–41, 236.

[74] Ibid., 237.

[75] Ibid., 239.

[76] Ibid., 240.

[77] Ibid., 241.

[78] Ibid., 241. Cf. a *Times* report of 14 October 1858 of the death of one Abraham Bold, a sergeant in the 7th Fusiliers and holder of a medal with eleven clasps representing service in the battles of Busaco, Albuera, Cuidad Rodrigo, Badajoz, Salamanca, Vittoria, Pyrnees, Nivelles, the Nive, Orthez and Toulouse: 'Nothing delighted Bold more in his later days than to get a few companions around him in an evening, to whom he would recount the story of his life. At such times his eye sparkled with all the vigour of youth, and his simple yet earnest delineation of the dangers he had encountered was sure to gain the undivided attention of his hearers' ('Death of a Veteran', *Times* (14 October 1858), 4 (The *Times* Digital Archive)).

[79] Aird, 'The Old Soldier', 241.

[80] Henry Metcalfe, *The Chronicle of Henry Metcalfe H. M. 32nd Regiment of Foot* [1858] (London: Cassell, 1953), 80

[81] Ibid., 88.

and Children'.[82] A fine reception. But Metcalfe concludes his account on a negative note:

> This was all very nice and grand and gratifying to the War-worn soldier and gave us to understand that we were not forgotten by a grateful public for our services. And so it would be if the same feeling always remained but our deeds like everything else were soon forgot by that grateful public [...] Such is the soldier and such is the grateful public.[83]

The fickleness of public attitudes to those who have fought in their name is Kipling's great theme – expressed in poems such as 'The Last of the Light Brigade' (1890) and 'The Absent-Minded Beggar' (1900) and, most famously, in his 1890 ballad 'Tommy': 'O it's Tommy this, an' Tommy that, an' "Tommy, go away"'; / But it's "Thank you, Mister Atkins", when the band begins to play.'[84]

The most telling couplet in 'Tommy' is 'We aren't no thin red 'eroes, nor we aren't no blackguards too, / But single men in barricks, most remarkable like you':[85] a veteran's plea to be treated neither as hero nor delinquent but as a working man meriting appropriate recompense for a dangerous job. But if, as Peter Reese reports, the Boer Wars brought 'a new level of sympathy for the British Soldier', official provision for returning troops remained inadequate.[86] 'Dedicated amateurism' remained 'the order of the day'.[87] And this mishmash of well-meaning, variously competent charitable organizations was the support system in place for veterans as Britain entered the First World War.

And now veterancy became the lot of a generation. The First World War produced almost 6 million British veterans.[88] Nearly a million of them – 12 times the strength of the original British Expeditionary Force – were disabled.[89] Some 30,000 had lost an eye, 34,000 had lost at least one limb.[90]

---

[82] Ibid., 88.
[83] Ibid., 89.
[84] Rudyard Kipling, *Selected Poems*, ed. Peter Keating (Harmondsworth: Penguin, 2000), 18–20: 18.
[85] Ibid., 19.
[86] Reese, *Homecoming Heroes*, 67.
[87] Ibid., 71.
[88] Ibid., 99.
[89] Ibid., 76, 99.
[90] Ibid., 95. The figures are notoriously difficult to ascertain. Sarah Cole states that 3.5 million men were on active duty in the British services at the time of the armistice; roughly 1.6 million had serious physical wounds and another 200,000 suffered from severe mental disorders (*Modernism, Male Friendship, and the First World War* (Cambridge: Cambridge University Press, 2003), 188). Joanna Bourke writes that 41,000 men had limbs amputated during the war, 272,000 had injuries to arms and legs that did not require amputation, 60,500 had injuries to the head and eyes, 89,000 had other serious injuries to the body (*Dismembering the Male: Men's Bodies, Britain and the Great War* (London: Reaktion, 1996), 33).

On demobilization, each former serviceman was entitled to unemployment benefits of 24 shillings a week for a maximum of 20 weeks.[91] For
the wounded, the Soldiers and Sailors Help Society, a charity, provided
convalescent facilities, training and sheltered employment.[92] Lord Roberts
Memorial Workshops, also charitably funded, were established in Fulham,
Colchester, Liverpool, Newcastle, Burnley, Lancaster and Bristol for those
too severely disabled to get work.[93] And in 1921, as an amalgamation of
various existing groups of ex-servicemen and their supporters, the British
Legion – from 1925, the *Royal* British Legion – was founded. Copying
the Memorial Poppy programme begun in the United States, the Legion
organized the first Poppy Appeal in 1921, raising £10,400.[94] In 1922 the
first Poppy Factory, offering work to severely disabled veterans, began production. Nearly 23 million poppies were made in the first year.[95] Together
with the Two Minutes' Silence and the Tomb of the Unknown Warrior,
the poppy – a simple assemblage of two pieces of paper, red and green,
and two pieces of plastic, green and black – has become indissociable from
veterancy in British minds. These voluntary, philanthropic initiatives by
the Legion and other bodies were as important symbolically as they were
substantively. Veterans *noticed*, and appreciated, them. It was evidence,
as Deborah Cohen puts it, that 'their fellow citizens had honored their
sacrifices'.[96] So much could not be said of the British state.

For, valiant as philanthropic efforts were, they weren't enough.[97] Despite
the charitable initiatives, in mid-1924 Britain had 600,000 unemployed
veterans.[98] Housing was another problem; rents were rising, as were
prices.[99] The 'penniless veteran begging on the pavement' became 'one of

---

[91] Peter Reese, *Homecoming Heroes*, 103.
[92] Ibid., 93.
[93] Ibid., 93–5.
[94] Ibid., 127.
[95] www.poppyfactory.org/history-timeline/#timeline; Reese, *Homecoming Heroes*, 127.
[96] Deborah Cohen, *The War Come Home: Disabled Veterans in Britain and Germany, 1914–1939*
(Berkeley, CA: University of California Press, 2001), 7. On the re-integration of disabled veterans in
Britain after the First World War, see further C. W. [Cecil William] Hutt, *The Future of the Disabled
Soldier* (New York: William Wood, 1917); Jeffrey S. Reznick, 'Work-Therapy and the Disabled
British Soldier in Great Britain in the First World War: The Case of Shepherd's Bush Military
Hospital, London', *Disabled Veterans in History*, ed. Gerber, 185–203.
[97] Peter Reese cites a number of ways in which demobilization arrangements were 'bungled': in-
service training opportunities were inadequate; the voluntary associations were overwhelmed by
the numbers; employment opportunities for disabled veterans depended on the public spirit of
employers, which was wanting; housing was in too short supply; the British Legion's relatively late
formation was a 'tragedy' (*Homecoming Heroes*, 136–7).
[98] Ibid., 130.
[99] Ibid., 104.

the characteristic motifs' of post-First World War Britain.[100] In this land fit for heroes to live in – Lloyd George's ringing promise to ex-servicemen on Armistice Day – the 'heroes' were moved to protest. Early 1919 saw demonstrations: 10,000 at Folkestone on 3 January, 2,000 at Dover the following day, 8,000 at Brighton two days later.[101] Serious strikes followed.[102] Most agonizing was the division between civilian and combatant. Peter Reese quotes Charles Quinnell, who had lost a leg in France, on the point: 'One thing I really noticed was that after being with the young fellows in the Army we were a race apart from civilians. You couldn't talk to civilians about war, they hadn't got the slightest conception of what conditions were and so forth. So after a time you didn't talk about it.'[103] But some did talk about it, and others talked about it on their behalf. Anger and bitterness at civilians' treatment of veterans erupt in poems such as Ivor Gurney's 'Strange Hells' (1917), in which former members of the Gloucestershire Regiment, their hearts burning with shame, are reduced to 'showing shop-patterns / Or walking town to town sore in borrowed tatterns',[104] and Vera Brittain's 'The Lament of the Demobilised' (1920), in which the veteran speakers returning after four years' service to their country find that 'we / Must just go back and start again once more'.[105] ' "The more fool you!" ' cry Brittain's complacent citizens, and, in a long, dry, extra-metrical line – it's as if the poetry suddenly stops being poetry and starts being something altogether more menacing – her veterans take note: 'we're beginning to agree with them'.[106]

The ravages of the First World War – the millions dead, the millions harmed, the global reach, the longevity, the industrialized nature of its weaponry, the political, economic and social consequences – are still being grappled with. In very practical literary terms, as D. J. Taylor points out, it meant that no male character could be introduced into a text with a contemporary setting 'without a description of what he had or had not done in the war'.[107] This makes it a nigh-impossible task to enumerate

---

[100] Alan Allport, *Demobbed: Coming Home After the Second World War* (New Haven, CT: Yale University Press, 2009), 5.

[101] Ibid., 103.

[102] Ibid., 104.

[103] Imperial War Museum Sound Records 554/18, Pte Quinnell, Charles Robert; quoted in Peter Reese, *Homecoming Heroes*, 148.

[104] Ivor Gurney, *Collected Poems of Ivor Gurney*, ed. Pat Kavanagh (Oxford: Oxford University Press, 1984), 140–1: 141.

[105] Vera Brittain, 'The Lament of the Demobilised' [1920], *Scars Upon My Heart. Women's Poetry and Verse of the First World War*, ed. Catherine Reilly (London: Virago, 1981), 14.

[106] Ibid.

[107] D. J. Taylor, *The Prose Factory: Literary Life in England Since 1918* (London: Chatto and Windus, 2016), 4.

the appearances of the First World War veteran in literature (extricating the figure from accounts of the war more generally is a problem in itself), but some examples can be picked out. Scathing accounts of the war by veterans themselves, autobiographically based but couched in a variety of genres, began to appear some ten years after the war – Edmund Blunden's *Undertones of War* in 1928, R. C. Sherriff's *Journey's End* in 1928, Robert Graves's *Good-Bye to All That* in 1929, Siegfried Sassoon's *Memoirs of an Infantry Officer* and Frederic Manning's *Her Privates We* in 1930. The First World War veteran also appears in the works of literary modernists – Richard Aldington, Mary Butts, T. S. Eliot, Ford Madox Ford, D. H. Lawrence, John Rodker, Rebecca West and Virginia Woolf – most famously in the guise of the shell-shocked Septimus Warren Smith (discussed in Chapter 5).

Lawrence, in particular, was unable to let the figure alone. He wrote about veterans before the First World War in stories such as 'In the Shadow of a Rose Garden' and 'The Prussian Officer' (both published in 1914). Thereafter, having been found physically unfit for military service himself (an experience recorded in all its deep humiliation in *Kangaroo* (1923)), he strove, in pieces such as his poetry sequence *All Of Us*, to demystify the Western Front, drawing connections between men engaged in trench warfare, land-workers in rural Egypt and the miners of his native Nottinghamshire.[108] In *Lady Chatterley's Lover* (1928) his complex attitude to veterancy receives its richest treatment. Clifford Chatterley and Oliver Mellors are both ex-officers but, while Clifford is the relict of the industrialized First World War, Mellors has served in Egypt and India, apparently without seeing actual combat. Mellors thinks back fondly on his military service as time spent with 'the colonel who had loved him and whom he had loved':[109] he is the embodiment of the elemental life forces that Lawrence so valued. But in his wheelchair, 'a hurt thing', 'not in actual touch with anybody', Clifford is aligned with what Lawrence saw as the evil of both Bolshevism and Capitalism – their ineluctable tendency to render '[e]ach man a machine-part'; the feared and sterile detritus of an industrialized war machine.[110]

Eliot, whose attempts to join the military were also, for different reasons, unsuccessful,[111] plays off veterancy and non-veterancy. Though the speaker

---

[108] See Kate McLoughlin, '*All of Us*: D. H. Lawrence's First World War Poems for the People', *Journal of D. H. Lawrence Studies* 4 (2015), 45–66.

[109] D. H. Lawrence, *Lady Chatterley's Lover* [1928] (Harmondsworth: Penguin, 1961), 147.

[110] Ibid., 16, 40.

[111] See Robert Crawford, *Young Eliot: From St Louis to The Waste Land* (London: Jonathan Cape, 2015), 303–6.

of 'Gerontion' (1920) is an old man, his advanced age is not matched by commensurate experience. So much is evident in the poem's opening section in which veterancy is – as though in some biblical parody – thrice denied:

> I was neither at the hot gates
> Nor fought in the warm rain
> Nor knee deep in the salt marsh, heaving a cutlass,
> Bitten by flies, fought.
>
> (ll. 3–6)[112]

But this little old man[113] who has not fought here and not fought there and not fought in that place either is a talker. In Vincent Sherry's shrewd analysis, he belongs to 'the senescence of contemporary Liberalism', a generation that 'authored in words a war' that it did not fight in body and so deserved the label of 'garrulous gerontocracy'.[114] Nothing but an empty old chatterbox, then (if a lethal one), and an anti-Semitic chatterbox at that, who, lacking experience, 'lacks the wisdom to teach'.[115] Nonetheless, this discredited character has the temerity to tell other people what to think. Five times the imperative is issued – and this to an age sick of being given orders. The thrust of the commands is the evasion of responsibility, attempted variously by blaming history ('Think now / History has many cunning passages' (ll. 33–4); 'Think now / She gives when our attention is distracted' (ll. 36–7)); embracing fatalism ('Think / Neither fear nor courage saves us' (ll. 43–4)); suggesting that what is at work is larger than any individual ('Think at last / We have not reached conclusion, when I / Stiffen in a rented house' (ll. 48–50)); and making a last desperate claim of good faith ('Think at last / I have not made this show purposelessly / And it is not by any concitation / Of the backward devils' (ll. 50–3)). After such knowledge, why should anyone think any of these things? Eliot defined 'Gerontion' as 'a kind of preliminary stage'

---

[112] The edition of Eliot's poem used is *The Poems of T. S. Eliot. Volume I: Collected and Uncollected Poems*, ed. Christopher Ricks and Jim McCue (London: Faber and Faber, 2015). Line numbers are given in the text.

[113] A diminutive of γέρων (Eliot, *The Poems of T. S. Eliot. Volume I*, ed. Ricks and McCue, 46).

[114] Vincent Sherry, *The Great War and the Language of Modernism* (Oxford: Oxford University Press, 2003), 208. As Sherry indicates, the phrase derives from C. K. Ogden, who criticized the conscription campaign that had 'once more let loose upon the world that gerontocratic garrulity which seemed for a time to have been shamed into silence by the holocausts of young men' ('The One Thing Needful: A Suggestion to Members of Parliament', *The Cambridge Magazine* 5.11 (29 January 1915), 240–1).

[115] Anthony Julius, *T. S. Eliot, Anti-Semitism and Literary Form* (Cambridge: Cambridge University Press, 1996), 42.

to *The Waste Land* (1922),[116] and the injunction to 'Think' by the non-veteran Gerontion finds its response in that poem in the section entitled 'A Game of Chess'. Here, a veteran is yet again told to 'Think':

> My nerves are bad tonight. Yes, bad. Stay with me.
> Speak to me. Why do you never speak. Speak.
> What are you thinking of? What thinking? What?
> I never know what you are thinking. Think.
>
> (ll. 111–14)

But there is no audible reply. Instead, we hear a veteran *not* speaking, since all we are given are the spaces where his replies should be and his inner thoughts:

> I think we are in rats' alley
> Where the dead men lost their bones.
>
> (ll. 115–16)

'Rats' alley' is the hint that the consciousness represented here has First World War experience – it was the nickname of one of the trenches on the Gallipoli peninsula.[117] Urged to 'Think', this consciousness turns, not to the grand revolutions of the wheels of history, but to the personal memory of men dying in mud. The importance of this representation cannot be overstated: we actually hear a silent veteran thinking.

Beyond literary modernism, there are portrayals of veterans in the decades after the First World War in works as various as A. E. Housman's 'Soldier from the Wars Returning' (1922), Dorothy L. Sayers's Lord Peter Wimsey detective novels (1923–37) (discussed in Chapter 3), Nan Shepherd's little-known melancholy novel *The Weatherhouse* (1930) and Nancy Mitford's comic *The Pursuit of Love* (1945). Memorably, the representation of veterancy in this last is Uncle Matthew with his entrenching tool. Ted Hughes's father served at Gallipoli and in France in the Lancashire Fusiliers and the First World War haunts Hughes's poetry. Hughes is writing about the war even when he doesn't appear to be, which may owe something to his veteran father's 'refusal to tell' of his experiences in it.[118] Addressing his father directly in 'For the Duration' (1985), the poet remarks 'what alarmed me most / Was your silence'.[119] In the last decade of the twentieth century,

---

[116] Eliot, *The Poems of T. S. Eliot. Volume I*, ed. Ricks and McCue, 468.

[117] See Sandra Gilbert, ' "Rats' Alley": The Great War; Modernism, and the (Anti)Pastoral Elegy', *New Literary History* 30 (1999), 179–201: 198.

[118] Ted Hughes, *Collected Poems*, ed. Paul Keegan (London: Faber and Faber, 2003), 760–1: 760.

[119] Ibid., 760.

the First World War veteran enjoyed a literary renaissance in Pat Barker's enormously successful *Regeneration* trilogy. In their fictionalization of the experiences of Wilfred Owen and Siegfried Sassoon at Craiglockhart Hydropathic Hospital, the three novels powerfully reinforce the nexus between veterancy, trauma and writing.

Less than twenty-one years later they were at it again. This time, the numbers were even greater. On VE Day in 1945, over 5 million Britons were in uniform, nine-tenths of them male.[120] Most had been in the forces since at least 1941.[121] Millions were abroad, scattered across the globe 'from Norway to the Kenyan highlands to the fringes of Antarctica'.[122] More than 250,000 had been overseas continuously for over five years.[123] Forty thousand had been held in captivity for the same length of time.[124] Not surprisingly, dismantling this gargantuan military machine was voted 'the most urgent postwar challenge facing the nation'.[125] *The Journey Home*, a report prepared for Mass-Observation in 1944, warned that the exercise would require 'prolonged social discipline among millions of people'.[126] The task of organizing the demobilization fell to the Labour politician Ernest Bevin, wartime Minister of Labour and National Service.[127] Bevin's demob plan was simple. The release date of those in Class A was worked out by age and length of service, with the oldest and longest serving brought home first. Those in Class B – men in 'vital' occupations (coal-mining, building and civil engineering, teaching, the police) – were discharged ahead of their Class A comrades. Demobilization began on Monday 18 June 1945 but progress was slow: four-fifths of men serving on VE Day would still be in the forces on 1 January 1946 and one-fifth of them on 31 December of that year.

Lessons had been learnt from the First World War. Attempts were made to prepare servicemen for civilian life through training before release and what Peter Reese calls 'sound and workable plans' were put in place to help the disabled.[128] Alongside the official Forces Resettlement Service,

---

[120] Allport, *Demobbed*, 3. Alan Allport's book is the definitive guide to Second World War demobilization in Britain.

[121] Ibid., 3.

[122] Ibid., 3.

[123] Ibid., 3.

[124] Ibid., 223 n7.

[125] This is cited in Anthony Burgess, *Little Wilson and Big God* (London: Heinemann, 1987), 85; quoted in Allport, *Demobbed*, 4.

[126] Anonymous, *The Journey Home: A Report Prepared by Mass-Observation for the Advertising Service Guild* (London: John Murray, 1944), 23.

[127] The data in this paragraph are derived from Allport, *Demobbed*, 23–48.

[128] Reese, *Homecoming Heroes*, 209.

there existed a 'vast mosaic' of regimental associations, benevolent funds and voluntary charities, the last including the Royal British Legion, whose membership passed the million mark in 1947.[129] The government issued booklets – *Release and Resettlement* and *For Your Guidance* – explaining to veterans their rights and giving practical advice, and these were supplemented by a host of other publications. Indeed, Alan Allport suggests that it was the Second World War and its attendant problems that gave 'the self-help guide a wholly respectable place on the nation's bookshelves' and accelerated 'the British embrace of therapy culture'.[130]

Help, whether of the self-administered variety or otherwise, was needed, for when Britain's Second World War veterans did eventually return, it was to a nation reeling from six years of total war. Britain had changed 'from the world's second largest creditor to its greatest debtor'.[131] After President Truman ended financial support in August 1945, the country was left to manage with a 'completely inadequate' $3.75 billion loan from the United States negotiated by John Maynard Keynes and some assistance via the Marshall Plan. Attempts to bolster its war-torn economy comprised a severe devaluation of the pound in 1949 and 'years of pinched consumerism'.[132] David Kynaston sums up 'Austerity Britain' in a long list of un-availables: 'Meat rationed, butter rationed, lard rationed, margarine rationed, sugar rationed, tea rationed, cheese rationed, jam rationed, eggs rationed, sweets rationed, soap rationed, clothes rationed. Make do and mend.'[133]

Barely recognizable, then, was the country that Second World War veterans came home to. They were greeted, not very enthusiastically, by '[t]hin, threadbare' civilians.[134] And this is where the experience of returning veterans differs from those in any previous war. Between 1939 and 1945, 62,464 civilians died from war-related causes in Britain – the majority from German bombing – and 86,000 were seriously wounded.[135] Their daily lives had also been disrupted by the war, whether in the form of requisitioning or rationing or being called up in auxiliary occupations. As Allport writes, '[t]he war's equality of sacrifice undermined the discharged

[129] Ibid., 217.

[130] Allport, *Demobbed*, 55.

[131] Joanna Bourke, *The Second World War: A People's History* (Oxford: Oxford University Press, 2001), 203.

[132] Allport, *Demobbed*, 29–30.

[133] David Kynaston, *Austerity Britain 1945–51* (London: Bloomsbury, 2007), 20.

[134] Allport, *Demobbed*, 111.

[135] Ibid., 3.

man's entitlement to special treatment'.[136] Civilians were *tired* – 'physically
and mentally exhausted', says Allport; 'fatigue[d]' says Kynaston[137] – and
'not in the best or most generous of spirits'.[138] Maurice Merritt, who had
been a driver in the Eighth Army, got the impression that 'a soldier wearing
his medals' was liable 'to annoy civilians'.[139] The writer Anthony Burgess
had 'to apologise for being in the army'.[140] An anonymous veteran writing
in the *Manchester Guardian* in September 1945 described how two taxi-
drivers refused to give him a ride from Euston Station after the arduous
journey back from his Mediterranean posting. 'I […] mentioned that after
a long period of foreign service one was not unanxious to get home,' he
noted, adding drily that, at least, '[n]o conductress has yet fainted on any
bus I have boarded'.[141] There was a suspicion that those away in the military
had actually had it *easier* than civilians, a suspicion that hardened attitudes
in already straitened circumstances. The *Guardian* thought that everyone
should loosen up a little. 'What should go,' advised an editorial in July
1945, 'is the control mentality – the fondness for saying no, the refusal to
take a little trouble to adjust restrictive routine, the reluctance to discrim-
inate between controls that are necessary for reconstruction and controls
which were justified only by exigencies of war.'[142]

But the 'control mentality' wasn't the only source of frustration.
Employment was a major problem – this was, after all, the return-to-work
of over 4 million men.[143] The Reinstatement in Civil Employment Act
1944 required employers to rehire for at least six months ex-workers who
had served in the forces. The Ministry of Labour's Resettlement Advice
Service also tried to help, its centres receiving 2.5 million visits from veterans by the end of 1946. The government distributed grants to would-be
veteran small businessmen, and veterans also received gratuities, postwar
credits and back pay. Nonetheless, civilian suspicion, reluctant employers,
non-transferrable military skills and the difficulties of reporting to younger
men who had been promoted in the interim all hampered the process of
re-employment. And, as the Australian psychiatrist Reginald Ellery noted

---

[136] Ibid., 76.
[137] Ibid., 11; Kynaston, *Austerity Britain*, 97.
[138] Allport, *Demobbed*, 11.
[139] Maurice Merritt, *Eighth Army Driver* (Tunbridge Wells: Midas Books, 1981), 180; quoted in Allport, *Demobbed*, 108.
[140] Burgess, *Little Wilson and Big God*, 333.
[141] Anonymous, 'Things Are Tricky', *Guardian* (17 September 1945), 4.
[142] Anonymous, 'Impatience', *Guardian* (15 July 1945), 4.
[143] Allport, *Demobbed*, 134. The data on veteran employment in this paragraph derive from Allport, *Demobbed*, 134–57.

in *Psychiatric Aspects of Modern Warfare* (1945), the veteran had problems even when employment had been found:

> It is not easy [for an ex-serviceman] to settle down to study or to apply himself to constant work. The life he has led in uniform has unfitted him for steady application; he is easily distracted by trifles. He looks instinctively for diversion or becomes apathetic and a little bewildered at the tasks which confront him. His routine is broken; he can neither pick up his tools nor open his text-books.[144]

If working-life was problematic, so too was family life. The Britain of 1945, writes Allport, 'was a country quietly tormented by sexual suspicion'.[145] William Franklin, an ex-POW, described a reunion with his wife very different to that which he had imagined in captivity: ' "*You have changed!*" was her comment, with a brief embrace. I was embarrassed, and could not reply [...] I realized that after four years, with no communication, we were total strangers. It was difficult to convey to my buddies just how awful an experience it was. Mine was not a case of falling into each other's arms.'[146] The difficulties produced by long separation were compounded by sexual jealousy of the American GIs stationed in Britain in such large numbers – more than 1.5 million by June 1944. British servicemen began 'to nurse what became an increasingly rancorous inferiority complex towards these allegedly oversexed, certainly overpaid interlopers'.[147] Attempts were made to help – by the Marriage Guidance Council (established in 1938) and by publications such as Phoebe D. and Laurence J. Bendit's *Living Together Again* (1946) and Kenneth Howard's *Sex Problems of the Returning Soldier* (1945). (Howard recommended 'continence' to the soldier posted overseas.)[148] But the immediate postwar period saw a 'skyrocketing divorce rate': a tenfold rise in divorce petitions between 1935 and 1947.[149]

Feeling unwelcome and misunderstood, facing shortages, unemployment, homelessness and domestic problems, many of Britain's Second World War veterans suffered from mental health disorders. The Services' After-Care Scheme, organized by the National Association of Mental

---

[144] Reginald Ellery, *Psychiatric Aspects of Modern Warfare* (Melbourne: Reed and Harris, 1945), 150; quoted in Allport, *Demobbed*, 140.

[145] Allport, *Demobbed*, 85.

[146] William A. Franklin, *Through Adversity to Attainment* (Victoria, BC: Trafford, 2005), 128; quoted in Allport, *Demobbed*, 57.

[147] Allport, *Demobbed*, 91.

[148] Kenneth Howard, *Sex Problems of the Returning Soldier* (Manchester: Sydney Pemberton, 1945), 43.

[149] Allport, *Demobbed*, 87, 11.

Health, was looking after 10,000 cases in 15 centres by 1946.[150] In particular, the shift between the camaraderie of military service and the meanness, in every sense, of Civvy Street was hard to bear. The sense of loss in demobilization was noted contemporaneously by Ellery in *Psychiatric Aspects of Modern Warfare* and by the sociologist Ferdinand Zweig in *Labour, Life and Poverty* (1948). But the point is made most vividly by a P. J. Salfeld, writing in the *Manchester Guardian*:

> Yes, the years of war seem golden now that they are gone. I know that in some ways I shall not be so contented again. [...] I have never laughed so much in my life – the rather childish but very fundamental laughter springing, for instance, from the confusion that follows when a class leader mistakes his right hand for his left and thirty men march eagerly into a blank wall. [...] They will never come again [...] those times when life seemed almost too full.[151]

The pain, frustration and disappointment spilled over: as Allport notes, '[v]iolent reactions were not uncommon' among demobbed veterans. Such reactions fed the all-too-familiar view of ex-soldiers as a social threat. Even before the end of the war, an editorial in *The People* conjured up a vision of 'browned-off warriors – lauded to the skies in war, unprovided for in peace, disillusioned, cynical, angry – marching again at home this time, say on London'.[152] Something of this veteran anger, disillusionment and cynicism may have contributed to the shock Labour victory in the July 1945 General Election – the *Daily Mirror* urged readers to 'vote the soldier's way' (i.e. for Clement Attlee)[153] – but Allport notes that 'barely half' the eligible service personnel registered to vote and two-fifths of them didn't bother to vote on election day.[154] Not a 'Forces' Victory', then, but the political potential of the veteran did not go unnoticed. J. B. Priestley, for example, wrote a *Letter to a Returning Serviceman* in 1945 in which, speaking as one (First World War) veteran to another (Second World War) veteran, he described the 'citizen-soldier' as made up of a 'red' (politically active) half and a 'blue' (domestically orientated) half.[155] The 'blue half' may simply want 'to wear his own clothes, to eat what he fancies and to do no more parades', but

---

[150] Ibid., 208.

[151] P. J. Salfeld, 'Farewell to Liberty', *Guardian* (9 January 1946), 4.

[152] 'Philosopher', 'When the Boys Come Back', *The People* (14 January 1945), 2; quoted in Allport, *Demobbed*, 6.

[153] George McCarthy, '"Vote Our Way", The Soldiers Tell Relatives', *Daily Mirror* (13 June 1945), 3; quoted in Allport, *Demobbed*, 27.

[154] Allport, *Demobbed*, 28.

[155] J. B. Priestley, *Letter to a Returning Serviceman* (London: Home and Van Thal, 1945), 3.

Priestley enjoins the 'red half' to be 'a real citizen' in a world threatened by the atom bomb.[156] The veteran as social threat and source of political subversion is explored in Chapter 2.

'Demobbed ex-servicemen had become two a penny', writes Allport, justifying the public indifference and even antipathy that set in after the initial fêting of the first troops to return.[157] In literature, the figure turns up in places both expected and unexpected in the five decades after the conflict, from middle-brow fiction (B. Ifor Evans's *The Shop on the King's Road* (1946), Michael Harrison's *Treadmill* (1946), Pamela Hansford Johnson's *An Avenue of Stone* (1947), Stuart B. Jackman's *Portrait in Two Colours* (1948), Gilbert Frankau's *Michael's Wife* (1948), Jack Aistrop's *Pretend I Am A Stranger* (1949), Mary Renault's *North Face* (1949), Arthur Barker's *Nobby and Pincher in Civvy Street* (1950), Hammond Innes's *The Angry Mountain* (1950), to give a selection of examples in addition to the works discussed in Chapter 2) to philosophical novels (Iris Murdoch's *An Unofficial Rose* (1962), *The Sacred and Profane Love Machine* (1974) and *Jackson's Dilemma* (1995)) to historiographical metafiction (Henry Green's *Back* (1946) and Graham Swift's *Waterland* (1983)).[158] But, though the genre may differ, the figure has a certain consistency: deracinated, demoralized, depleted. A number of veteran returnees are awkward misfits in the communities to which they return: examples include Charley Summers in Green's *Back* (discussed in Chapter 4), Broadbent and Toothill in Rayner Heppenstall's 'Local Boy' (1946)[159] and the semi-alcoholic Freddie Page in Terence Rattigan's *The Deep Blue Sea* (1952). To these can be added another dismal figure – identified by Allport as the 'unromantic, passionless, commercial m[a]n' – a figure embodied by the always-on-the-make Arthur Middlewitch in Green's *Back* and by the Hooper Charles Ryder so despises in Evelyn Waugh's *Brideshead Revisited* (1945).[160] And then there are cases like the quietly hurting Felix Milne in Nigel Balchin's *Mine Own Executioner* (1945) (discussed in Chapter 2) and the passive, defeated Felix Meecham in Murdoch's *An Unofficial Rose*. These are all notably damaged

---

[156] Ibid., 4, 29.

[157] Allport, *Demobbed*, 52.

[158] On the prevalence of the veteran in post-Second World War fiction, see Victoria Stewart, *Narratives of Memory: British Writing of the 1940s* (Basingstoke: Palgrave Macmillan, 2006), 135, 137, and N. H. Reeve, 'Away from the Lighthouse: William Sansom and Elizabeth Taylor in 1949', *The Fiction of the 1940s: Stories of Survival*, ed. Rod Mengham and N. H. Reeve (Basingstoke: Palgrave Macmillan, 2001), 152–68: 162.

[159] Allport acutely identifies their social type as 'de-mobilised ex-officer of modest background left *sui generis* by [the] war' (*Demobbed*, 150).

[160] Ibid., 150, 154.

characters, representatives of, as Gill Plain puts it, 'a deep anxiety about masculinity and the male role', which was itself an indicator of wider concerns about Britain's role in the postwar world.[161]

Britain goes on producing veterans. In the 70-odd years since 1945, the nation's armed forces have been in action in Malaya, Korea, Kenya, Egypt, Kuwait, Brunei, Northern Ireland, the Falkland Islands, Iraq, Bosnia, Kosovo, Sierra Leone, Iraq (again), Afghanistan and Syria. In the twenty-first century itself, 220,560 individuals have served in Afghanistan and Iraq.[162] An article published in the *Guardian* in February 2014 speculated that, after the withdrawal of troops from Afghanistan later that year, 2015 might be the first year 'since at least 1914' that British soldiers, sailors and air crews would 'not be engaged in fighting somewhere'.[163] It wasn't: there were airstrikes against Islamic State, part of the ongoing Operation Shader against ISIL in Iraq and Syria. At the time of writing, British troops are, according to the Ministry of Defence's website, on 'operational duties' in Afghanistan, Africa, Brunei, Canada, Cyprus, Gibraltar, Iraq and the South Atlantic Islands; these duties range from 'peacekeeping' to 'providing humanitarian aid' to 'enforcing anti-terrorism measures' to 'helping combat the international drugs trade'.[164] The most recent survey by the Royal British Legion – in 2014 – estimated that there were some 2.83 million veterans in the UK.[165]

Supporting them is an array of state-sponsored and charitable services. In 2009, Alan Allport, was writing that 'we still do a disgracefully inadequate job of demobilising our young men and women'.[166] There have been some, limited initiatives since then. The nation's obligations to those who have fought on its behalf are recognized in the Armed Forces Covenant of 2011. The Covenant, according to the official website, is 'a promise by the nation ensuring that those who serve or have served in the armed forces' are 'treated fairly'.[167] £10 million a year has been allocated in perpetuity

[161] Gill Plain, *Literature of the 1940s: War, Postwar and 'Peace'* (Edinburgh: Edinburgh University Press, 2013), 210.

[162] www.bbc.co.uk/news/uk-29294337.

[163] Ewen MacAskill and Ian Cobain, 'British Forces' Century of Unbroken Warfare Set to End With Afghanistan Exit', *Guardian* (11 February 2014), www.theguardian.com/uk-news/2014/feb/11/british-forces-century-warfare-end.

[164] www.army.mod.uk/Operations-Deployments/Operations-Deployments.Aspx.

[165] www.gov.uk/government/uploads/system/uploads/attachment_data/file/516051/HOCS_FOI_2016_01145___Number_of_soldiers_becoming_veterans_in_the_UK_Armed_Forces_2014.pdf.

[166] Allport, *Demobbed*, 221.

[167] On the genesis of the covenant, see Anthony Forster, 'The Military Covenant and British Civil–Military Relations: Letting the Genie out of the Bottle', *Armed Forces and Society* 38.2 (2011), 273–90.

to ensure the achievement of the government's Covenant commitments, a sum afforced by a further £170 million since 2011.[168] To put this in context, the annual defence budget for 2016–17 was £35.1 *billion*.[169] Veterans UK, which is part of the Ministry of Defence, administers the armed forces' pension schemes and compensation payments for those injured or bereaved through military service,[170] and the Veterans Welfare Service and the Veterans Advisory and Pensions Committee provide further support and advice.

In addition to the state provisions, there exists a plethora of veteran charities, from Help for Heroes to Troop Aid to Blind Veterans UK.[171] At the head of them all is still the Royal British Legion, promoter of the annual Poppy Day Appeal, provider of care homes, respite centres, medical funds, legal advice, grants and loans, household adaptation, care phones and even 'handy vans' to help with repairs.[172] Much less well known are the niche charities such as Surf Action, which brings the health and recreational benefits of surfing to former members of the military.[173] Sport is at the centre of a number of initiatives aimed at restoring the health and self-esteem of ex-servicemen and women, notably the Invictus Games, founded in 2014 by Prince Harry. Titled with the Latin word for 'unconquered', the Games declare themselves to embody 'the fighting spirit of the wounded, injured and sick service personnel'.[174] For all this support, it is still estimated that ex-service personnel make up 5 per cent of the prison population and 10 per cent of rough sleepers.[175] The Ministry of Defence, unlike its American counterpart, does not record suicide attempts among former members of the armed forces, but the BBC's *Panorama* programme established in 2013 that at least twenty-nine veterans took their own lives the previous year.[176]

The veteran continues to be a much-contested figure in national life. To a large extent, the perception of subversive potential which clustered around

[168] www.gov.uk/government/publications/armed-forces-covenant-2015-to-2020/armed-forces-covenant.
[169] www.gov.uk/Government/News/Defence-Budget-Increases-for-the-First-Time-in-Six-Years.
[170] www.gov.uk/government/organisations/veterans-uk.
[171] A list of UK veterans' charities is given here: www.gov.uk/government/publications/veterans-welfare-service-useful-links-for-service-personnel/useful-links-for-the-service-community.
[172] www.britishlegion.org.uk/veterans-and-families/.
[173] www.surfaction.co.uk/index.php.
[174] https://invictusgamesfoundation.org/foundation/story.
[175] www.gov.uk/government/uploads/system/uploads/attachment_data/file/389856/the-needs-of-ex-service-personnel-in-the-cjs-analytical-summary.pdf; www.supportbritishsoldiers.co.uk/?p=197.
[176] Anonymous, 'UK Soldier and Veteran Suicides "Outstrip Afghan Deaths"', www.bbc.co.uk/news/uk-23259865.

the Second World War returnee has given way to the 'unconquered hero' of the Invictus Games. There are undoubted advantages to this revised conception, from a reinforced sense of worth, both on the part of the veteran and on the part of the watching civilians, to the benefits of physical rehabilitation. But it is hard to have to be a hero and, as one columnist observed about the South Pole Allied Challenge of 2013 (an event in which wounded soldiers from Britain, America, Canada and Australia competed to reach the Pole first), '[i]t is good to be reminded of the hardship they endure on our (sort of) behalf, even if putting them through another, fresh hardship is a curious way to go about it'.[177] More ominously, the figure is vulnerable to appropriation by the right-wing tabloids, which enlist 'our boys' in support of what they deem 'traditional' values, though are not averse to running stories about ' "trained killer[s] going bananas" '.[178] The left-leaning press is more interested in the damaged individual who is another victim of war, both let down by society and a social problem.[179] The doublethink of the veteran as hero/delinquent has become triplethink, with 'victim' forming the third term. These issues are discussed at greater length in Chapter 2.

The veterans who feature in twenty-first-century literary texts have seen service in a variety of armed conflicts: from the Mau Mau Uprising and the Troubles in Northern Ireland (Rachel Seiffert's *Afterwards* (2007)) to Afghanistan and Iraq (Jon McGregor's *Even the Dogs* (2010) and the Cormoran Strike novels by J. K. Rowling writing as Robert Galbraith (discussed in Chapter 3)). But it is those of the First and Second World Wars who dominate. In the works about the former conflict, broadly speaking, with Pat Barker's *Regeneration* trilogy still very influential, these figures express concerns about representation. So, Andrew Motion's 'The Five Acts of Harry Patch' (2008) and Carol-Ann Duffy's 'Last Post' (2009) chop up and rearrange time, mixing memory and desire. Barker's own *Life Class* (2007) and *Toby's Room* (2012) and Louisa Young's *My Dear,*

---

[177] Zoe Williams, 'Why Posh People Mind About "Toughness of Mind" ', *Guardian* (20 April 2013), 9.

[178] Richard Littlejohn, 'The Proof We Live in Two Britains', *MailOnline* (7 November 2014), www.dailymail.co.uk/columnists/article-2824520/While-millions-pay-silent-tribute-Tower-London-anarchists-bring-chaos-Westminster-proof-live-two-Britains-writes-RICHARD-LITTLEJOHN.html; Lydia Willgress, 'Chilling Footage Reveals Moment Ex-Army Sniper Threatened to Kill a Family While on Bail For Firing an Air Pistol at Guests During His Partner's Ann Summers Party', *MailOnline* (15 October 2015), www.dailymail.co.uk/news/article-3273942/Ex-Army-sniper-29-gas-mask-opened-fire-Ann-Summers-party-hitting-one-woman-bottom-taking-offence-conversation-heard.html.

[179] See, for example, Simon Hattenstone and Eric Allison, 'Collateral Damage', *Guardian* (18 October 2014), 42–53.

*I Wanted To Tell You* (2011) use the pioneering facial reconstruction surgery performed on First World War veterans to explore ideas about war, identity and aesthetics, while Alan Hollinghurst's *The Stranger's Child* (2011) and Kate Atkinson's *Life After Life* (2013) experiment with and question narrative techniques for retrieving and conveying what is past. In Andrew Cowan's *Worthless Men* (2013), Walter Barley, presumed missing, has returned from the trenches, but, in a brilliant move on Cowan's part, this is a ghostly homecoming, as most people cannot see him. To portray the returned soldier as invisible to the society on behalf of which he has been fighting conveys, at a stroke, more about the veteran's condition than pages of recollected trauma.

Since 2000, Second World War veterans have featured in novels including Zadie Smith's *White Teeth* (2000) (discussed in the Conclusion), Jon McGregor's *If Nobody Speaks of Remarkable Things* (2002), A. L. Kennedy's *Day* (2007) and Gerard Woodward's *Nourishment* (2013). A passage from the first of these is a good illustration of how the veteran figures in the national psyche. Samad Iqbal, a waiter in an Indian restaurant, is chatting up his children's music teacher, Poppy Burt-Jones:

> 'No, the fact is I work in a restaurant. I did some study
>     in younger days, but the war came and … […].'
> 'War?' she said, as if he had said wireless or pianola or
>     water-closet. 'The Falklands?'
> 'No,' said Samad flatly. 'The Second World.'
> 'Oh, Mr Iqbal, you'd never guess. You must have
>     been ever so young.'[180]

A Bengali Muslim immigrant, Samad is a rarity of pianola proportions in British fictional representations of veterans. However, the civilian response to his veterancy, as summed up in Poppy's comment, is standard: disconcerted, ill-informed, but quickly flattering. Veterans are valued – at least as long as they conform to national narratives – but not known well. Richard Jennyns, home from the wars in 1594, would have nodded in recognition.

[180] Zadie Smith, *White Teeth* (London: Hamish Hamilton, 2000), 118.

# Bibliography

Abel, Elizabeth, *Virginia Woolf and the Fictions of Psychoanalysis* (Chicago: The University of Chicago Press, 1989).

Adams, M. Ray, 'Robert Merry, Political Romanticist', *Studies in Romanticism* 2.1 (Fall 1962), 23–37.

Adorno, Théodor, 'In Memory of Eichendorff' ('Zum Gedächtnis Eichendorffs') [1958], trans. Shierry Weber Nicholsen, *Notes to Literature*, ed. Rolf Tiedemann (New York: Columbia University Press, 1991), 55–79.

*Beethoven: The Philosophy of Music. Fragments and Texts* (*Philosophie der Musik: Fragmente und Texte*) [1938–], trans. Edmund Jephcott, ed. Rolf Tiedemann (Cambridge: Polity, 1998).

*Negative Aesthetics* (*Negative Dialektik*) [1966], trans. Robert Hullot-Kentor, ed. Gretel Adorno and Rolf Tiedemann (London: Continuum, 2004).

Adorno, Théodor and Max Horkheimer, *Dialectic of Enlightenment* (*Dialektik der Aufklärung*) [1944], trans. John Cumming (London: Verso, 1979).

*Dialektik der Aufklärung: Philosophische Fragmente* [1944] (Frankfurt-am-Main: S. Fischer, 1988).

Agamben, Giorgio, *Infancy and History: Essays on the Destruction of Experience* (*Infanzia e storia: Distruzione dell'esperienza e origine della storia*) [1979], trans. Liz Heron (London: Verso, 1993).

Aird, Thomas, 'The Old Soldier', *Blackwood's Edinburgh Magazine* 71.436 (February 1852), 236–41.

Aldington, Richard, 'Introduction', *Walter Pater: Selected Works*, ed. Richard Aldington (London: William Heinemann, 1948), 1–27.

Alexopoulou, Marigo, *The Theme of Returning Home in Ancient Greek Literature: The Nostos of the Epic Heroes* (Lewiston, ON: The Edwin Mellen Press, 2009).

Alighieri, Dante, *The Divine Comedy of Dante Alighieri. Volume 1. Inferno*, trans. and ed. Robert M. Durling (Oxford: Oxford University Press, 1996).

Allport, Alan, *Demobbed: Coming Home After the Second World War* (New Haven, CT: Yale University Press, 2009).

Anonymous, 'Lisbon, July th 5th. 1695', *Post Boy and Historical Account* (6–8 August 1695) (17th–18th Century Burney Collection Newspapers).

'An Angry Boy and a Calm Veteran', *An Asylum for Fugitive Pieces, In Prose and Verse, Not in Any Other Collection: With Several Pieces Never Before Published* (London: J. Debrett, 1789), 79–80.

'Classified Advertising', *Times* (14 July 1791), 1 (The *Times* Digital Archive).

'Advertisement', *Diary or Woodfall's Register* (14 February 1793) (17th–18th Century Burney Collection Newspapers).

'The Diary', *Diary or Woodfall's Register* (14 February 1793) (17th–18th Century Burney Collection Newspapers).

'Rowlandson's Edition of Smollet's [sic] Novels', *Diary or Woodfall's Register* (14 February 1793) (17th–18th Century Burney Collection Newspapers).

'Exhibition of Pictures', *Times* (30 April 1793) (17th–18th Century Burney Collection Newspapers).

'Country News', *Sun* (11 June 1793), unpaginated (17th–18th Century Burney Collection Newspapers).

Untitled, *Diary or Woodfall's Register* (26 June 1793) (17th–18th Century Burney Collection Newspapers).

'Dr. Knox', *Morning Chronicle* (10 September 1793) (17th–18th Century Burney Collection Newspapers).

'Brussels, Oct. 28.', *Sun* (30 October 1793) (17th–18th Century Burney Collection Newspapers).

'Elegy', *Sun* (18 January 1794) (17th–18th Century Burney Collection Newspapers).

Untitled, *Lloyd's Evening Post* (12–14 February 1794) (17th–18th Century Burney Collection Newspapers).

'British Parliament: House of Commons', *Morning Chronicle* (22 January 1795), 2.

'The Wounded Soldier', *The Muse in Good Humour; or Momus's Banquet: A Collection of Choice Songs, Including the Modern* (London: Printed for William Lane, 1795?), 71.

'Lieutenant-Colonel Malcolm', *Evening Mail* (22–4 June 1796) (17th–18th Century Burney Collection Newspapers).

'Advertisement', *True Briton* (6 August 1796), unpaginated (17th–18th Century Burney Collection Newspapers).

'London, August 18', *Oracle and Public Advertiser* (18 August 1796), 1.

'Further Extracts from the New Edition of Pratt's Gleanings, Etc.: State of Methodism in Catholic Countries; and the Wakes or Fairs of Germany', *St. James's Chronicle or the British Evening Post* (8 September 1796) (17th–18th Century Burney Collection Newspapers).

'The Naval Subaltern', *Star* (30 September 1796), unpaginated (17th–18th Century Burney Collection Newspapers).

Untitled, *Telegraph* (5 January 1797), 3.

'Postscript', *London Packet* (4–7 August 1797), 4.

'The Age of War', *Courier* (8 November 1798) (17th–18th Century Burney Collection Newspapers).

'London', *Whitehall Evening Post* (9 September 1800), unpaginated (17th–18th Century Burney Collection Newspapers).

'Illuminations', *E. Johnson's British Gazette and Sunday Monitor* (2 May 1802), unpaginated (17th–18th Century Burney Collection Newspapers).

'The Soldier's Return', *The Scots Magazine* LXVI (April 1804), 297.
'Art III: *Der Krieg der Tyroler Landleute im Jahre* 1809 von J. L. S. Bartholdy', *Edinburgh Review* 27.53 (1816), 67–86.
'Old Soldiers', *Times* (25 September 1857), 10 (The *Times* Digital Archive).
'Death of a Veteran', *Times* (14 October 1858), 4 (The *Times* Digital Archive).
'An Amorous Old Gentleman is the Stock Property', *Times* (30 November 1858), 6 (The *Times* Digital Archive).
'The Danger of the Crisis in the North-Western', *Times* (16 July 1875), 9 (The *Times* Digital Archive).
*Soldiers' Grievances* (London: Kegan Paul, Trench, Trübner, 1891).
'Chelsea, Part IV: The Royal Hospital: History of the Foundation', *Survey of London*, ed. Walter Godfrey (1927) (British History Online).
*The Journey Home: A Report Prepared by Mass-Observation for the Advertising Service Guild* (London: John Murray, 1944).
'Impatience', *Guardian* (15 July 1945), 4.
'Things Are Tricky', *Guardian* (17 September 1945), 4.
'The Analyst Analysed', *The Irish Times* (10 November 1945), 2.
'Helen Ashton, M.B., B.S.', *British Medical Journal* (12 July 1958), 110.
*The Armed Forces Covenant* (London: Ministry of Defence, 2011).
'UK Soldier and Veteran Suicides "Outstrip Afghan Deaths"', www.bbc.co.uk/news/uk-23259865
Anselme, Daniel, *On Leave (La Permission)* [1957], trans. David Bellos (London: Penguin, 2014).
Appleby, David, 'Veteran Politics in Restoration England, 1660–1670', *The Seventeenth Century* 28.3 (September 2013), 323–42.
Appleton, Jay, *The Experience of Landscape* [1975] (Chichester: John Wiley, 1996).
Aristotle, 'Poetics', trans. Stephen Halliwell, *Aristotle. Poetics; Longinus on the Sublime; Demetrius On Style*, Loeb Classical Library (Cambridge, MA: Harvard University Press, 1995).
Ashcroft, Michael, 'The Veterans' Transition Review', www.veteranstransition.co.uk/vtrreport.pdf
Ashton, Helen, *The Captain Comes Home* (London: Collins, 1947).
Aubin, Robert A., *Topographical Poetry in XVIII-Century England* (New York: Modern Language Association of America, 1936).
Auden, W. H., 'The Guilty Vicarage', *Detective Fiction: A Collection of Critical Essays*, ed. Robin W. Winks (Woodstock, VT: Foul Play Press, 1980), 15–24.
Auerbach, Erich, *Mimesis: The Representation of Reality in Western Literature* (Princeton, NJ: Princeton University Press, 1953).
Austen, Jane, *Mansfield Park* [1814], ed. Tony Tanner (Harmondsworth: Penguin, 1985).
*Persuasion* [1818], ed. D. W. Harding (Harmondsworth: Penguin, 1965, 1985).
*Catharine and Other Writings*, ed. Margaret Anne Doody (Oxford: Oxford University Press, 1993).
*Jane Austen's Letters*, ed. Deirdre Le Faye (Oxford: Oxford University Press, 1995).

*Pride and Prejudice* [1813], ed. James Kinsley (Oxford: Oxford University Press, 2004).

Austen-Leigh, J. E., *A Memoir of Jane Austen and Other Family Recollections*, ed. Kathryn Sutherland (Oxford: Oxford University Press, 2002).

Badworth, Jos[eph], 'Half-Pay', *The Gentleman's Magazine* 64 (December 1794), 1129.

Bainbridge, Simon, *Napoleon and English Romanticism* (Cambridge: Cambridge University Press, 1995).

*British Poetry and the Revolutionary and Napoleonic Wars: Visions of Conflict* (Oxford: Oxford University Press, 2003).

Balchin, Nigel, *Mine Own Executioner* [1945] (London: The Reprint Society, 1947).

*A Sort of Traitors* (London: Collins, 1949).

Balzac, Honoré de, *Le Colonel Chabert* [1832] (Paris: Librio, 2013).

Baring-Gould, William S., 'Two Doctors and a Detective', *The Annotated Sherlock Holmes*, ed. William S. Baring-Gould, vol. 1/2 (London: John Murray, 1968), 1–104.

' "Your Hand Stole Towards Your Old Wound ..." ', *The Annotated Sherlock Holmes*, ed. William S. Baring-Gould, vol. 1/2 (London: John Murray, 1968), 606–9.

Baron, Michael, *Language and Relationship in Wordsworth's Writing* (London: Longman, 1995).

Barrett, Gerard, 'Souvenirs from France: Textual Traumatism in Henry Green's *Back*', *The Fiction of the 1940s: Stories of Survival*, ed. Rod Mengham and N. H. Reeve (Basingstoke: Palgrave, 2001), 169–84.

Barsham, Diana, *Conan Doyle and the Meaning of Masculinity* (Aldershot: Ashgate, 2000).

Barth, John, *Lost in the Funhouse* (New York: Anchor Books, 1988).

Barthes, Roland, *S/Z* [1970], trans. Richard Miller (New York: Hill and Wang, 1974).

Listening' ('Écoute') [1977], trans. Richard Howard, *The Responsibility of Forms: Critical Essays on Music, Art, and Representation* (Oxford: Basil Blackwell, 1986), 245–60.

Batchelor, John, *Tennyson: To Strive, To Seek, To Find* (London: Chatto and Windus, 2012).

Baxendale, John, *Priestley's England: J. B. Priestley and English Culture* (Manchester: Manchester University Press, 2007).

Beaumont, Sir Harry [Joseph Spence], *Crito: Or, A Dialogue on Beauty*, ed. Edmund Goldsmid (Edinburgh: privately printed, 1885).

Bell, David A., *The First Total War: Napoleon's Europe and the Birth of Modern Warfare* (London: Bloomsbury, 2007).

Benis, Toby R., *Romanticism on the Road: The Marginal Gains of Wordsworth's Homeless* (Basingstoke: Macmillan, 2000).

Benjamin, Walter, 'Der Erzähler' [1936], *Gesammelte Schriften. Band II.2. Literarische und Ästhetische Essays (Forsetzung) / Ästhetische Fragmente / Vorträge und Reden / Enzyklopädieartikel / Kulturpolitische Artikel und Aufsätze*, ed.

Rolf Tiedemann and Hermann Schweppenhäuser (Frankfurt-am-Main: Suhrkamp, 1977), 438–65.

'Erfahrung' [1913–14], *Gesammelte Schriften. Band II.1. Aufsätze, Essays, Vorträge*, ed. Rolf Tiedemann and Hermann Schweppenhäuser (Frankfurt-am-Main: Suhrkamp, 1977), 54–6.

'Erfahrung und Armut' [1933], *Gesammelte Schriften. Band II.1. Aufsätze, Essays, Vorträge*, ed. Rolf Tiedemann and Hermann Schweppenhäuser (Frankfurt-am-Main: Suhrkamp, 1977), 213–19.

'Die Waffen von Morgen: Schlachten mit Chlorazetophenol, Diphenylaminchlorasin und Dichloräthylsulfid' [1925], *Gesammelte Schriften. Band IV.1, 2. Kleine Prosa. Baudelaire-Übertragungen. Werkausgabe*, ed. Théodor W. Adorno, Gershom Scholem, Rolf Tiedemann and Hermann Schweppenhäuser (Frankfurt-am-Main: Suhrkamp, 1980), 473–6.

'Kriminalromane, auf Reisen' [1930], *Gesammelte Schriften. Band IV.1, 2. Kleine Prosa. Baudelaire-Übertragungen. Werkausgabe*, ed. Théodor W. Adorno, Gershom Scholem, Rolf Tiedemann and Hermann Schweppenhäuser (Frankfurt-am-Main: Suhrkamp, 1980), 381–2.

'Experience' ('Erfahrung') [1913–14], trans. Lloyd Spencer and Stefan Jost, *Selected Writings. Volume 1: 1913–1926*, ed. Marcus Bullock and Michael W. Jennings (Cambridge, MA: The Belknap Press of Harvard University Press, 1996), 3–5.

'The Handkerchief' ('Das Taschentuch') [1932], trans. Rodney Livingstone, *Selected Writings. Volume 2, Part 2: 1931–1934*, ed. Michael W. Jennings, Howard Eiland and Gary Smith (Cambridge, MA: The Belknap Press of Harvard University Press, 1999), 658–61.

'On Some Motifs in Baudelaire' ('Über einige Motive bei Baudelaire') [1939], trans. Harry Zohn, *Selected Writings. Volume 4: 1938–40*, ed. Michael W. Jennings, Howard Eiland and Gary Smith (Cambridge, MA: The Belknap Press of Harvard University Press, 1999), 313–55.

'The Storyteller' ('Der Erzähler') [1936], trans. Harry Zohn, *Selected Writings. Volume 3: 1935–38*, ed. Michael W. Jennings and Howard Eiland (Cambridge, MA: The Belknap Press of Harvard University Press, 1999), 143–66.

'The Work of Art in the Age of Its Technological Reproducibility (Second Version)' ('Das Kunstwerk im Zeitalter seiner technischen Reproduzierbarkeit') [1935–6], trans. Edmund Jephcott and Harry Zohn, *Selected Writings. Volume 3: 1935–38*, ed. Michael W. Jennings and Howard Eiland (Cambridge, MA: The Belknap Press of Harvard University Press, 1999), 101–33.

Bennett, Betty T., ed., *British War Poetry in the Age of Romanticism: 1793–1815* (New York: Garland, 1976).

'Introduction', *British War Poetry in the Age of Romanticism: 1793–1815*, ed. Betty T. Bennett (New York: Garland, 1976), 1–67.

Bennett, J. A. W., 'Lewis, Clive Staples (1898–1963)', rev. Emma Plaskitt, *Oxford Dictionary of National Biography* (Oxford University Press, 2004), online edition.

Bennett, J. H. E. and Dewhurst, J. C., eds, *Quarter Sessions Records, with Other Records of the Justices of the Peace for the County Palatine of Chester 1559–1760* (place of publication unknown: publisher unknown, 1940).

Benson, E. F., *As We Are: A Modern Revue* (London: Longmans, Green, 1932).

Benveniste, Émile, *Indo-European Language and Society (Le Vocabulaire des institutions indo-européennes)* [1969], trans. Elizabeth Palmer (London: Faber and Faber, 1973).

Berendzen, J. C., 'Max Horkheimer', *The Stanford Encyclopedia of Philosophy* (Winter 2016), ed. Edward N. Zalta, https://plato.stanford.edu/archives/win2016/entries/horkheimer/

Berenhorst, Georg Heinrich von, *Betrachtungen über die Kriegskunst, über ihre Fortschritte, ihre Widersprüche und ihre Zuverlässigkeit* [1797–9], 3/3 vols (Osnabrück: Biblio, 1978).

Bergonzi, Bernard, 'Blunden, Edmund Charles (1896–1974)', *Oxford Dictionary of National Biography* (Oxford University Press, 2004), online edition.

Berry, Francis, 'Knight, (George) Richard Wilson (1897–1985)', *Oxford Dictionary of National Biography* (Oxford University Press, 2004), online edition.

Bevis, Matthew, *The Art of Eloquence: Byron, Dickens, Tennyson, Joyce* (Oxford: Oxford University Press, 2007).

Bewell, Alan, *Romanticism and Colonial Disease* (Baltimore, MD: The Johns Hopkins University Press, 1999).

Binyon, Laurence, 'For the Fallen' (1914), *The Oxford Book of War Poetry*, ed. Jon Stallworthy (Oxford: Oxford University Press, 2003), 209.

Blair, Hugh, *Lectures on Rhetoric and Belles Lettres* [1783], 2/2 vols (London: A. Strahan and T. Cadell, 1783).

Blamire, Susanna, 'Stoklewath; or, The Cumbrian Village', *British Women Poets of the Romantic Era: An Anthology*, ed. Paula R. Feldman (Baltimore, MD: The Johns Hopkins University Press, 2000), 115–47.

Boehm, Katharina, Farkas, Anna and Zwierlein, Anne-Julia, 'Introduction', *Interdisciplinary Perspectives on Victorian Old Age*, ed. Katharina Boehm, Anna Farkas and Anne-Julia Zwierlein (London: Routledge, 2014), 1–17.

Boitani, Piero, *The Shadow of Ulysses: Figures of a Myth (L'Ombre di Ulisse: Figure di un Mito)* [1992], trans. Anita Wilson (Oxford: The Clarendon Press, 1994).

Boltanski, Luc, *Mysteries and Conspiracies: Detective Stories, Spy Novels and the Making of Modern Societies (Énigmes et complots: Une enquête à propos d'enquêtes)* [2012], trans. Catherine Porter (Cambridge: Polity Press, 2014).

Bonikowski, Wyatt, 'The Return of the Soldier Brings Death Home', *Modern Fiction Studies* 51.3 (Fall 2005), 513–35.

Borradori, Giovanna, *Philosophy in a Time of Terror: Dialogues with Jürgen Habermas and Jacques Derrida* (Chicago: The University of Chicago Press, 1994).

Bourke, Joanna, *Dismembering the Male. Men's Bodies, Britain and the Great War* (London: Reaktion, 1996).

*The Second World War: A People's History* (Oxford: Oxford University Press, 2001).

Boxall, Peter, *The Value of the Novel* (Cambridge: Cambridge University Press, 2015).

Bradley, F. H., *Appearance and Reality: A Metaphysical Essay* (Oxford: The Clarendon Press, 1897).

Brantlinger, Patrick, *Rule of Darkness: British Literature and Imperialism, 1830–1914* (Ithaca, NY: Cornell University Press, 1988).

Brittain, Vera, 'The Lament of the Demobilised' [1920], *Scars Upon My Heart. Women's Poetry and Verse of the First World War*, ed. Catherine Reilly (London: Virago, 1981), 14.

   *Testament of Youth: An Autobiographical Study of the Years 1900–1925* [1933] (London: Virago, 2008).

Brodey, Inger S. B., 'On Pre-Romanticism or Sensibility: Defining Ambivalences', *A Companion to European Romanticism*, ed. Michael Ferber (London: Blackwell, 2005), 10–28.

Broers, Michael, 'Changes in War: The French Revolutionary and Napoleonic Wars', *The Changing Character of War*, ed. Hew Strachan and Sibylle Scheipers (Oxford: Oxford University Press, 2011), 64–78.

Bromwich, David, *A Choice of Inheritance: Self and Community from Edmund Burke to Robert Frost* (Cambridge, MA: Harvard University Press, 1989).

   *Disowned by Memory: Wordsworth's Poetry of the 1790s* (Chicago: The University of Chicago Press, 1998).

Brooke, Rupert, *The Collected Poems of Rupert Brooke* (New York: Dodd, Mead, 1925).

Brooks, Peter, *Psychoanalysis and Storytelling* (Oxford: Blackwell, 1994).

Brown, Ivor, 'Theatre and Life', *London Observer* (11 February 1945), 2.

Broyles, William, *Brothers in Arms: A Journey from War to Peace* (New York: Alfred A. Knopf, 1986).

Brunsdale, Mitzi, *Dorothy L. Sayers: Solving the Mystery of Wickedness* (Oxford: Berg, 1990).

Buchan, David Steuart Erskine, *Letters on the Impolicy of a Standing Army in Time of Peace, and on the Unconstitutional and Illegal Measure of Barracks: With a Post[s]cript Illustrative of the Real Constitutional Mode of Defence for this Island; Containing Also a Short Review of the Effects Which are Produced by a Standing Army on Morality, Population and Labour* (London: Printed for D. J. Eaton, 1793).

Burdett, Howard, Woodhead, Charlotte, Iversen, Amy, Wessely, Simon, Dandeker, Christopher and Fear, Nicola T., ' "Are You a Veteran?": Understanding of the Term "Veteran" Among UK Ex-Service Personnel: A Research Note', *Armed Forces and Society* 39.4 (2013), 751–9.

Burgess, Anthony, *Little Wilson and Big God* (London: Heinemann, 1987).

Burney, Charles, '*Lyrical Ballads*, With a Few Other Poems', *The Monthly Review* 29 (June 1799), 202–10.

Burrow, J. A., *The Ages of Man: A Study of Medieval Writing and Thought* (Oxford: Oxford University Press, 1988).

Butler, Judith, 'Values of Difficulty', *Just Being Difficult: Academic Writing in the Public Arena*, ed. Jonathan Culler and Kevin Lamb (Stanford, CA: Stanford University Press, 2003), 199–215.

Campbell, James, 'Coming Home: Difference and Reconciliation in Narratives of Return to the "World"', *The United States and Viet Nam from War to Peace: Papers from an Interdisciplinary Conference on Reconciliation*, ed. Robert M. Slabey (Jefferson, NC: McFarland, 1996), 198–207.

Combat Gnosticism: The Ideology of First World War Criticism', *New Literary History* 30 (1999), 203–15.

Caputo, John D., *The Prayers and Tears of Jacques Derrida: Religion Without Religion* (Bloomington, IN: Indiana University Press, 1997).

Carey, John, 'Coghill, Nevill Henry Kendal Aylmer (1899–1980)', *Oxford Dictionary of National Biography* (Oxford University Press, 2004), online edition.

Carfore, Kimberly, 'The Paradox of Homecoming: Home Is Where the Haunt Is', *Resisting the Place of Belonging: Uncanny Homecomings in Religion, Narrative and the Arts*, ed. Daniel Boscaljon (Farnham: Ashgate, 2013), 61–72.

Carlyle, Thomas, *The Life of John Sterling* 11/30 vols (London: Chapman and Hall, 1897).

*Selected Writings*, ed. Alan Shelston (London: Penguin, 1986).

*Sartor Resartus*, ed. Kerry McSweeney and Peter Sabor (Oxford: Oxford University Press, 1987).

Caruth, Cathy, *Unclaimed Experience. Trauma, Narrative, and History* (Baltimore, MD: Johns Hopkins University Press, 1996).

Cave, Terence, *Recognitions: A Study in Poetics* (Oxford: The Clarendon Press, 1988).

Cawelti, John G., 'Detecting the Detective', *ANQ: A Quarterly Journal of Short Articles, Notes and Reviews* 12.3 (1999), 44–55.

Cawthorn, Caroline, 'The Soldier as Hero: Images of the Military in the Novel 1815–1860', unpublished DPhil thesis (University of Oxford, 2006).

Chakrabarty, Dipesh, *Provincializing Europe: Postcolonial Thought and Historical Difference* (Princeton, NJ: Princeton University Press, 2000).

Charlesworth, Michael, 'The Ruined Abbey: Picturesque and Gothic Values', *The Politics of the Picturesque: Literature, Landscape and Aesthetics Since 1770*, ed. Stephen Copley and Peter Garside (Cambridge: Cambridge University Press, 1994), 62–80.

Chase, Karen, *The Victorians and Old Age* (Oxford: Oxford University Press, 2009).

Childs, John, *The British Army of William III, 1689–1702* (Manchester: Manchester University Press, 2007).

Clausewitz, Carl von, *On War* (*Vom Kriege*) [1832], trans. Michael Howard and Peter Paret (Princeton, NJ: Princeton University Press, 1976).

Cohen, Deborah, 'Will to Work: Disabled Veterans in Britain and Germany After the First World War', *Disabled Veterans in History*, ed. David A. Gerber (Ann Arbor, MI: The University of Michigan Press, 2000), 295–321.

*The War Come Home: Disabled Veterans in Britain and Germany, 1914–1939* (Berkeley, CA: University of California Press, 2001).

Cohen, Debra Rae, *Remapping the Home Front: Locating Citizenship in British Women's Great War Fiction* (Boston: Northeastern University Press, 2002).

Cohen, Samuel, *After the End of History: American Fiction in the 1990s* (Iowa City: University of Iowa Press, 2009).

Cole, Sarah, *Modernism, Male Friendship, and the First World War* (Cambridge: Cambridge University Press, 2003).

'The Poetry of Pain', *The Oxford Handbook of British and Irish War Poetry*, ed. Tim Kendall (Oxford: Oxford University Press, 2007), 483–503.

Coleridge, Samuel Taylor, *The Watchman*, ed. Lewis Patton, *The Collected Works of Samuel Taylor Coleridge*, 2/16 vols (Princeton, NJ: Princeton University Press, 1970).

*Lectures 1795 on Politics and Religion*, ed. Lewis Patton and Peter Mann, *The Collected Works of Samuel Taylor Coleridge*, 1/16 vols (Princeton, NJ: Princeton University Press, 1971).

*Biographia Literaria I*, ed. James Engell and W. Jackson Bate, *The Collected Works of Samuel Taylor Coleridge*, 7/16 vols (Princeton, NJ: Princeton University Press, 1983).

*Biographia Literaria II*, ed. James Engell and W. Jackson Bate, *The Collected Works of Samuel Taylor Coleridge*, 7/16 vols (Princeton, NJ: Princeton University Press, 1983).

*Table Talk II*, ed. Carl Woodring, *The Collected Works of Samuel Taylor Coleridge*, 14/16 vols (Princeton, NJ: Princeton University Press, 1990)

*Poetical Works I: Poems (Reading Text), Part 1*, ed. J. C. C. Mays, *The Collected Works of Samuel Taylor Coleridge*, 16:I:1/16 vols (Princeton, NJ: Princeton University Press, 2001).

*Poetical Works I: Poems (Reading Text), Part 2*, ed. J. C. C. Mays, *The Collected Works of Samuel Taylor Coleridge*, 16:I:2/16 vols (Princeton, NJ: Princeton University Press, 2001).

*Poetical Works II: Poems (Variorum Text), Part 1*, ed. J. C. C. Mays, *The Collected Works of Samuel Taylor Coleridge*, 16:3/16 vols (Princeton, NJ: Princeton University Press, 2001).

Colley, Linda, *Britons: Forging the Nation 1707–1837* [1992] (New Haven, CT: Yale University Press, 2009).

Comay, Rebecca, 'Gifts Without Presents: Economies of "Experience" in Bataille and Heidegger', *Yale French Studies* 78 (1995), 66–89.

Connell, P. J., 'Rieu, Emile Victor (1887–1972)', *Oxford Dictionary of National Biography* (Oxford University Press, 2004), online edition.

Cooke, John, *An Historical Account of the Royal Hospital for Seamen at Greenwich* (London: publisher unknown, 1789).

Cowan, Andrew, *Worthless Men* (London: Sceptre, 2013).

Crawford, Robert, *Young Eliot: From St Louis to The Waste Land* (London: Jonathan Cape, 2015).

Critchley, Simon, 'Emmanuel Levinas: A Disparate Inventory', *The Cambridge Companion to Levinas*, ed. Simon Critchley and Robert Bernasconi (Cambridge: Cambridge University Press, 2002), xv–xxx.

Curr, Matthew, *The Consolation of Otherness: The Male Love Elegy in Milton, Gray and Tennyson* (London: McFarland, 2002).

Currie, Mark, *About Time. Narrative, Fiction and the Philosophy of Time* (Edinburgh: Edinburgh University Press, 2007).

D'Israeli, Isaac, *A Dissertation on Anecdotes* (London: C. and G. Kearsley and J. Murray, 1793).

Dandeker, Christopher, Wessely, Simon, Iversen, Amy and Ross, John, '*Improving the Delivery of Cross Departmental Support and Services for Veterans. Joint Report*' (London: Department of War Studies and Institute of Psychiatry, 2003).

'What's in a Name? Defining and Caring for "Veterans": The United Kingdom in International Perspective', *Armed Forces and Society* 32.2 (January 2006), 161–77.

Darlington, Beth, 'Two Early Texts: *A Night-Piece* and *The Discharged Soldier*', *Bicentenary Wordsworth Studies in Memory of John Alban Finch*, ed. Jonathan Wordsworth and Beth Darlington (Ithaca, NY: Cornell University Press, 1970), 425–48.

Dauncey, Sarah, 'Crime, Forensics, and Modern Science', *A Companion to Crime Fiction*, ed. Charles J. Rzepka and Lee Horsley (Chichester: Wiley-Blackwell, 2010), 164–74.

Dawes, James, *The Language of War: Literature and Culture in the U. S. from the Civil War Through World War II* (Cambridge, MA: Harvard University Press, 2002).

Dawson, Graham, *Soldier Heroes: British Adventure, Empire and the Imagining of Masculinities* (London: Routledge, 1994).

de Kock, Leon, 'Interview with Gayatri Chakravorty Spivak: New Nation Writers Conference in South Africa', *ARIEL: A Review of International English Literature* 23.3 (1992), 29–47.

de Lamartine, Alphonse, *Biographies and Portraits of Some Celebrated People. Volume 1: Lord Chatham. William Pitt. Shakespeare* (London: Tinsley Brothers, 1866).

de Saussure, Ferdinand, *Course in General Linguistics* (*Cours de Linguistique Générale*) [1916], trans. Roy Harris (London: Duckworth, 1983).

Dean, C. G. T., *The Royal Hospital, Chelsea* (London: Hutchinson, 1950).

Decker, Christopher, 'Tennyson's Limitations', *Tennyson Among the Poets: Bicentenary Essays*, ed. Robert Douglas-Fairhurst and Seamus Perry (Oxford: Oxford University Press, 2009), 57–75.

Deeming, David, 'Henry Green's "The Lull" and the Postwar Demise of Green's Modernist Aesthetic', *Modern Fiction Studies* 44.4 (Winter 1998), 865–87.

DeFalco, Amelia, *Uncanny Subjects: Aging in Contemporary Narrative* (Columbus, OH: The Ohio State University Press, 2010).

deMeester, Karen, 'Trauma and Recovery in Virginia Woolf's *Mrs Dalloway*', *Modern Fiction Studies* 44.3 (1998), 649–73.

Derrida, Jacques, *Specters of Marx: The State of the Debt, the Work of Mourning and the New International* (*Spectres de Marx: L'État de la dette, le travail du deuil et la nouvelle Internationale*) [1993], trans. Peggy Kamuf (New York and London: Routledge, 1994).

'HOSTIPITALITY', trans. Barry Stocke and Forbes Morlock, *Angelaki* 5.3 (2000), 3–18.

Derrida, Jacques and Dufourmantelle, Anne, *Of Hospitality: Anne Dufourmantelle Invites Jacques Derrida to Respond* (Stanford, CA: Stanford University Press, 2000).

Dickens, Charles, *Bleak House* [1852–3], ed. Stephen Gill (Oxford: Oxford University Press, 2008).

Dickens, Monica, *The Happy Prisoner* (London: Michael Joseph and The Book Society, 1946).

Disraeli, Benjamin, *Sybil* [1845], ed. Sheila M. Smith (Oxford: Oxford University Press, 1998).

Doan, Laura L., 'Recuperating the Postwar Moment: Green's *Back* and Bacon's *Three Studies for Figures at the Base of a Crucifixion*', *Mosaic* 23.3 (Summer 1990), 113–24.

Dove, George N., *The Reader and the Detective Story* (Bowling Green, OH: Bowling Green State University Popular Press, 1997).

Dove, Mary, *The Perfect Age of Man's Life* (Cambridge: Cambridge University Press, 1986).

Doyle, Arthur Conan, *Memories and Adventures* [1924] (London: John Murray, 1930).

*The Annotated Sherlock Holmes*, ed. William S. Baring-Gould, 2 vols (London: John Murray, 1968).

*The Complete Brigadier Gerard* [1924], ed. Owen Dudley Edwards (Edinburgh: Canongate Classics, 1995).

E., F., 'To the Conductor of the Sun', *Sun* (29 November 1793) (17th–18th Century Burney Collection Newspapers).

Eagleton, Terry, ' "Sylvia's Lovers" and Legality', *Essays in Criticism* 26.1 (January 1976), 17–27.

Early, Emmett, *The War Veteran in Film* (Jefferson, NC: McFarland, 2003).

Edelstein, Dan, *The Enlightenment: A Genealogy* (Chicago: The University of Chicago Press, 2014).

Eilenberg, Susan, *Strange Power of Speech: Wordsworth, Coleridge, and Literary Possession* (Oxford: Oxford University Press, 1992).

Eliot, George, *Adam Bede* [1859], ed. Stephen Gill (Oxford: Oxford University Press, 1986).

*Felix Holt* [1866], ed. Lynda Mugglestone (Oxford: Oxford University Press, 1995).

Eliot, T. S., *Knowledge and Experience in the Philosophy of F. H. Bradley* (London: Faber and Faber, 1964).

*Selected Prose of T. S. Eliot*, ed. Frank Kermode (London: Faber and Faber, 1984).

*The Poems of T. S. Eliot. Volume I: Collected and Uncollected Poems*, ed. Christopher Ricks and Jim McCue (London: Faber and Faber, 2015).

Ellery, Reginald, *Psychiatric Aspects of Modern Warfare* (Melbourne: Reed and Harris, 1945).

Emsley, Clive, *British Society and the French Wars 1793–1815* (London: Macmillan, 1979).

Engberg-Pedersen, Anders, *Empire of Chance: The Napoleonic Wars and the Disorder of Things* (Cambridge, MA: Harvard University Press, 2015).

Ezard, John, 'Richard Hoggart Obituary', *Guardian* (10 April 2014), www.theguardian.com/books/2014/apr/10/richard-hoggart

Faflak, Joel, *Romantic Psychoanalysis: The Burden of the Mystery* (Albany, NY: State University of New York Press, 2008).

Faulkner, Thomas, *An Historical and Descriptive Account of the Royal Hospital, and the Royal Military Asylum, at Chelsea* (London: publisher unknown, 1805).

Faust, Ron, 'Vets: "Not Home Yet"', *The Nation* 235.21 (18 December 1982), 642.

Favret, Mary, 'Coming Home: The Public Spaces of Romantic War', *Studies in Romanticism* 33.4 (Winter 1994), 539–48.

*War at a Distance: Romanticism and the Making of Modern Wartime* (Princeton, NJ: Princeton University Press, 2010).

'A Feeling for Numbers: Representing the Scale of the War Dead', *War and Literature*, ed. Laura Ashe and Ian Patterson (Cambridge: D. S. Brewer, 2014), 185–204.

Feldman, Paula R., 'Susanna Blamire (1747–1794)', *British Women Poets of the Romantic Era: An Anthology*, ed. Paula R. Feldman (Baltimore, MD: The Johns Hopkins University Press, 2000), 103–7.

Felski, Rita, 'Context Stinks!', *New Literary History* 42.4 (Autumn 2011), 573–91.

Ferguson, Rex, 'Blind Noise and Deaf Visions: Henry Green's *Caught*, Synaesthesia and the Blitz', *Journal of Modern Literature* 33 (Fall 2009), 102–16.

*Criminal Law and the Modernist Novel: Experience on Trial* (Cambridge: Cambridge University Press, 2013).

Festa, Lynn, 'Cosmetic Differences: The Changing Faces of England and France', *Studies in Eighteenth-Century Culture* 34 (2005), 25–54.

Finch, Charles, 'The Master is Back in "The Cuckoo's Calling"', *USA Today* (16 July 2013), www.usatoday.com/story/life/books/2013/07/24/the-cuckoos-calling/2581907/

Finkel, David, *Thank You For Your Service* (New York: Sarah Crichton Books, 2013).

Fordham, Finn, *I Do I Undo I Redo: The Textual Genesis of Modernist Selves in Hopkins, Yeats, Conrad, Forster, Joyce, and Woolf* (Oxford: Oxford University Press, 2010).

Forster, Anthony, 'The Military Covenant and British Civil-Military Relations: Letting the Genie out of the Bottle', *Armed Forces and Society* 38.2 (2011), 273–90.

Forster, E. M., *The BBC Talks of E. M. Forster 1929–1960: A Selected Edition*, ed. Mary Lago, Linda K. Hughes and Elizabeth Macleod Walls (Columbia, MO: University of Missouri Press, 2008).

Foster, John, *Poems, Chiefly on Religious Subjects* (London: publisher unknown, 1797).

Foucault, Michel, *The Order of Things: An Archeology of the Human Sciences* (*Les mots et les choses: Une archéologie des sciences humaines*) [1966], translator unknown (New York: Vintage, 1973).

Foucault, Michel and Deleuze, Gilles, '*Intellectuals and Power: A Conversation between Michel Foucault and Gilles Deleuze*' (*Les Intellectuels et le pouvoir*) [1972], trans. Donald F. Bouchard and Sherry Simon, *Language, Counter-Memory,*

*Practice: Selected Essays and Interviews*, ed. Michel Foucault (Ithaca, NY: Cornell University Press, 1977), 205–17.

Frank, Arthur W., *Letting Stories Breathe: A Socio-Narratology* (Chicago: The University of Chicago Press, 2010).

Frank, Laurence, *Victorian Detective Fiction and the Nature of Evidence: The Scientific Investigations of Poe, Dickens and Doyle* (Basingstoke: Palgrave Macmillan, 2003).

Franklin, William A., *Through Adversity to Attainment* (Victoria, BC: Trafford, 2005).

Fraser, Lindsey, *An Interview with J. K. Rowling* (London: Mammoth, 2000).

Freeman, Nick, 'Sensational Ghosts, Ghostly Sensations', *Women's Writing* 20.2 (2013) (Special Issue: Beyond Braddon: Re-Assessing Female Sensationalists), 186–201.

Freud, Sigmund, *Beyond the Pleasure Principle* (*Jenseits des Lustprinzips*) [1920], trans. C. J. M. Hubback, ed. Ernest Jones (London: The Hogarth Press/The Institute for Psycho-Analysis, 1922).

'The Uncanny' ('Das Unheimliche') [1919], *An Infantile Neurosis and Other Works*, ed. James Strachey in collaboration with Anna Freud, assisted by Alix Strachey and Alan Tyson (London: The Hogarth Press/Institute of Psycho-Analysis, 1955), 219–52.

'Fragment of an Analysis of a Case of Hysteria (1905 [1901])' ('Traum und Hysterie'), *'A Case of Hysteria', 'Three Essays on Sexuality' and Other Works*, ed. James Strachey in collaboration with Anna Freud, assisted by Alix Strachey and and Alan Tyson (London: Vintage, 2001), 7–122.

Frevert, Ute, 'War', *A Companion to Nineteenth-Century Europe: 1789–1914*, ed. Stefan Berger (Oxford: Blackwell Reference Online, 2006), unpaginated.

Furneaux, Holly, *Queer Dickens: Erotics, Families, Masculinities* (Oxford: Oxford University Press, 2009).

Fussell, Paul, *Thank God for the Atom Bomb and Other Essays* (New York: Summit Books, 1988).

Gale, Maggie B., *J. B. Priestley* (London: Routledge, 2008).

Gates, David, 'The Transformation of the Army 1783–1815', *The Oxford History of the British Army*, gen. ed. David G. Chandler, assoc. ed. Ian Beckett (Oxford: Oxford University Press, 2007), 132–60.

Gerber, David A., 'Heroes and Misfits: The Troubled Social Reintegration of Disabled Veterans of World War II in *The Best Years of Our Lives*', *Disabled Veterans in History*, ed. David A. Gerber (Ann Arbor, MI: The University of Michigan Press, 2000), 70–95.

'Introduction: Finding Disabled Veterans in History', *Disabled Veterans in History*, ed. David A. Gerber (Ann Arbor, MI: The University of Michigan Press, 2000), 1–51.

Gibson, Andrew, 'Henry Green as Experimental Novelist', *Studies in the Novel* 16.2 (Summer 1984), 197–212.

Gifford, Terry, *Pastoral* (London and New York: Routledge, 1999).

Gilbert, Sandra, '"Rats' Alley": The Great War; Modernism, and the (Anti) Pastoral Elegy', *New Literary History* 30 (1999), 179–201.

Ginzburg, Carlo, *Myths, Emblems, Clues [Miti, Emblemi, Spie]* [1986], trans. John Tedeschi and Anne C. Tedeschi (London: Hutchinson Radus, 1990).

Girard, René, *Violence and the Sacred (Violence et le sacré)* [1972], trans. Patrick Gregory (Baltimore, MD: Johns Hopkins University Press, 1977).

Gladstone, Sir John ('Mercator'), 'To The Right Honourable William Pitt', *Diary or Woodfall's Register* (18 January 1792), 2.

Glotz, Gustave, *Histoire Grecque* (Paris: Presses Universitaires de France, 1939).

Godwin, William, *Caleb Williams* [1794], ed. Pamela Clemit (Oxford: Oxford University Press, 2009).

Goldman, Mark, 'Robert Henriques, *The Journey Home*', *Modern Language Studies* 21.1 (Winter 1991), 22–36.

Goldsmith, Oliver, *Selected Writings of Oliver Goldsmith*, ed. John Lucas (Manchester: Carcanet, 1988/2003).

Goody, Jack, 'The Time of Telling and the Telling of Time in Written and Oral Cultures', *Chronotypes: The Construction of Time*, ed. John Bender and David E. Wellbery (Stanford, CA: Stanford University Press, 1991), 77–96.

Goren, Elizabeth, 'Society's Use of the Hero Following a National Trauma', *American Journal of Psychoanalysis* 67.1 (2007), 37–52.

Goslee, David F., 'Three Stages of Tennyson's "Tiresias"', *The Journal of English and Germanic Philology* 75.1/2 (January–April 1976), 154–67.

Gramsci, Antonio, *Selections from the Prison Notebooks (Quaderni del Carcere)* [1948], trans. Geoffrey Nowell Smith and Quintin Hoare (London: Lawrence and Wishart, 1971).

Graves, Robert, *Good-Bye to All That* [1929] (New York: Anchor, 1957).

Green, Henry, *Surviving: The Uncollected Writings of Henry Green*, ed. Matthew Yorke (London: Chatto and Windus, 1992).

   *Back* [1946] (London: Harvill, 1998).

Greenblatt, Stephen, 'Psychoanalysis and Renaissance Culture', *Literary Theory / Renaissance Texts*, ed. Patricia Parker and David Quint (Baltimore, MD: The Johns Hopkins University Press, 1986), 210–24.

Grimstad, Paul, *Experience and Experimental Writing: Literary Pragmatism from Emerson to the Jameses* (Oxford: Oxford University Press, 2013).

Grosz, Elizabeth, *Jacques Lacan: A Feminist Introduction* (New York: Routledge, 1990).

Guha, Ranajit, 'The Prose of Counter-Insurgency', *Subaltern Studies II*, ed. Ranajit Guha (Delhi: Oxford University Press, 1983), 1–42.

Gurney, Ivor, *Collected Poems of Ivor Gurney*, ed. Pat Kavanagh (Oxford: Oxford University Press, 1984).

Gustar, Jennifer J., '*The Tempest* in an English Teapot: Colonialism and the Measure of a Man in Zadie Smith's *White Teeth*', *Changing English: An International Journal of English Teaching* 17.4 (2010), 333–43.

Gwilliam, Tassie, 'Cosmetic Poetics: Coloring Faces in the Eighteenth Century', *Body and Text in the Eighteenth Century*, ed. Veronica Kelly and Dorothea von Mücke (Stanford, CA: Stanford University Press, 1994), 144–62.

Habermas, Jürgen, 'Towards a Theory of Communicative Competence', *Inquiry* 13.1 (1970), 360–75.

*Communication and the Evolution of Society* (*Sprachpragmatik und Philosophie; Zur Rekonstruktion des historischen Materialismus*) [1976], trans. Thomas McCarthy (London: Heinemann, 1979).

*The Philosophical Discourse of Modernity: Twelve Lectures* (*Der philosophische Diskurs der Moderne: Zwölf Vorlesungen*) [1985], trans. Frederick G. Lawrence (Cambridge, MA: The MIT Press, 1985).

*The Inclusion of the Other: Studies in Political Theory* (*Die Einbeziehung des Anderen: Studien zur politischen Theorie*) [1988], trans. Ciaran Cronin, ed. Ciaran Cronin and Pablo De Greiff (Cambridge, MA: The MIT Press, 1989).

*The Structural Transformation of the Public Sphere* (*Strukturwandel der Öffentlichkeit*) [1962], trans. Thomas Burge (Cambridge, MA: The MIT Press, 1989).

*Postmetaphysical Thinking: Philosophical Essays* (*Nachmetaphysisches Denken: Philosophische Aufsätze*) [1988], trans. William Mark Hohengarten (Cambridge, MA: The MIT Press, 1994).

Hack, Daniel, 'Wild Charges: The Afro-Haitian "Charge of the Light Brigade"', *Victorian Studies* 54.2 (Winter 2012), 199–225.

Haggerty, George E., 'Desire and Mourning: The Ideology of the Elegy', *Ideology and Form in Eighteenth Century Literature*, ed. David H. Richter (Lubbock: Texas Tech University Press, 1999), 184–206.

'Love and Loss: An Elegy', *GLQ: A Journal of Lesbian and Gay Studies* 10.3 (2004), 385–405.

Halberstam, Judith, *In a Queer Time and Place: Transgender Bodies, Subcultural Lives* (New York: New York University Press, 2005).

Hale, Dorothy J., 'Aesthetics and the New Ethics: Theorizing the Novel in the Twenty-First Century', *PMLA* 124.3 (May 2009), 896–905.

Hale, Lionel, 'Soldiers Come Home', *Observer* (10 December 1944), 3.

Hallam, Arthur, *Remains in Verse and Prose* (London: John Murray, 1863).

*Hansard, House of Commons* (24 June 1831), series 3, vol. 4.

Harari, Yuval Noah, *The Ultimate Experience: Battlefield Revelations and the Making of Modern War Culture, 1450–2000* (Basingstoke: Palgrave Macmillan, 2008).

Hardy, Thomas, *The Dynasts: An Epic-Drama of the War with Napoleon* [1908] (London: Macmillan, 1965).

*The Life and Work of Thomas Hardy*, ed. Michael Millgate (London: Macmillan, 1984).

Hareven, Tamara K., 'Synchronizing Individual Time, Family Time, and Historical Time', *Chronotypes: The Construction of Time*, ed. John Bender and David E. Wellbery (Stanford, CA: Stanford University Press, 1991), 167–82.

Hartman, Geoffrey, *Wordsworth's Poetry 1787–1814* (New Haven, CT: Yale University Press, 1964).

Hartmann, Susan M., 'Prescriptions for Penelope: Literature on Women's Obligations to Returning World War II Veterans', *Women's Studies* 5.3 (January 1978), 223–39.

Hartog, François, *Régimes d'historicité: présentisme et expériences du temps* (Paris: Seuil, 2003).

Hattenstone, Simon and Allison, Eric, 'Collateral Damage', *Guardian* (18 October 2014), 42–53.

Heaney, Seamus, *The Cure at Troy: A Version of Sophocles' Philoctetes* (New York: Farrar, Straus and Giroux, 1991).

'Dylan the Durable? On Dylan Thomas', *Salmagundi* 100 (Fall 1993), 66–85.

Heidegger, Martin, *Sein und Zeit* [1927], 7th ed. (Tübingen: Neomarius Verlag, 1953).

*Being and Time (Sein und Zeit)* [1927], trans. John Macquarrie and Edward Robinson (San Francisco, CA: HarperSanFrancisco, 1962).

Hemingway, Ernest, *A Farewell to Arms* [1929] (London: Vintage, 1999).

Henriques, Robert, *The Journey Home* (London: William Heinemann, 1944).

*From a Biography of Myself: A Posthumous Selection of the Autobiographical Writings of Robert Henriques* (London: Secker and Warburg, 1969).

Hentea, Marius, 'Fictional Doubles in Henry Green's *Back*', *The Review of English Studies* 61.251 (September 2010), 614–26.

Herman, Judith Lewis, *Trauma and Recovery* (London: HarperCollins, 1992).

Hern, Alex, 'Sales of "The Cuckoo's Calling" Surge by 150,000% After JK Rowling Revealed as Author', *New Statesman* (14 July 2013), www.newstatesman.com/2013/07/sales-cuckoos-calling-surge-150000-after-jk-rowling-revealed-author

Hichberger, J. W. M., *Images of the Army: The Military in British Art, 1815–1914* (Manchester: Manchester University Press, 1988).

Higonnet, Margaret, 'Authenticity and Art in Trauma Narratives of World War I', *Modernism/Modernity* 9.1 (January 2002), 91–107.

Higonnet, Margaret R. and Higonnet, Patrice L.-R., 'The Double Helix', *Behind the Lines: Gender and the Two World Wars*, ed. Margaret R. Higonnet, Jane Jenson, Sonya Michel and Margaret Collins Weitz (New Haven, CT: Yale University Press, 1987), 31–48.

Hirsch, Marianne, *Family Frames: Photography, Narrative, and Postmemory* (Cambridge, MA: Harvard University Press, 1997).

Hoa, Jen Hui Bon, 'Totality and the Common: Henri Lefebvre and Maurice Blanchot on Everyday Life', *Cultural Critique* 88 (Fall 2014), 54–78.

Holmes, Richard, *Redcoat: The British Soldier in the Age of Horse and Musket* (London: HarperCollins, 2001).

Holquist, Michael, 'Whodunit and Other Questions: Metaphysical Detective Stories in Postwar Fiction', *The Poetics of Murder: Detective Fiction and Literary Theory*, ed. Glenn W. Most and William W. Stowe (New York: Harcourt Brace Jovanovich, 1983), 149–74.

Home, Henry (Lord Kames), *Elements of Criticism* [1762], ed. Peter Jones, vol. 1/2 (Indianapolis, IN: Liberty Fund, 2005).

Hopkins, Nick, 'MPs Block Military Covenant', *Guardian* (17 February 2011), www.gov.uk/government/organisations/veterans-uk

Hopkins, Robert, 'Moral Luck and Judgment in Jane Austen's *Persuasion*', *Nineteenth-Century Literature* 42.2 (September 1987), 143–58.

Horsley, Lee, 'From Sherlock Holmes to the Present', *A Companion to Crime Fiction*, ed. Charles J. Rzepka and Lee Horsley (Chichester: Wiley-Blackwell, 2010), 28–42.

Howard, Kenneth, *Sex Problems of the Returning Soldier* (Manchester: Sydney Pemberton, 1945).

Howard, Michael, *War in European History* (Oxford: Oxford University Press, 1976/2009).

Hudson, Geoffrey, 'Disabled Veterans and the State in Early Modern England', *Disabled Veterans in History*, ed. David A. Gerber (Ann Arbor, MI: The University of Michigan Press, 2000), 117–44.

'Arguing Disability: Ex-Servicemen's Own Stories in Early Modern England, 1590–1790', *Medicine, Madness and Social History: Essays in Honour of Roy Porter*, ed. Roberta Bivins and John V. Pickstone (Basingstoke: Palgrave Macmillan, 2007), 105–17.

Hughes, Ted, *Collected Poems*, ed. Paul Keegan (London: Faber and Faber, 2003).

Huhn, Tom, 'Introduction: Thoughts Beside Themselves', *The Cambridge Companion to Adorno*, ed. Tom Huhn (Cambridge: Cambridge University Press, 2002), 1–18.

Hume, David, *Essays and Treatises on Several Subjects* (London: A. Millar, 1758).

Hussey, Mark, ed., *Virginia Woolf and War: Fiction, Reality, and Myth* (Syracuse, NY: Syracuse University Press, 1991).

Hutchison, Hazel, *The War That Used Up Words: American Writers and the First World War* (New Haven, CT: Yale University Press, 2015).

Hutt, C. W. [Cecil William], *The Future of the Disabled Soldier* (New York: William Wood, 1917).

Innes, Joanna, 'The Domestic Face of the Military-Fiscal State: Government and Society in Eighteenth-Century Britain', *An Imperial State at War: Britain from 1689–1815*, ed. Lawrence Stone (London: Routledge, 1994), 96–127.

Jackson, M. W., 'Rousseau's Discourse on Heroes and Heroism', *Proceedings of the American Philosophical Society* 133.3 (1989), 434–46.

Jacobson, Howard, 'Howard Jacobson on Being Taught by F. R. Leavis', *Telegraph* (23 April 2011), www.telegraph.co.uk/culture/books/8466388/Howard-Jacobson-on-being-taught-by-FRLeavis.html

Jakobson, Roman, 'Two Types of Language and Two Types of Aphasic Disturbances', *Fundamentals of Language*, ed. Roman Jakobson and Morris Halle ('s-Gravenhage: Mouton, 1956), 53–82.

James, Clive, *At the Pillars of Hercules* (London: Picador, 1979).

Jay, Martin, 'Experience Without A Subject: Walter Benjamin and the Novel', *New Formations* 20 (Summer 1993), 145–55.

'The Limits of Limit-Experience: Bataille and Foucault', *Constellations* 2.2 (1995), 155–74.

*Songs of Experience: Modern American and European Variations on a Universal Theme* (Berkeley, CA: University of California Press, 2004).

Johnson, Samuel, *A Dictionary of the English Language* [1755] (London: Time Books, 1983).

Johnstone, Charles, *Chrysal: Or, The Adventures of a Guinea. Wherein are Exhibited Views of Several Striking Scenes, with Curious and Interesting Anecdotes of the Most Noted Persons in Every Rank of Life, Whose Hands It Passed Through, in America, England, Holland, Germany and Portugal* (Dublin: Printed by Dillon Chamberlaine, in Smock-Alley, 1760).

Julius, Anthony, *T. S. Eliot, Anti-Semitism and Literary Form* (Cambridge: Cambridge University Press, 1996).

Kakutani, Michiko, 'A Murder Is Solved, A Sleuth Is Born', *New York Times* (17 July 2013), www.nytimes.com/2013/07/18/books/in-j-k-rowlings-cuckoos-calling-model-dies-but-why.html?pagewanted=all&_r=1&

Kant, Immanuel, *Practical Philosophy*, trans. and ed. Mary J. Gregor, *The Cambridge Edition of the Works of Immanuel Kant* (Cambridge: Cambridge University Press, 1999).

  *Critique of Pure Reason* (*Kritik der reinen Vernunft*) [1781], trans. Norman Kemp Smith (London: Palgrave, 2003).

  *Anthropology from a Pragmatic Point of View* (*Die Anthropologie in pragmatischer Hinsicht*) [1796–7], trans. and ed. Robert B. Louden, *The Cambridge Edition of the Works of Immanuel Kant* (Cambridge: Cambridge University Press, 2006).

Kavka, Misha, 'Men in (Shell-)Shock: Masculinity, Trauma, and Psychoanalysis in Rebecca West's *The Return of the Soldier*', *Studies in Twentieth Century Literature* 22 (1998), 151–71.

Keats, John, *John Keats: The Major Works*, ed. Elizabeth Cook (Oxford: Oxford University Press, 2001).

Keen, Suzanne, *Empathy and the Novel* (Oxford: Oxford University Press, 2014).

Keith, A. L., 'The Taunt in Homer and Vergil', *The Classical Journal* 19.9 (1924), 554–60.

Kelly, John, 'Ellmann, Richard David (1918–1987)', *Oxford Dictionary of National Biography* (Oxford University Press, 2004), online edition.

Kiernan, Victor, 'Tennyson, King Arthur and Imperialism', *Culture, Ideology and Politics: Essays for Eric Hobsbawm*, ed. Raphael Samuel and Gareth Stedman Jones (London: Routledge and Kegan Paul, 1983), 126–48.

Kipling, Rudyard, *Many Inventions* (London: Macmillan, 1913).

  *Rudyard Kipling's Verse: Inclusive Edition. 1885–1918* (New York: Doubleday, 1922).

  *Selected Poems*, ed. Peter Keating (Harmondsworth: Penguin, 2000).

  *Kipling and War: From 'Tommy' to 'My Boy Jack'*, ed. Andrew Lycett (London: I. B. Tauris, 2015).

Knight, Stephen, *Crime Fiction 1800–2000: Detection, Death, Diversity* (Basingstoke: Palgrave Macmillan, 2004).

Knox, Ronald, *Essays in Satire* (New York: E. P. Dutton, 1930).

Koerner, Joseph Leo, *Caspar David Friedrich and the Subject of Landscape* (London: Reaktion, 2009).

Kracauer, Siegfried, *Der Detektiv-Roman: Ein philosophisches Fragment* (Frankfurt-am-Main: Suhrkamp, 1979).

Kristeva, Julia, *Revolution in Poetic Language* (*La Révolution du langage poétique*) [1974], trans. Leon S. Roudiez (New York: Columbia University Press, 1984).

*Strangers to Ourselves* (*Étrangers à nous-mêmes*) [1988], trans. Leon S. Roudiez (New York: Columbia University Press, 1994).

Kukil, Karen V., ed., *Woolf in the Real World. Selected Papers From the Thirteenth International Conference on Virginia Woolf* (Clemson, SC: Clemson University Digital Press, 2005).

Kynaston, David, *Austerity Britain 1945–51* (London: Bloomsbury, 2007).

Kyriakou, Poulheria, 'Warrior Vaunts in the "Iliad"', *Rheinisches Museum für Philologie* 144.3/4 (2001), 250–77.

Langan, Celeste, *Romantic Vagrancy: Wordsworth and the Simulation of Freedom* (Cambridge: Cambridge University Press, 1995).

Langbaum, Robert, *The Poetry of Experience: The Dramatic Monologue in Modern Literary Tradition* (London: Chatto and Windus, 1957).

'Wordsworth's Lyrical Characterisations', *Studies in Romanticism* 21.3 (Fall 1982), 319–39.

Lawrence, D. H., *Lady Chatterley's Lover* [1928] (Harmondsworth: Penguin, 1961).

Lefebvre, Henri, *Critique of Everyday Life: The One-Volume Edition* (*Critique de la vie quotidienne*) *[1947–81], trans. John Moore (London: Verso, 2014).*

Leighton, Angela, 'Thresholds of Attention: On Listening in Literature', *Thinking on Thresholds: The Poetics of Transitive Spaces*, ed. Subha Mukherji (London: Anthem, 2011), 199–212.

Levenback, Karen, *Virginia Woolf and the Great War* (Syracuse, NY: Syracuse University Press, 1999).

Lévi-Strauss, Claude, *The Savage Mind* (*La Pensée sauvage*) [1962], translator unknown (London: Weidenfeld and Nicolson, 1966).

Levinas, Emmanuel, *Nine Talmudic Readings* (*Quatre lectures talmudiques*, 1968; *Du sacré au saint: cinq lectures talmudiques*, 1977), trans. Annette Aronowicz (Bloomington, IN: Indiana University Press, 1968/1990).

*Totality and Infinity: An Essay on Exteriority* (*Totalité et Infini: essai sur l'extériorité*) [1969], trans. Alphonso Lingis (Pittsburgh, PA: Duquesne University Press, 2007).

Lewis, C. S., *The Allegory of Love: A Study in Medieval Tradition* (Oxford: The Clarendon Press, 1936).

*Surprised by Joy: The Shape of My Life* (London: Fontana, 1955/1959).

Light, Alison, *Forever England: Femininity, Literature and Conservatism Between the Wars* (London: Routledge, 1991).

Lin, Patricia, 'Extending Her Arms: Military Families and the Transformation of the British State, 1793–1815', unpublished PhD thesis (University of California Berkeley, 1997).

Littlejohn, Richard, 'The Proof We Live in Two Britains', *MailOnline* (7 November 2014). www.dailymail.co.uk/columnists/article-2824520/While-millions-pay-silent-tribute-Tower-London-anarchists-bring-chaos-Westminster-proof-live-two-Britains-writes-RICHARD-LITTLEJOHN.html

Lloyd, Genevieve, 'Providence as Progress: Kant's Variations on a Tale of Origins', *Kant's Idea for a Universal History with a Cosmopolitan Aim: A Critical Guide*, ed. Amélie Oksenberg Rorty and James Schmidt (Cambridge: Cambridge University Press, 2009), 200–15.

Locke, John, *An Essay Concerning Human Understanding* [1689], ed. Roger Woolhouse (London: Penguin, 1997).

Lukács, Georg, *Essays on Realism* (*Essays über Realismus*) [1948], trans. David Fernbach, ed. Rodney Livingstone (London: Lawrence and Wishart, 1980).

*The Historical Novel* (*Der Historische Roman*) [1962], trans. Hannah Mitchell and Stanley Mitchell (Lincoln, NE: University of Nebraska Press, 1983).

Lynch, E., 'Copy of a Letter', London: National Army Museum, 9208–23 O/S 92.

MacAskill, Ewen and Cobain, Ian, 'British Forces' Century of Unbroken Warfare Set to End With Afghanistan Exit', *Guardian* (11 February 2014), www.theguardian.com/uk-news/2014/feb/11/british-forces-century-warfare-end

McCarthy, George, ' "Vote Our Way", The Soldiers Tell Relatives', *Daily Mirror* (13 June 1945), 3.

McClure, Helen Margaret, 'Alienated Patriots: A Sociological Portrait of Military Retirees', unpublished PhD thesis (University of California Berkeley, 1992).

McDermott, Jim, 'Old Soldiers Never Die: They Adapt Their Military Skills and Become Successful Civilians. What Factors Contribute to the Successful Transition of Army Veterans to Civilian Life and Work?', unpublished PhD thesis (University of Leicester, 2007).

'Struggling on Civvy Street', *Public Service Review: Transport, Local Government and the Regions* 8 (2009), unpaginated.

McGann, Jerome J., 'The Meaning of The Ancient Mariner', *Critical Inquiry* 8.1 (Autumn 1981), 35–67.

*The Poetics of Sensibility: A Revolution in Literary Style* (Oxford: Oxford University Press, 1996).

McHale, Brian, *Postmodern Fiction* (London: Routledge, 1987).

McHardy, Wallace B., *A Scheme For Establishing a Royal Army Society for Each County and Great City, In Order to Improve the Status of the British Soldier on his Return to Civil Life* (London: Harrison and Sons, 1893).

Mackay, Marina, 'The Lunacy of Men, the Idiocy of Women: Woolf, West, and War', *NWSA Journal* 15.3 (Autumn 2003), 124–44.

'The Wartime Rise of *The Rise of the Novel*', *Representations* 119.1 (2012), 119–43.

Mackenzie, Henry, *The Man of Feeling* [1771], ed. Brian Vickers (Oxford: Oxford University Press, 2001).

McKeon, Michael, *The Secret History of Domesticity: Public, Private and the Division of Knowledge* (Baltimore, MD: The Johns Hopkins University Press, 2007).

McKeown, Adam N., *English Mercuries: Soldier Poets in the Age of Shakespeare* (Nashville, TN: Vanderbilt University Press, 2009).

MacKillop, Ian, 'Leavis, Frank Raymond (1895–1978)', *Oxford Dictionary of National Biography* (Oxford University Press, 2004), online edition.

McLoughlin, Kate, *Martha Gellhorn: The War Writer in the Field and in the Text* (Manchester: Manchester University Press, 2007).

'Vera Lynn and the "We'll Meet Again" Hypothesis', *From Self to Shelf: The Artist Under Construction*, ed. Sally Bayley and William May (Newcastle: Cambridge Scholars Publishing, 2007), 109–25.

*Authoring War: The Literary Representation of War from the* Iliad *to* Iraq (Cambridge: Cambridge University Press, 2011).

'New Impressions XVI: *The Great War and Modern Memory*', *Essays in Criticism* 64.4 (October 2014), 436–58.

'*All of Us*: D. H. Lawrence's First World War Poems for the People', *Journal of D. H. Lawrence Studies* 4 (2015), 45–66.

'The Literature of Tiredness', *Postwar: British Writing in Transition Volume 3: 1940–1960*, ed. Gill Plain (Cambridge: Cambridge University Press, 2018) (forthcoming).

McMullan, Gordon, *Shakespeare and the Idea of Late Writing: Authorship in the Proximity of Death* (Cambridge: Cambridge University Press, 2007).

McMullin, Jaremey, 'Integration or Separation? The Stigmatization of Ex-Combatants after War', *Review of International Studies* 39.2 (April 2013), 385–414.

McNally, Richard J., *Remembering Trauma* (Cambridge, MA: The Belknap Press of Harvard University Press, 2003).

Mahaffey, Vicki, *Modernist Literature: Challenging Fictions* (Malden, MA: Blackwell, 2007).

Malcolm, Joyce, 'Charles II and the Reconstruction of Royal Power', *The Historical Journal* 35.2 (1992), 307–30.

Marcus, Laura, 'Detection and Literary Fiction', *The Cambridge Companion to Crime Fiction*, ed. Martin Priestman (Cambridge: Cambridge University Press, 2003), 245–68.

*Dreams of Modernity: Psychoanalysis, Literature, Cinema* (Cambridge: Cambridge University Press, 2014).

Marcus, Steve, *Freud and the Culture of Psychoanalysis: Studies in the Transition from Victorian Humanism to Modernity* (Boston: George Allen and Unwin, 1984).

Markley, A. A., *Stateliest Measures: Tennyson and the Literature of Greece and Rome* (Toronto: University of Toronto Press, 2004).

Masland, James Gillinder, 'Narratives of Romantic Masculinity Within the Long Eighteenth Century', unpublished PhD thesis (University of California Los Angeles, 2008).

Maycock, Christopher Hugh, *A Passionate Poet: Susanna Blamire, 1747–94* (Penzance: Hypatia, 2003).

Mayhew, Henry, *London Labour and the London Poor: Those That Will Not Work 4/* 4 vols (London: Griffin, Bone, 1862).

Mee, Jon, 'Merry, Robert', *An Oxford Companion to the Romantic Age: British Culture, 1776–1832*, ed. Iain McCalman (Oxford: Oxford University Press, 1999), 601–2.

'*The Magician No Conjuror*: Robert Merry and the Political Alchemy of the 1790s', *Unrespectable Radicals?: Popular Politics in the Age of Reform*, ed. Michael T. Davis and Paul A. Pickering (Aldershot: Ashgate, 2008), 41–55.

Meisenhelder, Susan Edwards, *Wordsworth's Informed Reader: Structures of Experience in His Poetry* (Nashville, TN: Vanderbilt University Press, 1988).

Melville, Peter, *Romantic Hospitality and the Resistance to Accommodation* (Waterloo, ON: Wilfred Laurier University Press, 2007).

Mengham, Rod, *The Idiom of the Time: The Writings of Henry Green* (Cambridge: Cambridge University Press, 1982).

Merivale, Patricia, 'Postmodern and Metaphysical Detection', *A Companion to Crime Fiction*, ed. Charles J. Rzepka and Lee Horsley (Chichester: Wiley-Blackwell, 2010), 308–20.

Merritt, Maurice, *Eighth Army Driver* (Tunbridge Wells: Midas Books, 1981).

Merry, Robert, 'Mustapha's Adoration of The Sublime Sultan Pittander the Omnipotent', *Cabinet of Curiosities* (London: publisher unknown, 1795), 26–30.

'Theatrical Extraordinary. Pittachio's Theatre Royal', *Cabinet of Curiosities* (London: publisher unknown, 1795), 87–90.

'Wonderful Exhibition', *Cabinet of Curiosities* (London: publisher unknown, 1795), 82–7.

'The Wounded Soldier', *The Spirit of the Public Journals* II (1799), 126–9.

Metcalfe, Henry, *The Chronicle of Henry Metcalfe H. M. 32nd Regiment of Foot* [1858] (London: Cassell, 1953).

Meyers, Jeffrey, *Edmund Wilson: A Biography* (Boston: Houghton Mifflin, 1995).

Mill, John Stuart, *Newspaper Writings*, ed. Ann P. Robson and John M. Robson (Toronto: University of Toronto Press, 1986).

Millar, Ruby, 'Home is the Soldier', *Times Literary Supplement* (16 August 1947), 413.

Miller, Betty, *On the Side of the Angels* [1945] (London: Capuchin Classics, 2012).

Miller, Jonathan, 'Foreword', *On the Side of the Angels* by Betty Miller (London: Capuchin Classics, 2012), 9–10.

Miller, Kristine, 'The War of the Roses: Sexual Politics in Henry Green's *Back*', *Modern Fiction Studies* 49.2 (Summer 2003), 228–45.

Miller, Sarah, 'Introduction', *On the Side of the Angels* by Betty Miller (London: Capuchin Classics, 2012), 11–23.

Milton, John, *The Major Works*, ed. Stephen Orgel and Jonathan Goldberg (Oxford: Oxford University Press, 1991/2003).

Miskimmins, Esme, 'Dorothy L. Sayers (1893–1957)', *A Companion to Crime Fiction*, ed. Charles J. Rzepka and Lee Horsley (Chichester: Wiley-Blackwell, 2010), 438–49.

Morello, Henry James, 'Time and Trauma in Ricardo Piglia's *The Absent City*', *The Comparatist* 37 (2013), 219–33.

Morris, Rosalind C., 'Introduction', *Can the Subaltern Speak?: Reflections on the History of an Idea*, ed. Rosalind C. Morris (New York: Columbia University Press, 2010), 1–18.

Moser, Joseph, *The Adventures of Timothy Twig, Esq. in a Series of Poetical Epistles*, 1/2 vols (London: printed for B. and T. Williams, 1794) (Eighteenth-Century Collections Online).

Motion, Andrew, 'The Five Acts of Harry Patch', *Daily Telegraph* (8 March 2008), www.telegraph.co.uk/culture/books/3671688/The-Five-Acts-of-Harry-Patch.html

Newlyn, Lucy, *Reading, Writing, and Romanticism: The Anxiety of Reception* (Oxford: Oxford University Press, 2000).

'The Wordsworths' Poetics of Hospitality', *Essays in Criticism* 66.1 (2016), 1–28.

Newton, Isaac, *Philosophiae Naturalis Principia Mathematica* [1687], trans. Andrew Motte, rev. Florian Cajori, 1/2 vols (Berkeley, CA: University of California Press, 1966).

Nicolson, Marjorie, 'The Professor and the Detective', *The Atlantic Monthly* 143.4 (April 1929), 484–93.

Nielsen, Caroline, 'Continuing to Serve: Representations of the Elderly Veteran Soldier in the Late Eighteenth and Early Nineteenth Centuries', *Men After War*, ed. Stephen McVeigh and Nicola Cooper (London: Routledge, 2013), 18–35.

Nietzsche, Friedrich, *The Gay Science (Die fröhliche Wissenschaft)* [1882], trans. Walter Kaufmann (New York: Vintage Books, 1974).

Norris, Margot, *Virgin and Veteran Readings of Ulysses* (Basingstoke: Palgrave Macmillan, 2010/2011).

Nowell Smith, Geoffrey and Hoare, Quintin, 'Preface', Antonio Gramsci, *Selections from the Prison Notebooks* (London: Lawrence and Wishart, 1971), ix–xv.

Nunokawa, Jeff, '*In Memoriam* and the Extinction of the Homosexual', *ELH* 58.2 (Summer 1991), 427–38.

Nussbaum, Martha C., *Love's Knowledge: Essays on Philosophy and Literature* (New York: Oxford University Press, 1990).

Nuttall, A. D., *A Common Sky: Philosophy and the Literary Imagination* (Berkeley, CA: University of California Press, 1974).

'O., T.', 'For the European Magazine: On a Late Victory at Sea', *European Magazine, and London Review* 26 (December 1794), 438–9.

O'Connell, Robert, *Of Arms and Men: A History of War, Weapons, and Aggression* (Oxford: Oxford University Press, 1989).

O'Gorman, Francis, 'Tennyson's "The Lotus-Eaters" and the Politics of the 1830s', *Victorian Review* 30.1 (2004), 1–20.

O'Grady, Kathleen, 'White Teeth: An Interview with Author Zadie Smith', *Atlantis: A Women's Studies Journal/Revue d'Études sur les Femmes* 27.1 (2002), 105–11.

Ogden, C. K., 'The One Thing Needful: A Suggestion to Members of Parliament', *The Cambridge Magazine* 5.11 (29 January 1915), 240–1.

Olmsted, Wendy, 'On the Margins of Otherness: Metamorphosis and Identity in Homer, Ovid, Sidney, and Milton', *New Literary History* 27.2 (1996), 167–84.

Ong, Walter, *Orality and Literacy: The Technologizing of the Word* (London: Routledge, 1982).

'Pacificus', 'Effects of War', *The Cambridge Intelligencer* (16 November 1793) (17th–18th Century Burney Collection Newspapers).

Paine, Thomas, *Rights of Man, Common Sense and Other Political Writings*, ed. Mark Philp (Oxford: Oxford University Press, 1998).

Palmer, Roy, ed., *The Rambling Soldier* (Gloucester: Alan Sutton, 1985).

Paret, Peter, *Understanding War: Essays on Clausewitz and the History of Military Power* (Princeton, NJ: Princeton University Press, 1992).

Parker, Geoffrey, *The Thirty Years War* (London: Routledge, 1998).

Parkes, Simon, 'Home from the Wars: the Romantic Revenant-Veteran of the 1790s', unpublished PhD thesis (University of Warwick, 2009).

'Cultural Transfer, Wartime Anxiety and the *Lenore* Translations of 1796', *Romanticism* 17 (2011), 175–85.

'"More Dead than Alive": The Return of Not-Orlando in Charlotte Smith's *The Old Manor House*', *European Romantic Review* 22.6 (2011), 765–84.

'Wooden Legs and Tales of Sorrow Done: The Literary Broken Soldier of the Late Eighteenth Century', *Journal for Eighteenth-Century Studies* 36.2 (June 2013), 191–207.

Parrish, Stephen, *The Art of the Lyrical Ballads* (Cambridge, MA: Harvard University Press, 1973).

Pater, Walter, *Studies in the History of the Renaissance* [1873], ed. Matthew Beaumont (Oxford: Oxford University Press, 2010).

Patočka, Jan, *Heretical Essays in the Philosophy of History* (*Kacířské eseje o filosofii dějin*) [1975], trans. Erazim Kohák, ed. James Dodd (Chicago: Open Court, 1996).

Pattison, Robert, *Tennyson and Tradition* (Cambridge, MA: Harvard University Press, 1979).

Peperzak, Adriaan, *To the Other: An Introduction to the Philosophy of Emmanuel Levinas* (West Lafayette, IN: Purdue University Press, 1993).

Perovic, Sanja, *The Calendar in Revolutionary France: Perceptions of Time in Literature, Culture, Politics* (Cambridge: Cambridge University Press, 2012).

Perry, Seamus, *Coleridge and the Uses of Division* (Oxford: Oxford University Press, 1999).

'The Talker', *The Cambridge Companion to Coleridge*, ed. Lucy Newlyn (Cambridge: Cambridge University Press, 2002), 103–25.

*Alfred Tennyson* (London: Northcote House, 2005).

'Philosopher', 'When the Boys Come Back', *The People* (14 January 1945), 2.

Philp, Mark, 'Revolution', *An Oxford Companion to The Romantic Age: British Culture 1776–1832*, ed. Iain McCalman (Oxford: Oxford University Press, 1999), 17–26.

Pinker, Steven, *The Better Angels of Our Nature: Why Violence Has Declined* (New York: Penguin, 2011).

Pinkerton, Steve, 'Trauma and Cure in Rebecca West's *The Return of the Soldier*', *Journal of Modern Literature* 32.1 (Fall 2008), 1–12.

Pippin, Robert B., *Modernism as a Philosophical Problem: On the Dissatisfactions of European High Culture* (Oxford: Blackwell, 1991/1999).

Plain, Gill, *Twentieth-Century Crime Fiction: Gender, Sexuality and the Body* (Edinburgh: Edinburgh University Press, 2001).

*Literature of the 1940s: War, Postwar and 'Peace'* (Edinburgh: Edinburgh University Press, 2013).

Poe, Edgar Allan, *Tales of Mystery and Imagination* (London: Dent, 1981).

Porter, Dennis, *The Pursuit of Crime: Art and Ideology in Detective Fiction* (New Haven, CT: Yale University Press, 1981).

Potkay, Adam, *The Fate of Eloquence in the Age of Hume* (Ithaca, NY: Cornell University Press, 1994).

Priestley, J. B., *Letter to a Returning Serviceman* (London: Home and Van Thal, 1945).

*Three Men in New Suits* (London: William Heinemann, 1945).

Prince, Michael, 'The Eighteenth-Century Beauty Contest', *MLQ* 55.3 (September 1994), 251–79.

Pritchett, V. S., *George Meredith and English Comedy* (London: Chatto and Windus, 1970).

Pyrhönen, Heta, 'Criticism and Theory', *A Companion to Crime Fiction*, ed. Charles J. Rzepka and Lee Horsley (Chichester: Wiley-Blackwell, 2010), 43–56.

Quintilian, *The Orator's Education (Institutio Oratoria)*, trans. Donald Russell, Loeb Classical Library (Cambridge, MA: Harvard University Press, 2001).

R., W., 'The Pensioner', *Lady's Monthly Museum* (1 April 1811), 229–32.

Rajan, Rajeswari Sunder, 'Death and the Subaltern', *Can the Subaltern Speak?: Reflections on the History of an Idea*, ed. Rosalind C. Morris (New York: Columbia University Press, 2010), 117–38.

Rajan, Tilottama, *The Supplement of Reading: Figures of Understanding in Romantic Theory and Practice* (Ithaca, NY: Cornell University Press, 1990).

Ramazani, Jahan, *Poetry of Mourning: The Modern Elegy from Hardy to Heaney* (Chicago: The University of Chicago Press, 1994).

Ramsey, Neil, *The Military Memoir and Romantic Literary Culture, 1780–1835* (Farnham: Ashgate, 2011).

'"A Real English Soldier": Suffering, Manliness and Class in the Mid-Nineteenth-Century Soldiers' Tale', *Soldiering in Britain and Ireland, 1750–1850*, ed. Catriona Kennedy and Matthew McCormack (Basingstoke: Palgrave Macmillan, 2013), 137–55.

Reese, Peter, *Homecoming Heroes: An Account of the Reassimilation of British Military Personnel into Civilian Life* (London: Leo Cooper, 1992).

Reeve, N. H., 'Away from the Lighthouse: William Sansom and Elizabeth Taylor in 1949', *The Fiction of the 1940s: Stories of Survival*, ed. Rod Mengham and N. H. Reeve (Basingstoke: Palgrave Macmillan, 2001), 152–68.

Reid, Fiona, *Broken Men: Shell Shock, Treatment and Recovery in Britain, 1914–1930* (London: Continuum, 2010).

Reznick, Jeffrey S., 'Work-Therapy and the Disabled British Soldier in Great Britain in the First World War: The Case of Shepherd's Bush Military Hospital, London', *Disabled Veterans in History*, ed. David A. Gerber (Ann Arbor, MI: The University of Michigan Press, 2000), 185–203.

Ricks, Christopher, *Tennyson* (Basingstoke: Macmillan, 1989).

Rizzuto, Nicole, 'Towards an Ethics of Witnessing: Traumatic Testimony in Rebecca West's *The Return of the Soldier*', *College Literature* 39.4 (Fall 2012), 7–33.

Robbins, Tony, 'Tennyson's "Ulysses": The Significance of the Homeric and Dantesque Backgrounds', *Victorian Poetry* 11.3 (Autumn 1973), 177–93.

Roberts, Warren, *Jane Austen and the French Revolution* (London: Macmillan, 1979).

Rogers, H. C. B., *The British Army of the Eighteenth Century* (London: George Allen and Unwin, 1977).

Rogers, Rachel, 'Vectors of Revolution: The British Radical Community in Early Republican Paris 1792–1794', unpublished PhD thesis (University of Toulouse, 2012).

Rorty, Richard, *Philosophy and the Mirror of Nature* (Oxford: Blackwell, 1980).

Rowland, Peter, 'Balchin, Nigel Marlin (1908–1970)', *Oxford Dictionary of National Biography* (Oxford University Press, 2004), online edition.

Rowland, Susan, 'The "Classical" Model of the Golden Age', *A Companion to Crime Fiction*, ed. Charles J. Rzepka and Lee Horsley (Chichester: Wiley-Blackwell, 2010), 117–27.

Rowling, J. K., *The Cuckoo's Calling* [2013] (London: Sphere Books, 2014).

*The Silkworm* (London: Sphere Books, 2014).

*Career of Evil* (London: Sphere Books, 2015).

'Frequently Asked Questions', www.robert-galbraith.com/#frequentlyAsked Questions

'Very Good Lives: The Fringe Benefits of Failure, and the Importance of Imagination', http://news.harvard.edu/gazette/story/2008/06/text-of-j-k-rowling-speech/

Rowlinson, Matthew, 'The Ideological Moment of Tennyson's "Ulysses"', *Victorian Poetry* 30.3/4 (Autumn–Winter 1992) (Centennial of Alfred, Lord Tennyson: 1809–1892), 265–76.

Rubenstein, Roberta, '"I Meant Nothing by the Lighthouse": Virginia Woolf's Poetics of Negation', *Journal of Modern Literature* 31.4 (Summer 2008), 36–53.

Rushing, Robert A., *Resisting Arrest: Detective Fiction and Popular Culture* (New York: Other Press, 2007).

Ruskin, John, *The Crown of Wild Olive: Three Lectures on Work, Traffic, and War* (New York: John Wiley, 1866).

*Selected Writings*, ed. Dinah Birch (Oxford: Oxford University Press, 2004).

Russell, Corinna, 'Merry, Robert (1755–1798)', *Oxford Dictionary of National Biography* (Oxford University Press, 2004), online edition.

Russell, Gillian, *The Theatres of War: Performance, Politics, and Society, 1793–1815* (Oxford: The Clarendon Press, 1995).

'The Army, the Navy, and the Napoleonic Wars', *A Companion to Jane Austen*, ed. Claudia L. Johnson and Clara Tuite (Chichester: Wiley-Blackwell, 2009), 261–71.

Rzepka, Charles J., 'What is Crime Fiction?', *A Companion to Crime Fiction*, ed. Charles J. Rzepka and Lee Horsley (Chichester: Wiley-Blackwell, 2010), 1–9.

Said, Edward, *On Late Style* (London: Bloomsbury, 2006).

Salfeld, P. J., 'Farewell to Liberty', *Guardian* (9 January 1946), 4.

Sampson, David, 'Wordsworth and the Poor: The Poetry of Survival', *Studies in Romanticism* 23.1 (Spring 1984), 31–59.

Saunders, Max, *Self Impression: Life-Writing, Autobiografiction, and the Forms of Modern Literature* (Oxford: Oxford University Press, 2010).

Savage, D. S., 'Fiction', *Spectator* (25 July 1947), 122.

Sayers, Dorothy L., *Begin Here: A War-Time Essay* (London: Victor Gollancz, 1940).

'Dr. Watson's Christian Name: A Brief Contribution to the Exegetical Literature of Sherlock Holmes', *Queen Mary's Book for India*, ed. Cornelia Sorabji (London: G. G. Harrap, 1943), 78–82.

*Unpopular Opinions* (London: Victor Gollancz, 1946).

*The Lost Tools of Learning: Paper Read at a Vacation Course in Education, Oxford 1947* (London: Methuen, 1948).

*Strong Poison* [1926] (London: Stodder, 1968).

*The Unpleasantness at the Bellona Club* [1921] (London: Hodder and Stoughton, 1977).

*Lord Peter Views the Body* [1928] (London: Hodder and Stoughton, 1979).

*Gaudy Night* [1935] (London: Hodder and Stoughton, 1987).

*The Letters of Dorothy L. Sayers: 1899–1936: The Making of a Detective Novelist*, ed. Barbara Reynolds (London: Hodder and Stoughton, 1995).

*Whose Body?* [1927] (London: Hodder and Stoughton, 2003).

Schmitt, Carl, *The Nomos of the Earth in the International Law of the Jus Publicum Europaeum* (*Der Nomos der Erde im Völkerrecht des Jus Publicum Europaeum*) [1950], trans. G. L. Ulmen (New York: Telos, 2006).

Scurati, Antonio, 'Dire addio alle armi: Forma giuridica e retorica della guerra in Schmitt e Hemingway', *Le Parole e le armi*, ed. Giorgio Mariani (Milan: Marcos y Marcos, 1999), 291–326.

Seigel, Jerrold, *The Idea of the Self: Thought and Experience in Western Europe since the Seventeenth Century* (Cambridge: Cambridge University Press, 2005).

Shaffer, Elinor, *'Kubla Khan' and the Fall of Jerusalem* (Cambridge: Cambridge University Press, 1975).

Shapiro, S. A., 'Henry Green's *Back*: The Presence of the Past', *Critique: Studies in Contemporary Fiction* 7.1 (Spring 1964), 87–96.

Shaw, Matthew, *Time and the French Revolution: The Republican Calendar, 1789–Year XIV* (Woodbridge: Royal Historical Society/Boydell Press, 2011).

Shaw, Philip, 'Introduction', *Romantic Wars: Studies in Culture and Conflict, 1793–1822*, ed. Philip Shaw (Aldershot: Ashgate, 2000), 1–12.

*Suffering and Sentiment in Romantic Military Art* (Farnham: Ashgate, 2013).

Shay, Jonathan, *Achilles in Vietnam: Combat Trauma and the Undoing of Character* (New York: Simon and Schuster Touchstone, 1995).

*Odysseus in America: Combat Trauma and the Trials of Homecoming* (New York: Scribner, 2002).

Shelley, Percy Bysshe, *The Major Works*, ed. Zachary Leader (Oxford: Oxford University Press, 2003).

Sherry, Vincent, *The Great War and the Language of Modernism* (Oxford: Oxford University Press, 2003).

*Modernism and the Reinvention of Decadence* (Cambridge: Cambridge University Press, 2015).

Shippey, T. A, 'Tolkien, John Ronald Reuel (1892–1973)', *Oxford Dictionary of National Biography* (Oxford University Press, 2004), online edition.

Sinfield, Alan, *Alfred Tennyson* (Oxford: Basil Blackwell, 1986).

Small, Helen, 'Tennyson and Late Style', *Tennyson Bulletin* 8.4 (2005), 226–50.

*The Long Life* (Oxford: Oxford University Press, 2007).

Smith, Adam, *The Theory of Moral Sentiments* (London: A. Millar, A. Kincaid, J. Bell, 1759).

Smith, Dai, 'Williams, Raymond Henry (1921–1988)', *Oxford Dictionary of National Biography* (Oxford University Press, 2004), online edition.

Smith, Goldwin, 'The War Passages in "Maud" ', *Saturday Review* 1.1 (3 November 1855), 14–15.

Smith, Zadie, *White Teeth* (London: Hamish Hamilton, 2000).

Sophocles, *Antigone. The Women of Trachis. Philoctetes. Oedipus at Colonus.* trans. and ed. Hugh Lloyd-Jones, Loeb Classical Library (Cambridge, MA: Harvard University Press, 2014).

Southam, Brian, *Jane Austen and the Navy* (London: National Maritime Museum, 2005).

Spivak, Gayatri Chakravorty, 'Can the Subaltern Speak?', *Marxism and the Interpretation of Culture*, ed. Cary Nelson and Lawrence Grossberg (Urbana, IL: University of Illinois Press, 1988), 271–313.

'"Can the Subaltern Speak?" Revised Edition, from the "History" Chapter of *Critique of Postcolonial Reason*', *Can the Subaltern Speak?: Reflections on the History of an Idea*, ed. Rosalind C. Morris (New York: Columbia University Press, 2010), 21–78.

Sprat, Thomas, *The History of the Royal Society of London, for the Improving of Natural Knowledge* (London: J. Martyn and T. Allestry, 1667).

Stafford, Fiona, *The Last of the Race: The Growth of a Myth from Milton to Darwin* (Oxford: The Clarendon Press, 1994).

Stanford, W. B., 'The Homeric Etymology of the Name Odysseus', *Classical Philology* 47.4 (October 1952), 209–13.

Stein, Gertrude, *Look At Me Now and Here I Am: Writings and Lectures 1911–1945*, ed. Patricia Meyerowitz (London: Peter Owen, 1967).

*Geography and Plays* (Madison, WI: University of Wisconsin Press, 1993).

Stewart, Victoria, *Narratives of Memory: British Writing of the 1940s* (Basingstoke: Palgrave Macmillan, 2006).

'Masculinity, Masquerade and the Second World War: Betty Miller's *On the Side of the Angels*', *Conflict, Nationhood and Corporeality in Modern Literature: Bodies-at-War*, ed. Petra Rau (Basingstoke: Palgrave Macmillan, 2010), 124–42.

Stonebridge, Lyndsey, *The Writing of Anxiety: Imagining Wartime in Mid-Century British Culture* (Basingstoke: Palgrave Macmillan, 2007).

Stoneman, Patsy, *Elizabeth Gaskell* (Manchester: Manchester University Press, 2006).

Stoyle, Mark, ' "Memories of the Maimed": The Testimony of Charles I's Former Soldiers, 1660–1730', *History* 88.290 (April 2003), 204–26.

Talbot Rice, R. H., *The Next Generation of Veterans: Their Critical Needs and Their Emerging Rights* (London: Royal College of Defence Studies, 2009).

Tani, Stefano, *The Doomed Detective: The Contribution of the Detective Novel to Postmodern American and Italian Fiction* (Carbondale, IL: Southern Illinois University Press, 1984).

Tate, Trudi, *Modernism, History and the First World War* (Manchester: Manchester University Press, 1998).

Taunton, Matthew. ' "The Radiant Future": The Bolshevik Revolution in Modernist Temporality', conference paper, British Association of Modernist

Studies Annual Conference: Modernism Now, Senate House, London (28 June 2014).

Taylor, D. J., *The Prose Factory: Literary Life in England Since 1918* (London: Chatto and Windus, 2016).

Tennyson, Alfred Lord, *The Poems of Tennyson*, ed. Christopher Ricks, 3 vols (Harlow: Longman, 1969/1987).

*The Letters of Alfred Lord Tennyson*, ed. Cecil Y. Yang, 3 vols (Oxford: The Clarendon Press, 1982–1990).

Tennyson, Charles, *Alfred Tennyson* (London: Macmillan, 1949).

Tennyson, Hallam, *Alfred, Lord Tennyson: A Memoir*, 1/2 vols (London: Macmillan, 1897).

Thelwall, John, 'The Lecture "On Barracks and Fortifications; with Sketches of the Character and Treatment of the British Soldiery." Delivered Wednesday, June 10th, 1795 (Issue 19)', *The Tribune, A Periodical Publication Consisting Chiefly of the Political Lectures of J. Thelwall* (London: printed for the author, 1795), 85–108.

Thomas, Ronald R., *Detective Fiction and the Rise of Forensic Science* (Cambridge: Cambridge University Press, 1999).

Thomas, Sue, 'Virginia Woolf's Septimus Smith and Contemporary Perceptions of Shell Shock', *English Language Notes* 25.2 (1987), 49–57.

Thompson, George, *Documentary History of the African Theatre* (Chicago: Northwestern University Press, 1998).

Thomson, James, *The Seasons and The Castle of Indolence*, ed. James Sambrook (Oxford: Oxford University Press, 1984).

*Liberty, The Castle of Indolence and Other Poems*, ed. James Sambrook (Oxford: Oxford University Press, 1986).

Todorov, Tzvetan, *The Poetics of Prose* (*Poétique de la prose*) [1971], trans. Richard Howard (Oxford: Basil Blackwell, 1977).

Tolkien, J. R. R., 'On Fairy-Stories', *The Monsters and the Critics and Other Essays*, ed. Christopher Tolkien (London: George Allen and Unwin, 1983), 109–61.

Tombs, Robert, *The English and Their History* (London: Allen Lane, 2014).

Tönnies, Ferdinand, *Community and Society* (*Gemeinschaft und Gesellschaft*) [1887, 1912] (New Brunswick, NJ: Transaction Books, 1957/1988).

Treglown, Jeremy, *Romancing: The Life and Work of Henry Green* (London: Faber and Faber, 2000).

Tritle, Lawrence A., *From Melos to My Lai: War and Survival* (London, New York: Routledge, 2000).

Trollope, Anthony, *Framley Parsonage* [1860], ed. David Skilton and Peter Miles (Oxford: Oxford University Press, 1986).

Trott, Nicola, 'Wordsworth: The Shape of the Poetical Career', *The Cambridge Companion to Wordsworth*, ed. Stephen Gill (Cambridge: Cambridge University Press, 2003), 5–21.

Vanden Bossche, Chris R., *Carlyle and the Search for Authority* (Columbus, OH: Ohio State University Press, 1991).

Varney, Susan, 'Oedipus and the Modernist Aesthetic: Reconceiving the Social in Rebecca West's *The Return of the Soldier*', *Naming the Father: Legacies,*

*Genealogies, and Explorations of Fatherhood in Modern and Contemporary Literature*, ed. Eva Paulino Bueno, Terry Caesar and William Hummel (Lanham, MD: Lexington, 2000), 253–75.

Waldman, Katy, 'Private "I"', *Slate* (16 July 2013), www.slate.com/articles/arts/books/2013/07/the_cuckoo_s_calling_by_j_k_rowling_or_robert_galbraith_reviewed.html

Walford, Edward, 'Greenwich: The Hospital for Seamen', *Old and New London* (London: publisher unknown, 1878) (British History Online).

Walker, Alexander, *Beauty; Illustrated Chiefly by an Analysis and Classification of Beauty in Woman* [1836] (New York: Henry G. Langley, 1845).

Waller, Willard, *The Veteran Comes Back* (New York: Dryden Press, 1944).

Watson, J. R., *Romanticism and War: A Study of British Romantic Period Writers and the Napoleonic Wars* (Basingstoke: Palgrave Macmillan, 2003).

Watt, Ian, *Essays on Conrad* (Cambridge: Cambridge University Press, 2000).

Weinstein, Philip, *Unknowing: The Work of Modernist Fiction* (Ithaca, NY: Cornell University Press, 2005).

Welch, Denton, *Fragments of a Life Story: The Collected Short Stories of Denton Welch* (Harmondsworth: Penguin, 1987).

Wellek, René, 'Erich Auerbach (1892–1958)', *Comparative Literature* 10.1 (1958), 93–5.

Wenger, Etienne, *Communities of Practice. Learning, Meaning and Identity* (Cambridge: Cambridge University Press, 1999).

West, Rebecca, *Henry James* (London: Nisbet, 1916).
  *The Return of the Soldier* [1918] (London: Virago, 1980, 1990).
  'On "The Return of the Soldier"', *The Yale University Library Gazette* 57 (1983), 66–70.

Wheeler, Kathleen M., *Romanticism, Pragmaticism and Deconstruction* (Oxford: Basil Blackwell, 1993).

Whewell, William, *History of the Inductive Sciences, from the Earliest to the Present Times*, 3/3 vols (London: John W. Parker, 1837).

White, Simon J., *Robert Bloomfield, Romanticism and the Poetry of Community* (Aldershot: Ashgate, 2007).

Wilde, Oscar, *The Picture of Dorian Gray* [1890], ed. Joseph Bristow (Oxford: Oxford University Press, 2008).

Willgress, Lydia, 'Chilling Footage Reveals Moment Ex-Army Sniper Threatened to Kill a Family While on Bail for Firing an Air Pistol at Guests During His Partner's Ann Summers Party', *MailOnline* (15 October 2015), www.dailymail.co.uk/news/article-3273942/Ex-Army-sniper-29-gas-mask-opened-fire-Ann-Summers-party-hitting-one-woman-bottom-taking-offence-conversation-heard.html

Williams, Raymond, *Culture and Society 1780–1950* (London: Chatto and Windus, 1958).
  *Politics and Letters: Interviews with New Left Review* (London: New Left Books, 1979).

Williams, Zoe, 'Why Posh People Mind About "Toughness of Mind" ', *Guardian* (20 April 2013), 9.

Willis, Thomas, *The Remaining Medical Works of that Famous and Renowned Physician Dr. Thomas Willis* (London: T. Dring, 1681).

Wilson, Edmund, *The Wound and the Bow: Seven Studies in Literature* [1941] (London: Methuen, 1961).

Wilson, Emily R., *Mocked with Death: Tragic Overliving from Sophocles to Milton* (Baltimore, MD: The Johns Hopkins University Press, 2004).

Wise, Terence, *Artillery Equipments of the Napoleonic Wars* (Oxford: Osprey, 1979).

Wolfson, Susan J., *The Questioning Presence: Wordsworth, Keats, and the Interrogative Mode in Romantic Poetry* (Ithaca, NY: Cornell University Press, 1986).

Woods, R., 'Infant Mortality in Britain: A Survey of Current Knowledge on Historical Trends and Variations', *Infant and Child Mortality in the Past*, ed. Alain Bideau, Bertrand Desjardins and Héctor Pérez Brignoli (Oxford: Oxford University Press, 1997), 74–88.

Woodward, Kathleen, *Aging and Its Discontents: Freud and Other Fictions* (Bloomington, IN: Indiana University Press, 1991).

Woolf, Virginia, *Mrs Dalloway* [1925], ed. David Bradshaw (Oxford: Oxford University Press, 2000, 2009).

Wordsworth, Christopher, *Memoirs of William Wordsworth*, 1/2 vols (London: Edward Moxon, 1851).

Wordsworth, Dorothy, *Journals of Dorothy Wordsworth*, ed. Ernest de Selincourt, 1/2 vols (London: Macmillan, 1941).

Wordsworth, Jonathan, *The Music of Humanity: A Critical Study of Wordsworth's 'Ruined Cottage'* (New York: J and J Harper, 1969).

'The Five-Book "Prelude" of Early Spring 1804', *The Journal of English and Germanic Philology* 76.1 (January 1977), 1–25.

Wordsworth, William, *The Prose Works of William Wordsworth*, ed. W. J. B. Owen and Jane Worthington Smyser, 1/3 vols (Oxford: The Clarendon Press, 1974).

*The Cornell Wordsworth*, gen. ed. Stephen Maxfield Parris, 21 vols (Ithaca, NY: Cornell University Press, 1975–2007).

*The Prelude 1799, 1805, 1850*, ed. Jonathan Wordsworth, M. H. Abrams and Stephen Gill (New York: W. W. Norton, 1979).

*Lyrical Ballads and Other Poems, 1797–1800 by William Wordsworth*, ed. James Butler and Karen Green, *The Cornell Wordsworth* (Ithaca, NY: Cornell University Press, 1992).

Wordsworth, William and Wordsworth, Dorothy, *The Letters of William and Dorothy Wordsworth: The Early Years 1787–1805*, ed. Chester L. Shaver, 1/8 vols (Oxford: The Clarendon Press, 1967).

Worthington, Heather, *Key Concepts in Crime Fiction* (Basingstoke: Palgrave Macmillan, 2011).

Wu, Duncan, *Wordsworth's Reading 1770–1799* (Cambridge: Cambridge University Press, 1993).

Zemon Davis, Natalie, *The Return of Martin Guerre* (Cambridge, MA: Harvard University Press, 1983).


## Websites
### *BBC News*

www.bbc.co.uk/news/uk-29294337


### *Help for Heroes*

www.helpforheroes.org.uk/


### *Invictus Games*

https://invictusgamesfoundation.org/foundation/story


### *Ministry of Defence*

www.army.mod.uk/Operations-Deployments/Operations-Deployments.Aspx
www.gov.uk/government/news/defence-budget-increases-for-the-first-time-in-six-years
www.gov.uk/government/organisations/veterans-uk
www.gov.uk/government/publications/armed-forces-covenant-2015-to-2020/armed-forces-covenant
www.gov.uk/government/publications/veterans-welfare-service-useful-links-for-service-personnel/useful-links-for-the-service-community
www.gov.uk/government/uploads/system/uploads/attachment_data/file/389856/the-needs-of-ex-service-personnel-in-the-cjs-analytical-summary.pdf
www.gov.uk/government/uploads/system/uploads/attachment_data/file/516051/HOCS_FOI_2016_01145___Number_of_soldiers_becoming_veterans_in_the_UK_Armed_Forces_2014.pdf


### *Oxford English Dictionaries*

https://en.oxforddictionaries.com/word-of-the-year/word-of-the-year-2016


### *Penguin Group*

www.us.penguingroup.com/static/pages/classics/history.html

### The Poppy Factory

www.poppyfactory.org/history-timeline/#timeline

### Royal British Legion

www.britishlegion.org.uk/veterans-and-families/

### Support British Soldiers

www.supportbritishsoldiers.co.uk/?p=197

### Surf Action

www.surfaction.co.uk/index.php

### Theater of War

www.theaterofwar.com/projects/theater-of-war/overview

# Index

Abraham, 7
Abraham, Karl, 217n93
actor-network theory, 8–9, 239
Addison, Joseph, 194, 228n124
Adler, Alfred, 217n93
Adorno, Théodor, 6, 6n32, 57, 60, 60n139,
    109, 123n95
  and Horkheimer, Max
    *Dialectic of Enlightenment*, 2, 7, 8, 26, 185,
    192n38, 231–34
Aestheticism, 187
Agamben, Giorgio, 109
Aiken, Conrad, 230
Aird, Thomas
  'The Old Soldier', 258–59
Aistrop, Jack
  *Pretend I Am A Stranger*, 91n98, 271
Aldington, Richard, 187n12, 263
Algerian War, 236
Alighieri, Dante, 51
  *Inferno*, 53–54, 55n115
Allingham, Margery, 127
American Revolutionary War, 162, 249
*American Sniper*, 23
*anagnorisis* (recognition), 103–04, 222–23, 226
Anderson, Robert
  'Poor Will', 255
  'The Soldier: A Fragment', 254
Anglo-Dutch Wars, 248
Anselme, Daniel
  *On Leave*, 236
Aptel, Karl-Otto, 152
Aristotle
  *Nichomachean Ethics*, 58
  *Poetics*, 103
Armed Forces Covenant, 13–14, 272–73
Ashton, Helen, 78
  *The Captain Comes Home*, 24, 64, 69, 77–88,
    89, 96, 98, 134n142
Atkinson, Kate, 112
  *Life After Life*, 275

Auden, W. H., 113
Auerbach, Erich, 6, 6n32
  *Mimesis*, 7–8, 104
Augustine, 106
Austen, Jane, 42–43
  *Emma*, 42
  *Jack and Alice*, 43n69
  *Mansfield Park*, 43
  *Northanger Abbey*, 42
  *Persuasion*, 23, 34, 41–49, 62
  *Pride and Prejudice*, 43
  *Sense and Sensibility*, 42
Austen-Leigh, James Edward, 43

Bacon, Francis, 104
Badworth, Joseph
  'Half-Pay', 149, 255
*The Baffled Hero*, 252
Balchin, Nigel, 88, 94
  *A Sort of Traitors*, 24, 64, 69, 88, 94–96
  *Mine Own Executioner*, 24, 64, 69,
    88–94, 271
  *The Small Back Room*, 92n99
Balzac, Honoré de
  *Le Colonel Chabert*, 37n41
Bannerman, Anne
  'The Soldier', 254
Barker, Arthur
  *Nobby and Pincher in Civvy Street*, 271
Barker, Pat
  *Life Class*, 274
  *Regeneration* trilogy, 266, 274
  *Toby's Room*, 274
Barth, John
  *Lost in the Funhouse*, 147n4
Barthes, Roland, 116, 241
  'Listening', 239–40
*The Battle of the Somme*, 191
Baudelaire, Charles, 21
Beaumont, Sir Harry (aka Joseph Spence)
  *Crito: Or, A Dialogue on Beauty*, 45n70